The Way of the House Husband

KOUSUKE OONO

8

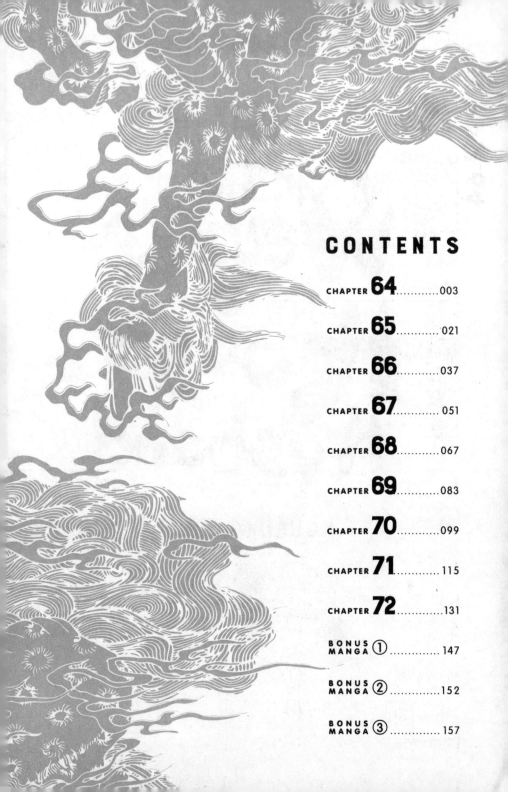

CONTENTS

CHAPTER 64

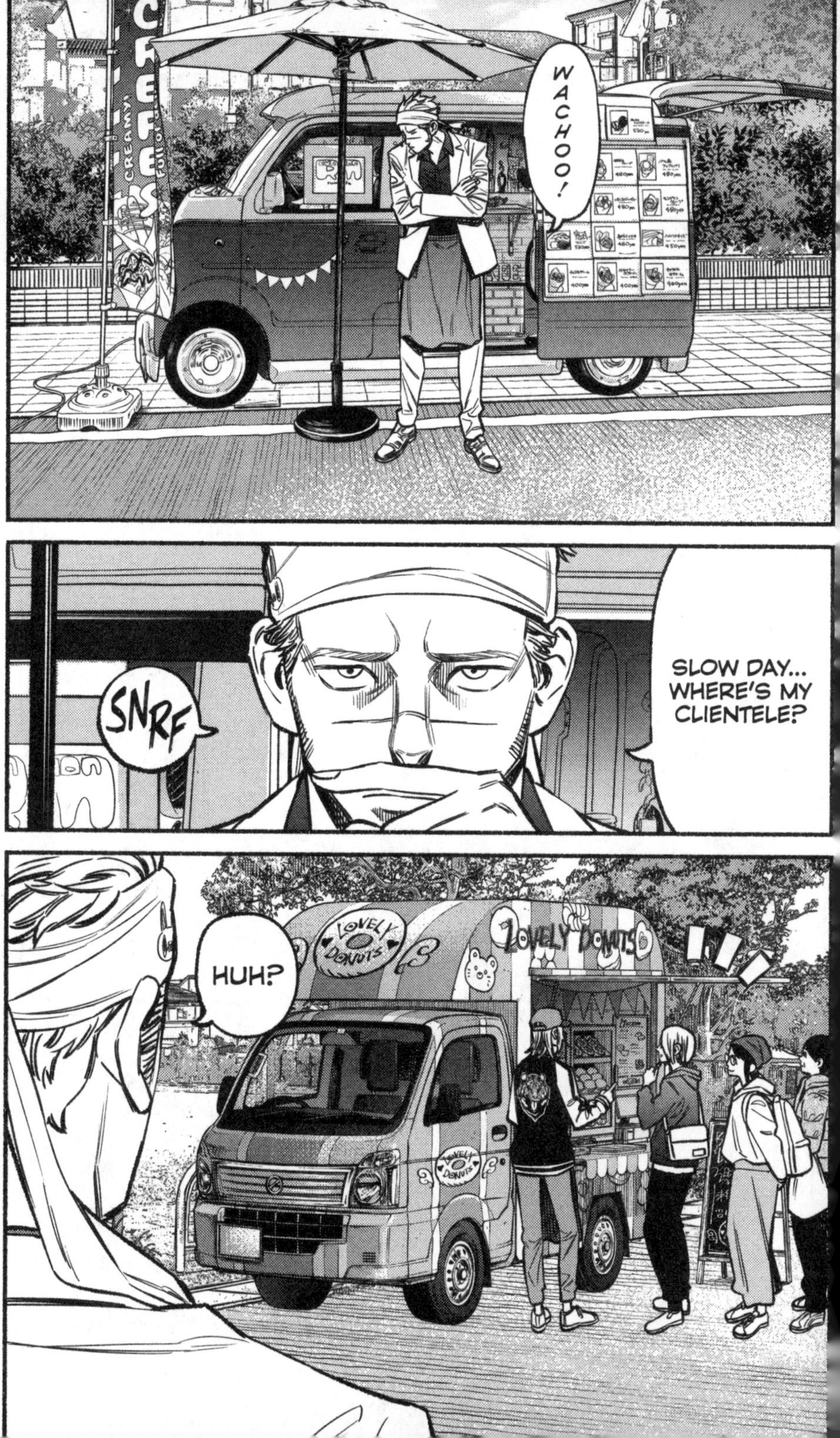
WACHOO!
SLOW DAY... WHERE'S MY CLIENTELE?
SNRF
LOVELY DONUTS
LOVELY DONUTS
HUH?
LOVELY DONUTS

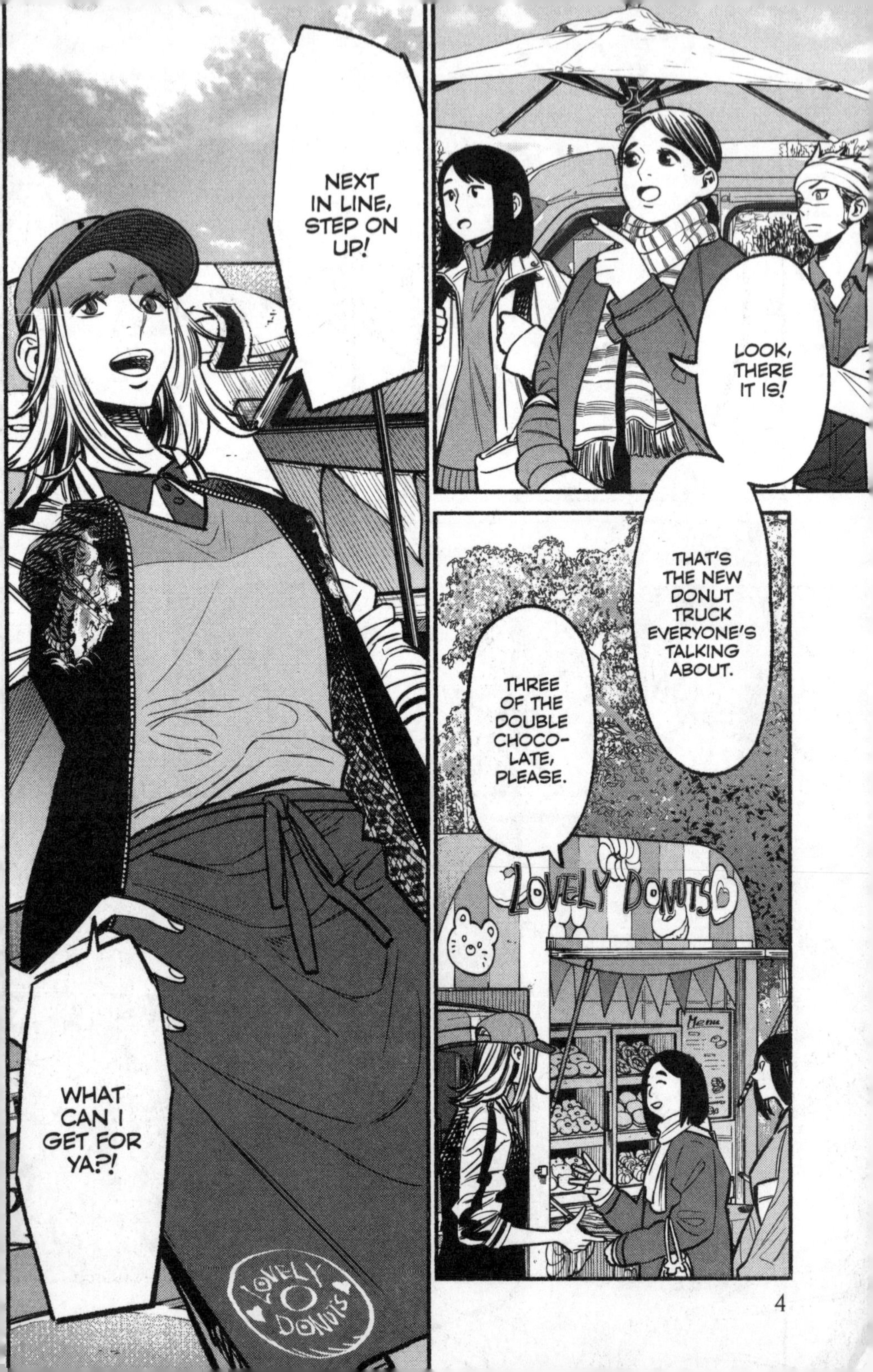
LOOK, THERE IT IS!
THAT'S THE NEW DONUT TRUCK EVERYONE'S TALKING ABOUT.
LOVELY DONUTS
THREE OF THE DOUBLE CHOCO-LATE, PLEASE.
NEXT IN LINE, STEP ON UP!
WHAT CAN I GET FOR YA?!

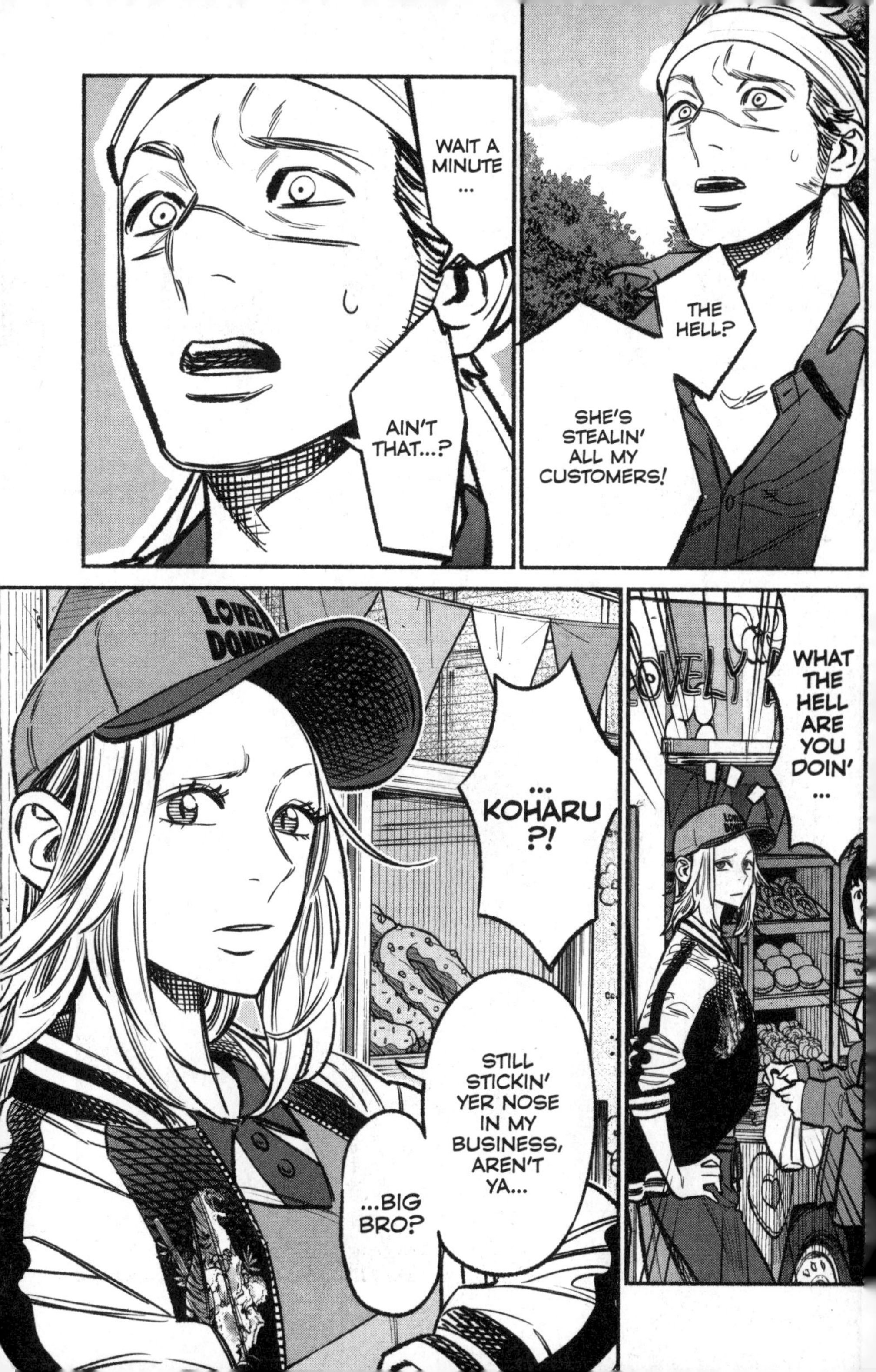
THE HELL?
SHE'S STEALIN' ALL MY CUSTOMERS!
WAIT A MINUTE ...
AIN'T THAT...?
WHAT THE HELL ARE YOU DOIN' ...
... KOHARU ?!
STILL STICKIN' YER NOSE IN MY BUSINESS, AREN'T YA...
...BIG BRO?

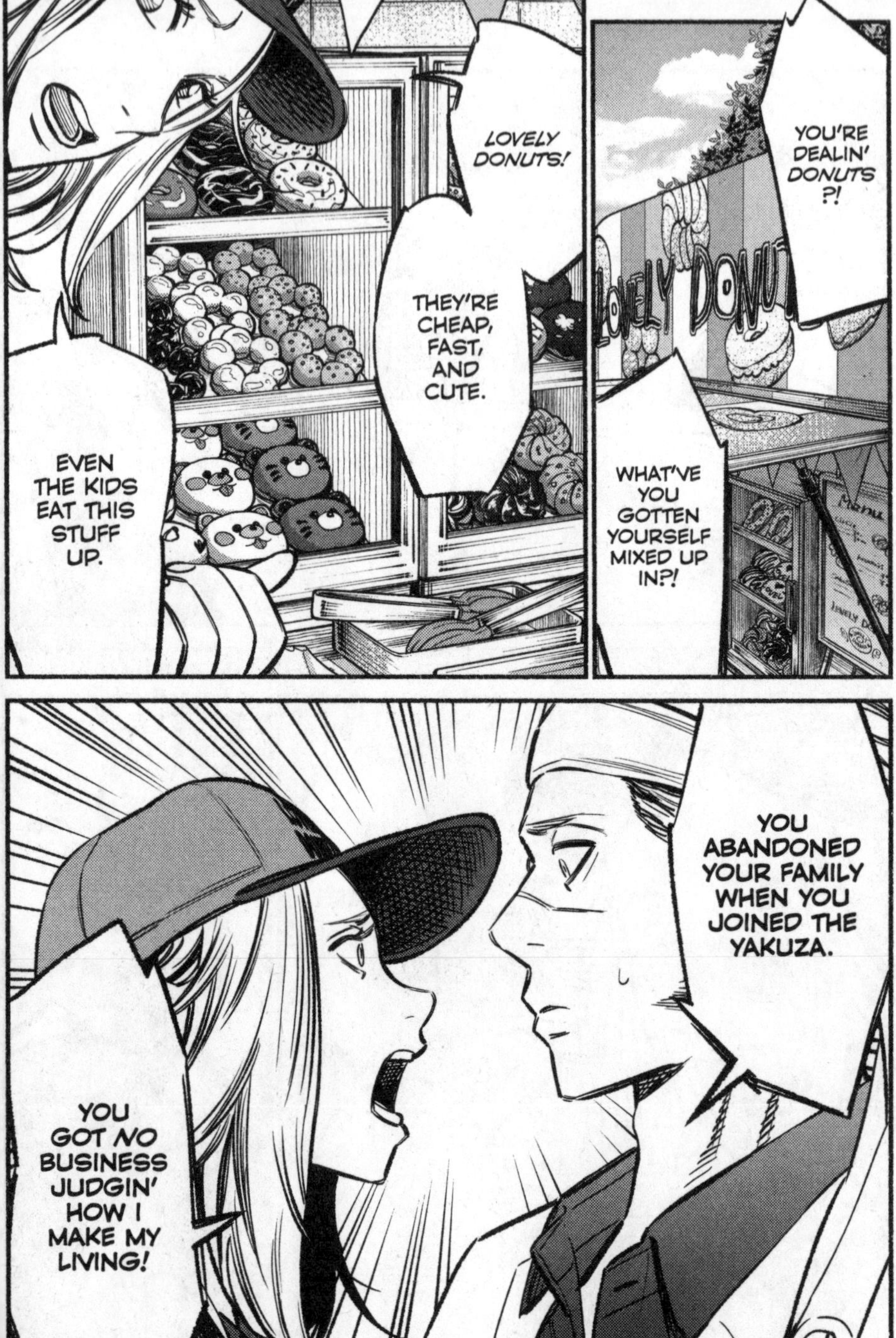
YOU'RE DEALIN' *DONUTS* ?!
WHAT'VE YOU GOTTEN YOURSELF MIXED UP IN?!
LOVELY DONUTS!
THEY'RE CHEAP, FAST, AND CUTE.
EVEN THE KIDS EAT THIS STUFF UP.
YOU ABANDONED YOUR FAMILY WHEN YOU JOINED THE YAKUZA.
YOU GOT *NO* BUSINESS JUDGIN' HOW I MAKE MY LIVING!

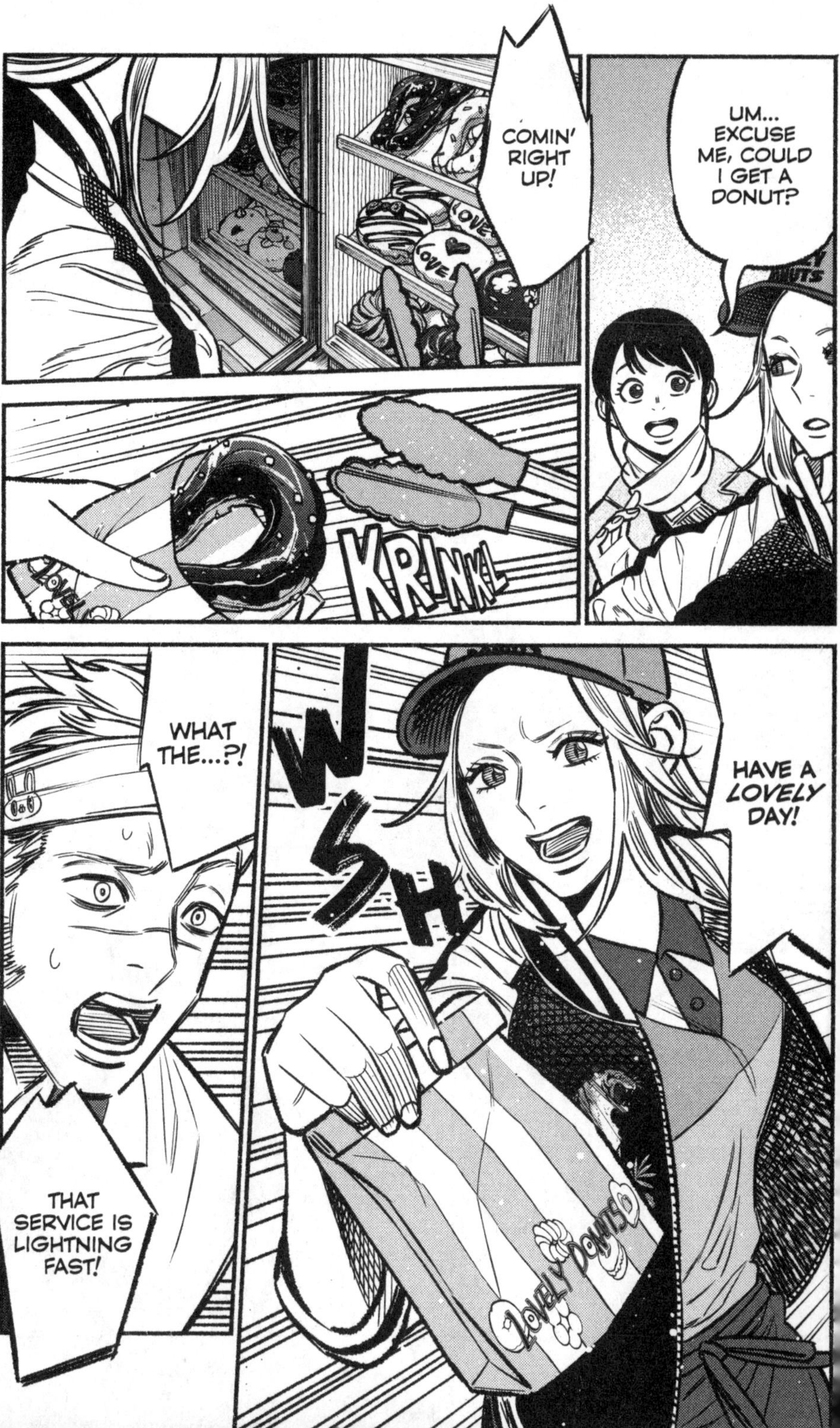
UM... EXCUSE ME, COULD I GET A DONUT?
COMIN' RIGHT UP!
KRINKL
HAVE A *LOVELY* DAY!
WSH
LOVELY DONUTS
WHAT THE...?!
THAT SERVICE IS LIGHTNING FAST!

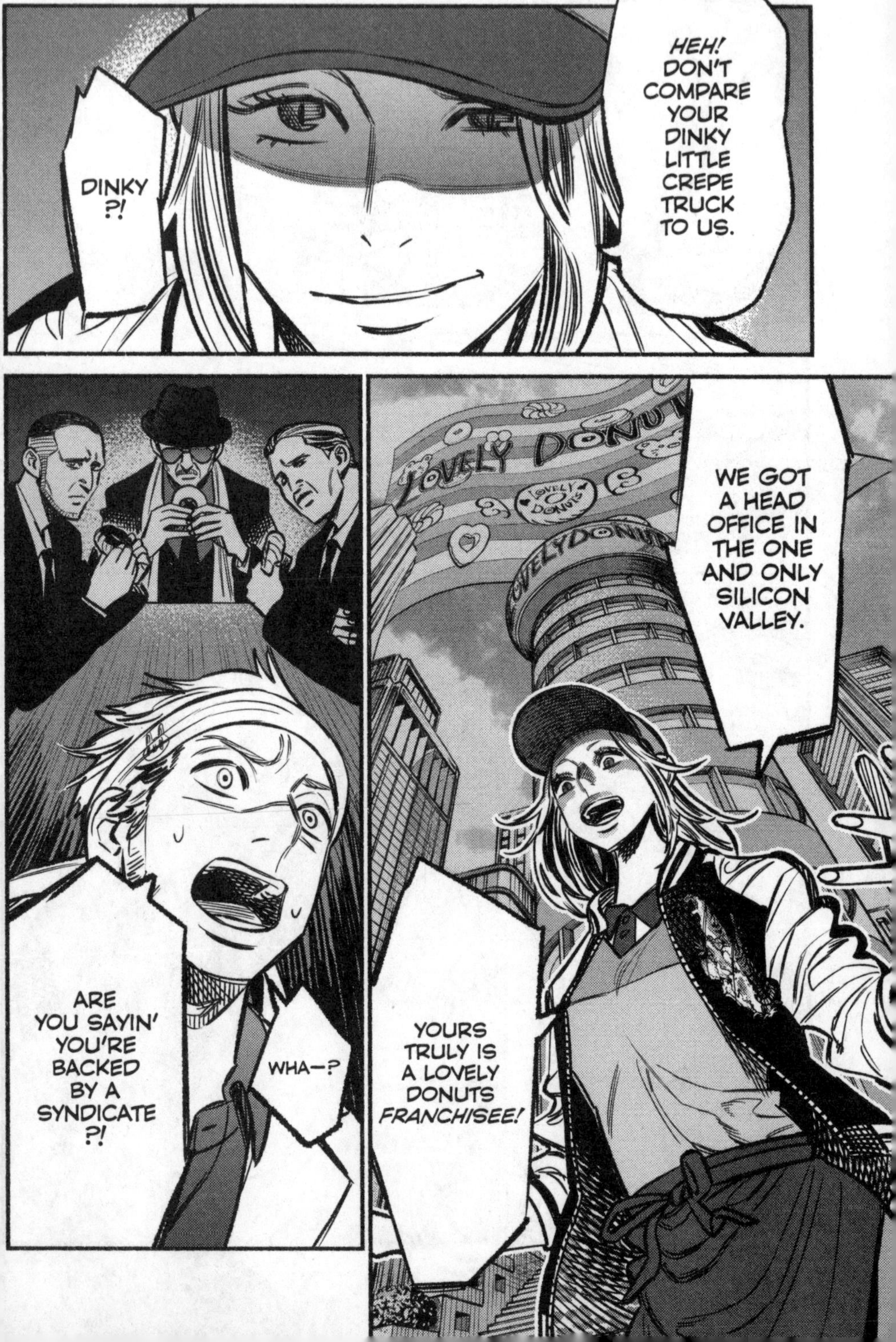
HEH! DON'T COMPARE YOUR DINKY LITTLE CREPE TRUCK TO US.
DINKY?!
WE GOT A HEAD OFFICE IN THE ONE AND ONLY SILICON VALLEY.
YOURS TRULY IS A LOVELY DONUTS *FRANCHISEE!*
WHA-?
ARE YOU SAYIN' YOU'RE BACKED BY A SYNDICATE?!

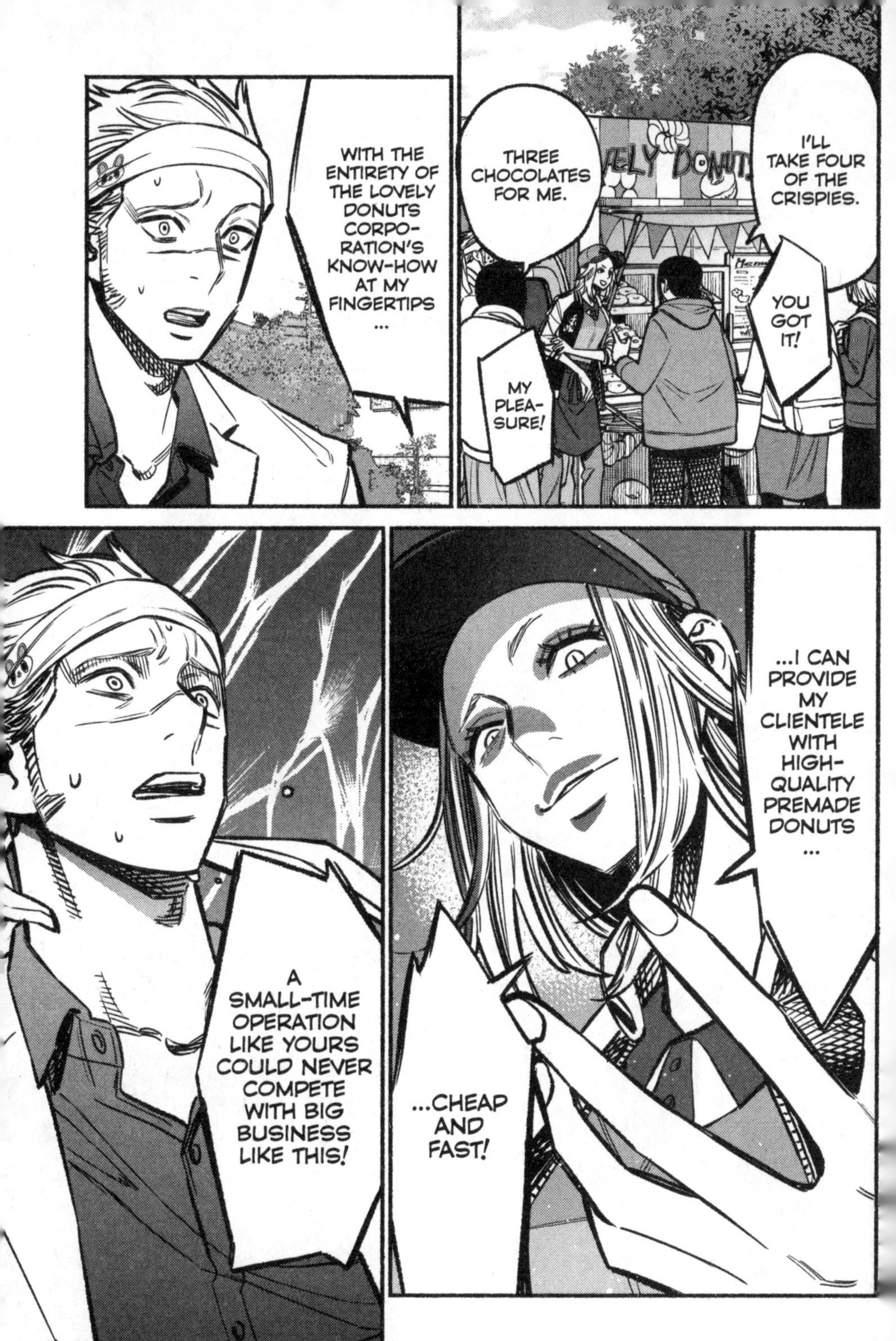
I'LL TAKE FOUR OF THE CRISPIES.
THREE CHOCOLATES FOR ME.
YOU GOT IT!
MY PLEASURE!
WITH THE ENTIRETY OF THE LOVELY DONUTS CORPORATION'S KNOW-HOW AT MY FINGERTIPS...
...I CAN PROVIDE MY CLIENTELE WITH HIGH-QUALITY PREMADE DONUTS...
...CHEAP AND FAST!
A SMALL-TIME OPERATION LIKE YOURS COULD NEVER COMPETE WITH BIG BUSINESS LIKE THIS!

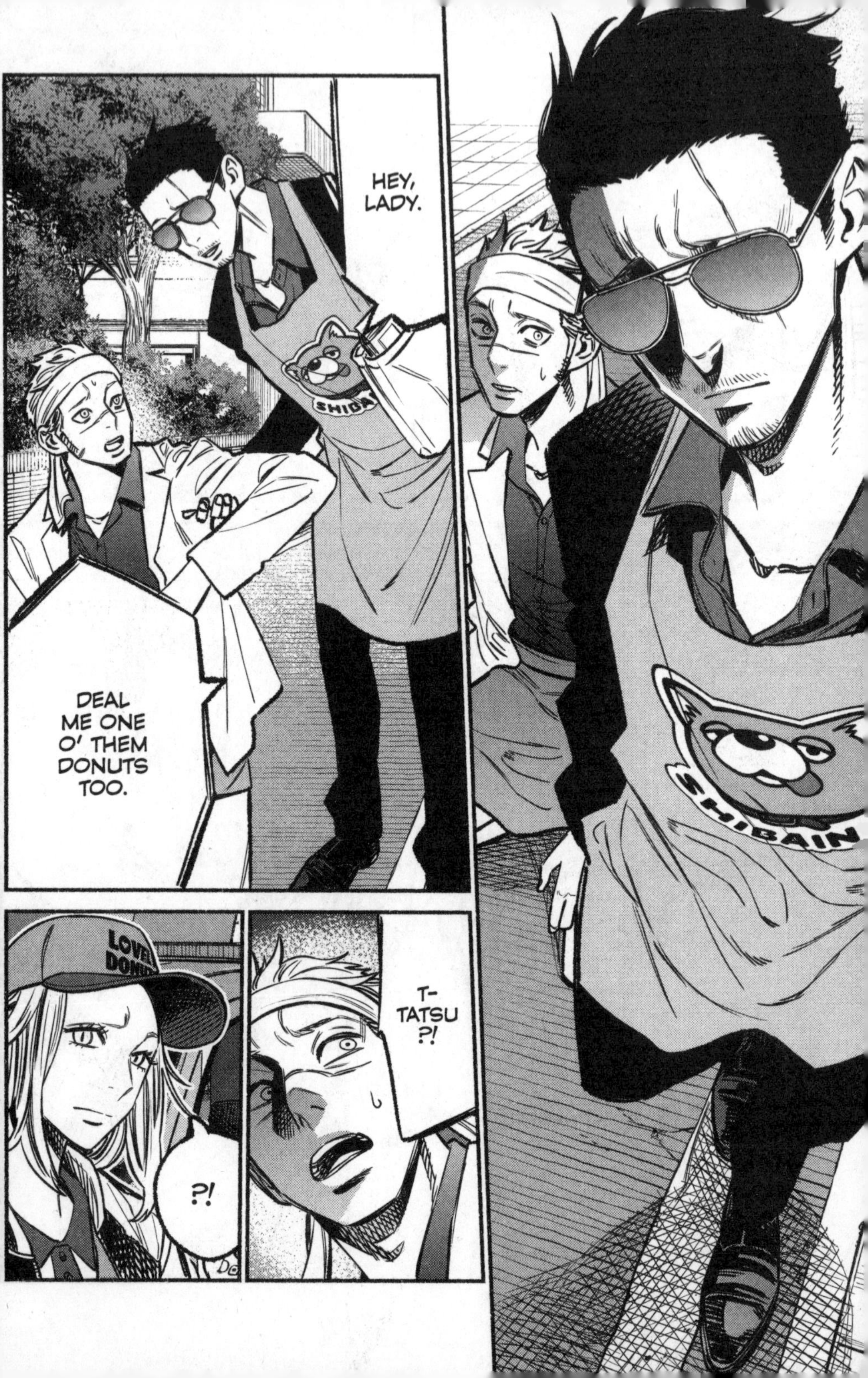
HEY, LADY.
DEAL ME ONE O' THEM DONUTS TOO.
T-TATSU?!
?!

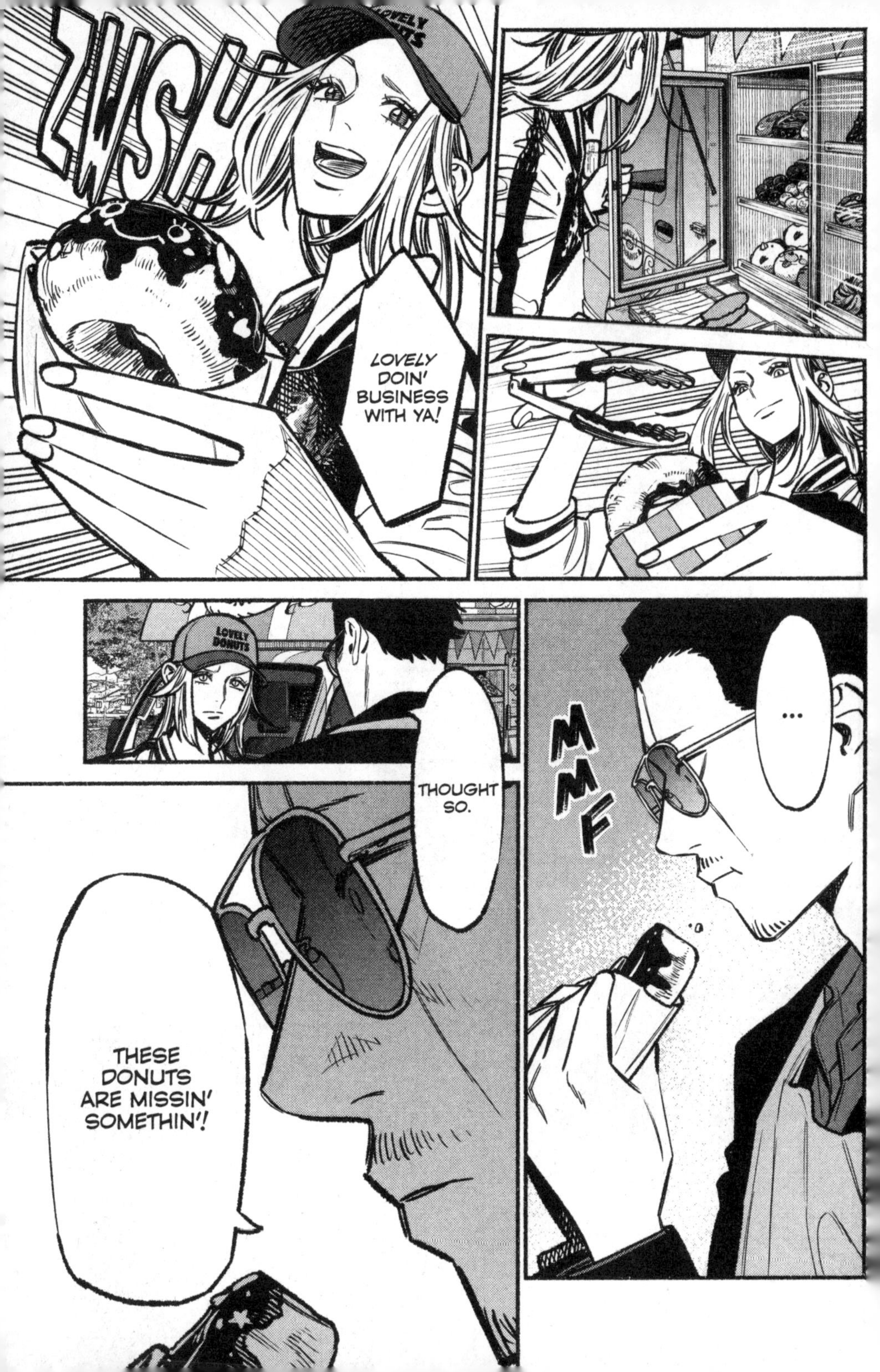
ZWSH
LOVELY DOIN' BUSINESS WITH YA!
...
MMF
THOUGHT SO.
THESE DONUTS ARE MISSIN' SOMETHIN'!

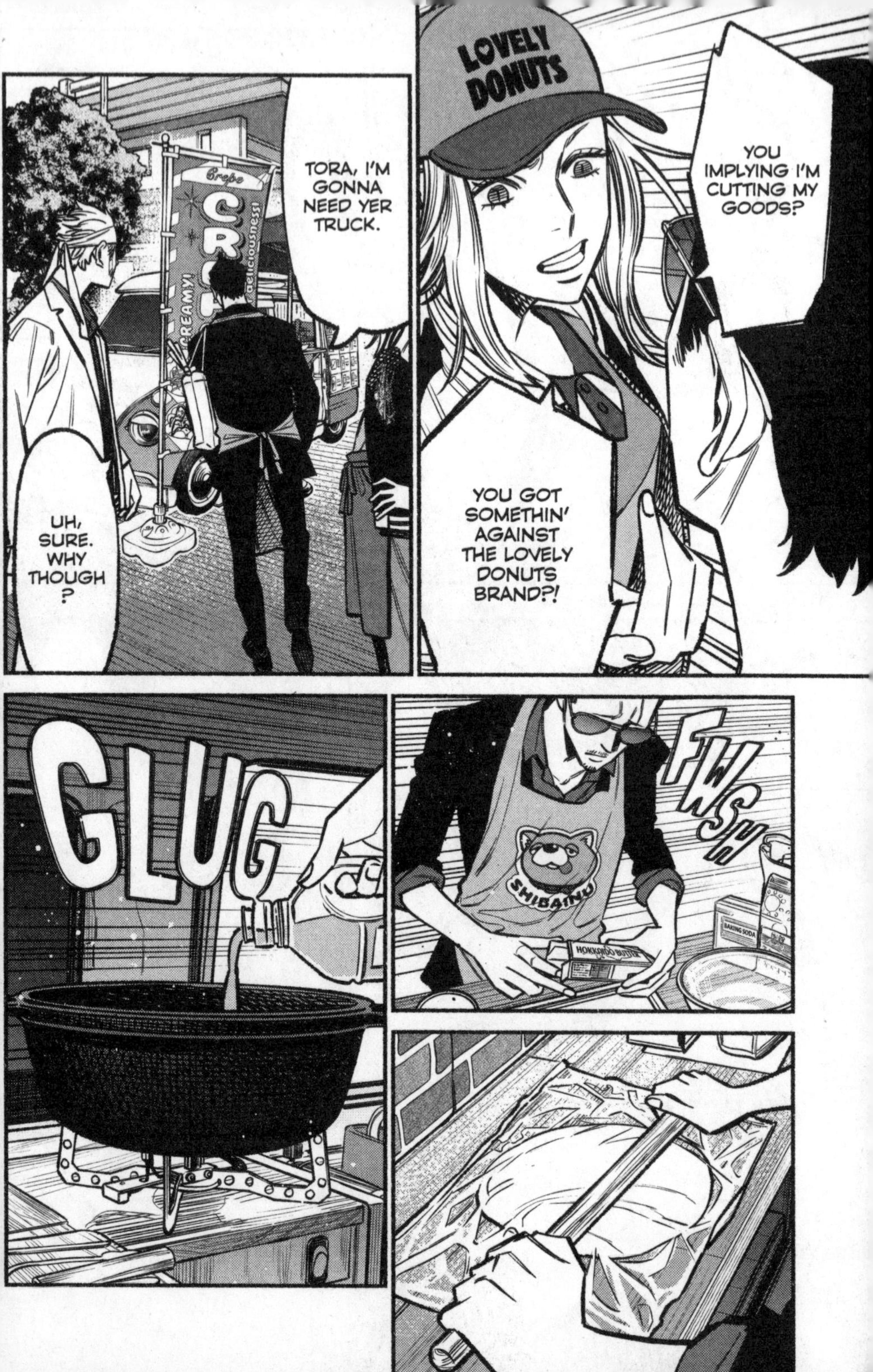
LOVELY DONUTS
YOU IMPLYING I'M CUTTING MY GOODS?
YOU GOT SOMETHIN' AGAINST THE LOVELY DONUTS BRAND?!
TORA, I'M GONNA NEED YER TRUCK.
Crepe
CREAMY!
deliciousness!
UH, SURE. WHY THOUGH?
FWSH
SHIBAINU
HOKKAIDO BUTTER
BAKING SODA
GLUG

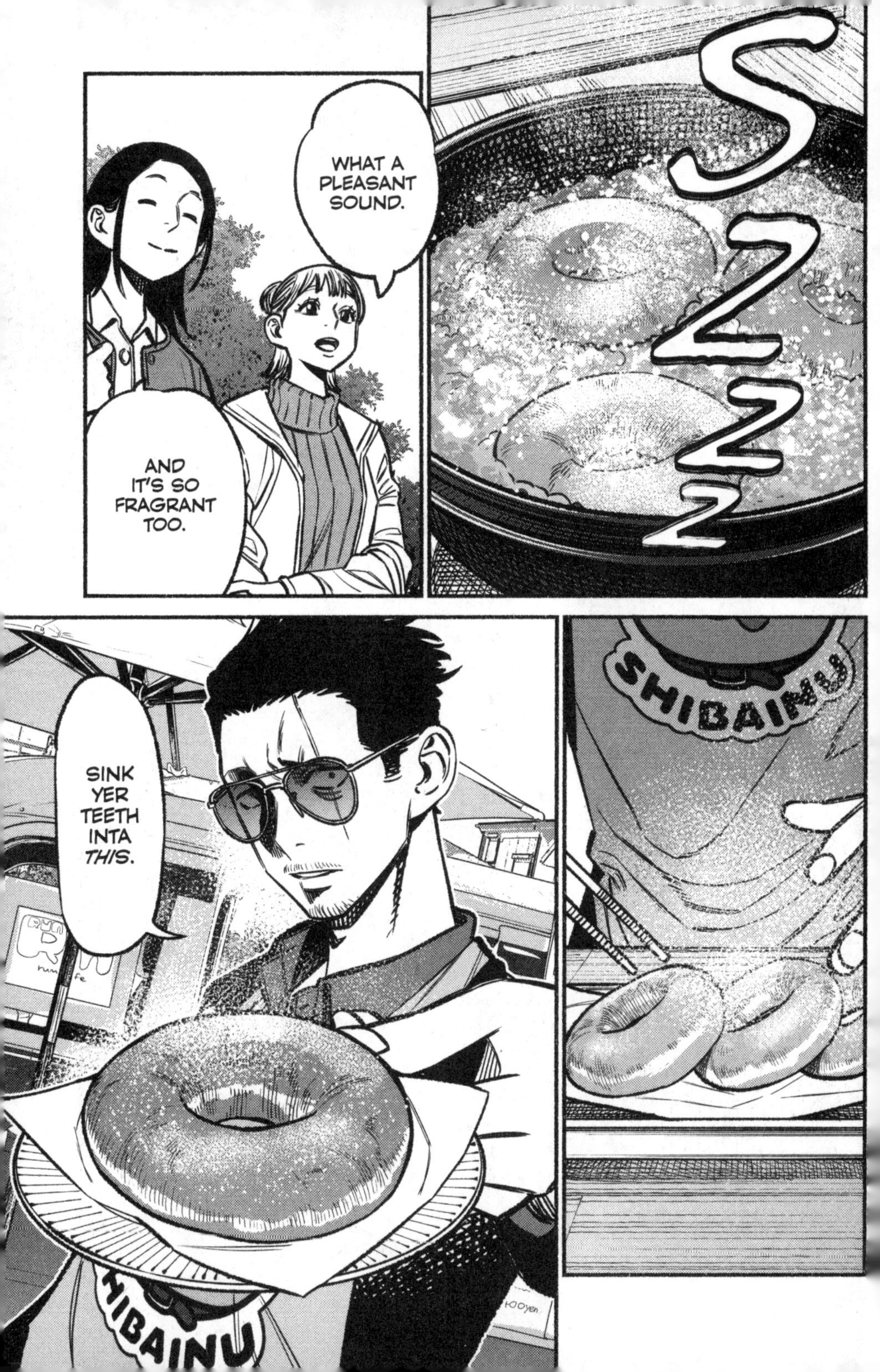
SZZZ
WHAT A PLEASANT SOUND.
AND IT'S SO FRAGRANT TOO.
SHIBAINU
SINK YER TEETH INTA *THIS*.
HIBAINU

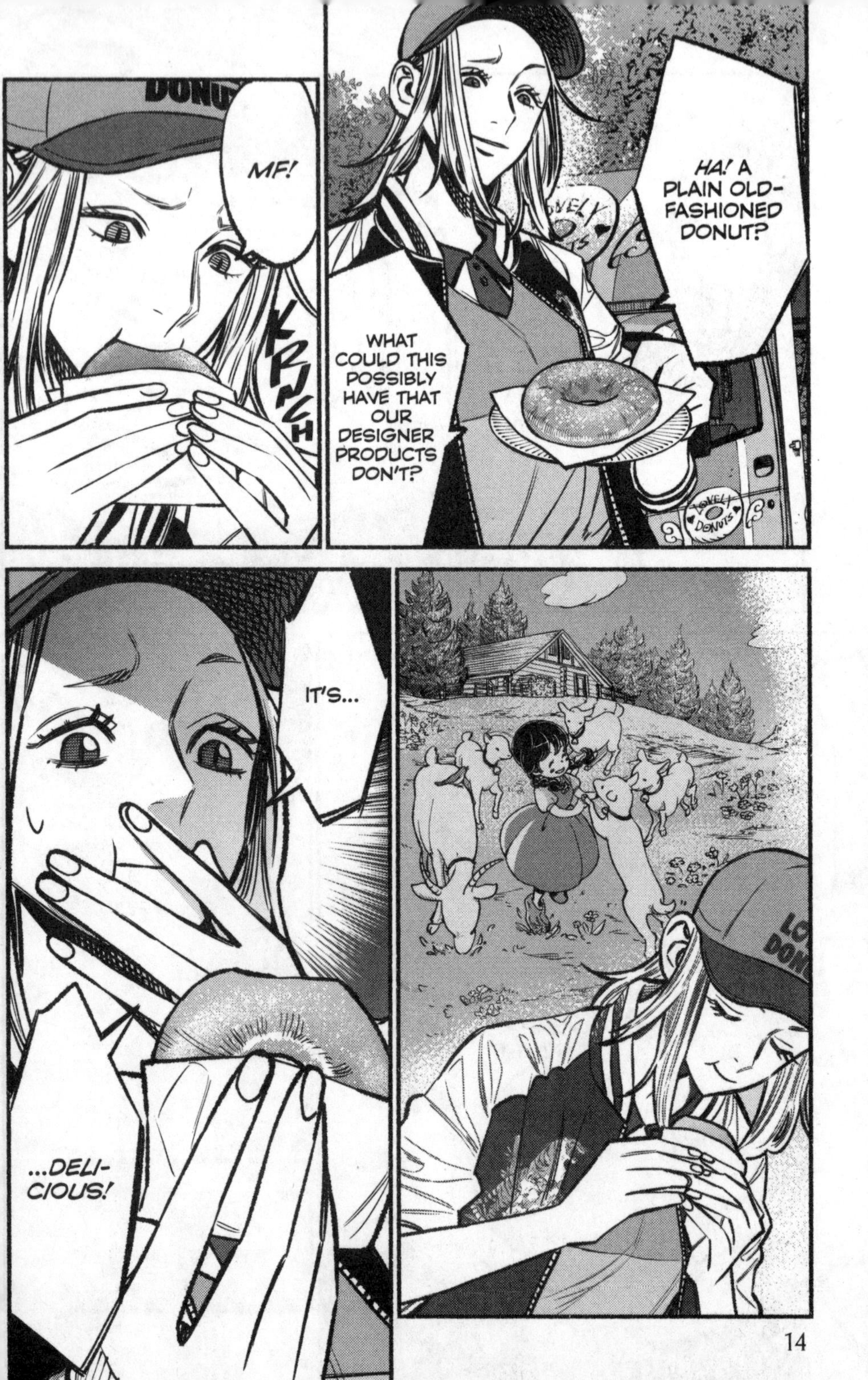
HA! A PLAIN OLD-FASHIONED DONUT?
WHAT COULD THIS POSSIBLY HAVE THAT OUR DESIGNER PRODUCTS DON'T?
MF!
KRUNCH
IT'S...
...DELI-CIOUS!

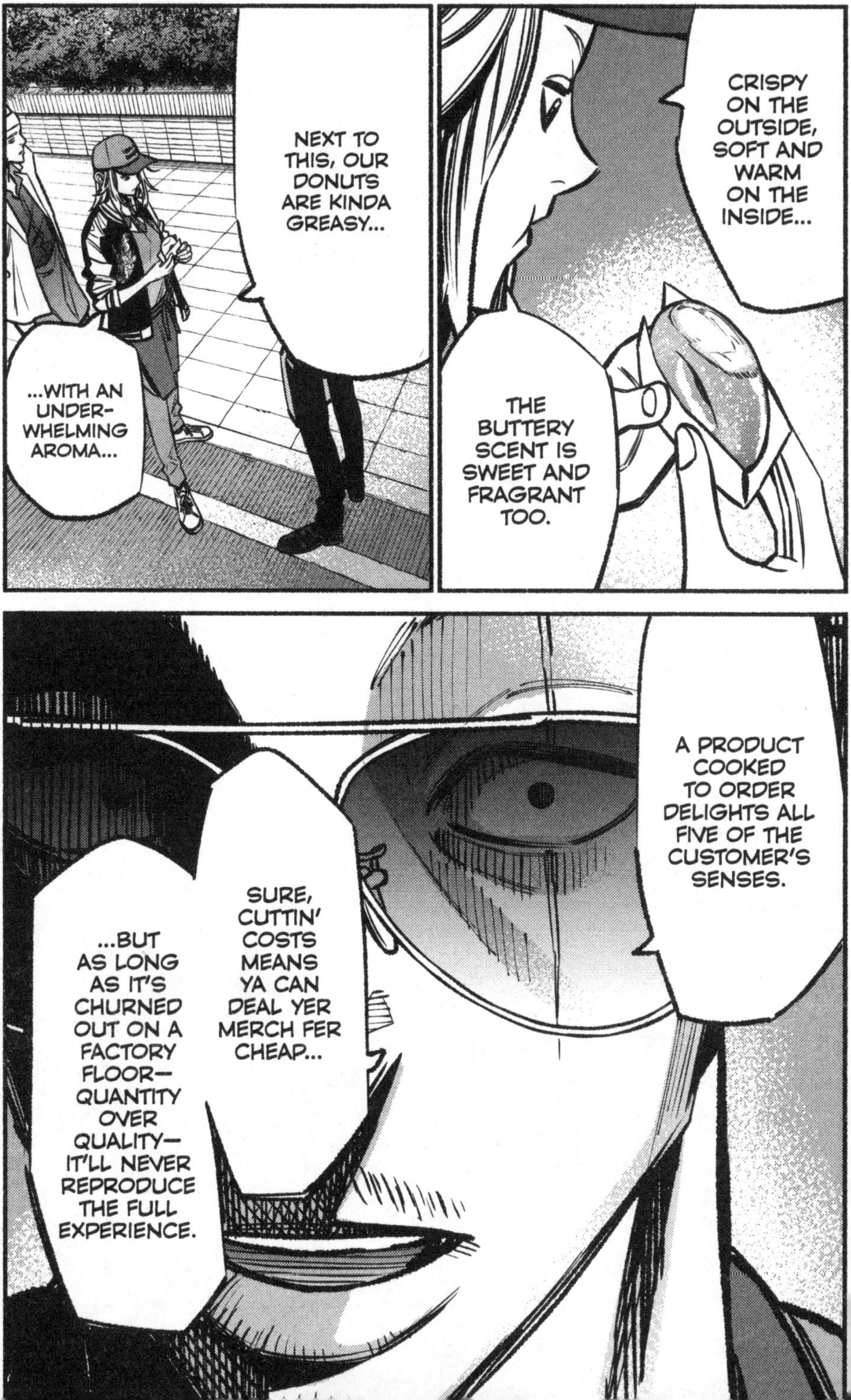
CRISPY ON THE OUTSIDE, SOFT AND WARM ON THE INSIDE...
THE BUTTERY SCENT IS SWEET AND FRAGRANT TOO.
NEXT TO THIS, OUR DONUTS ARE KINDA GREASY...
...WITH AN UNDER-WHELMING AROMA...
A PRODUCT COOKED TO ORDER DELIGHTS ALL FIVE OF THE CUSTOMER'S SENSES.
SURE, CUTTIN' COSTS MEANS YA CAN DEAL YER MERCH FER CHEAP...
...BUT AS LONG AS IT'S CHURNED OUT ON A FACTORY FLOOR—QUANTITY OVER QUALITY—IT'LL NEVER REPRODUCE THE FULL EXPERIENCE.

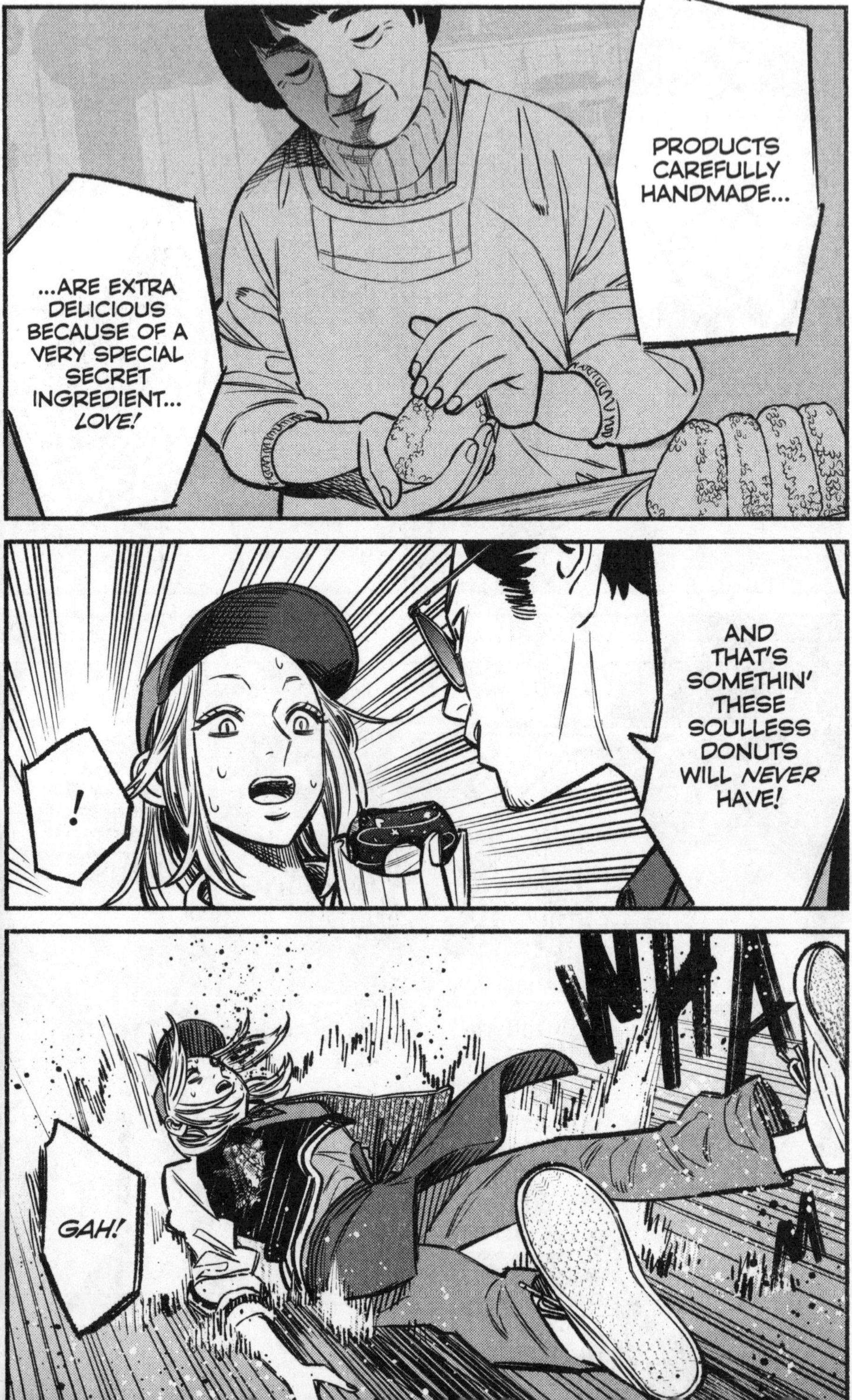
PRODUCTS CAREFULLY HANDMADE...
...ARE EXTRA DELICIOUS BECAUSE OF A VERY SPECIAL SECRET INGREDIENT... *LOVE!*
AND THAT'S SOMETHIN' THESE SOULLESS DONUTS WILL *NEVER* HAVE!
!
GAH!

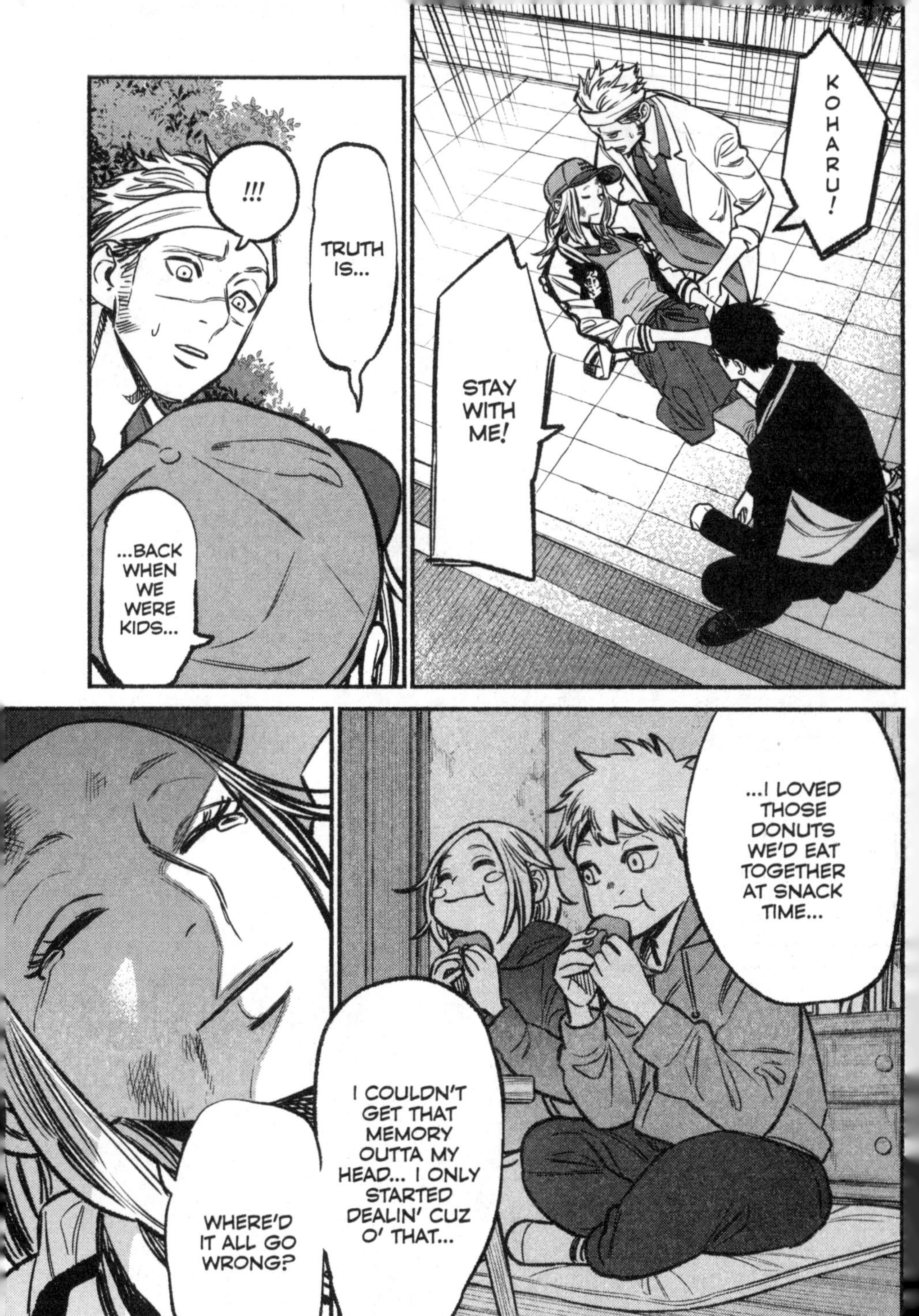
KOHARU!
STAY WITH ME!
!!!
TRUTH IS...
...BACK WHEN WE WERE KIDS...
...I LOVED THOSE DONUTS WE'D EAT TOGETHER AT SNACK TIME...
I COULDN'T GET THAT MEMORY OUTTA MY HEAD... I ONLY STARTED DEALIN' CUZ O' THAT...
WHERE'D IT ALL GO WRONG?

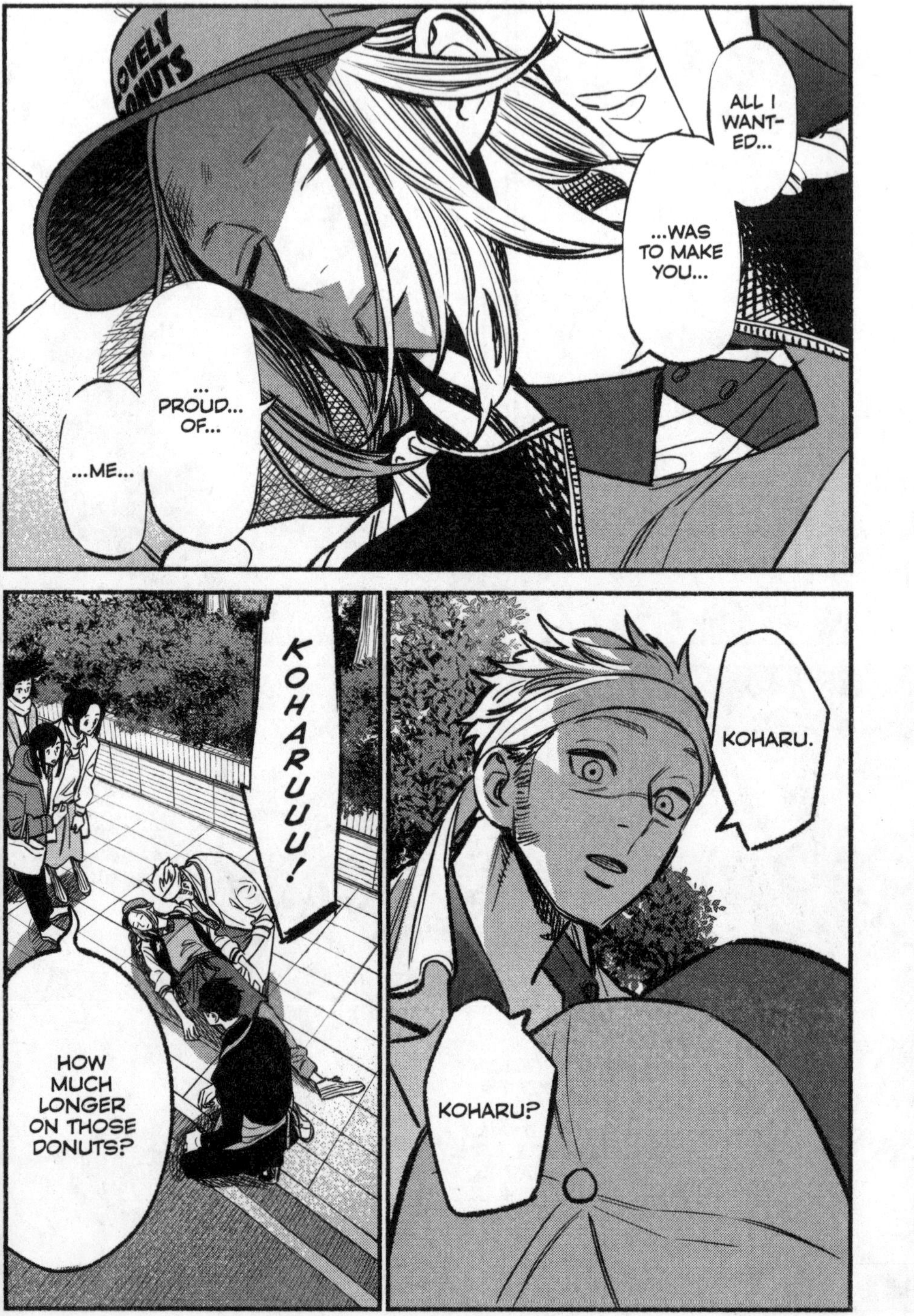
LOVELY
ALL I WANTED...
...WAS TO MAKE YOU...
... PROUD... OF...
...ME...
KOHARU.
KOHARU?
KOHARUUU!
HOW MUCH LONGER ON THOSE DONUTS?

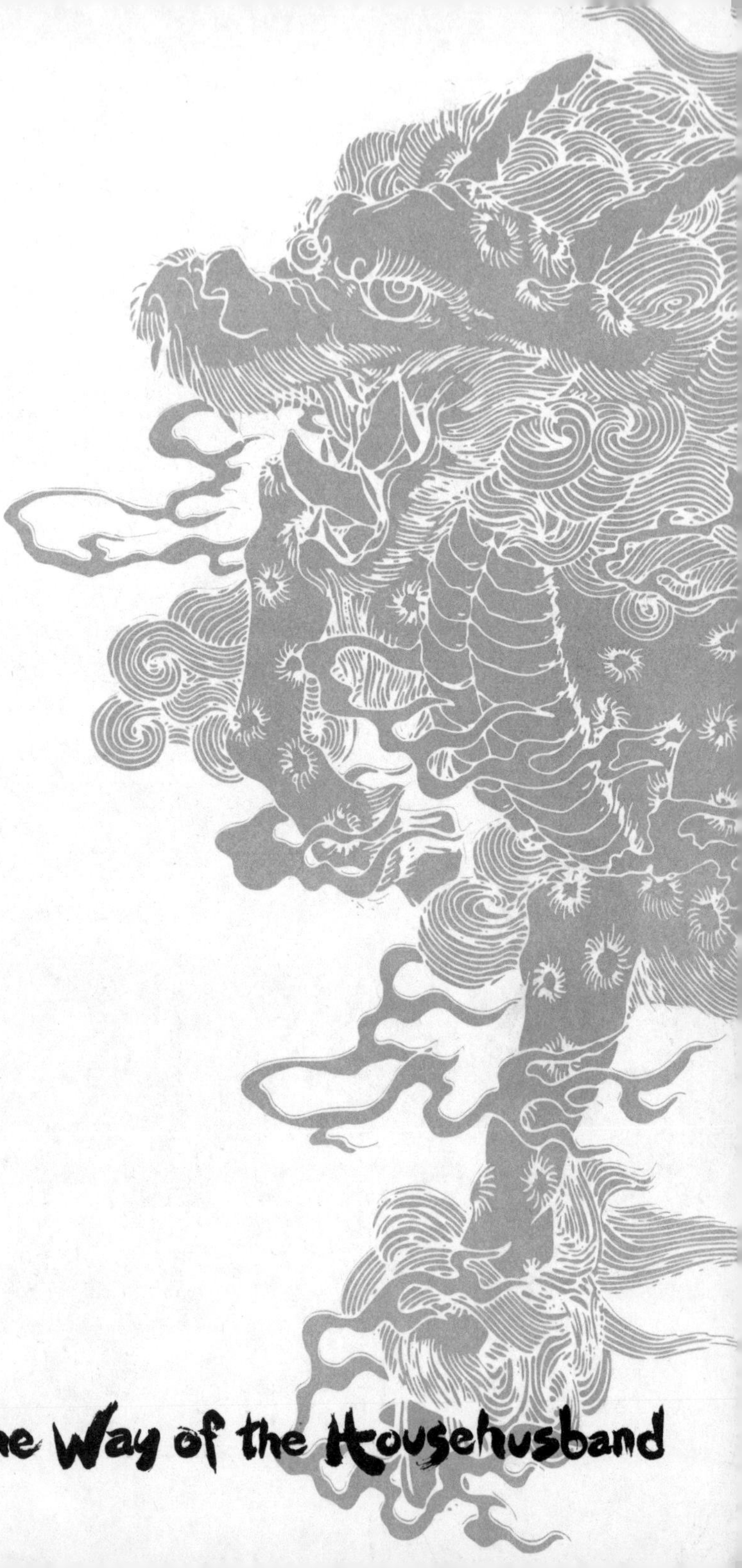

The Way of the Househusband

CHAPTER 65

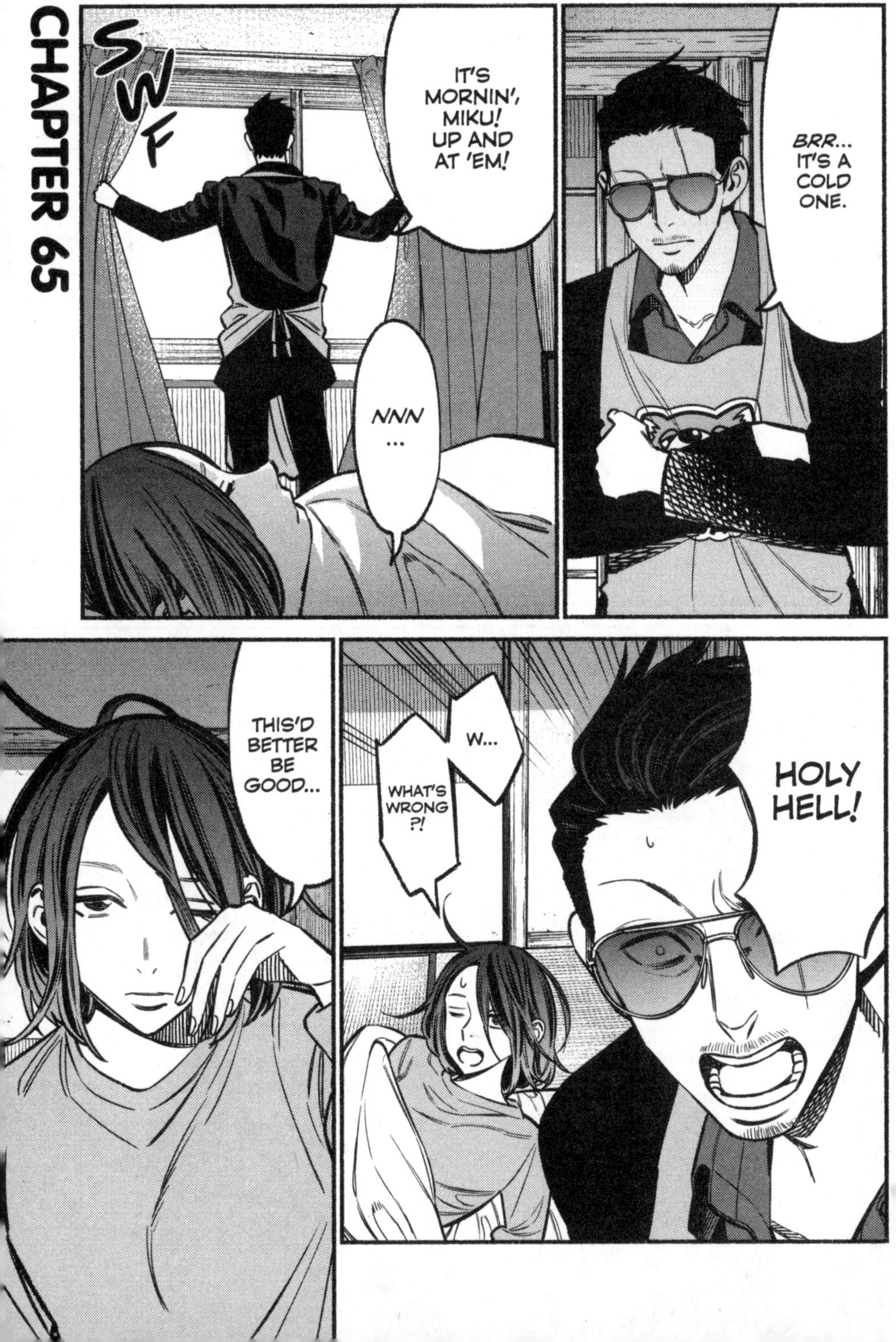
BRR... IT'S A COLD ONE.
SWF
IT'S MORNIN', MIKU! UP AND AT 'EM!
NNN...
HOLY HELL!
W...
WHAT'S WRONG?!
THIS'D BETTER BE GOOD...

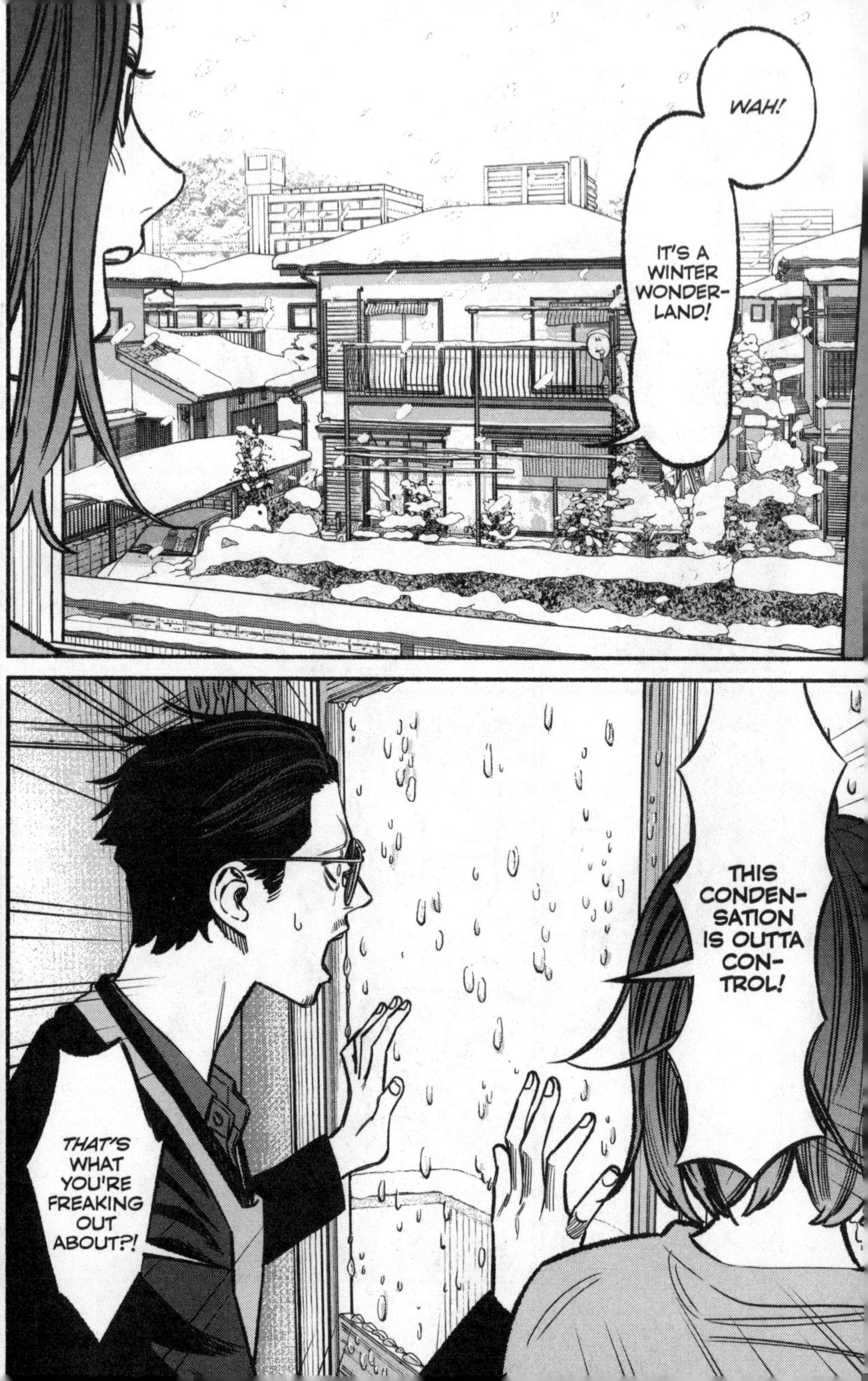
WAH!
IT'S A WINTER WONDER-LAND!
THIS CONDEN-SATION IS OUTTA CON-TROL!
THAT'S WHAT YOU'RE FREAKING OUT ABOUT?!

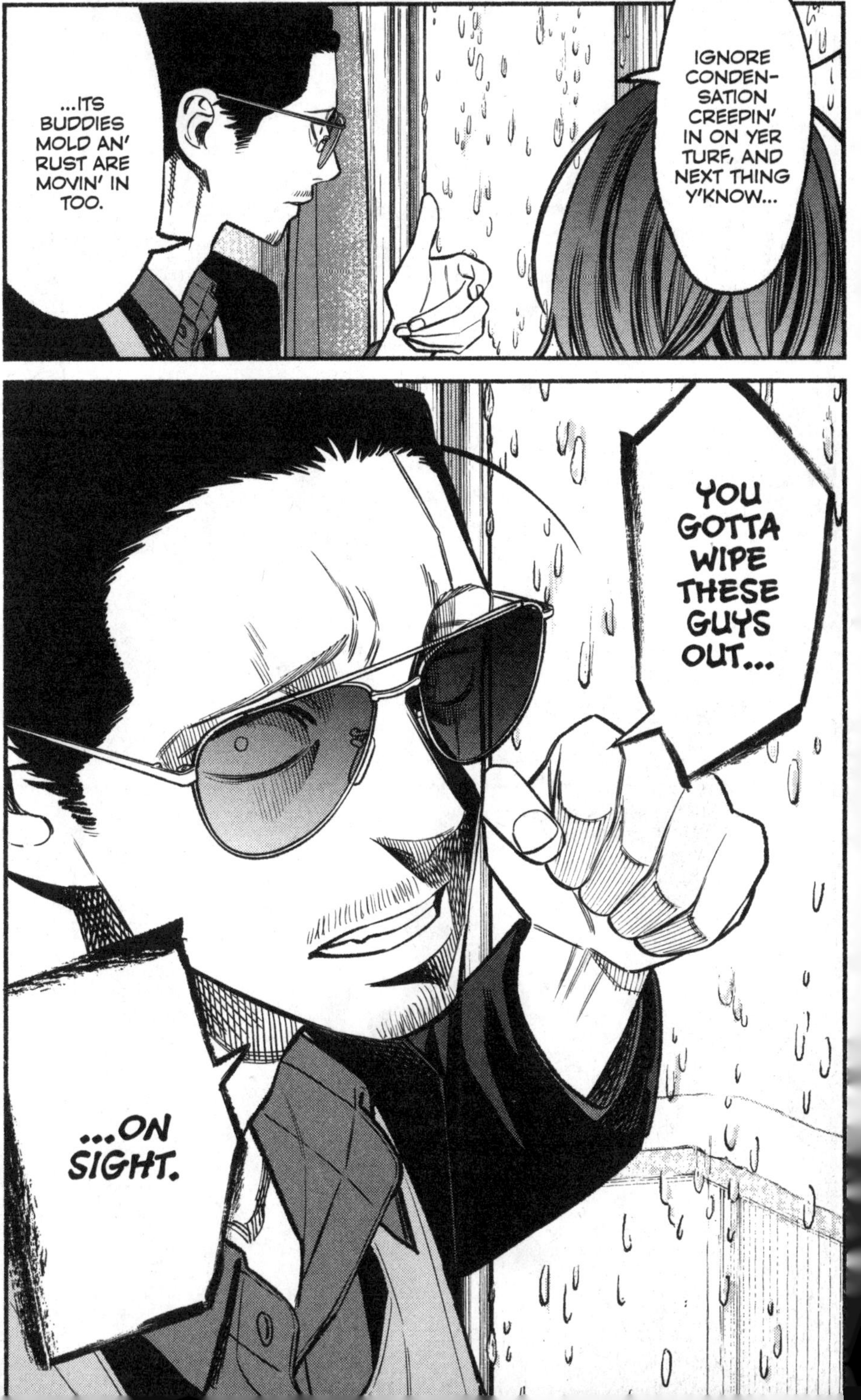
IGNORE CONDEN-SATION CREEPIN' IN ON YER TURF, AND NEXT THING Y'KNOW...
...ITS BUDDIES MOLD AN' RUST ARE MOVIN' IN TOO.
YOU GOTTA WIPE THESE GUYS OUT...
...ON SIGHT.

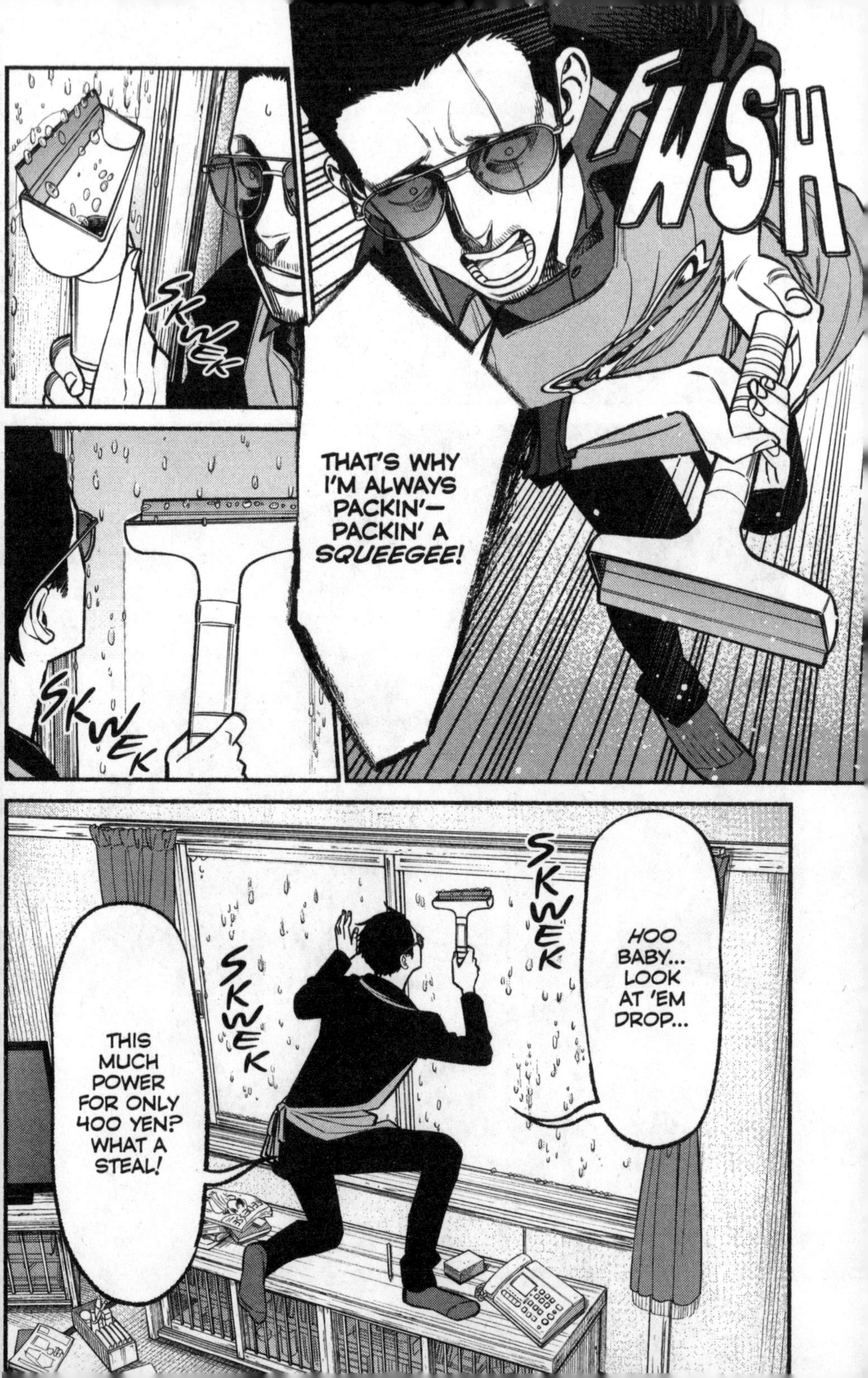
FWSH
THAT'S WHY I'M ALWAYS PACKIN'— PACKIN' A SQUEEGEE!
SKWEK
SKWEK
SKWEK
HOO BABY... LOOK AT 'EM DROP...
SKWEK
THIS MUCH POWER FOR ONLY 400 YEN? WHAT A STEAL!

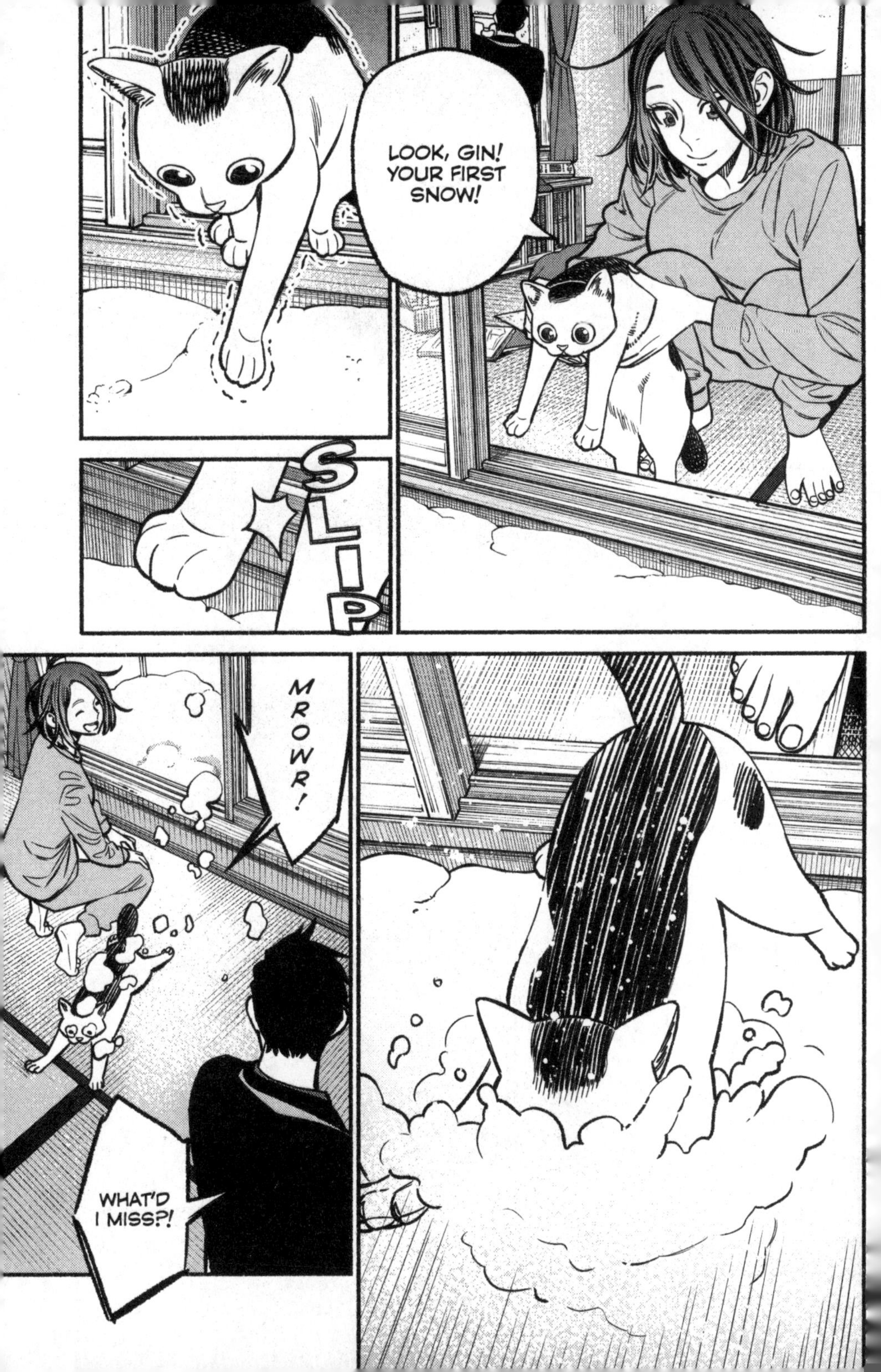
LOOK, GIN! YOUR FIRST SNOW!
SLIP
MROWR!
WHAT'D I MISS?!

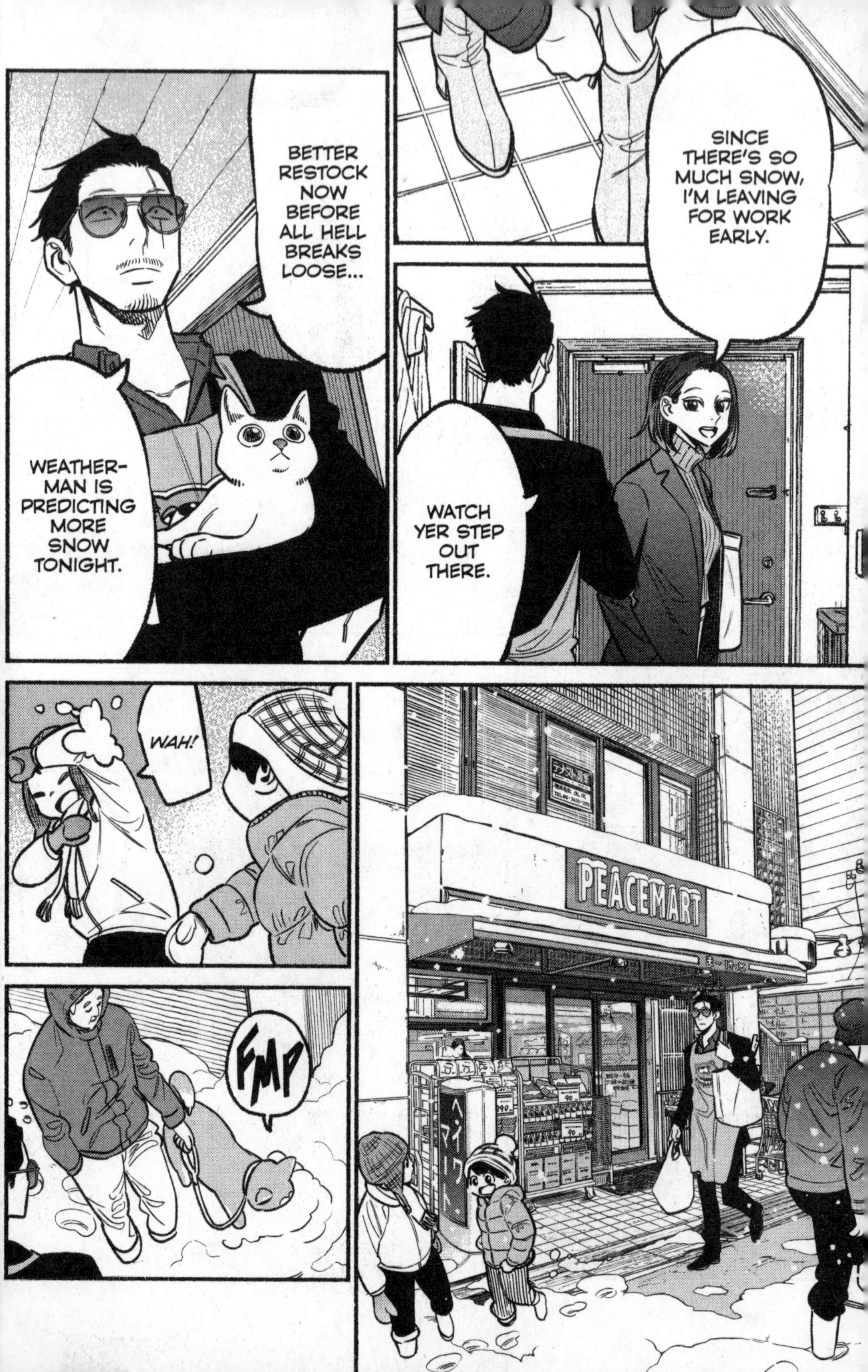
SINCE THERE'S SO MUCH SNOW, I'M LEAVING FOR WORK EARLY.
WATCH YER STEP OUT THERE.
BETTER RESTOCK NOW BEFORE ALL HELL BREAKS LOOSE...
WEATHER-MAN IS PREDICTING MORE SNOW TONIGHT.
PEACEMART
WAH!
FMP

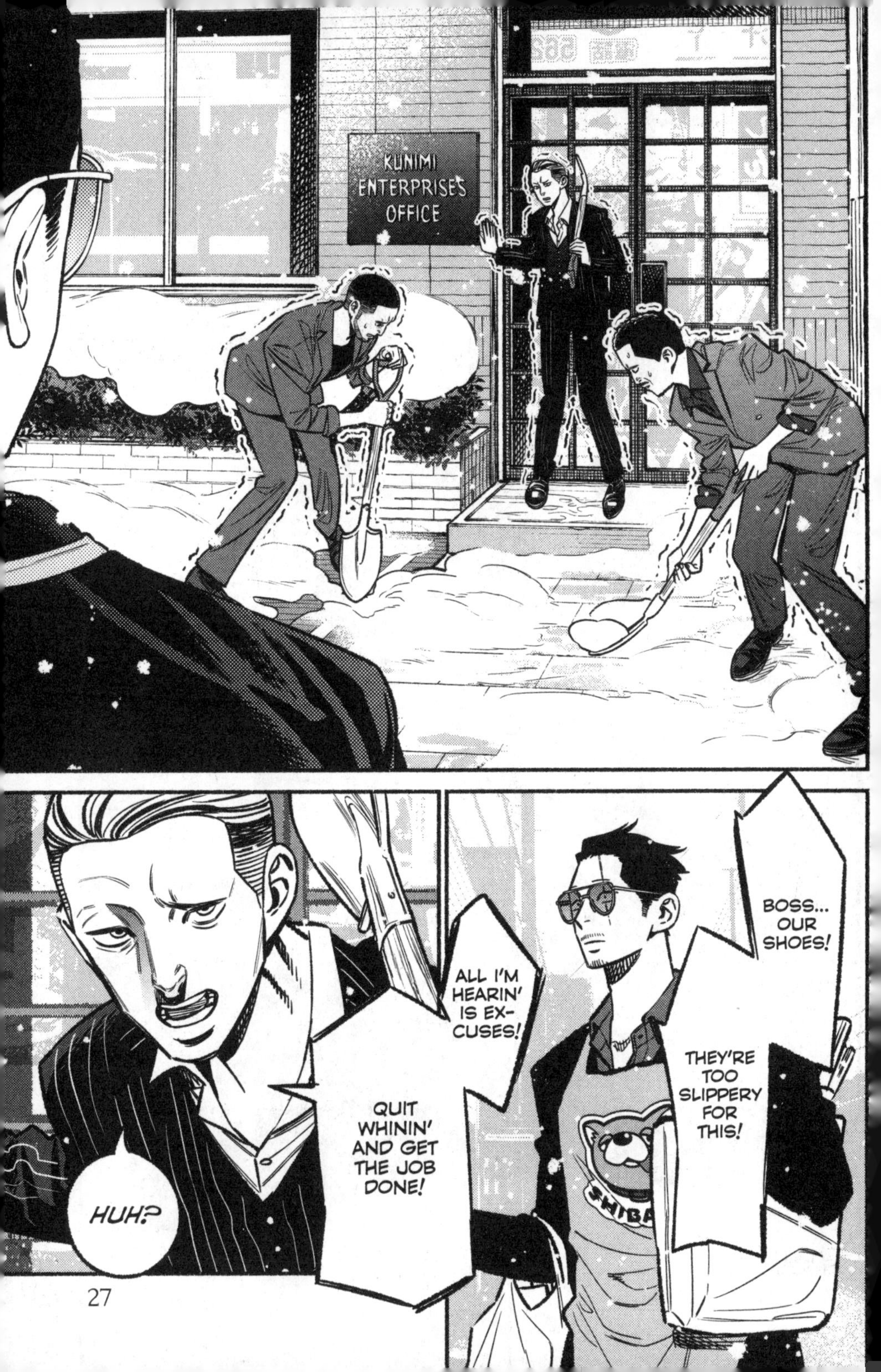
KUNIMI ENTERPRISES OFFICE
BOSS... OUR SHOES!
THEY'RE TOO SLIPPERY FOR THIS!
ALL I'M HEARIN' IS EX-CUSES!
QUIT WHININ' AND GET THE JOB DONE!
HUH?

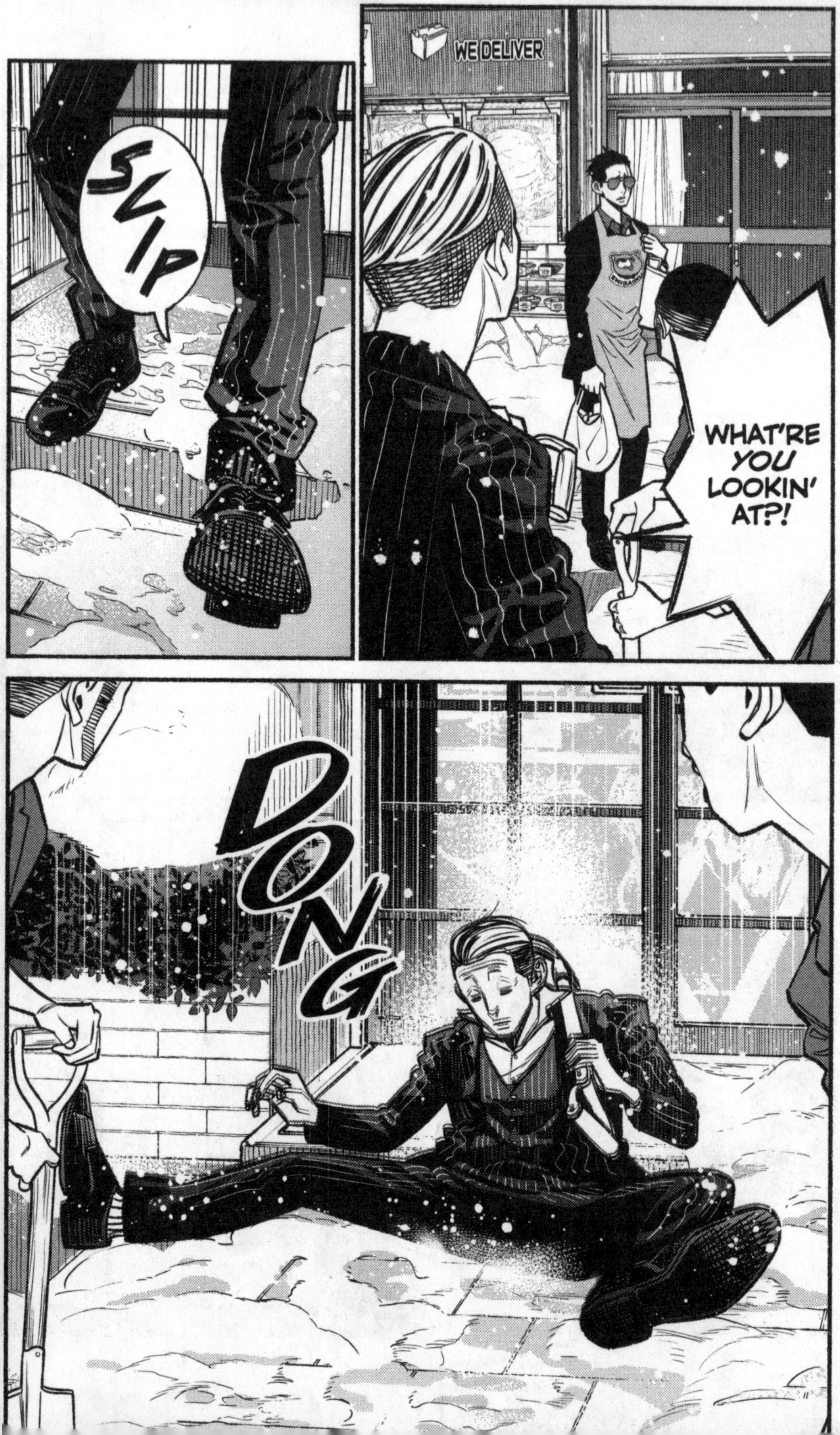
WE DELIVER
WHAT'RE *YOU* LOOKIN' AT?!
SLIP
DONG

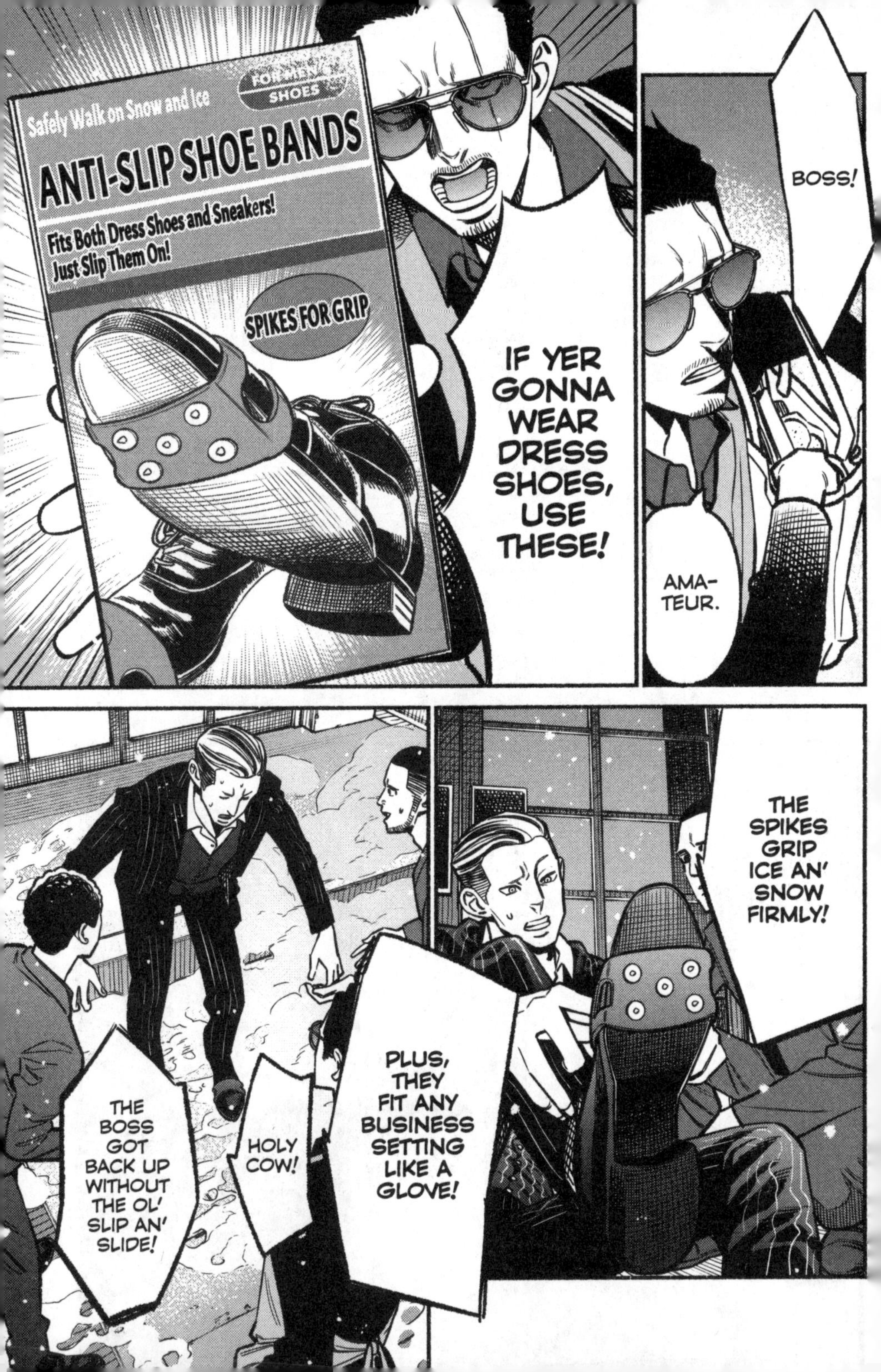
BOSS!
AMA-TEUR.
FOR MEN'S SHOES
Safely Walk on Snow and Ice
ANTI-SLIP SHOE BANDS
Fits Both Dress Shoes and Sneakers! Just Slip Them On!
SPIKES FOR GRIP
IF YER GONNA WEAR DRESS SHOES, USE THESE!
THE SPIKES GRIP ICE AN' SNOW FIRMLY!
PLUS, THEY FIT ANY BUSINESS SETTING LIKE A GLOVE!
HOLY COW!
THE BOSS GOT BACK UP WITHOUT THE OL' SLIP AN' SLIDE!

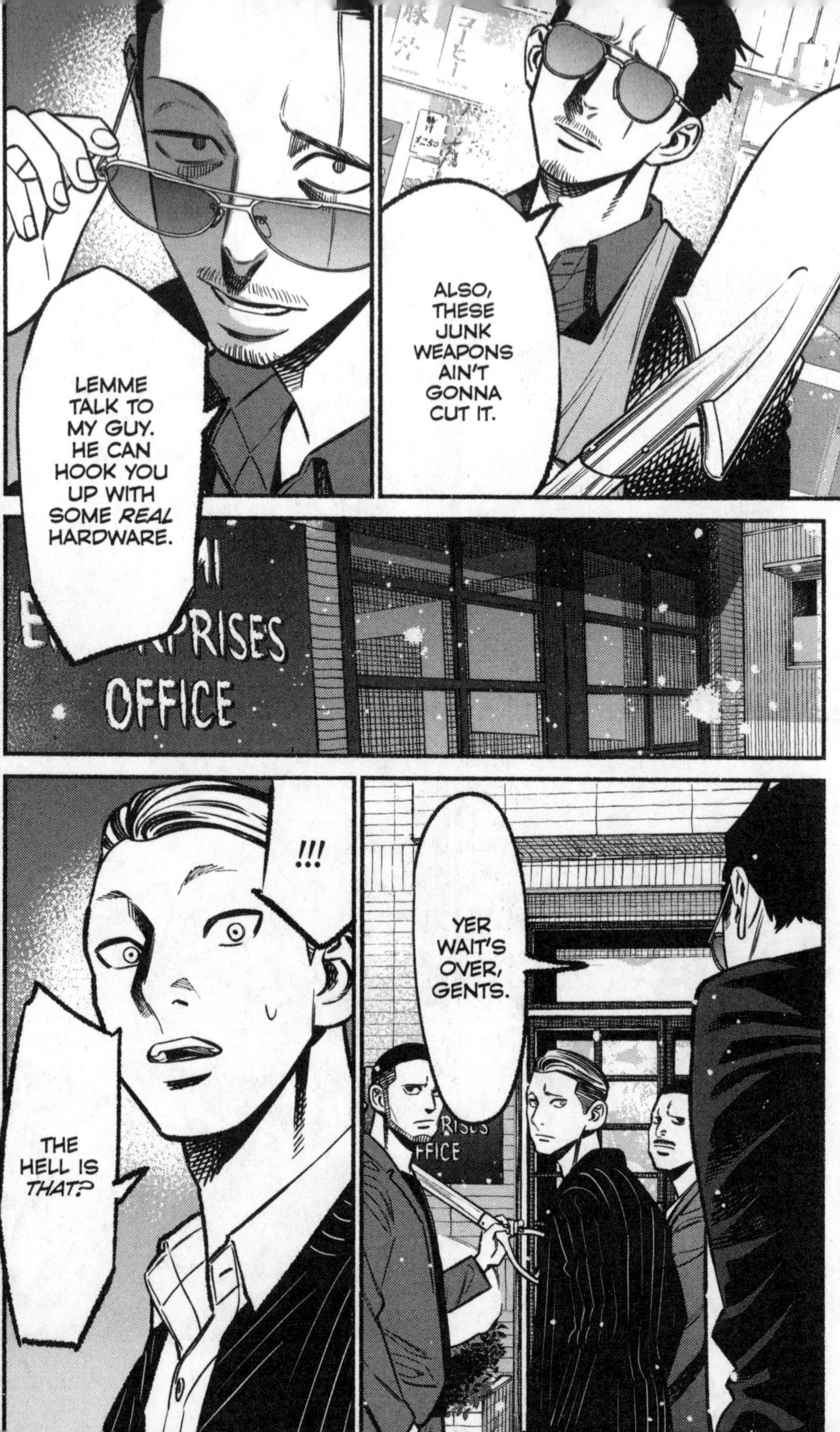
ALSO, THESE JUNK WEAPONS AIN'T GONNA CUT IT.
LEMME TALK TO MY GUY. HE CAN HOOK YOU UP WITH SOME *REAL* HARDWARE.
OFFICE
YER WAIT'S OVER, GENTS.
!!!
THE HELL IS *THAT?*

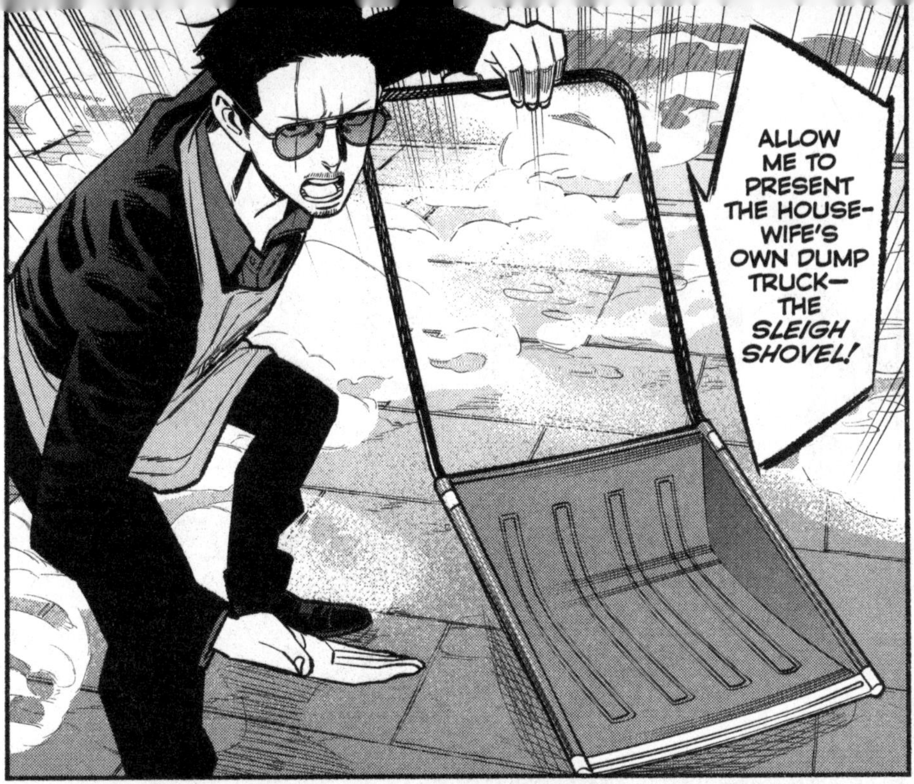
ALLOW ME TO PRESENT THE HOUSE-WIFE'S OWN DUMP TRUCK—THE *SLEIGH SHOVEL!*
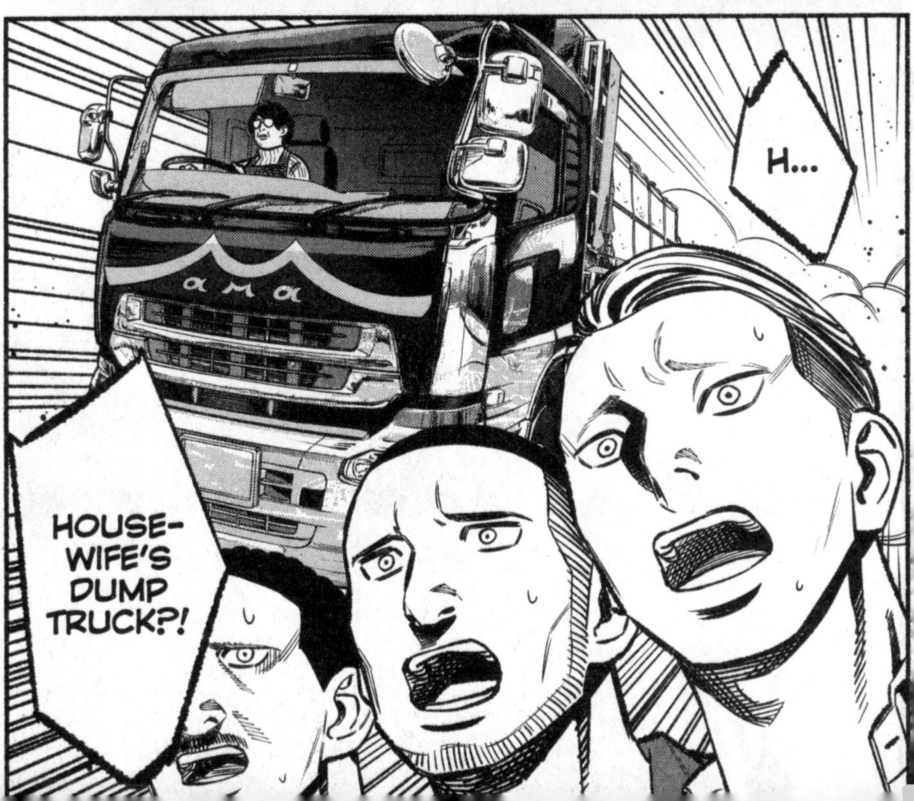
H...
HOUSE-WIFE'S DUMP TRUCK?!

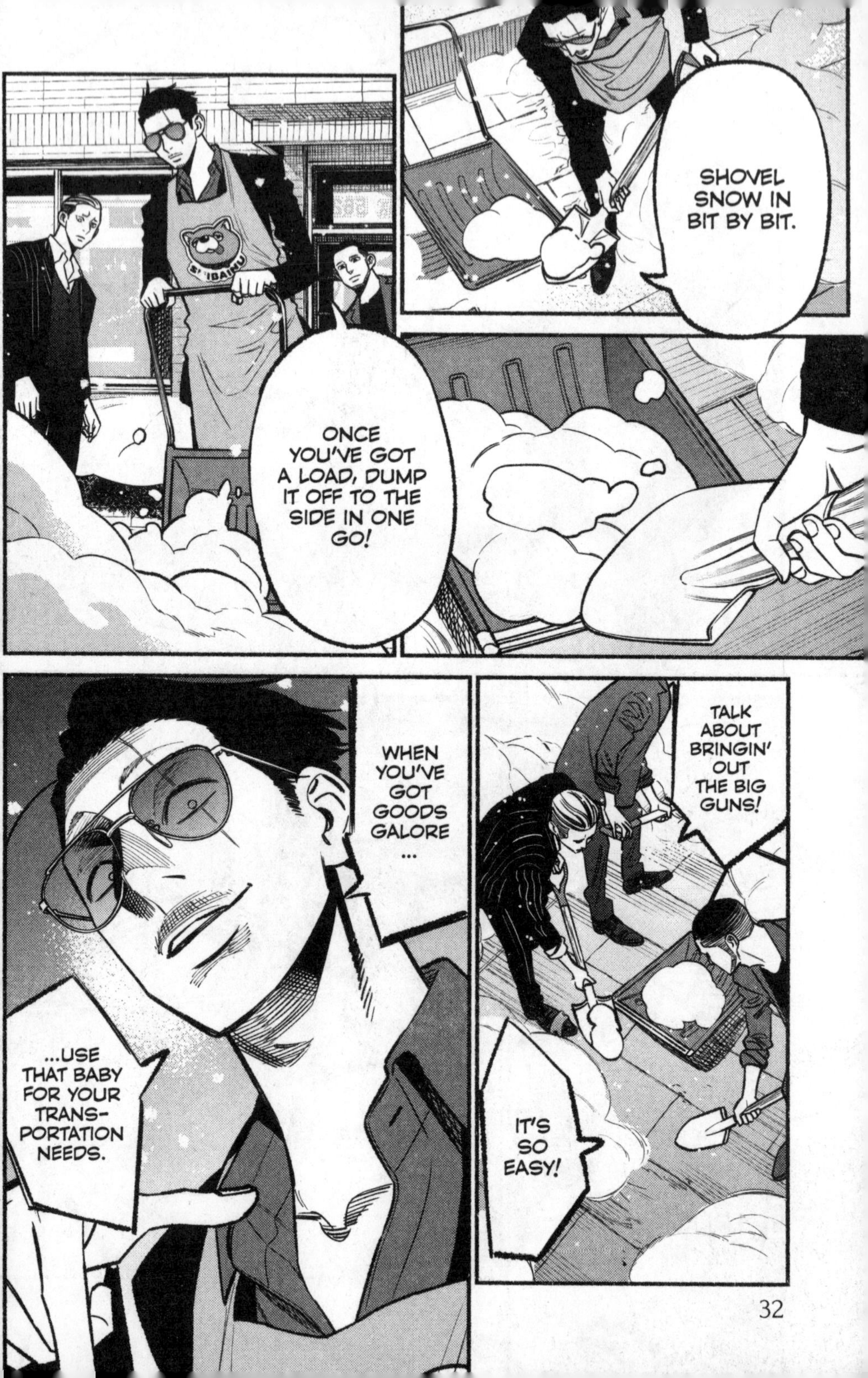
SHOVEL SNOW IN BIT BY BIT.
ONCE YOU'VE GOT A LOAD, DUMP IT OFF TO THE SIDE IN ONE GO!
TALK ABOUT BRINGIN' OUT THE BIG GUNS!
IT'S SO EASY!
WHEN YOU'VE GOT GOODS GALORE ...
...USE THAT BABY FOR YOUR TRANS-PORTATION NEEDS.

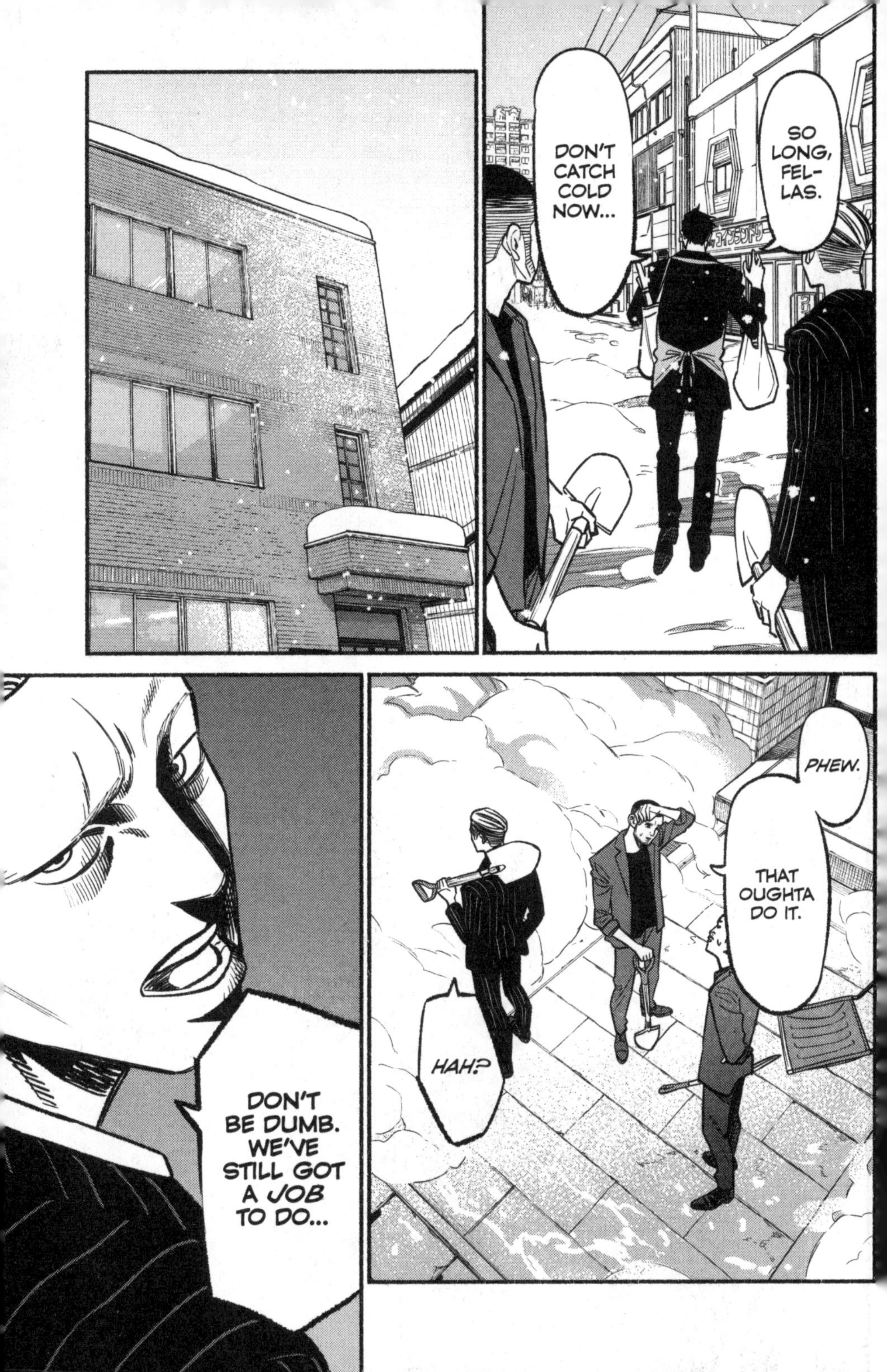
SO LONG, FEL-LAS.
DON'T CATCH COLD NOW...
PHEW.
THAT OUGHTA DO IT.
HAH?
DON'T BE DUMB. WE'VE STILL GOT A *JOB* TO DO...

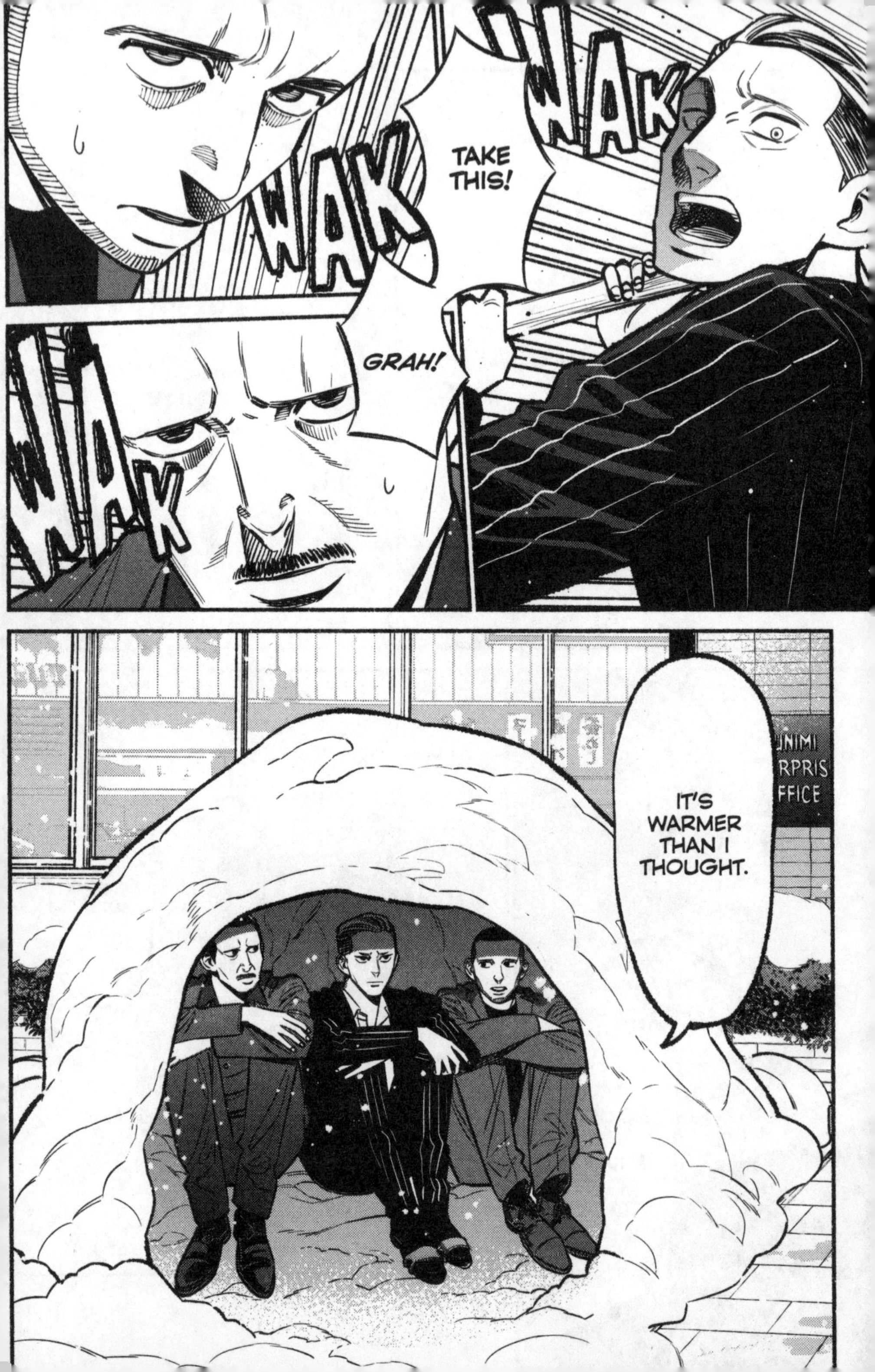
WAK
TAKE THIS!
WAK
GRAH!
WAK
IT'S WARMER THAN I THOUGHT.

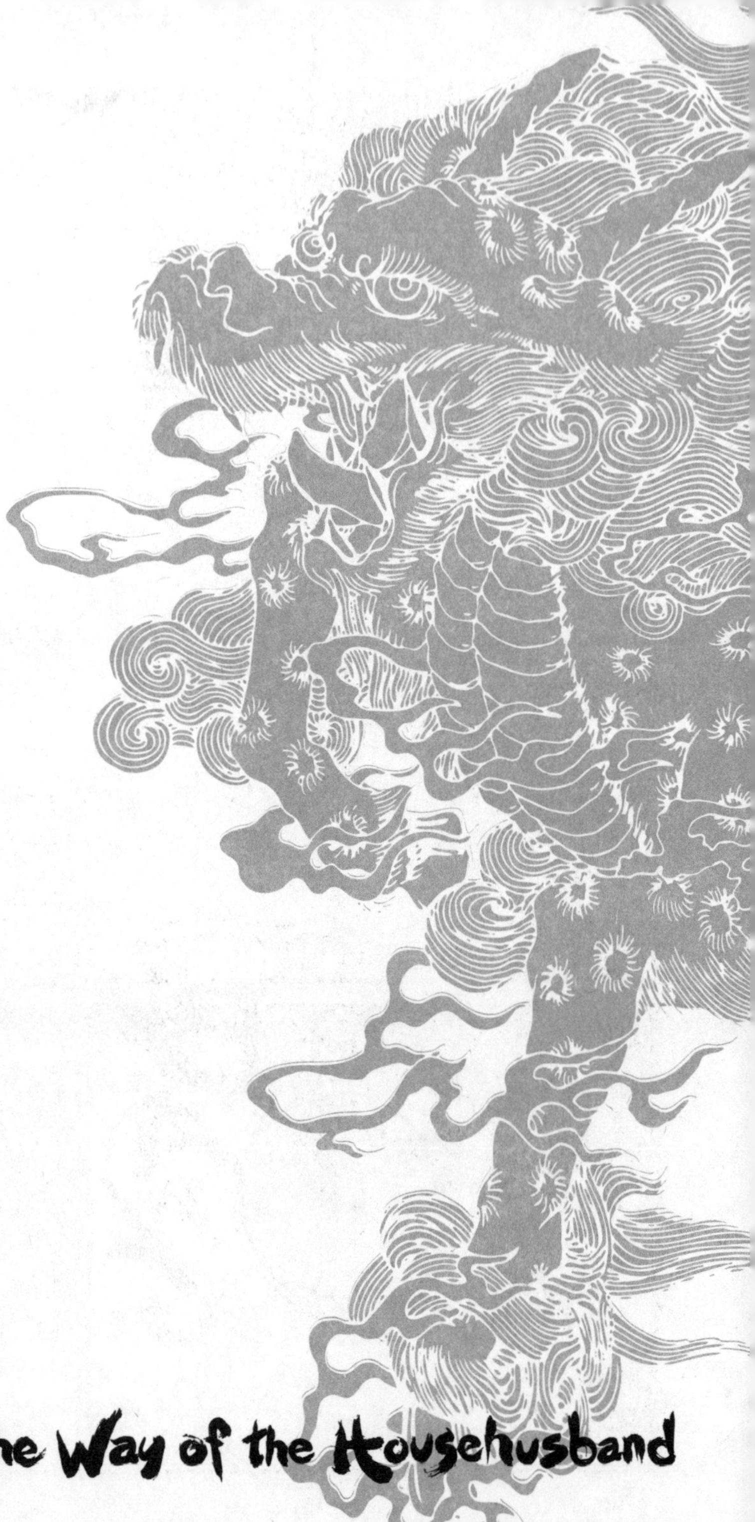

The Way of the Househusband

CHAPTER 66

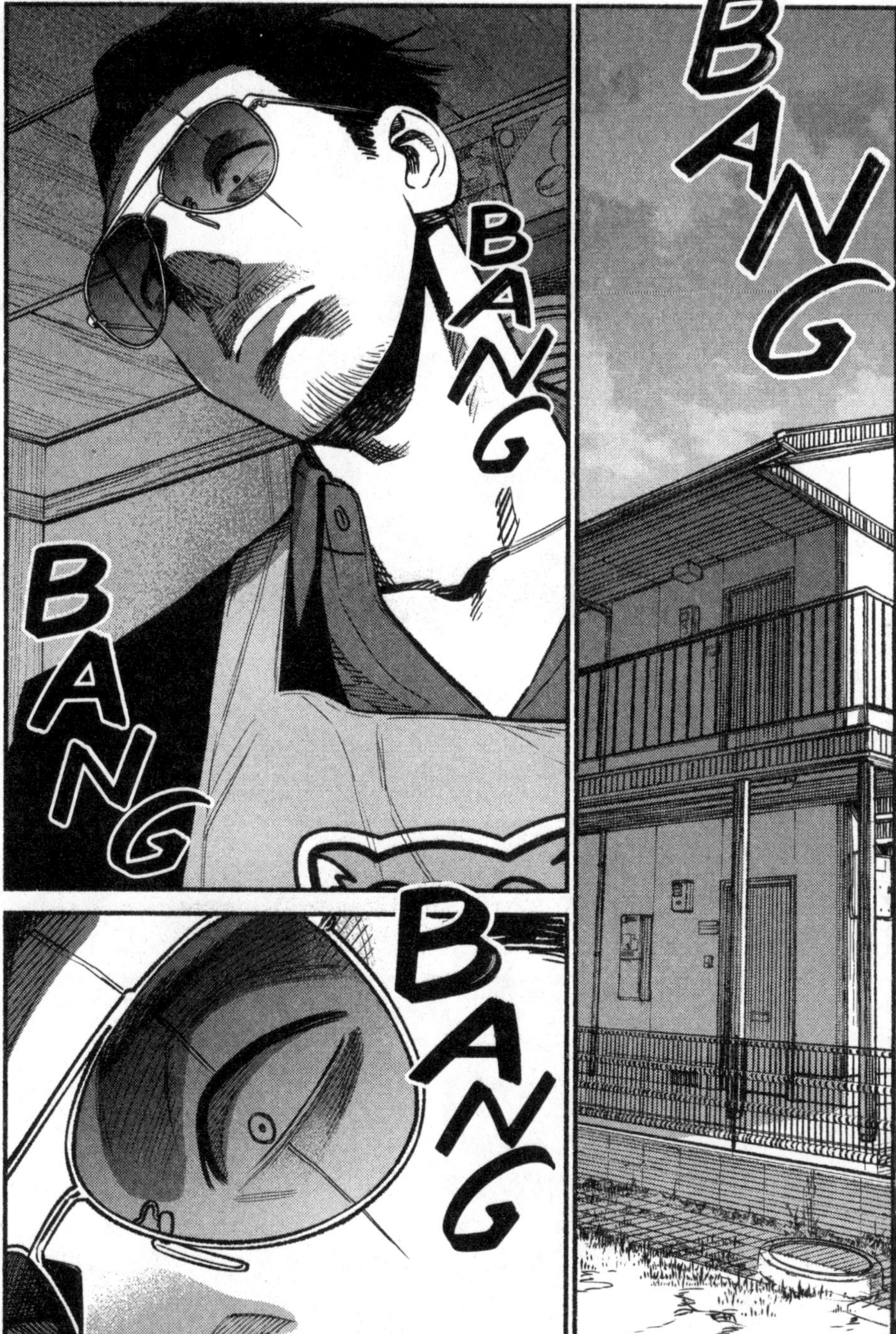
BANG
BANG
BANG
BANG

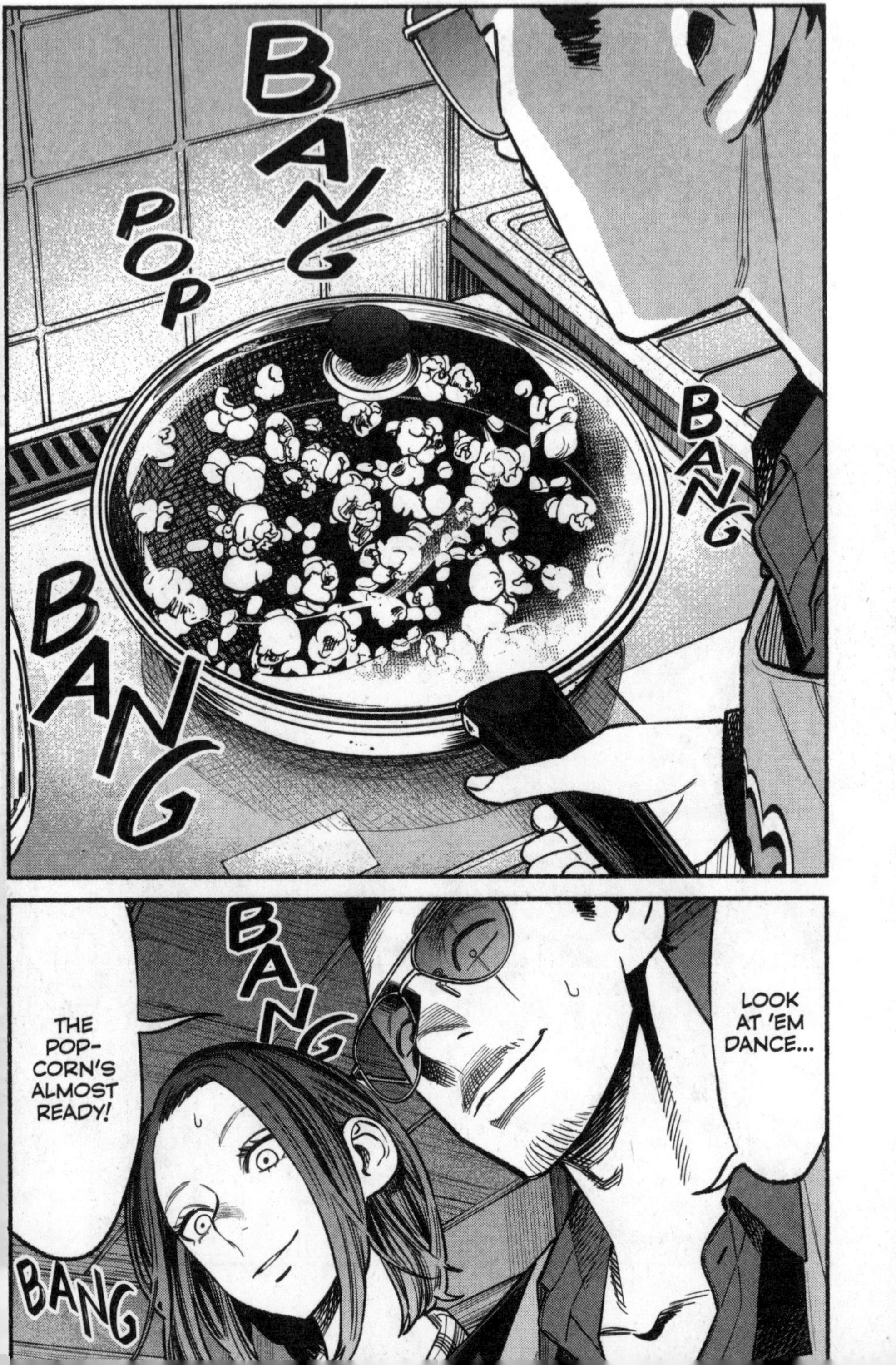
BANG
BANG
POP
POP
BANG
LOOK AT 'EM DANCE...
BANG
THE POP-CORN'S ALMOST READY!
BANG

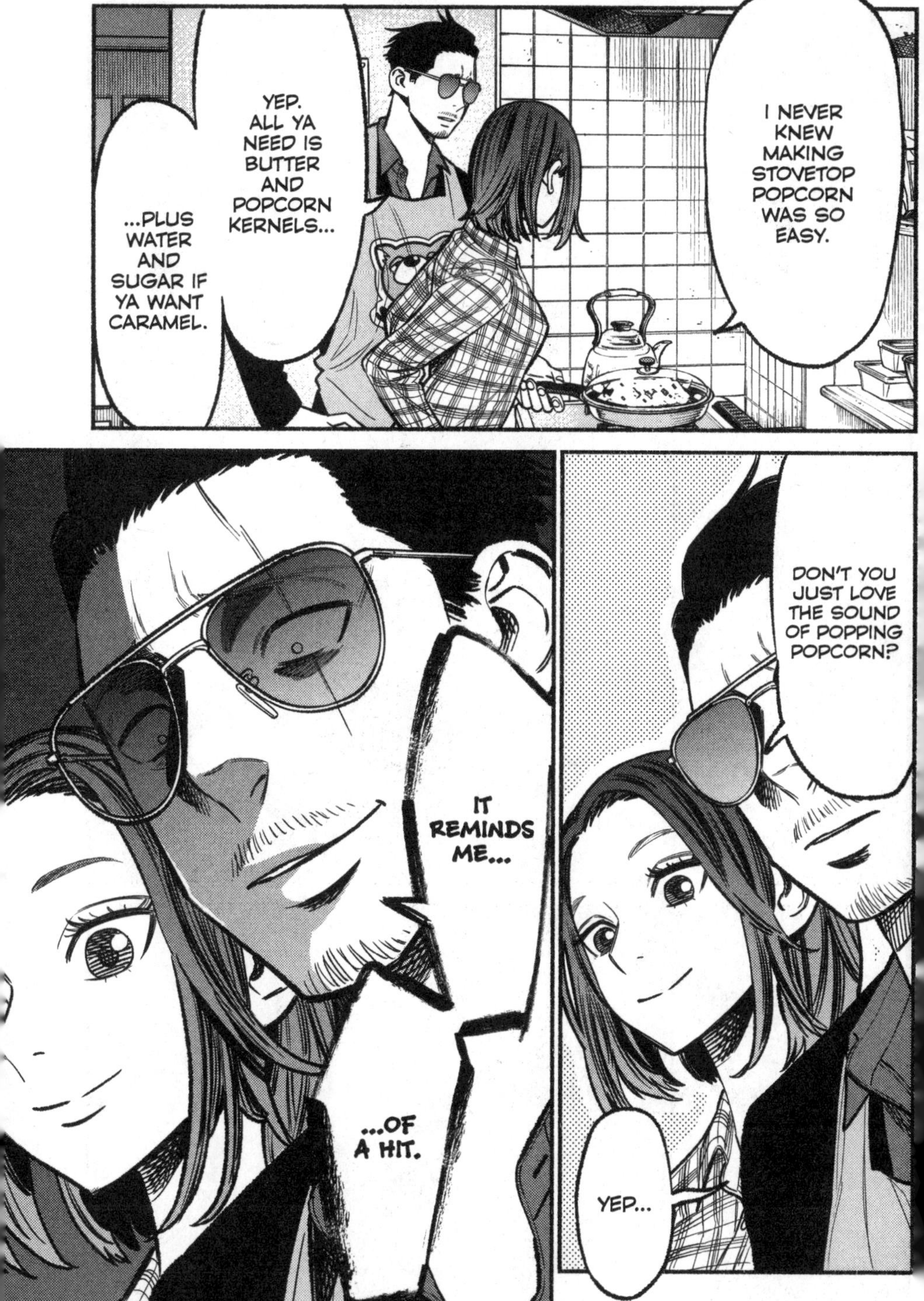
I NEVER KNEW MAKING STOVETOP POPCORN WAS SO EASY.
YEP. ALL YA NEED IS BUTTER AND POPCORN KERNELS...
...PLUS WATER AND SUGAR IF YA WANT CARAMEL.
DON'T YOU JUST LOVE THE SOUND OF POPPING POPCORN?
YEP...
IT REMINDS ME...
...OF A HIT.

A'IGHT!
TIME WE GOT DOWN TO BUSINESS. WE GOT A BIG DECISION TO MAKE.
WHAT ARE WE GONNA WATCH...
...FOR OUR FIRST TV NIGHT?!
I KNOW *MY* PICK!

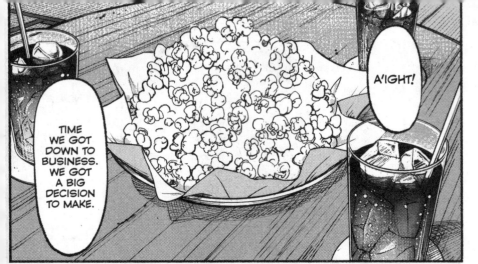

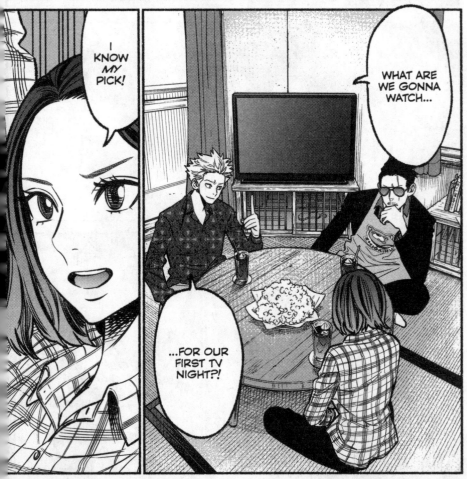

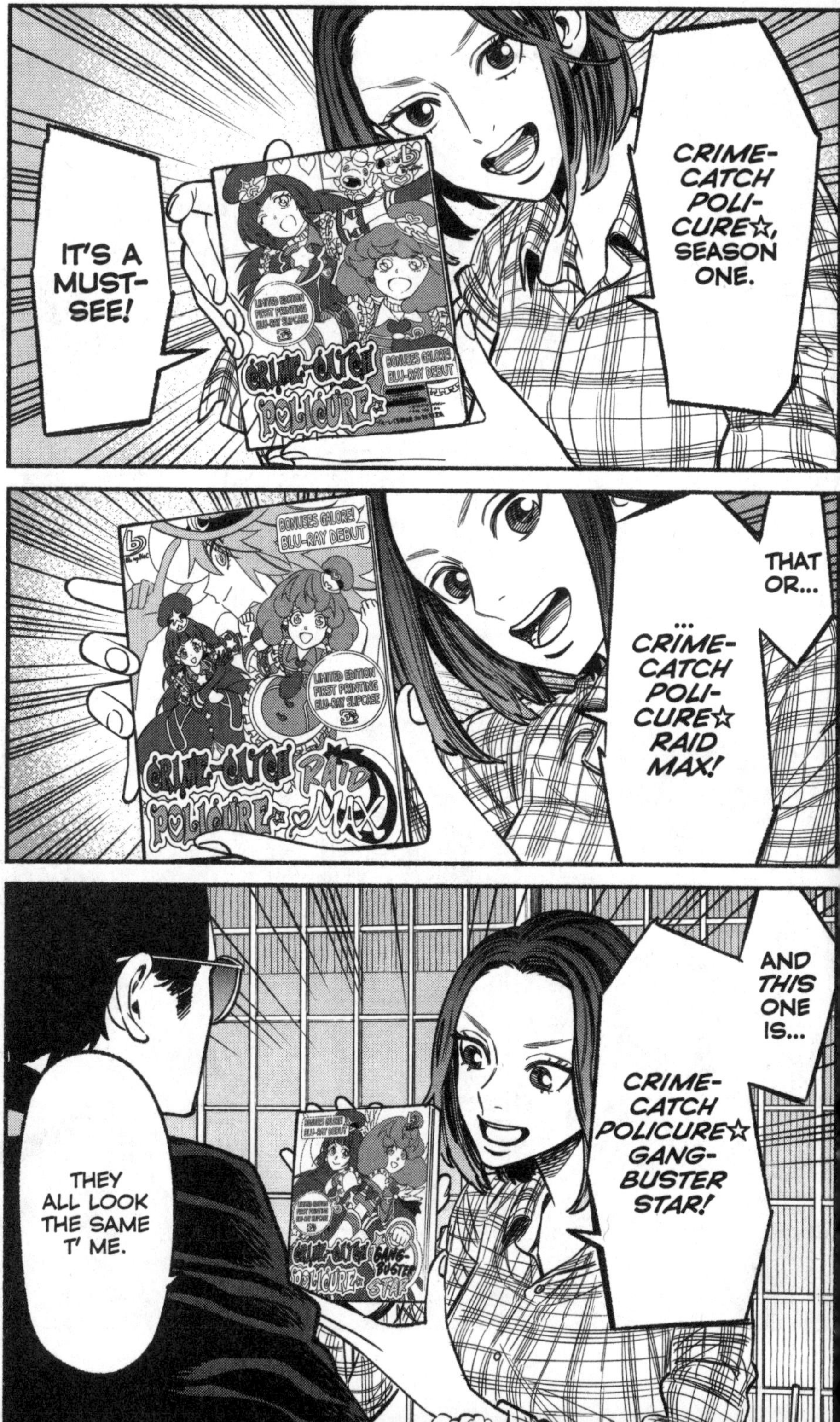
CRIME-CATCH POLICURE☆, SEASON ONE.
IT'S A MUST-SEE!
LIMITED EDITION FIRST PRINTING BLU-RAY SLIPCASE
BONUSES GALORE! BLU-RAY DEBUT
CRIME-CATCH POLICURE☆
THAT OR...
...CRIME-CATCH POLICURE☆ RAID MAX!
BONUSES GALORE! BLU-RAY DEBUT
LIMITED EDITION FIRST PRINTING BLU-RAY SLIPCASE
CRIME-CATCH POLICURE☆ RAID MAX
AND THIS ONE IS...
CRIME-CATCH POLICURE☆ GANG-BUSTER STAR!
THEY ALL LOOK THE SAME T' ME.

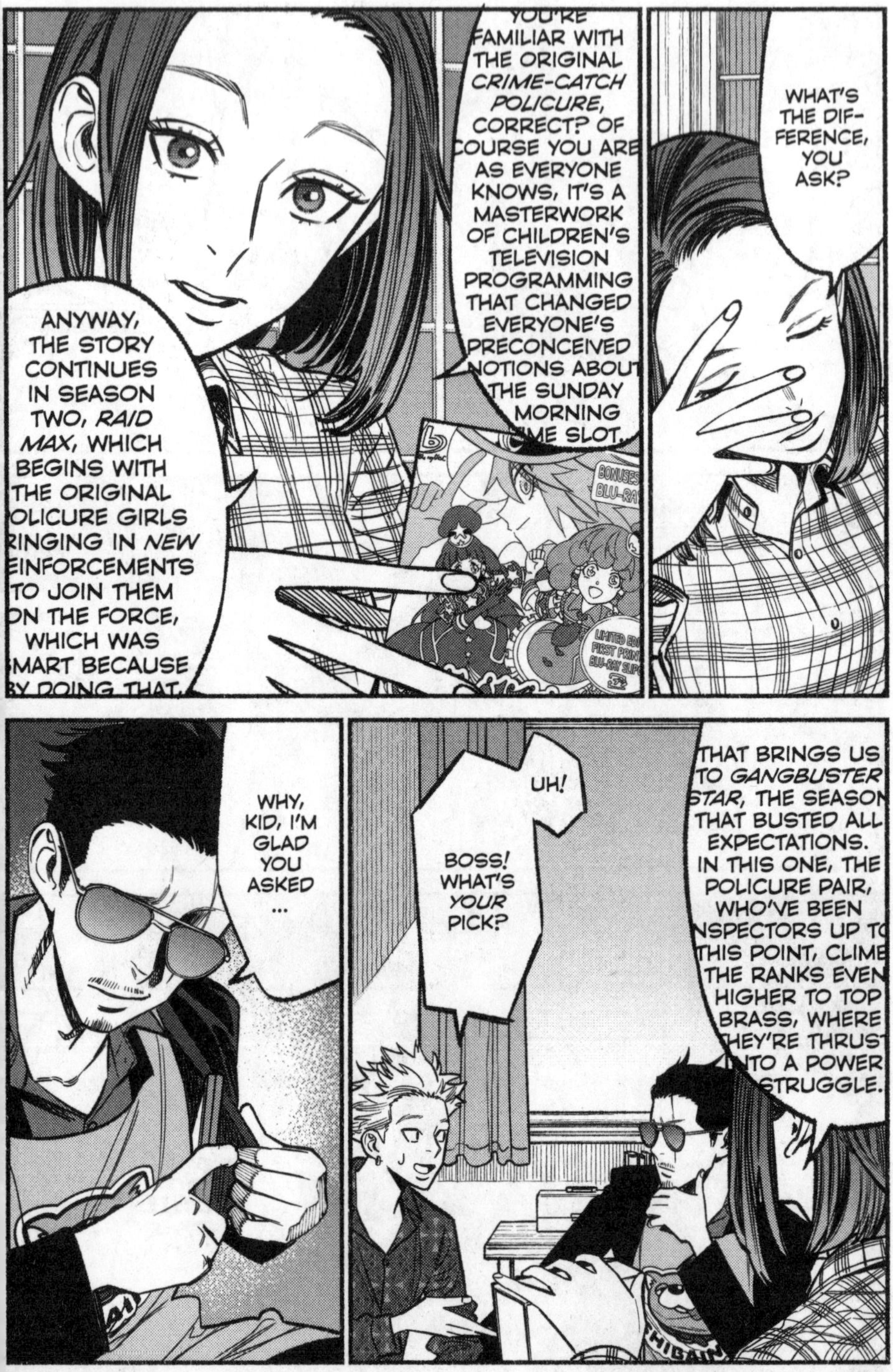
WHAT'S THE DIF- FERENCE, YOU ASK?
YOU'RE FAMILIAR WITH THE ORIGINAL *CRIME-CATCH POLICURE*, CORRECT? OF COURSE YOU ARE AS EVERYONE KNOWS, IT'S A MASTERWORK OF CHILDREN'S TELEVISION PROGRAMMING THAT CHANGED EVERYONE'S PRECONCEIVED NOTIONS ABOUT THE SUNDAY MORNING IME SLOT...
ANYWAY, THE STORY CONTINUES IN SEASON TWO, *RAID MAX*, WHICH BEGINS WITH THE ORIGINAL OLICURE GIRLS RINGING IN *NEW* EINFORCEMENTS TO JOIN THEM ON THE FORCE, WHICH WAS MART BECAUSE Y DOING THAT,
THAT BRINGS US TO *GANGBUSTER STAR*, THE SEASON THAT BUSTED ALL EXPECTATIONS. IN THIS ONE, THE POLICURE PAIR, WHO'VE BEEN NSPECTORS UP TO THIS POINT, CLIMB THE RANKS EVEN HIGHER TO TOP BRASS, WHERE HEY'RE THRUST NTO A POWER STRUGGLE.
UH!
BOSS! WHAT'S *YOUR* PICK?
WHY, KID, I'M GLAD YOU ASKED ...

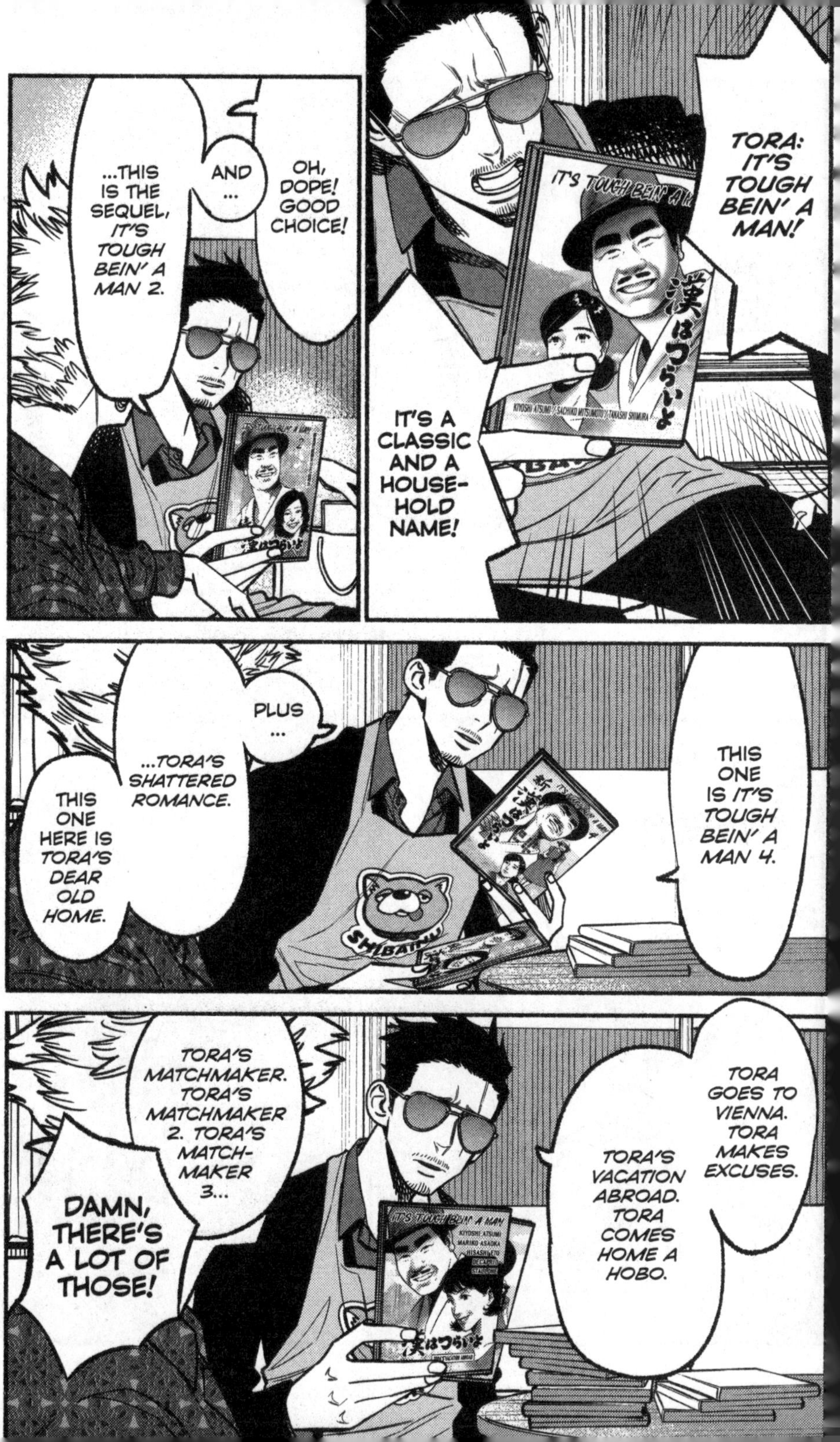
TORA: IT'S TOUGH BEIN' A MAN!
IT'S TOUGH BEIN' A MAN
漢はつらいよ
KIYOSHI ATSUMI / SACHIKO MITSUMOTO / TAKASHI SHIMURA
IT'S A CLASSIC AND A HOUSE-HOLD NAME!
OH, DOPE! GOOD CHOICE!
AND ...
...THIS IS THE SEQUEL, IT'S TOUGH BEIN' A MAN 2.
THIS ONE IS IT'S TOUGH BEIN' A MAN 4.
PLUS ...
...TORA'S SHATTERED ROMANCE.
THIS ONE HERE IS TORA'S DEAR OLD HOME.
SHIBAINU
TORA GOES TO VIENNA. TORA MAKES EXCUSES.
TORA'S VACATION ABROAD. TORA COMES HOME A HOBO.
IT'S TOUGH BEIN' A MAN
漢はつらいよ
TORA'S MATCHMAKER. TORA'S MATCHMAKER 2. TORA'S MATCH-MAKER 3...
DAMN, THERE'S A LOT OF THOSE!

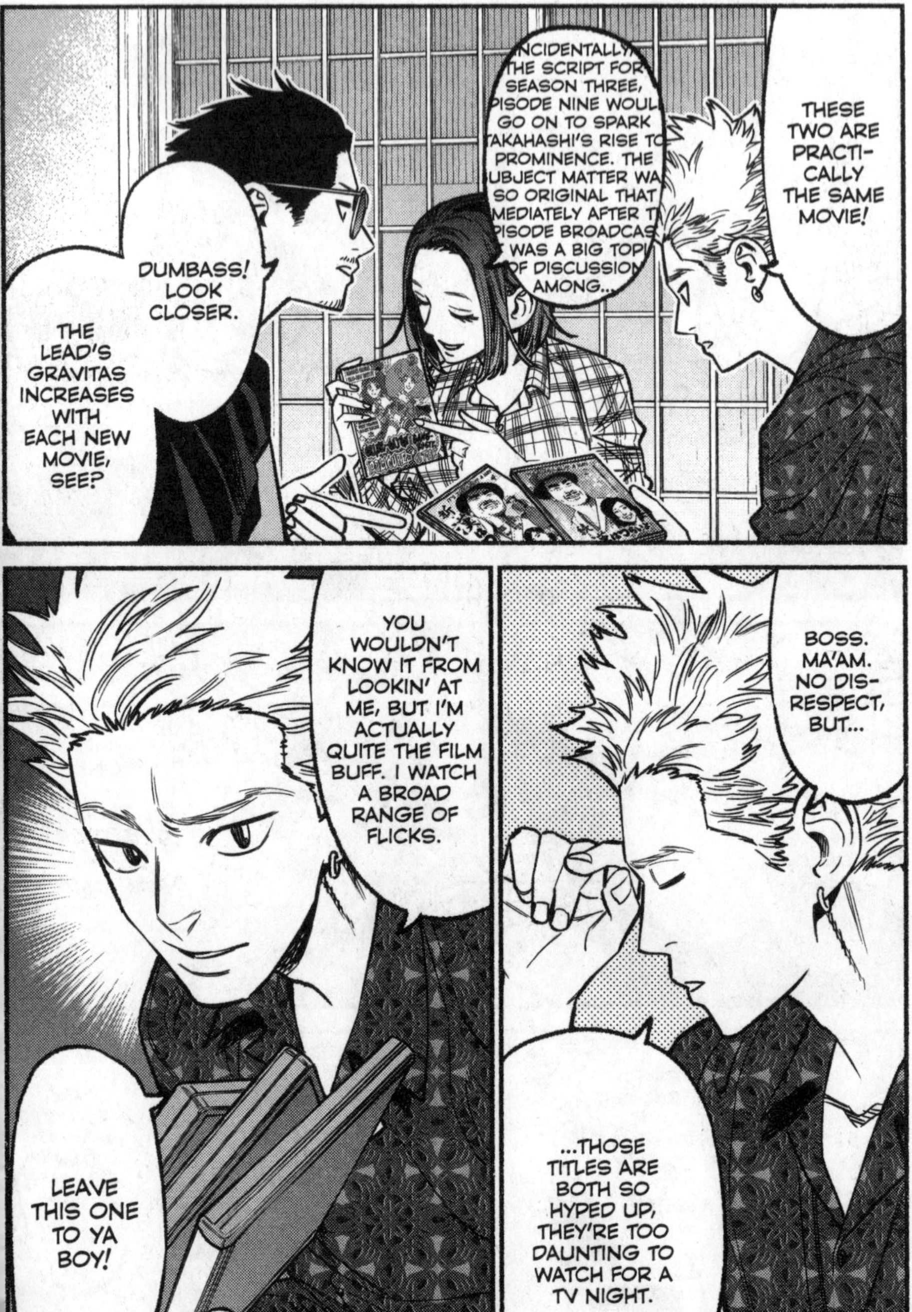
THESE TWO ARE PRACTICALLY THE SAME MOVIE!
NCIDENTALLY, THE SCRIPT FOR SEASON THREE, PISODE NINE WOUL GO ON TO SPARK TAKAHASHI'S RISE TO PROMINENCE. THE UBJECT MATTER WA SO ORIGINAL THAT MEDIATELY AFTER T PISODE BROADCAS T WAS A BIG TOPI OF DISCUSSION AMONG...
DUMBASS! LOOK CLOSER.
THE LEAD'S GRAVITAS INCREASES WITH EACH NEW MOVIE, SEE?
BOSS. MA'AM. NO DISRESPECT, BUT...
...THOSE TITLES ARE BOTH SO HYPED UP, THEY'RE TOO DAUNTING TO WATCH FOR A TV NIGHT.
YOU WOULDN'T KNOW IT FROM LOOKIN' AT ME, BUT I'M ACTUALLY QUITE THE FILM BUFF. I WATCH A BROAD RANGE OF FLICKS.
LEAVE THIS ONE TO YA BOY!

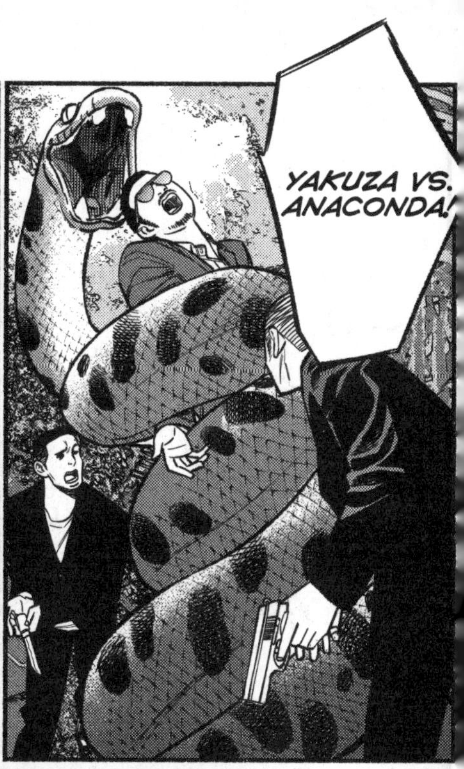
YAKUZA VS. ANACONDA!
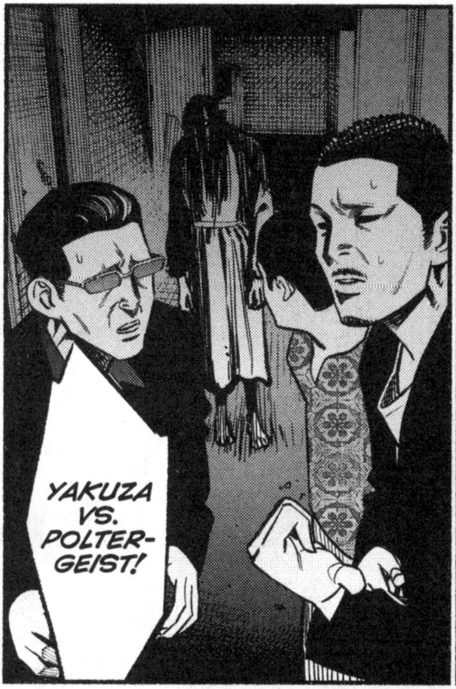
YAKUZA VS. POLTER-GEIST!
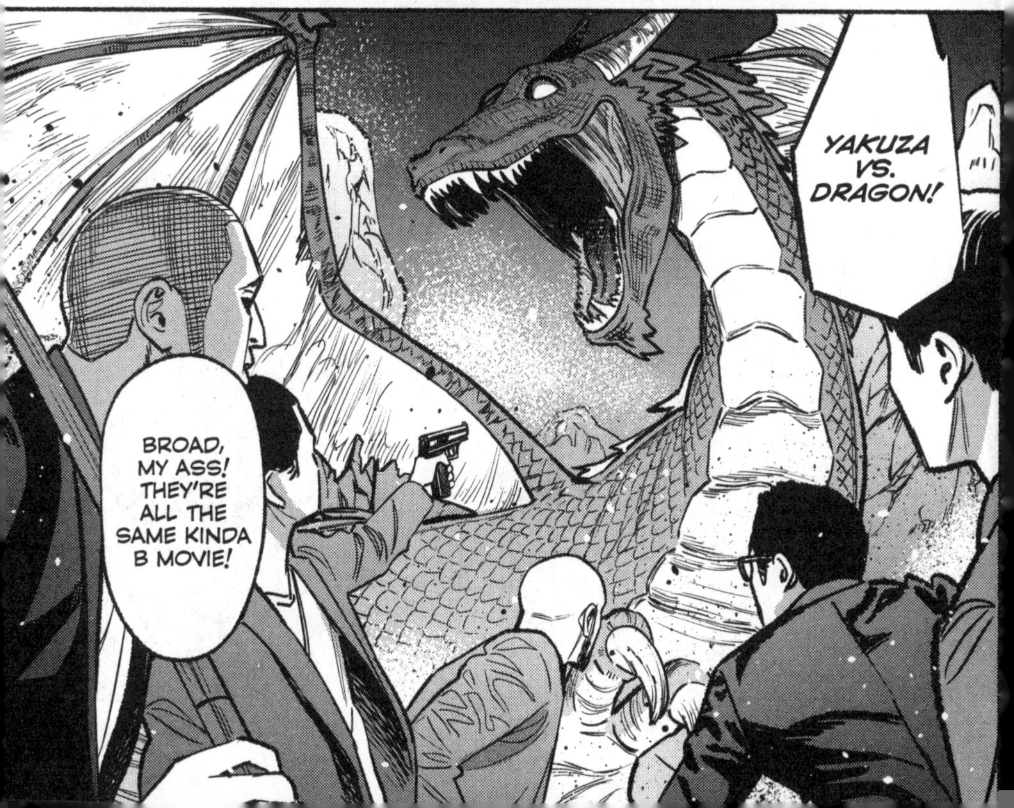
YAKUZA VS. DRAGON!
BROAD, MY ASS! THEY'RE ALL THE SAME KINDA B MOVIE!

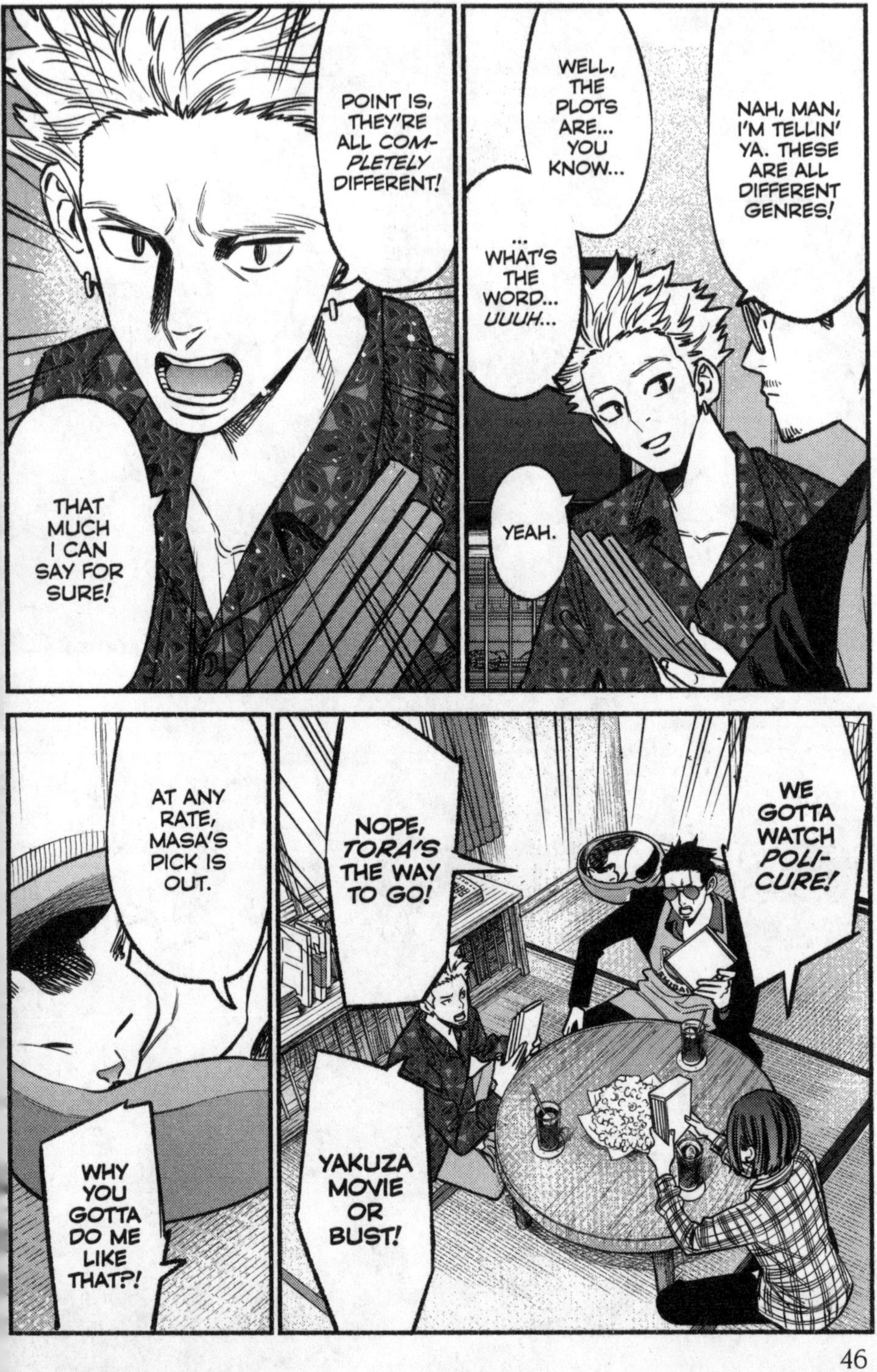
NAH, MAN, I'M TELLIN' YA. THESE ARE ALL DIFFERENT GENRES!
WELL, THE PLOTS ARE... YOU KNOW...
... WHAT'S THE WORD... UUUH...
YEAH.
POINT IS, THEY'RE ALL COM-PLETELY DIFFERENT!
THAT MUCH I CAN SAY FOR SURE!
WE GOTTA WATCH POLI-CURE!
NOPE, TORA'S THE WAY TO GO!
YAKUZA MOVIE OR BUST!
AT ANY RATE, MASA'S PICK IS OUT.
WHY YOU GOTTA DO ME LIKE THAT?!

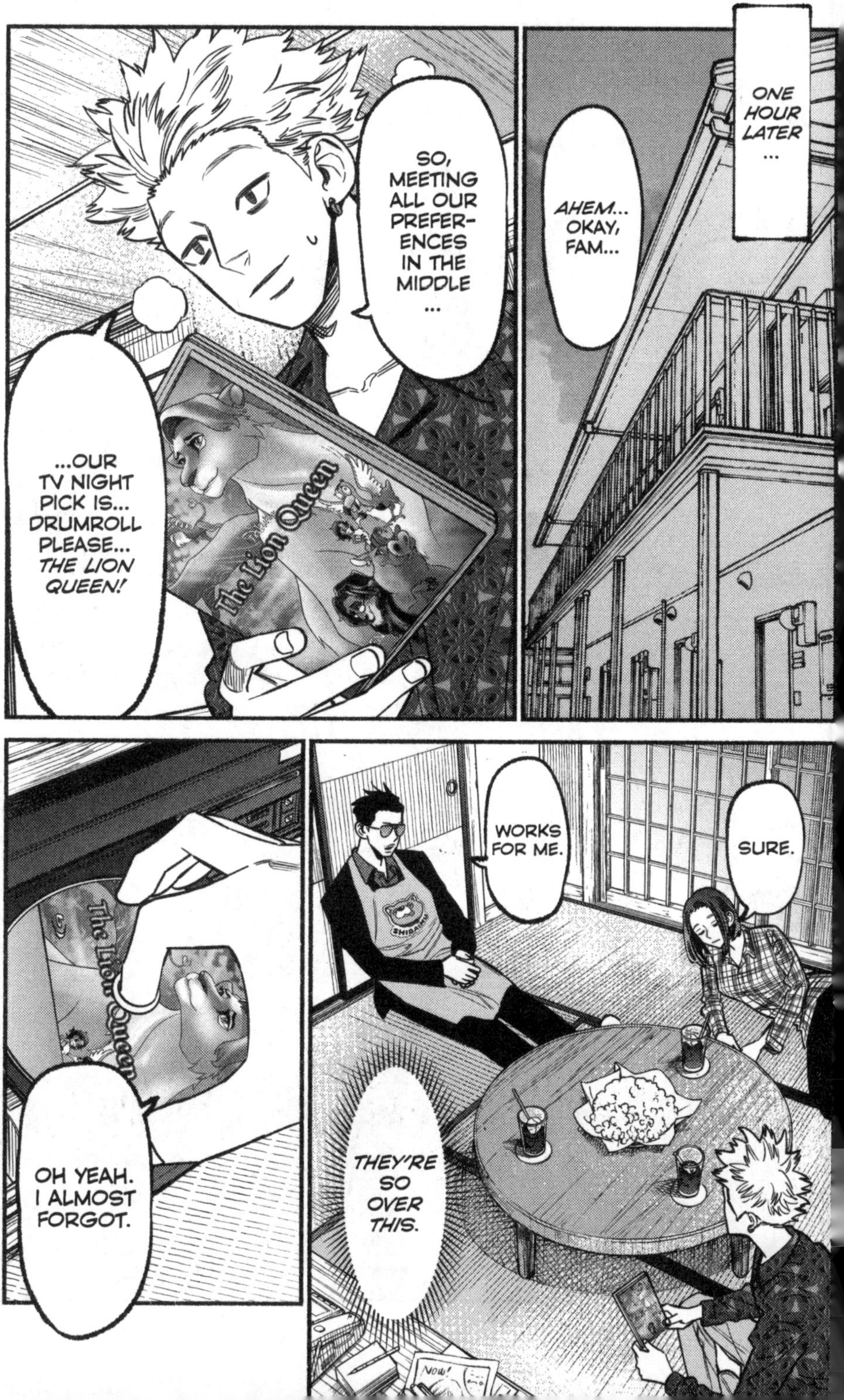
ONE HOUR LATER ...
AHEM... OKAY, FAM...
SO, MEETING ALL OUR PREFERENCES IN THE MIDDLE ...
...OUR TV NIGHT PICK IS... DRUMROLL PLEASE... *THE LION QUEEN!*
The Lion Queen
SURE.
WORKS FOR ME.
THEY'RE SO OVER THIS.
The Lion Queen
OH YEAH. I ALMOST FORGOT.

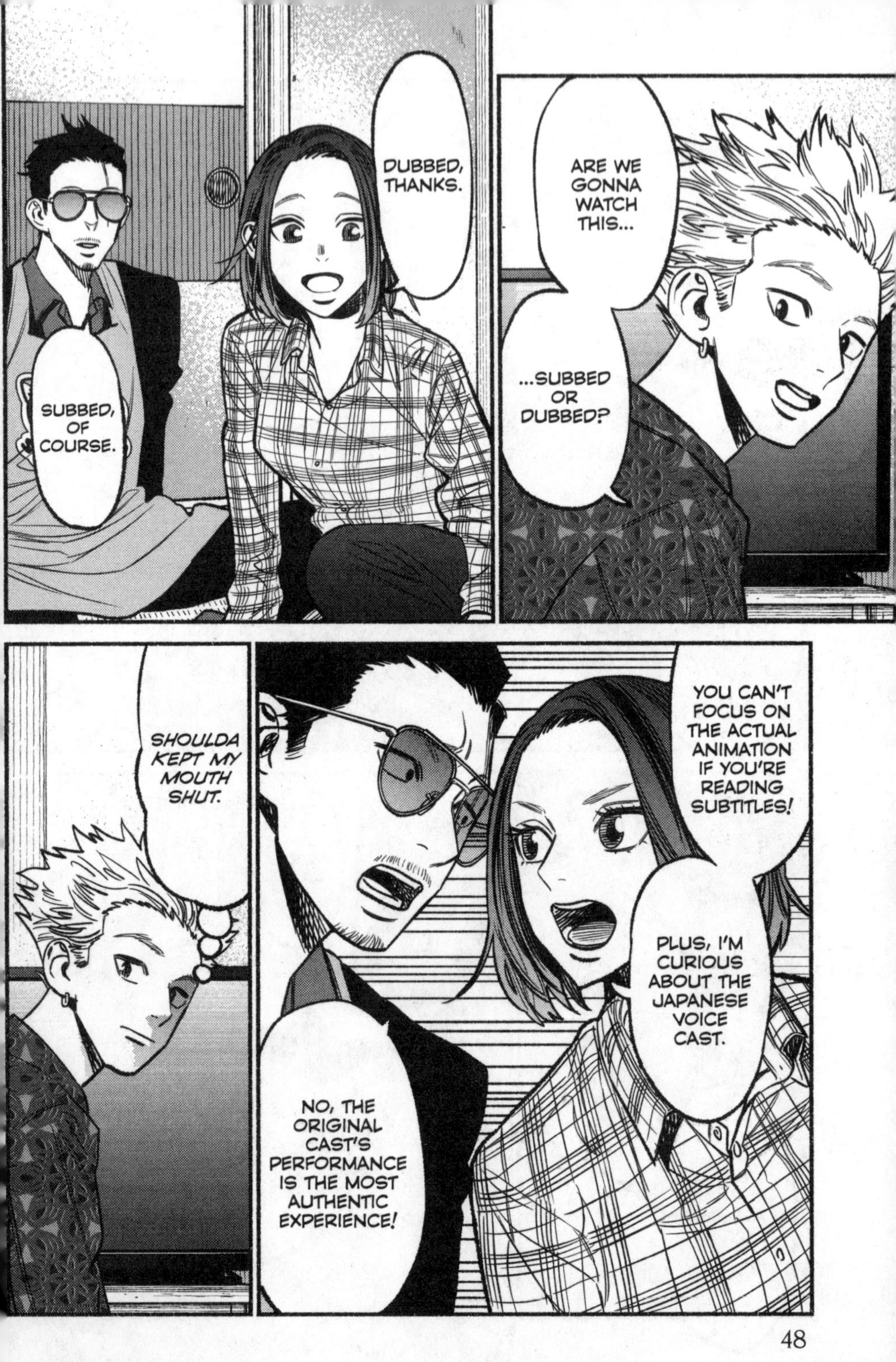
ARE WE GONNA WATCH THIS...
...SUBBED OR DUBBED?
DUBBED, THANKS.
SUBBED, OF COURSE.
YOU CAN'T FOCUS ON THE ACTUAL ANIMATION IF YOU'RE READING SUBTITLES!
PLUS, I'M CURIOUS ABOUT THE JAPANESE VOICE CAST.
NO, THE ORIGINAL CAST'S PERFORMANCE IS THE MOST AUTHENTIC EXPERIENCE!
SHOULDA KEPT MY MOUTH SHUT.

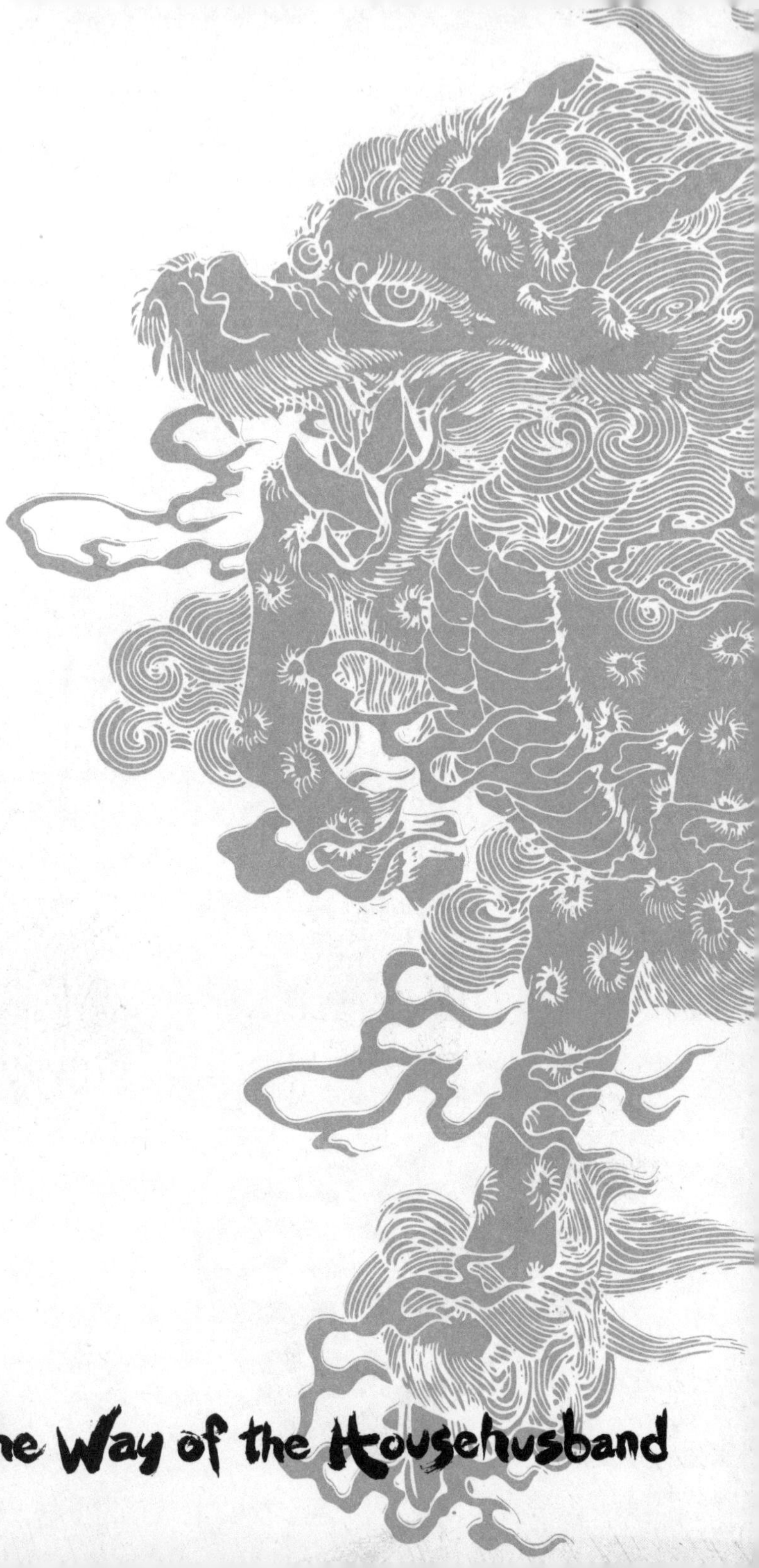

The Way of the Househusband

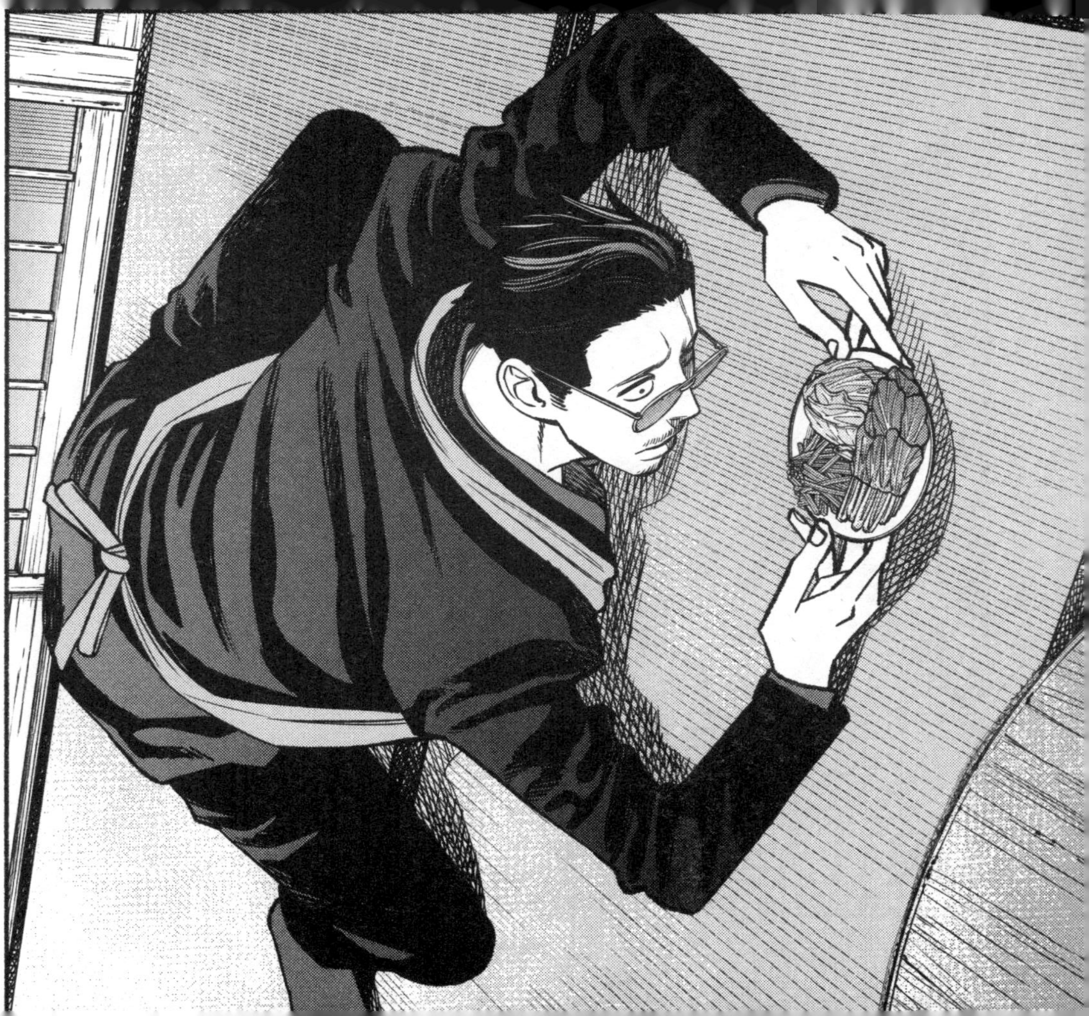

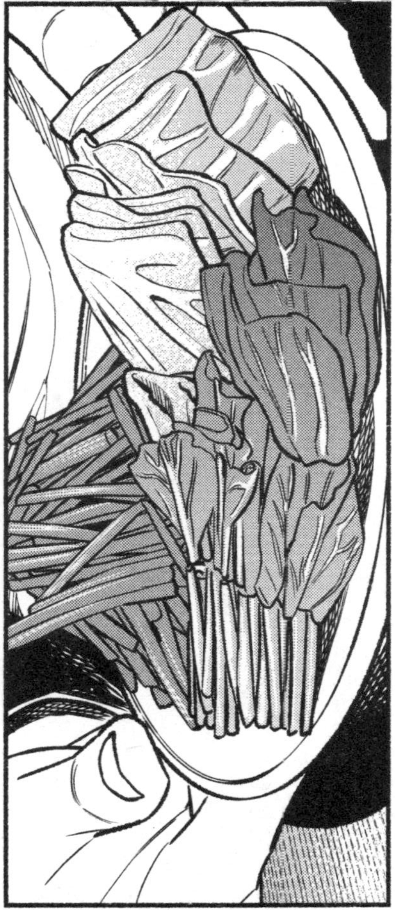

CHAPTER 67

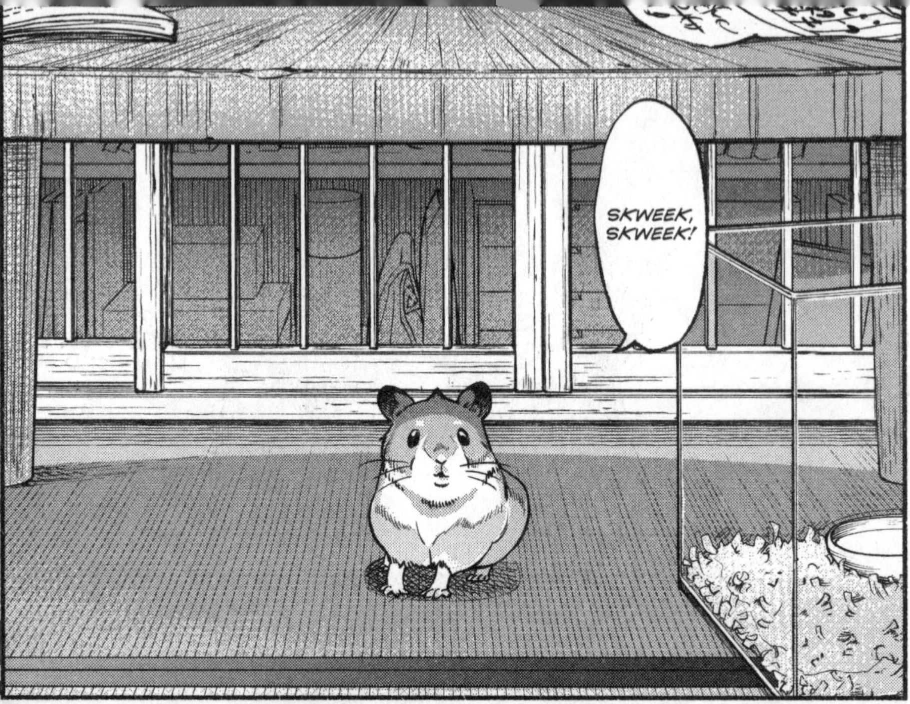
SKWEEK, SKWEEK!

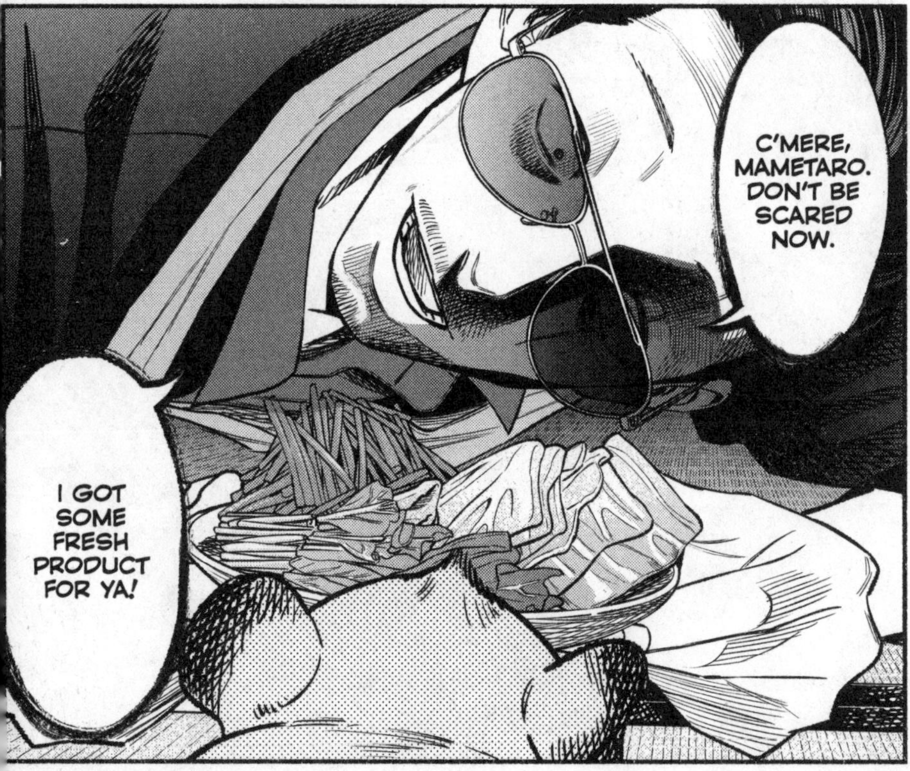
C'MERE, MAMETARO. DON'T BE SCARED NOW.
I GOT SOME FRESH PRODUCT FOR YA!

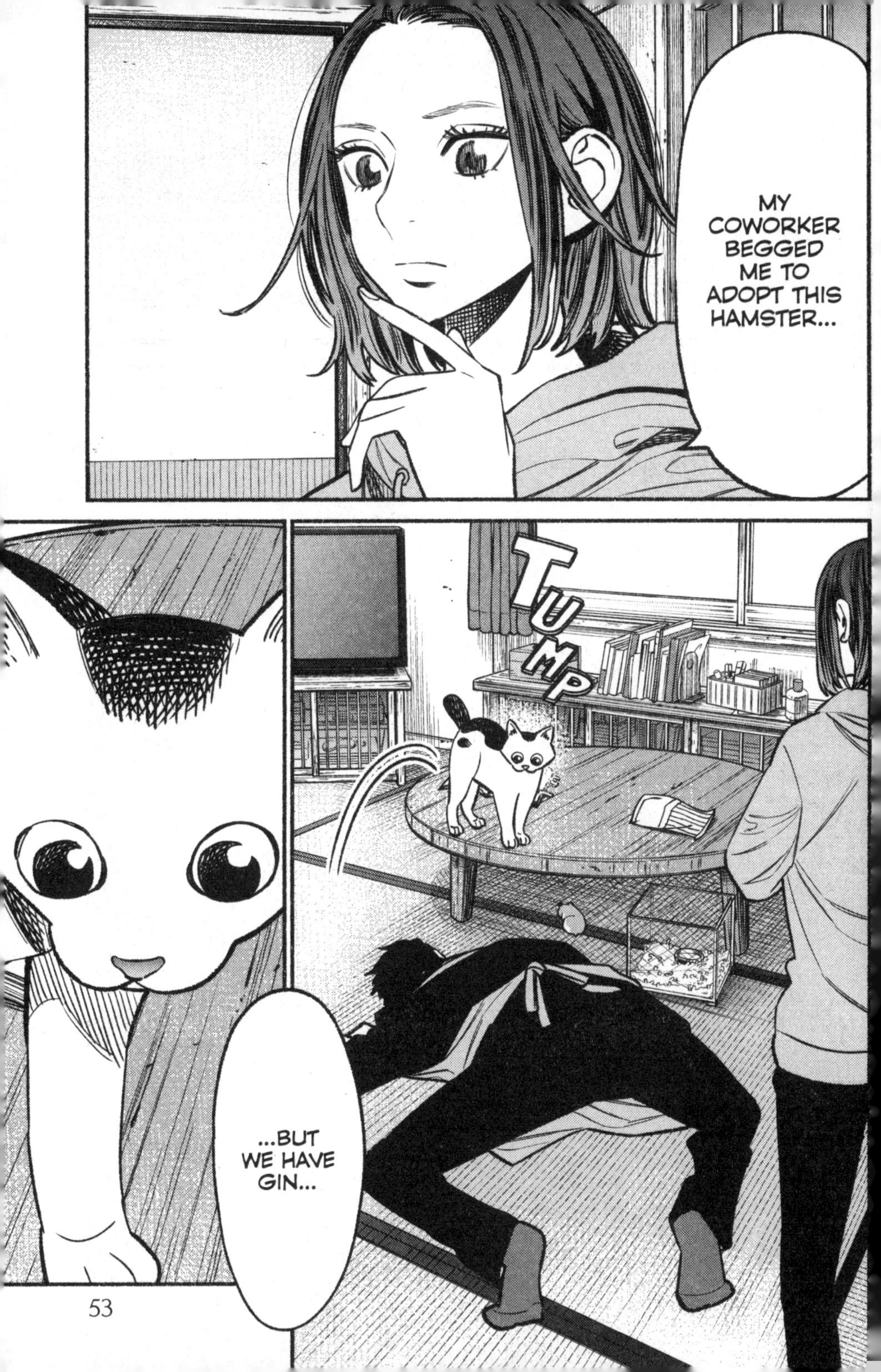
MY COWORKER BEGGED ME TO ADOPT THIS HAMSTER...
TUMP
...BUT WE HAVE GIN...

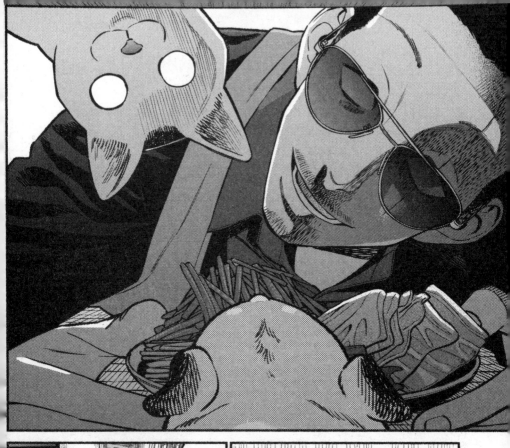

OKAY!

WE CAN'T
KEEP HIM.
NO WAY.

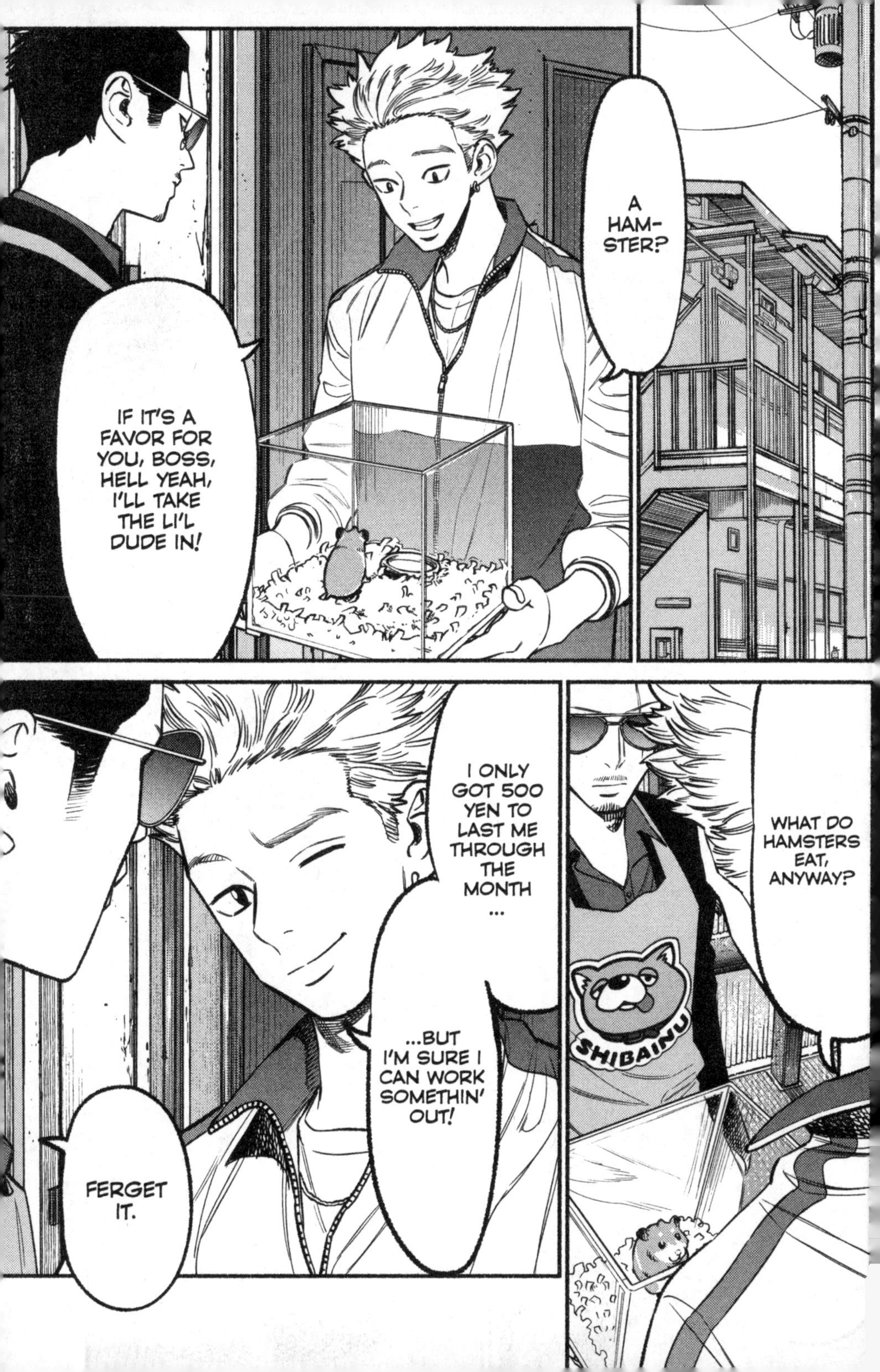
A HAM-STER?
IF IT'S A FAVOR FOR YOU, BOSS, HELL YEAH, I'LL TAKE THE LI'L DUDE IN!
WHAT DO HAMSTERS EAT, ANYWAY?
SHIBAINU
I ONLY GOT 500 YEN TO LAST ME THROUGH THE MONTH ...
...BUT I'M SURE I CAN WORK SOMETHIN' OUT!
FERGET IT.

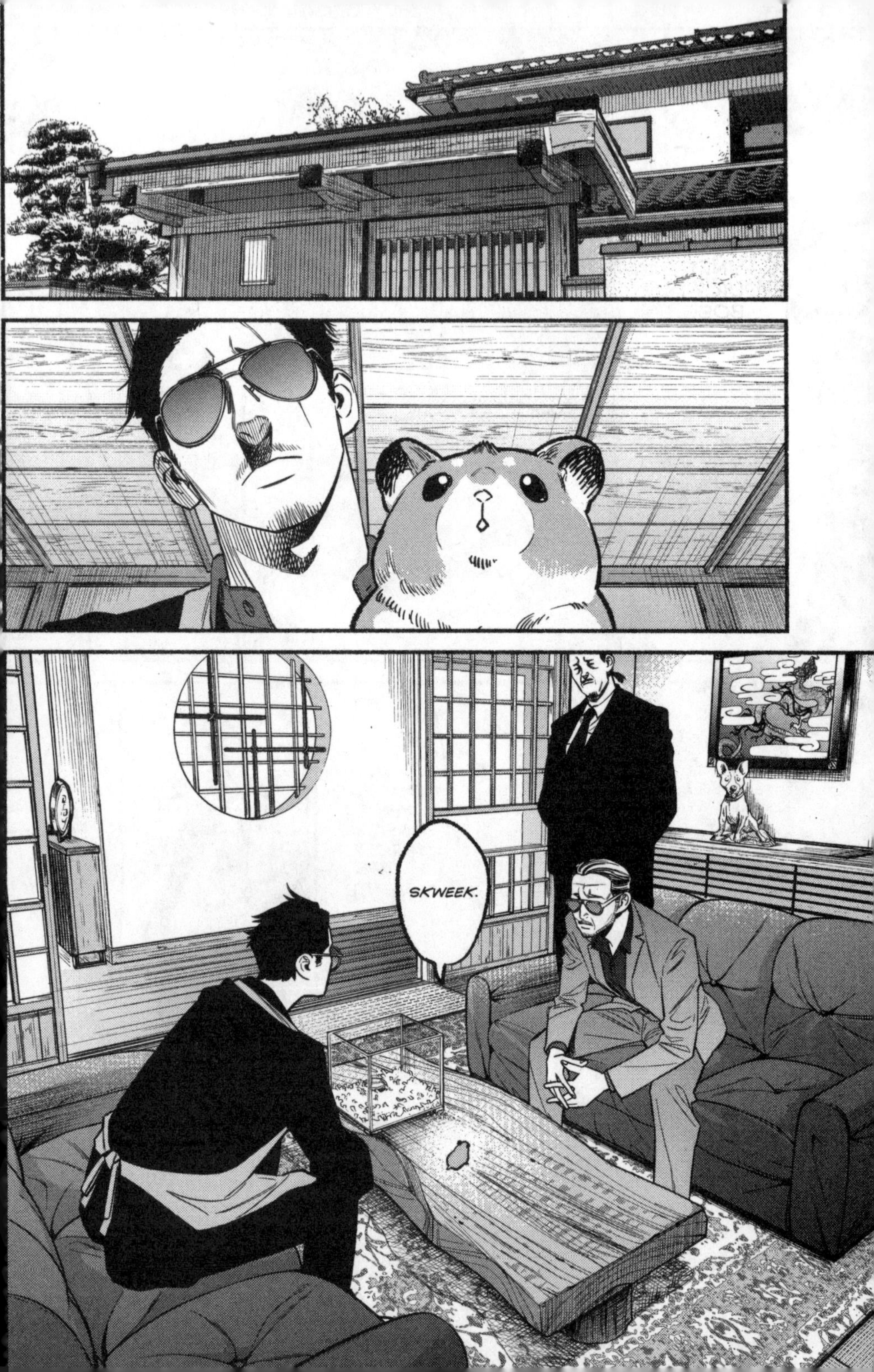
SKWEEK.

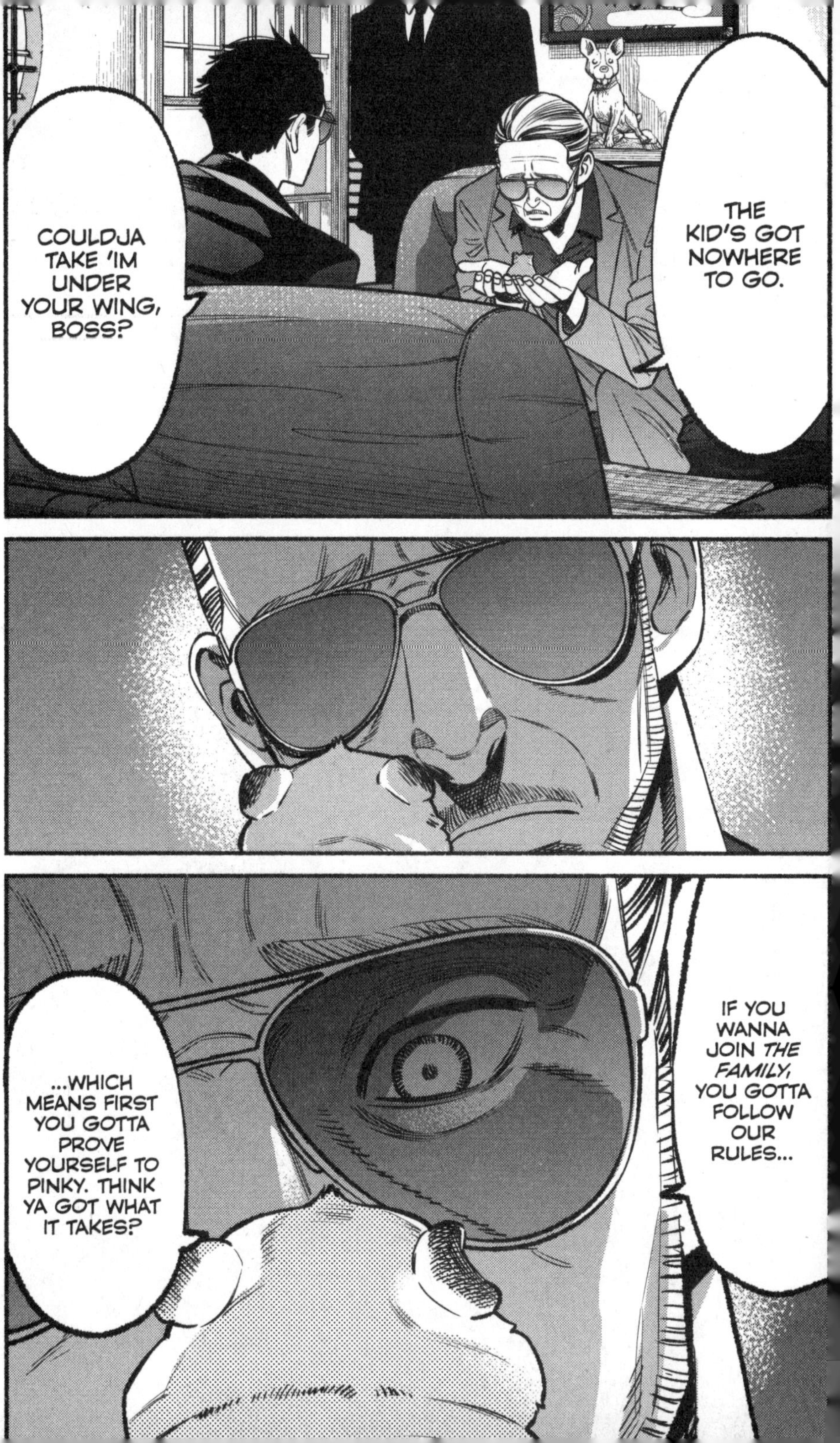
THE KID'S GOT NOWHERE TO GO.
COULDJA TAKE 'IM UNDER YOUR WING, BOSS?
IF YOU WANNA JOIN *THE FAMILY,* YOU GOTTA FOLLOW OUR RULES...
...WHICH MEANS FIRST YOU GOTTA PROVE YOURSELF TO PINKY. THINK YA GOT WHAT IT TAKES?

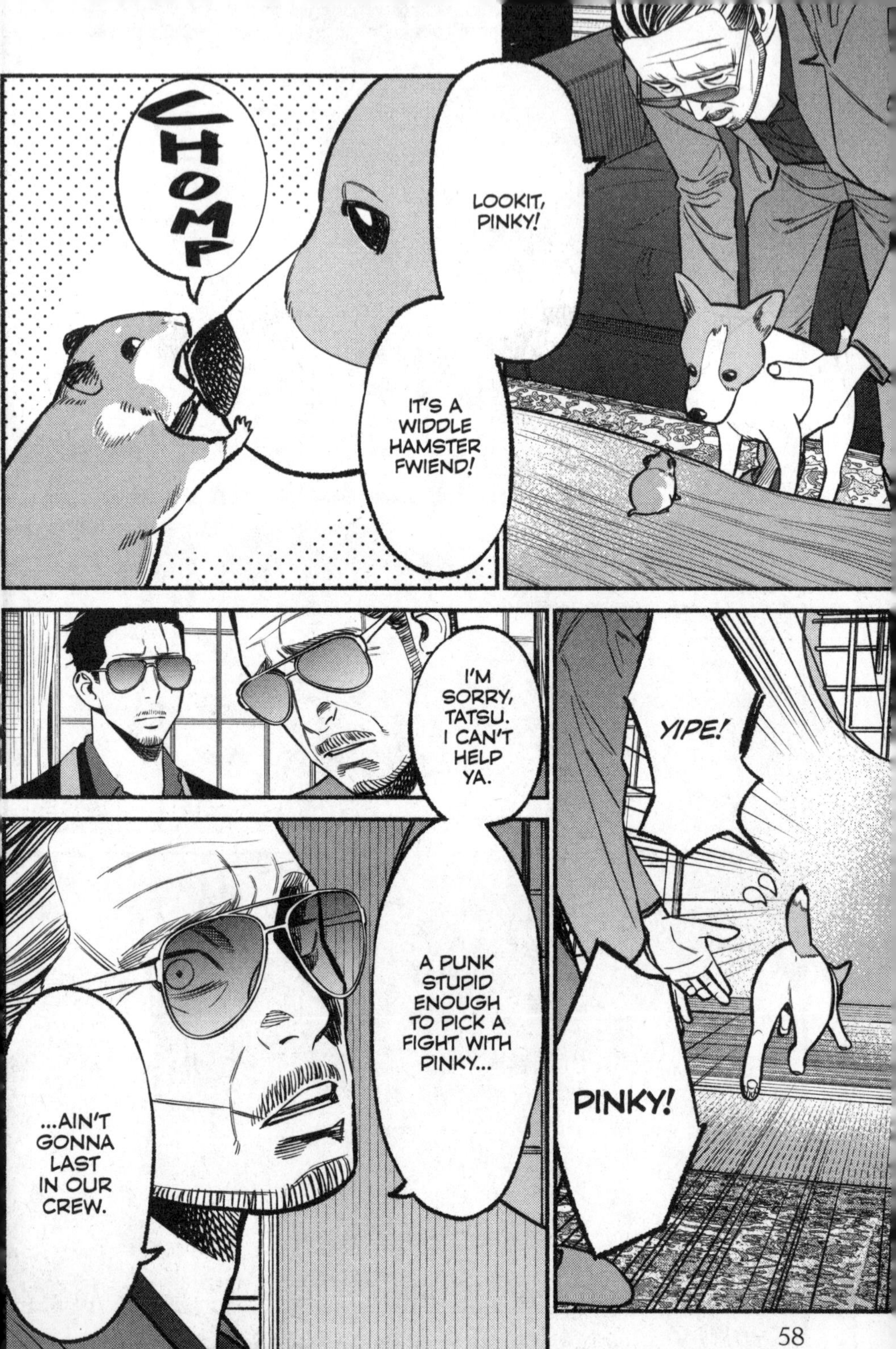
LOOKIT, PINKY!
IT'S A WIDDLE HAMSTER FWIEND!
CHOMP
YIPE!
PINKY!
I'M SORRY, TATSU. I CAN'T HELP YA.
A PUNK STUPID ENOUGH TO PICK A FIGHT WITH PINKY...
...AIN'T GONNA LAST IN OUR CREW.

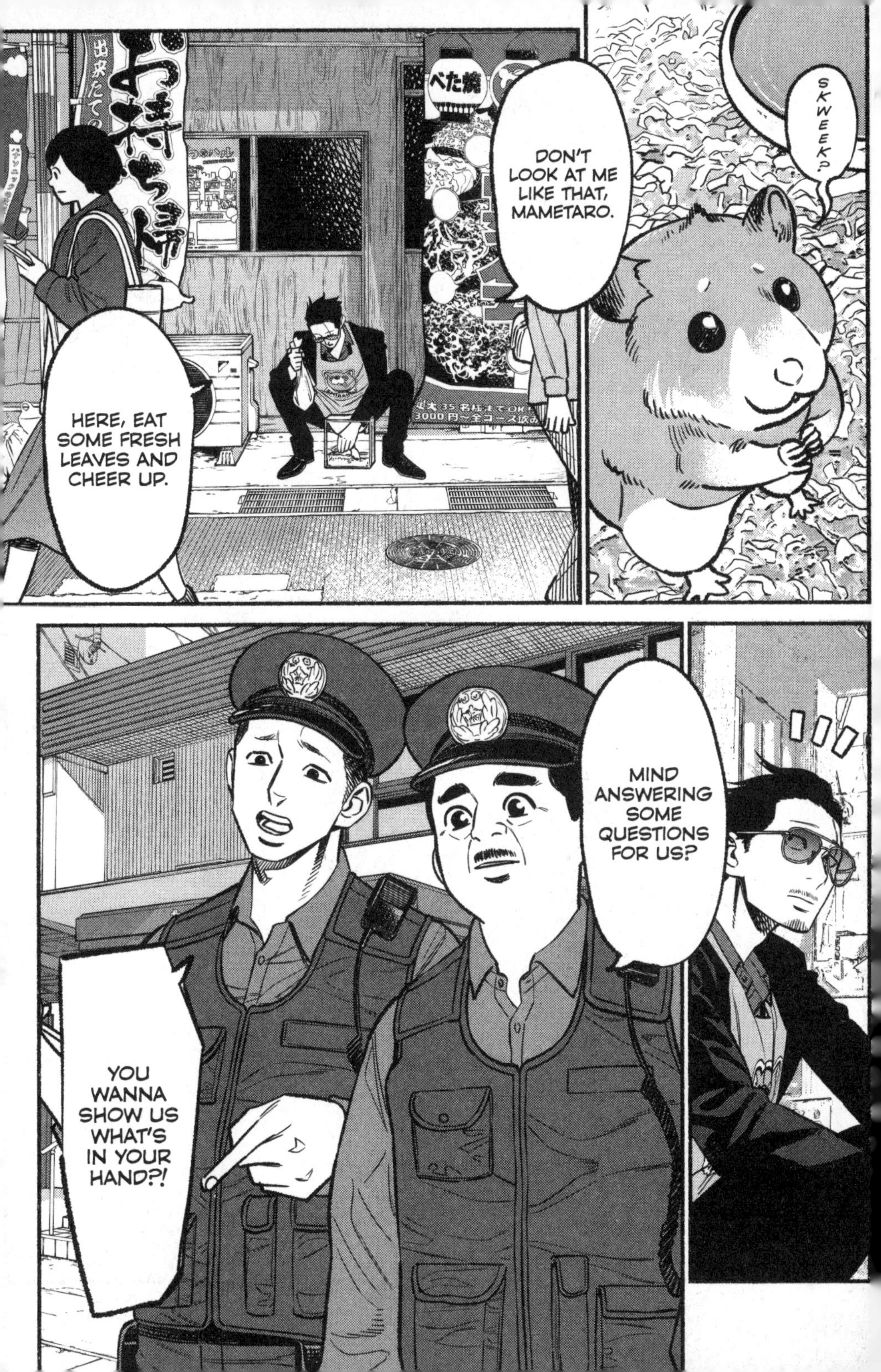
SKWEEK?
DON'T LOOK AT ME LIKE THAT, MAMETARO.
べた焼
HERE, EAT SOME FRESH LEAVES AND CHEER UP.
MIND ANSWERING SOME QUESTIONS FOR US?
YOU WANNA SHOW US WHAT'S IN YOUR HAND?!

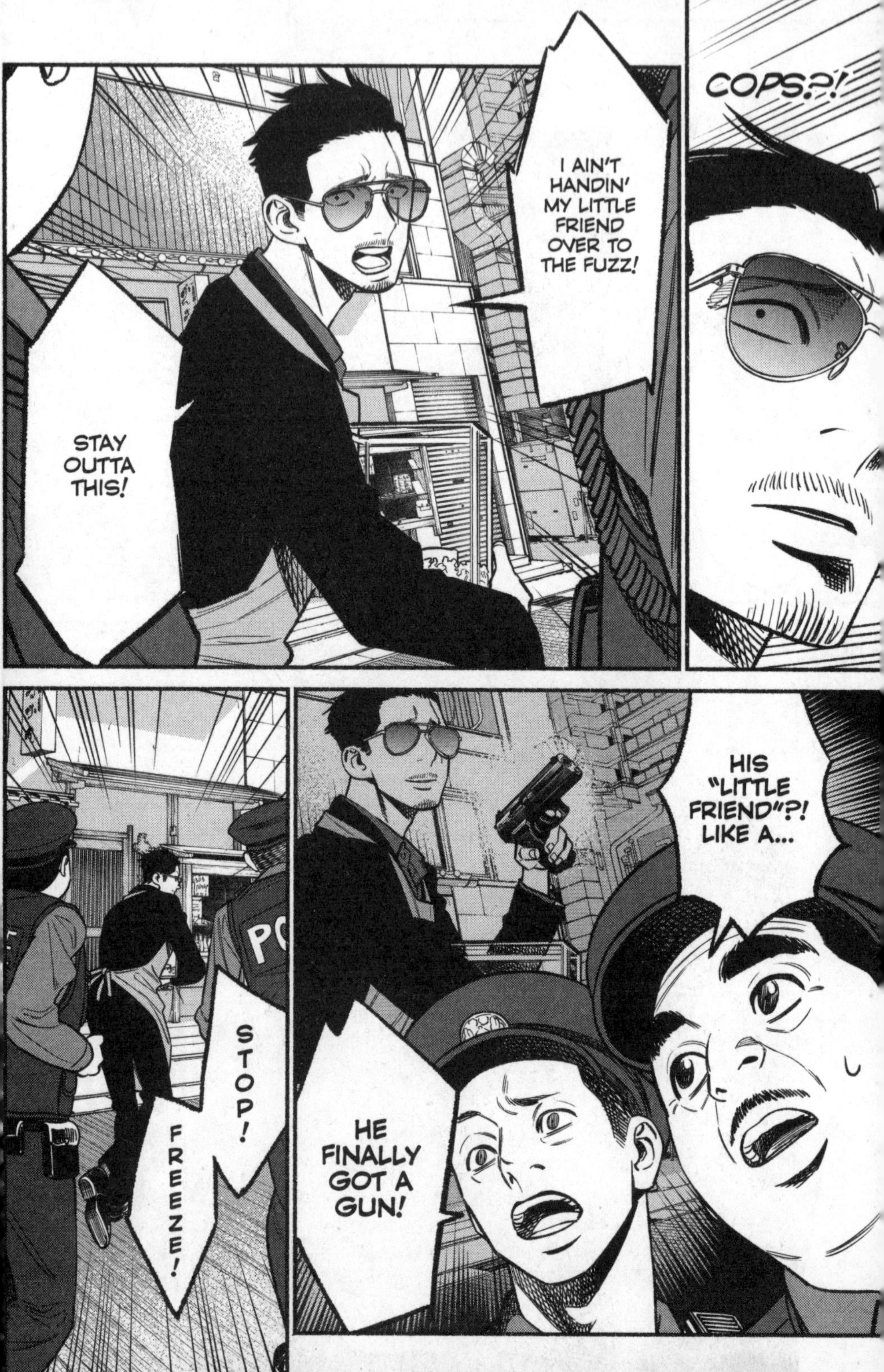
COPS?!
I AIN'T HANDIN' MY LITTLE FRIEND OVER TO THE FUZZ!
STAY OUTTA THIS!
HIS "LITTLE FRIEND"?! LIKE A...
HE FINALLY GOT A GUN!
STOP!
FREEZE!

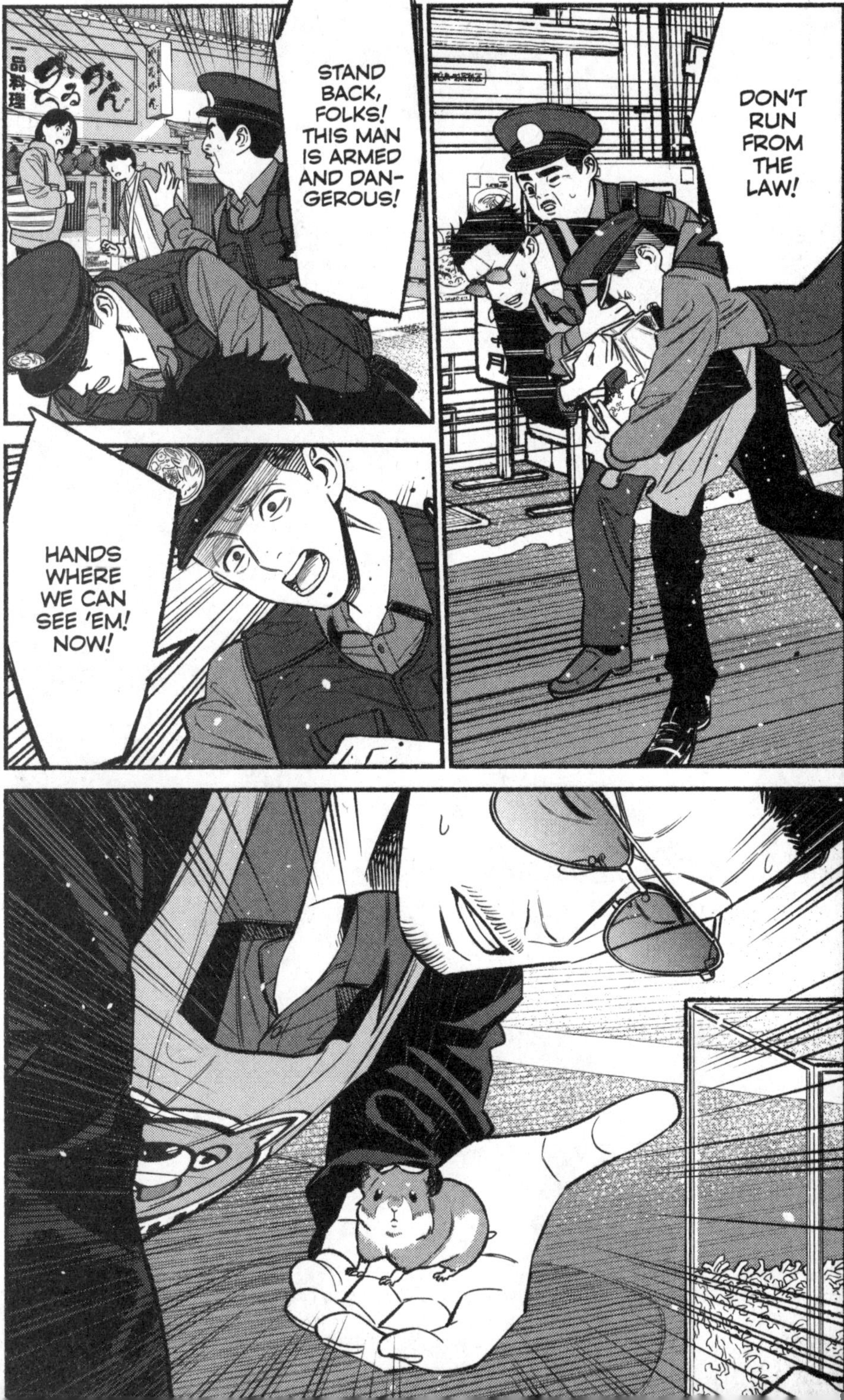
DON'T RUN FROM THE LAW!
STAND BACK, FOLKS! THIS MAN IS ARMED AND DAN-GEROUS!
HANDS WHERE WE CAN SEE 'EM! NOW!

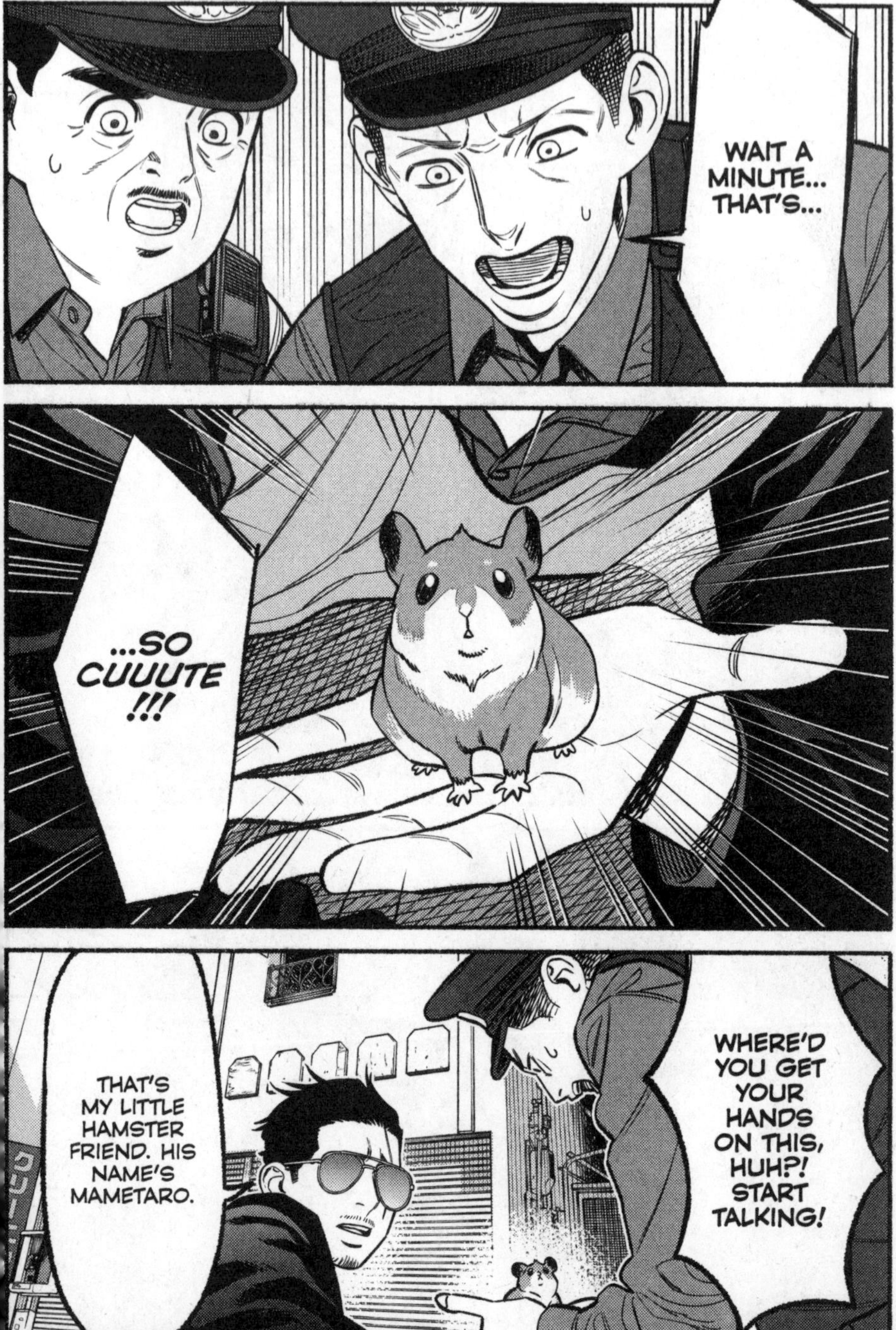
WAIT A MINUTE... THAT'S...
...SO CUUUTE!!!
WHERE'D YOU GET YOUR HANDS ON THIS, HUH?! START TALKING!
THAT'S MY LITTLE HAMSTER FRIEND. HIS NAME'S MAMETARO.

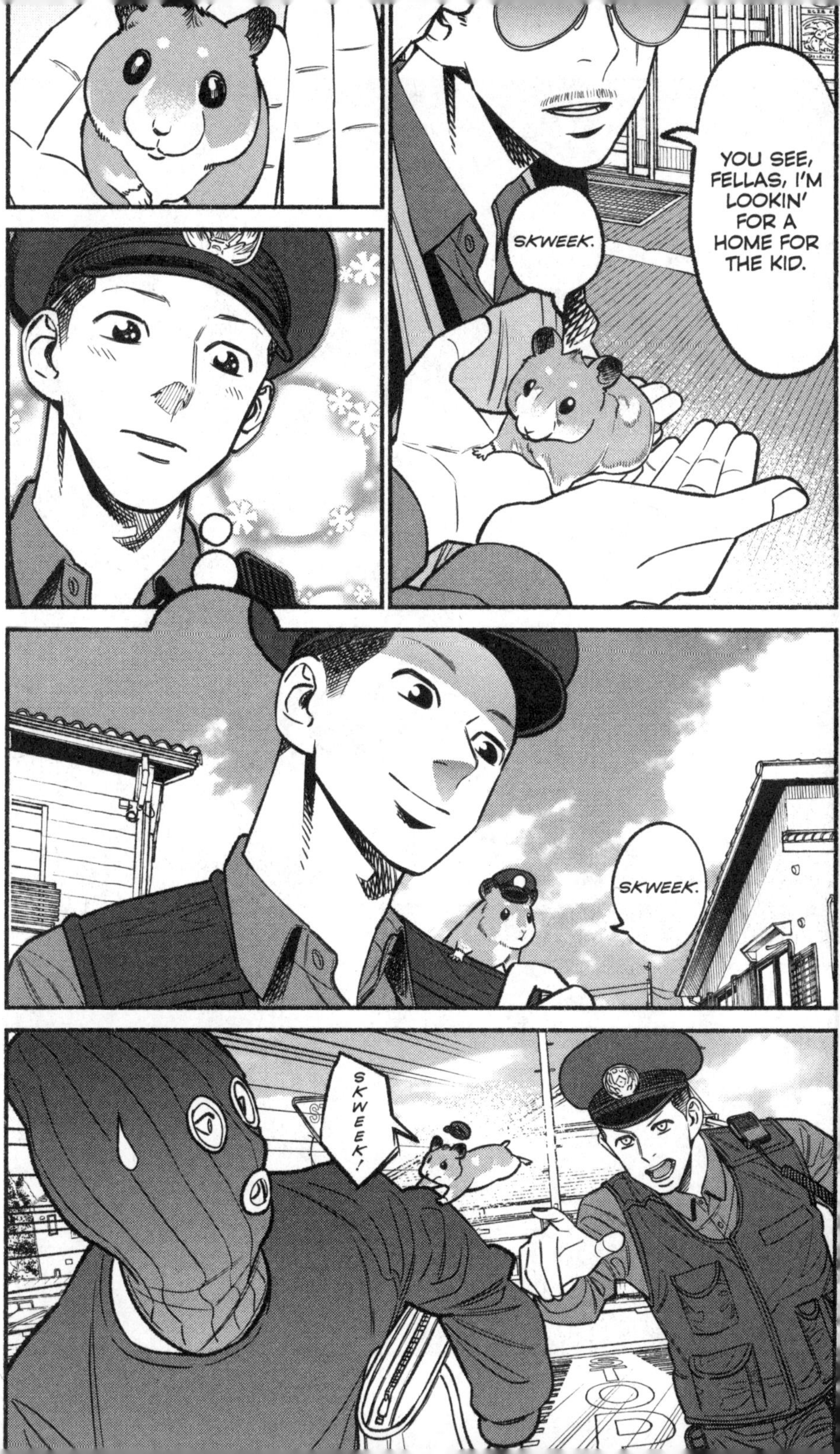
YOU SEE, FELLAS, I'M LOOKIN' FOR A HOME FOR THE KID.
SKWEEK.
SKWEEK.
SKWEEK!

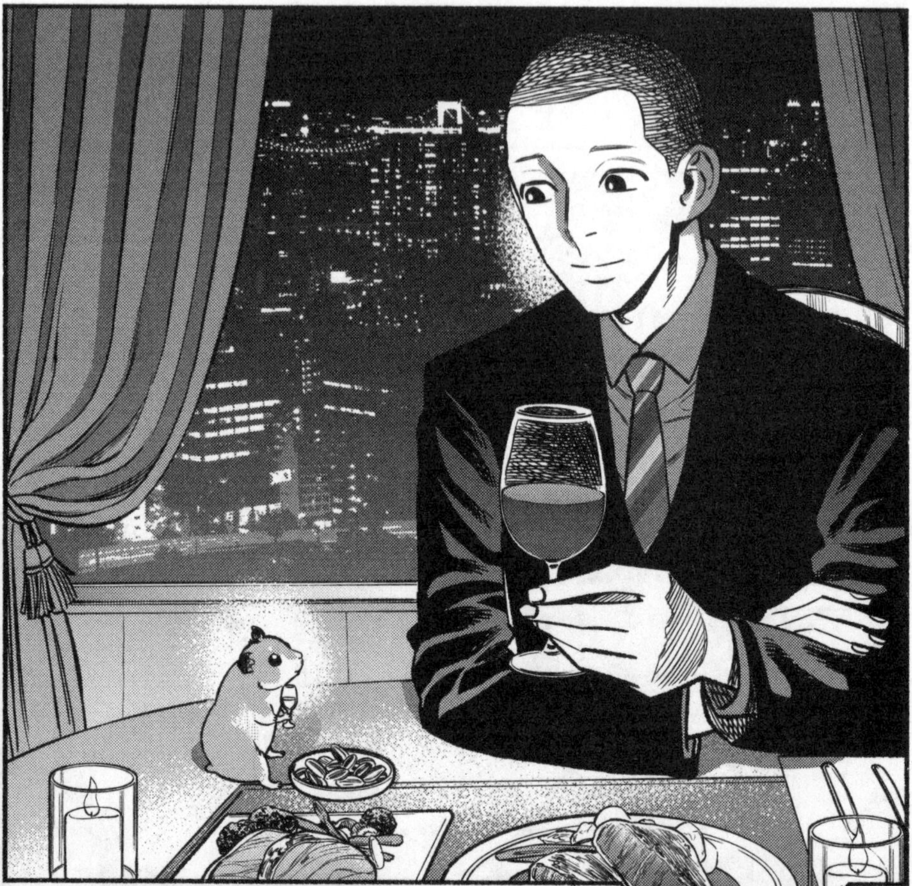

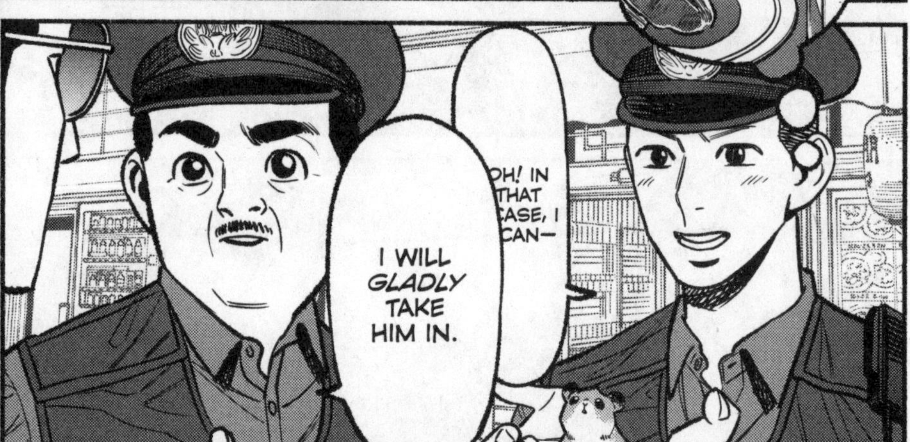
OH! IN THAT CASE, I CAN—
I WILL GLADLY TAKE HIM IN.

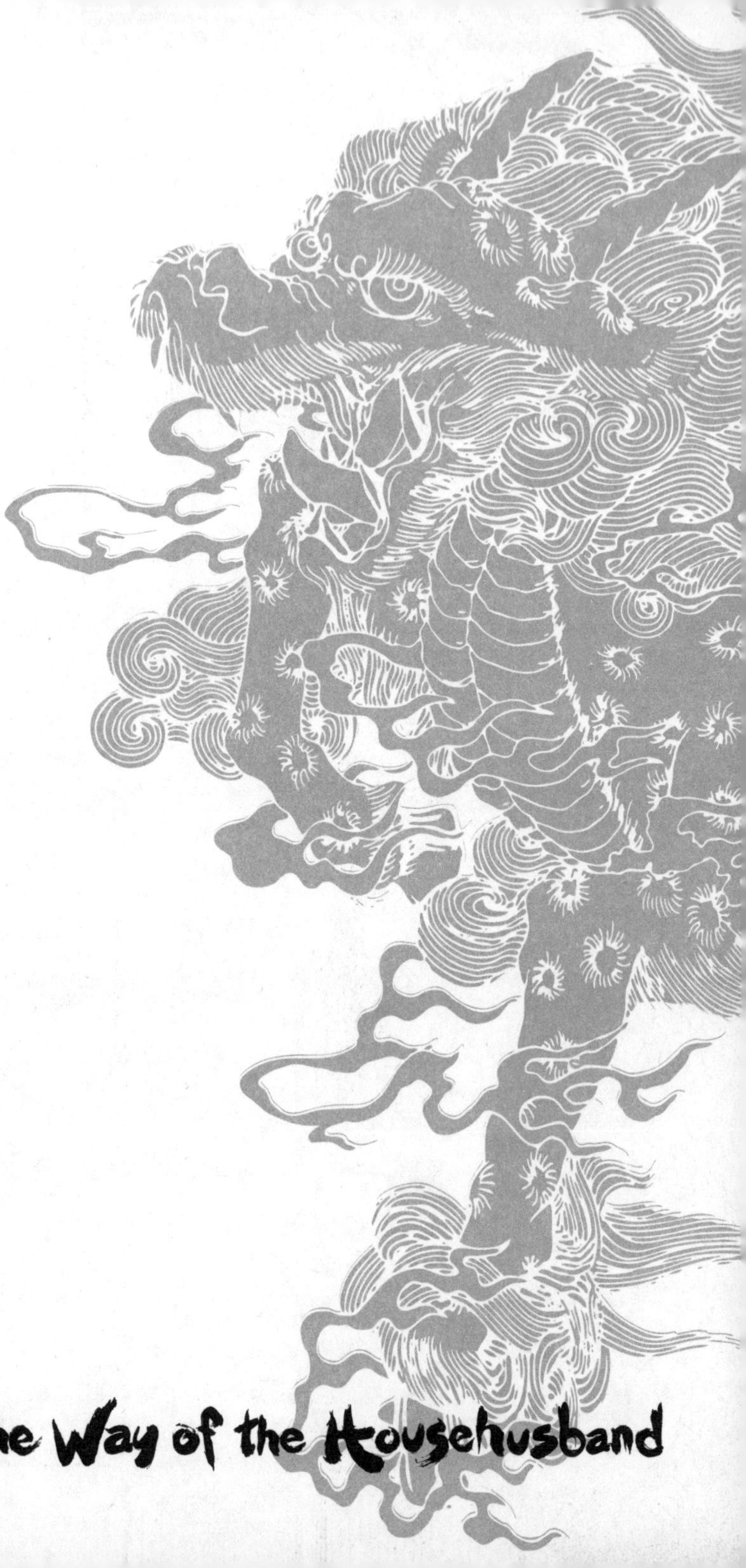

The Way of the Househusband

CHAPTER 68

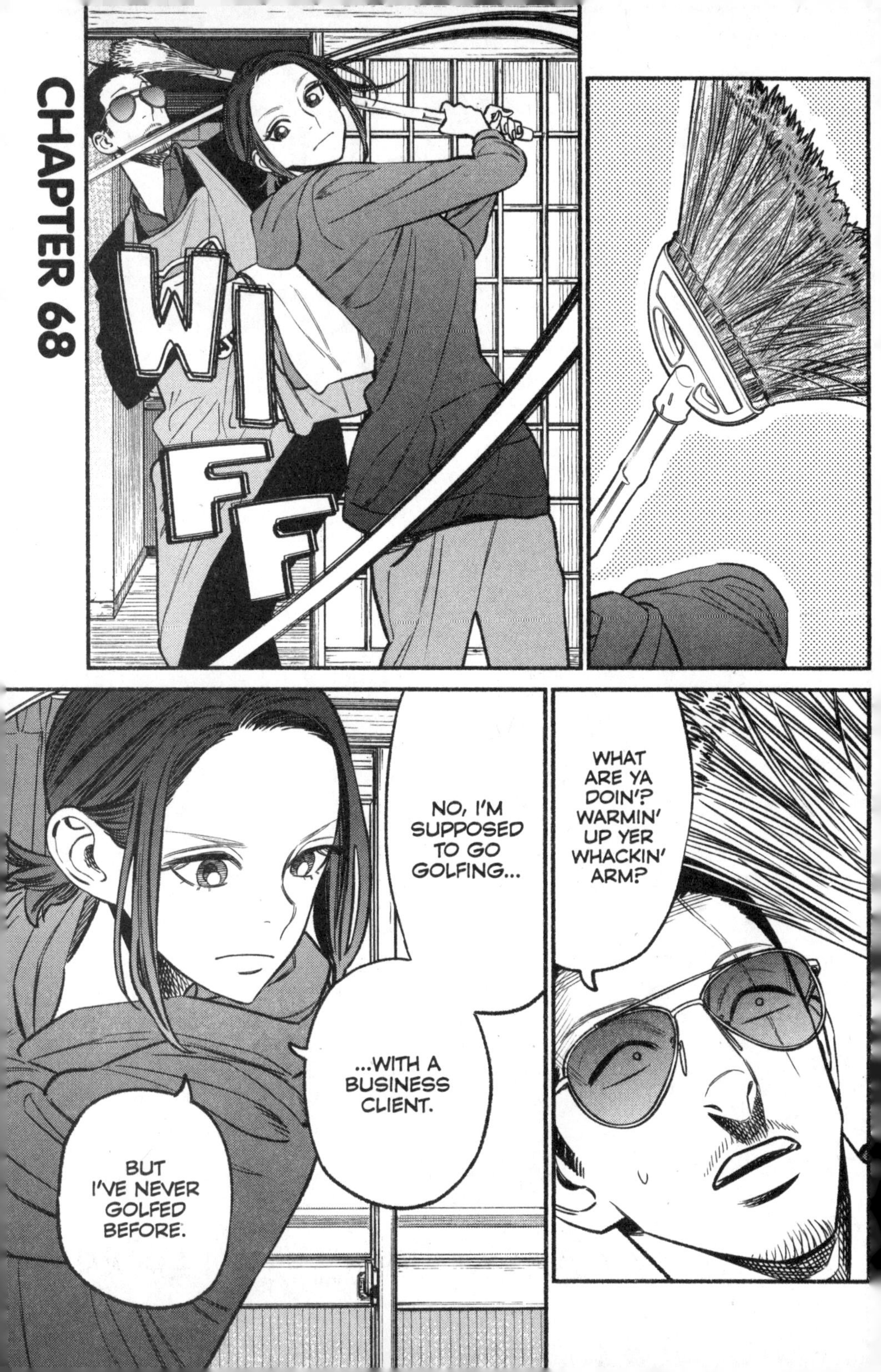
WIFF
WHAT ARE YA DOIN'? WARMIN' UP YER WHACKIN' ARM?
NO, I'M SUPPOSED TO GO GOLFING...
...WITH A BUSINESS CLIENT.
BUT I'VE NEVER GOLFED BEFORE.

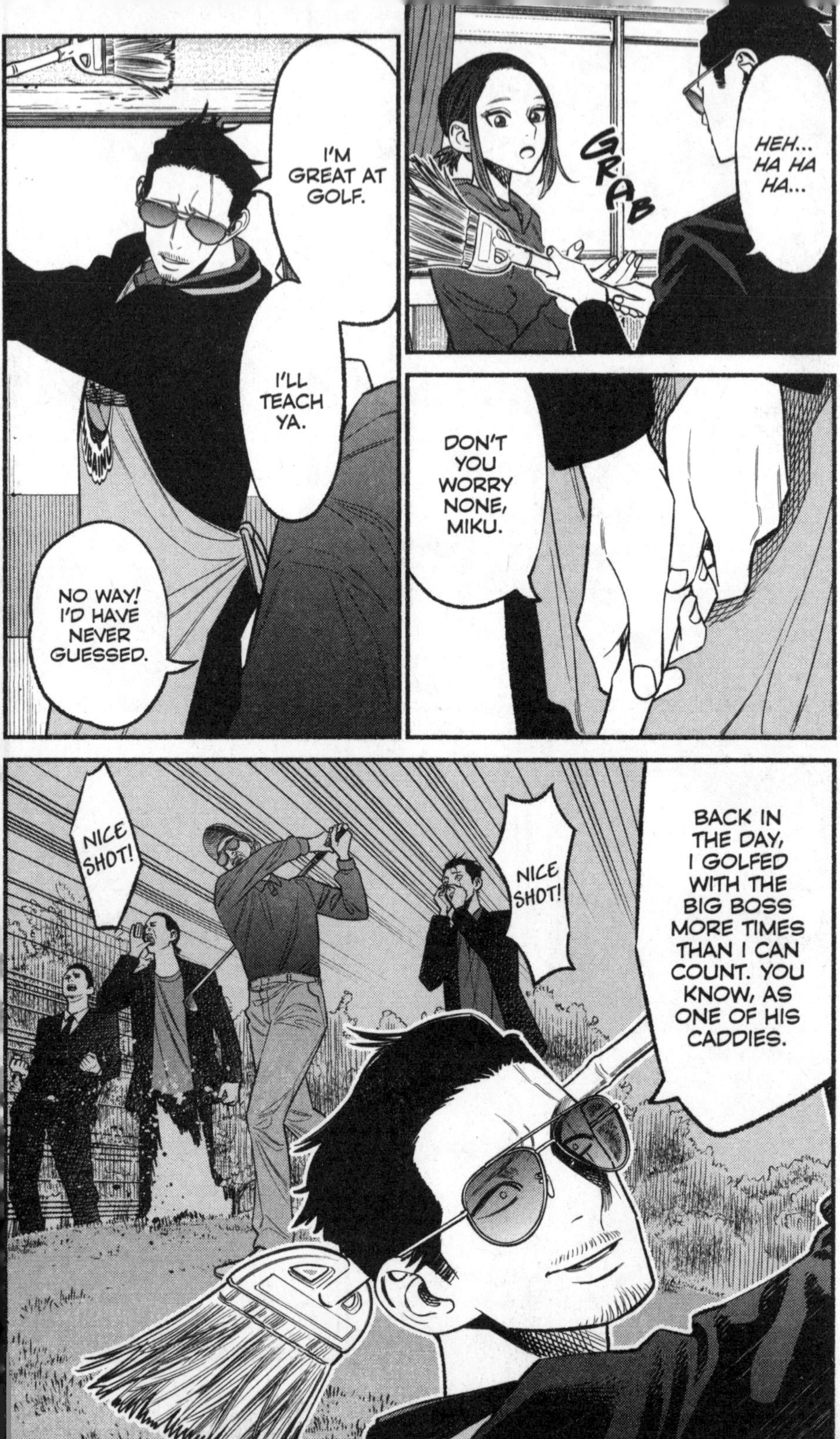
HEH... HA HA HA...
GRAB
DON'T YOU WORRY NONE, MIKU.
I'M GREAT AT GOLF.
I'LL TEACH YA.
NO WAY! I'D HAVE NEVER GUESSED.
BACK IN THE DAY, I GOLFED WITH THE BIG BOSS MORE TIMES THAN I CAN COUNT. YOU KNOW, AS ONE OF HIS CADDIES.
NICE SHOT!
NICE SHOT!

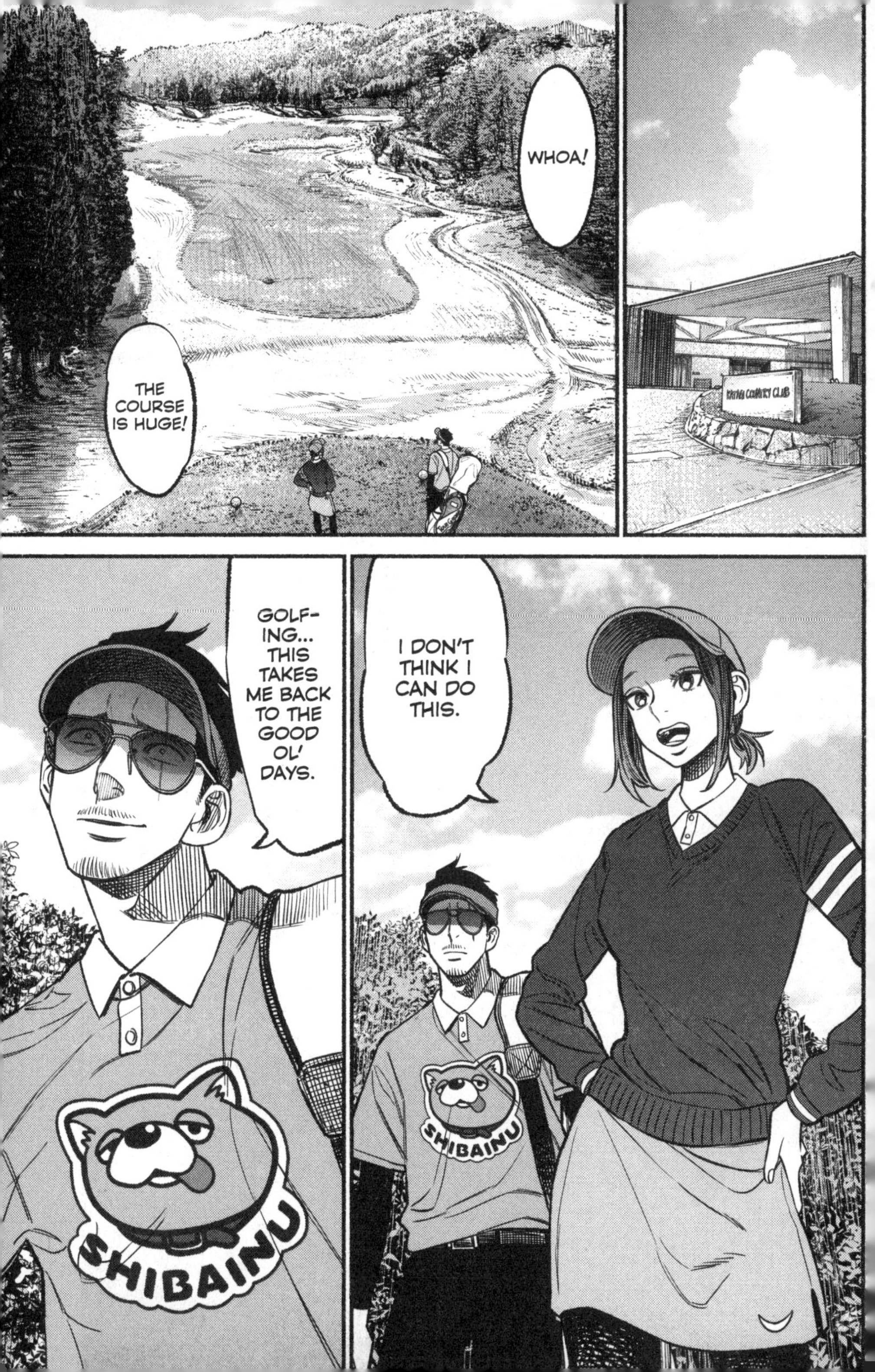
COUNTRY CLUB
WHOA!
THE COURSE IS HUGE!
I DON'T THINK I CAN DO THIS.
SHIBAINU
GOLF-ING... THIS TAKES ME BACK TO THE GOOD OL' DAYS.
SHIBAINU

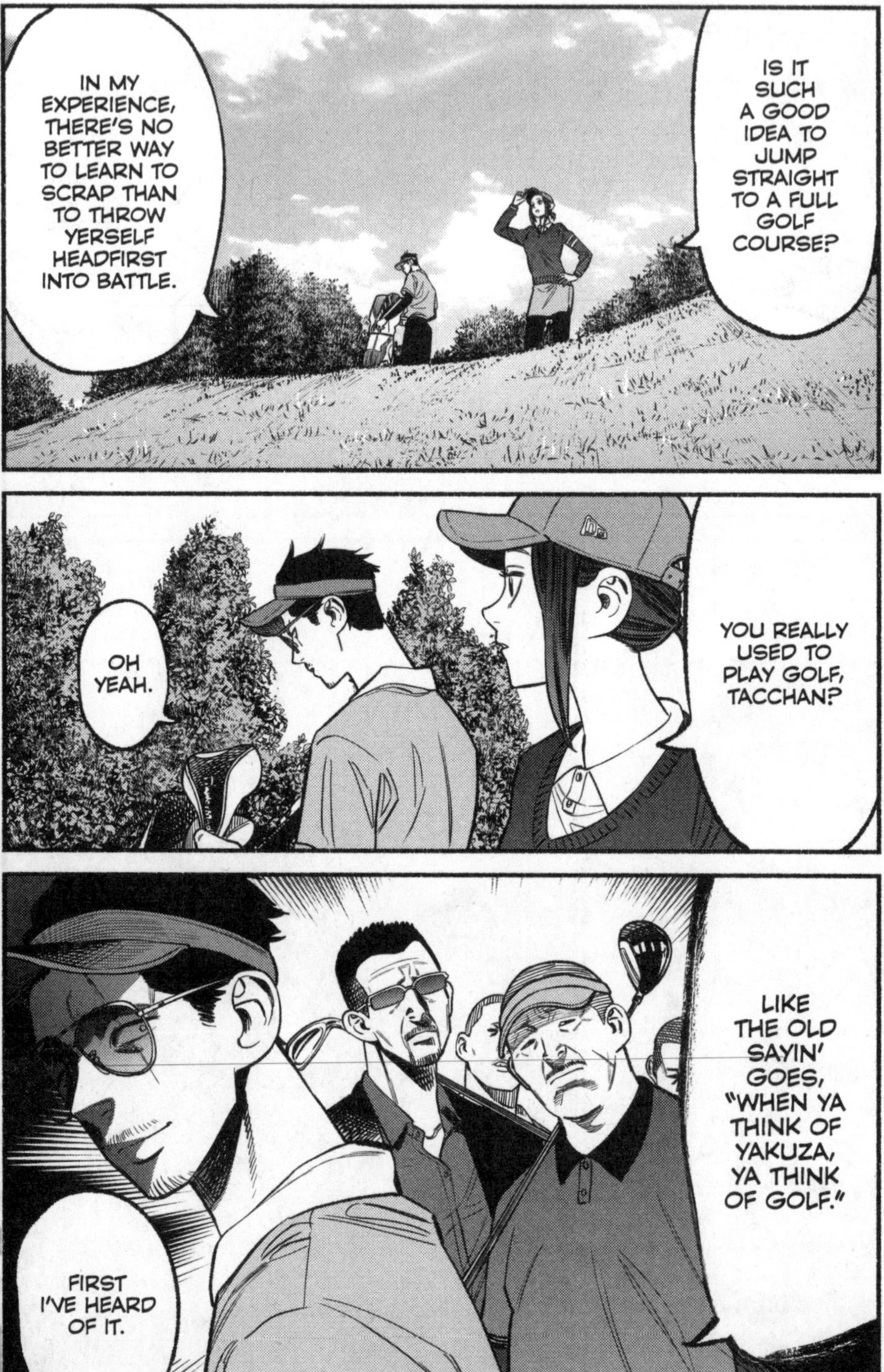
IS IT SUCH A GOOD IDEA TO JUMP STRAIGHT TO A FULL GOLF COURSE?
IN MY EXPERIENCE, THERE'S NO BETTER WAY TO LEARN TO SCRAP THAN TO THROW YERSELF HEADFIRST INTO BATTLE.
YOU REALLY USED TO PLAY GOLF, TACCHAN?
OH YEAH.
LIKE THE OLD SAYIN' GOES, "WHEN YA THINK OF YAKUZA, YA THINK OF GOLF."
FIRST I'VE HEARD OF IT.

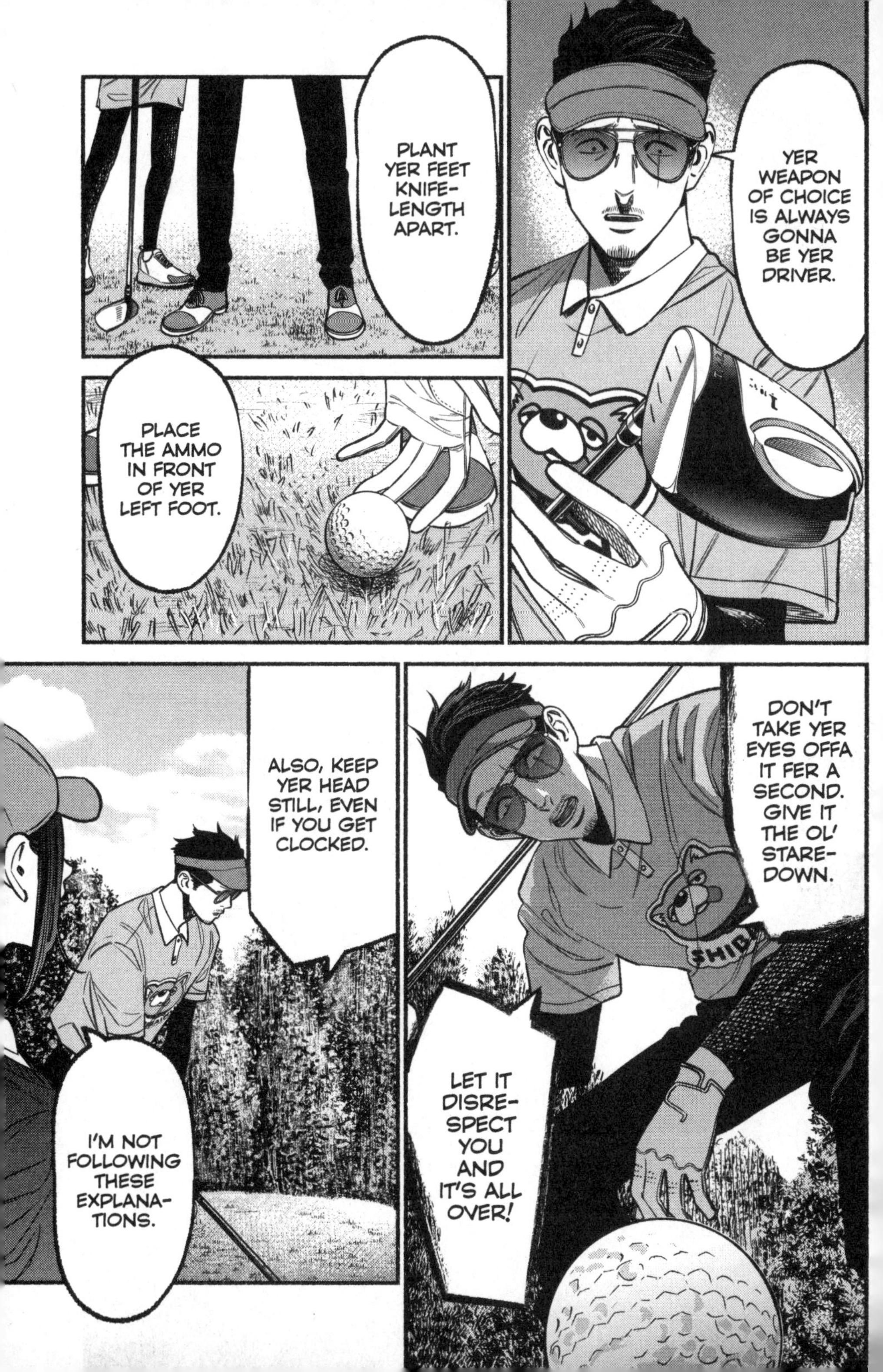
YER WEAPON OF CHOICE IS ALWAYS GONNA BE YER DRIVER.
PLANT YER FEET KNIFE-LENGTH APART.
PLACE THE AMMO IN FRONT OF YER LEFT FOOT.
DON'T TAKE YER EYES OFFA IT FER A SECOND. GIVE IT THE OL' STARE-DOWN.
LET IT DISRE-SPECT YOU AND IT'S ALL OVER!
ALSO, KEEP YER HEAD STILL, EVEN IF YOU GET CLOCKED.
I'M NOT FOLLOWING THESE EXPLANA-TIONS.

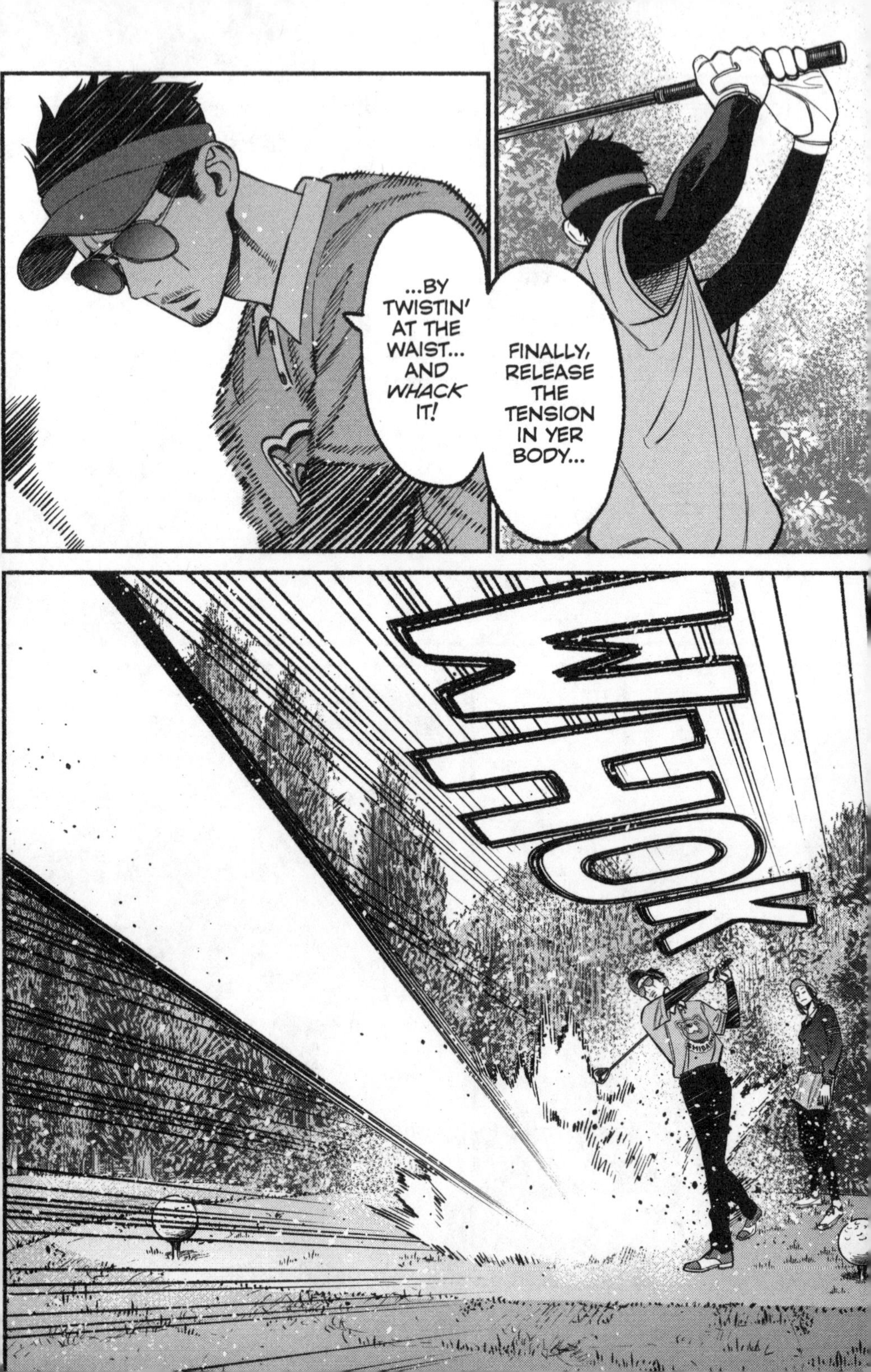
FINALLY, RELEASE THE TENSION IN YER BODY...
...BY TWISTIN' AT THE WAIST... AND *WHACK* IT!
WHOK

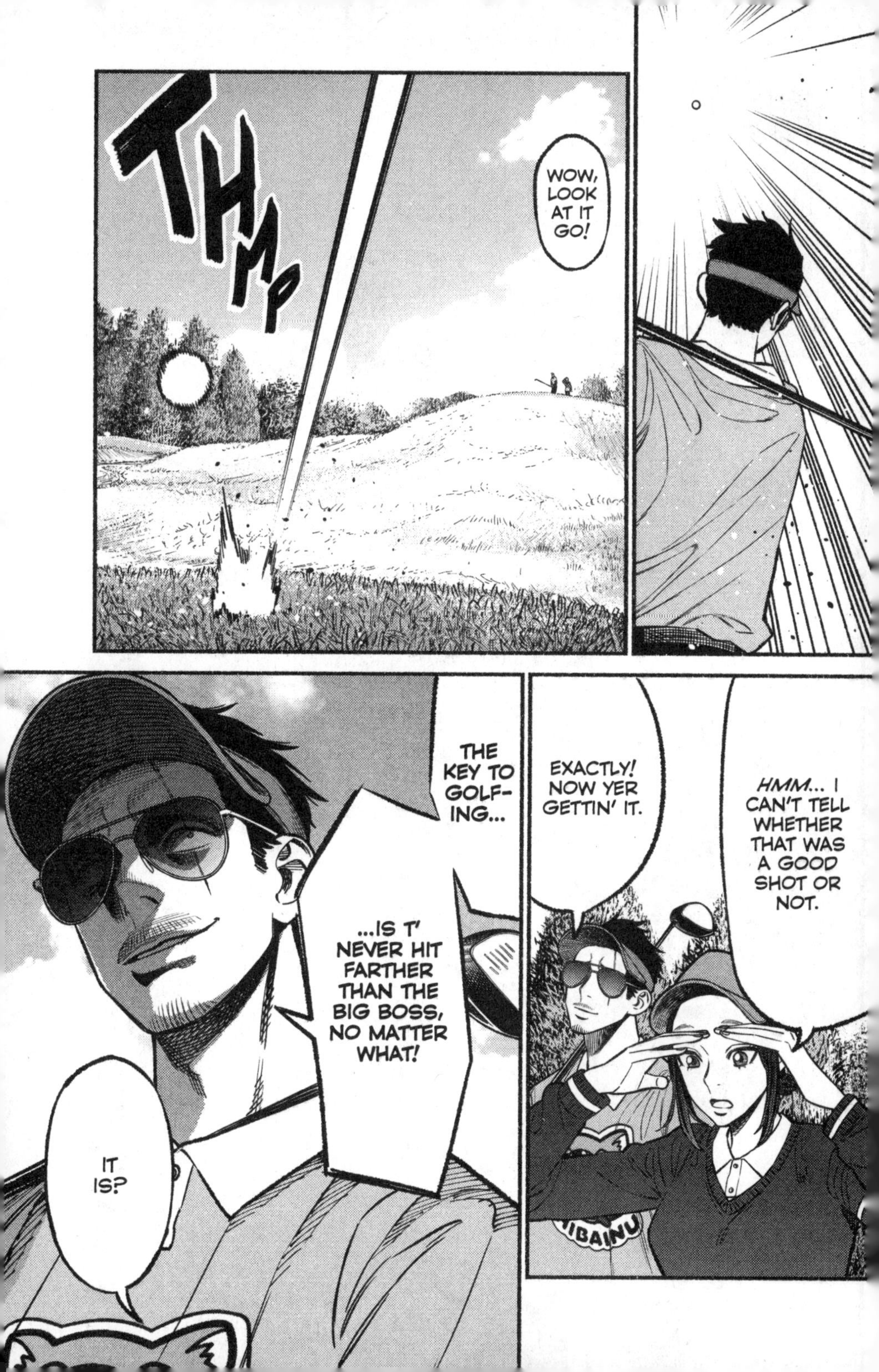
THMP
WOW, LOOK AT IT GO!
HMM... I CAN'T TELL WHETHER THAT WAS A GOOD SHOT OR NOT.
EXACTLY! NOW YER GETTIN' IT.
THE KEY TO GOLF-ING...
...IS T' NEVER HIT FARTHER THAN THE BIG BOSS, NO MATTER WHAT!
IT IS?

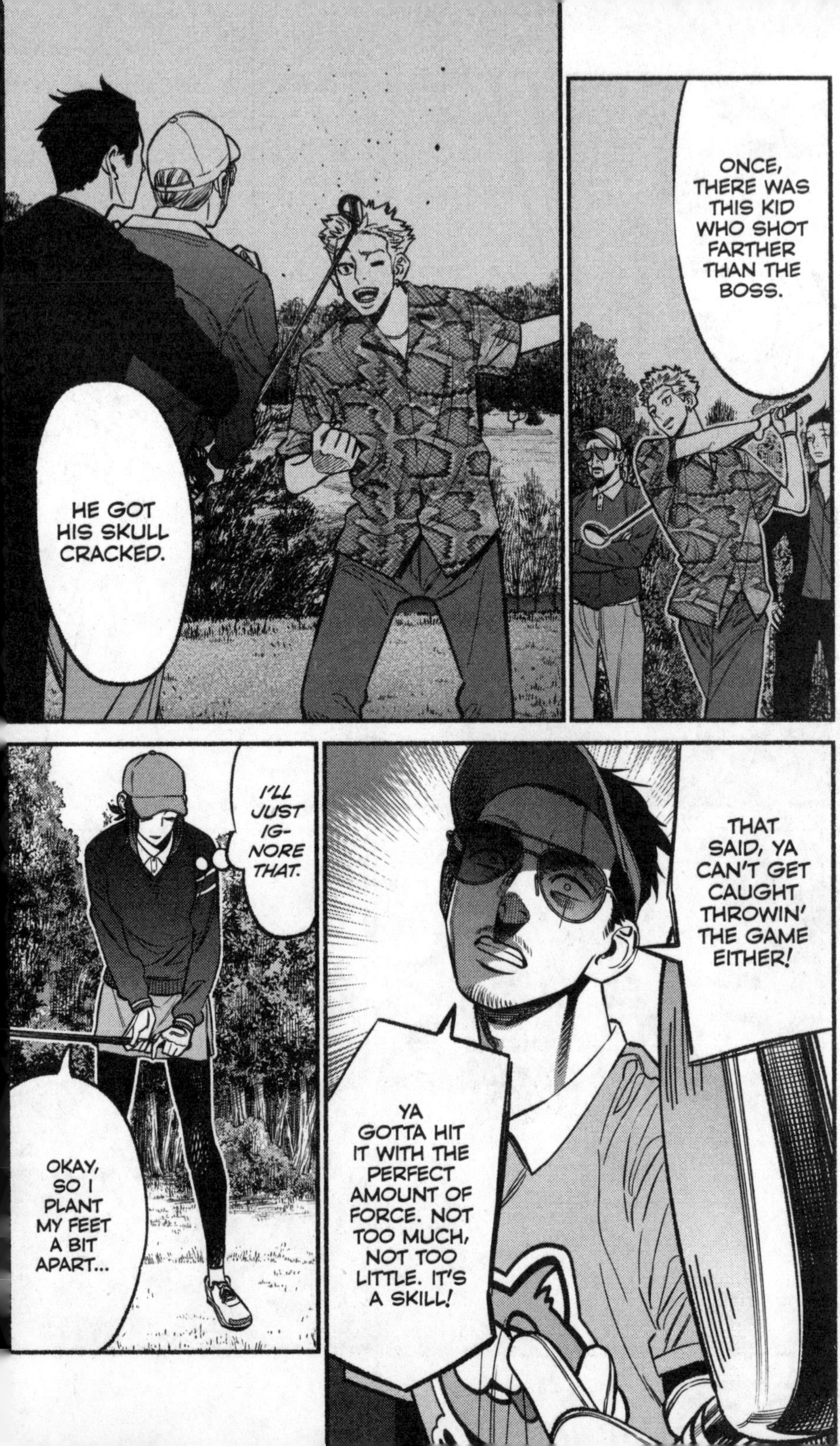
ONCE, THERE WAS THIS KID WHO SHOT FARTHER THAN THE BOSS.
HE GOT HIS SKULL CRACKED.
THAT SAID, YA CAN'T GET CAUGHT THROWIN' THE GAME EITHER!
YA GOTTA HIT IT WITH THE PERFECT AMOUNT OF FORCE. NOT TOO MUCH, NOT TOO LITTLE. IT'S A SKILL!
I'LL JUST IG- NORE THAT.
OKAY, SO I PLANT MY FEET A BIT APART...

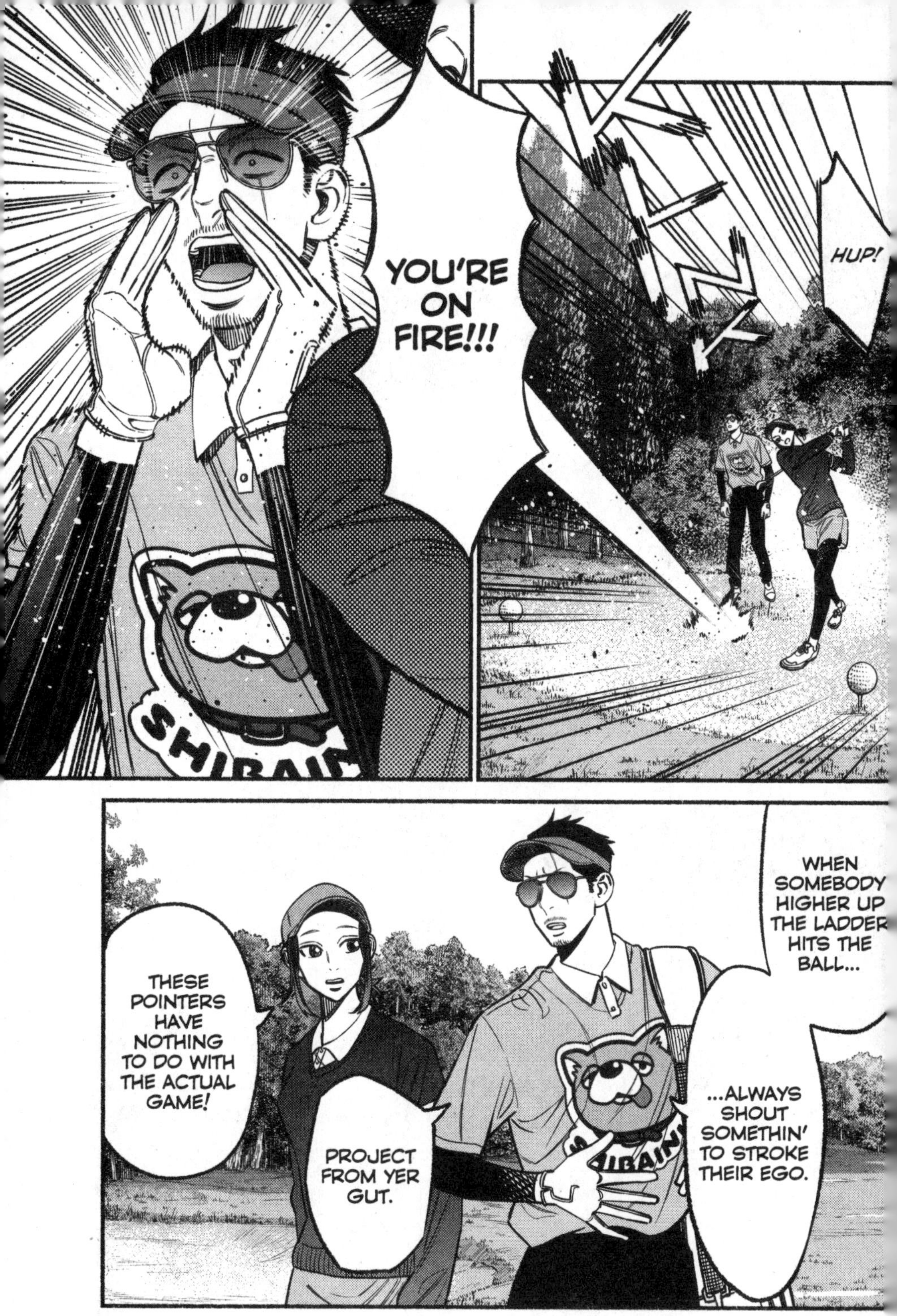
HUP!
YOU'RE ON FIRE!!!
WHEN SOMEBODY HIGHER UP THE LADDER HITS THE BALL...
...ALWAYS SHOUT SOMETHIN' TO STROKE THEIR EGO.
PROJECT FROM YER GUT.
THESE POINTERS HAVE NOTHING TO DO WITH THE ACTUAL GAME!

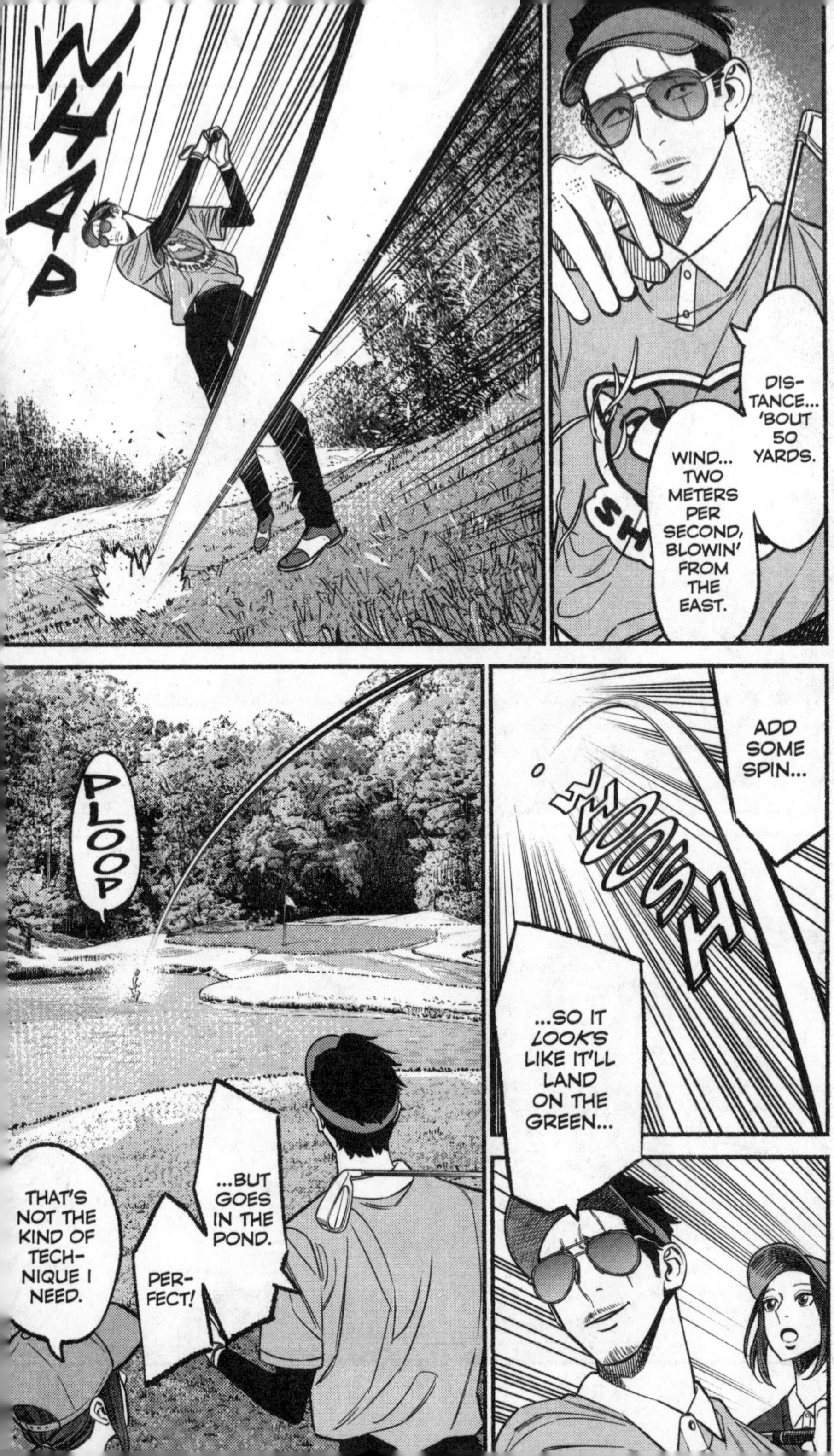
DIS-TANCE... 'BOUT 50 YARDS.
WIND... TWO METERS PER SECOND, BLOWIN' FROM THE EAST.
WHAP
ADD SOME SPIN...
WHOOSH
...SO IT *LOOKS* LIKE IT'LL LAND ON THE GREEN...
...BUT GOES IN THE POND.
PLOOP
PER-FECT!
THAT'S NOT THE KIND OF TECH-NIQUE I NEED.

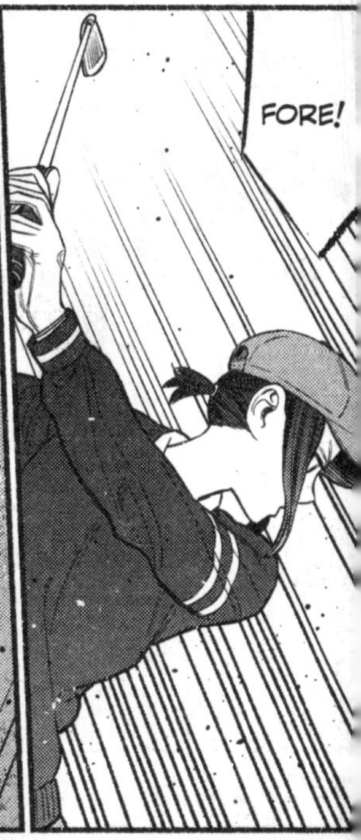
FORE!

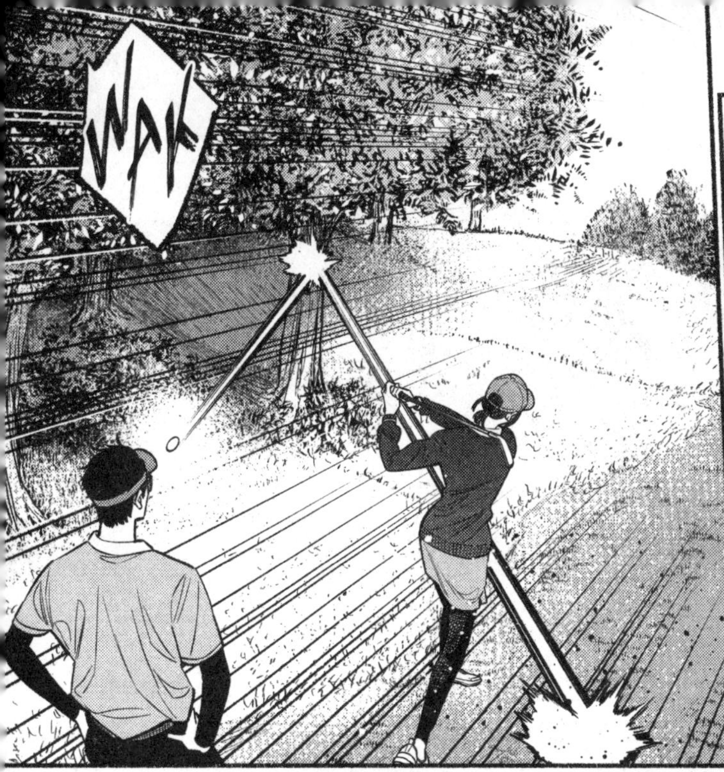
WAK

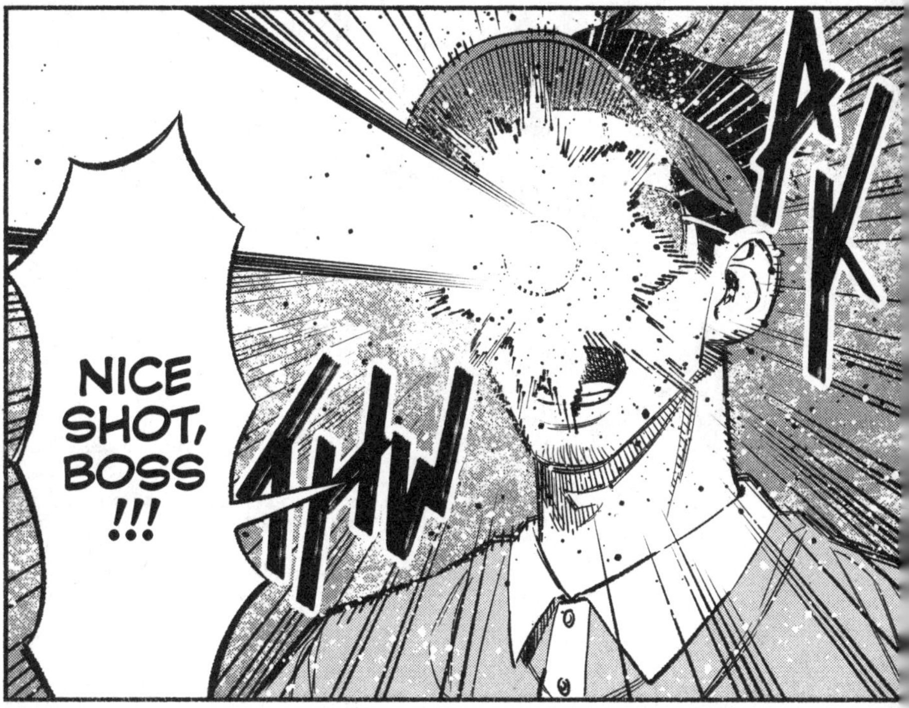
NICE SHOT, BOSS !!!

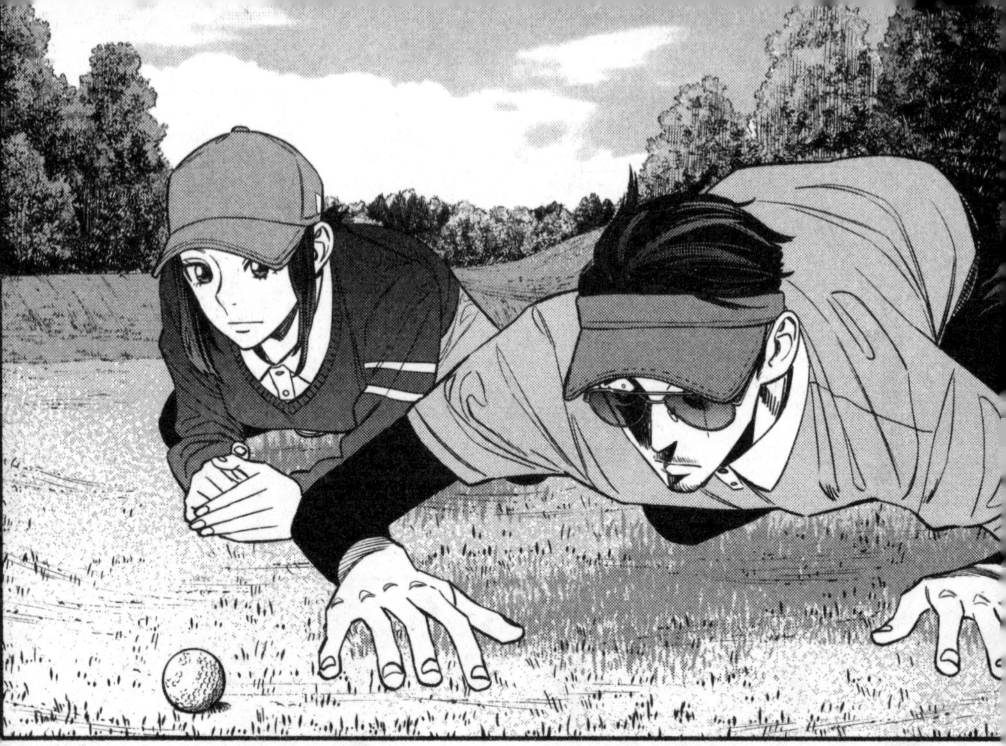

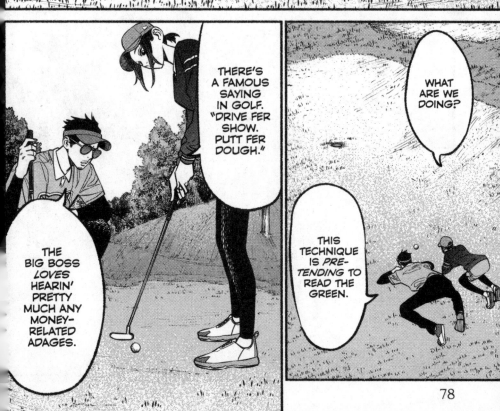

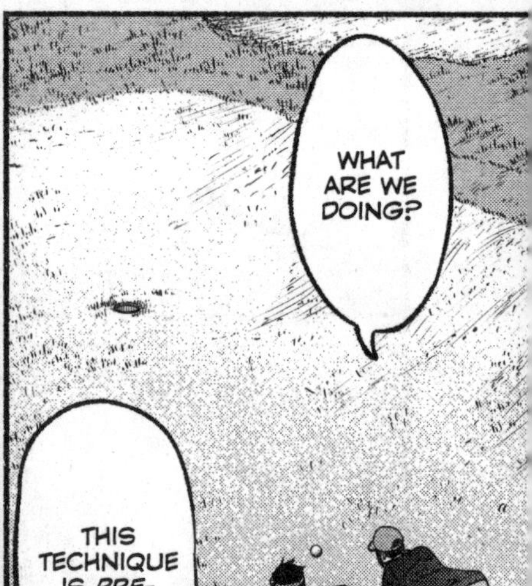
WHAT ARE WE DOING?
THIS TECHNIQUE IS *PRE-TENDING* TO READ THE GREEN.

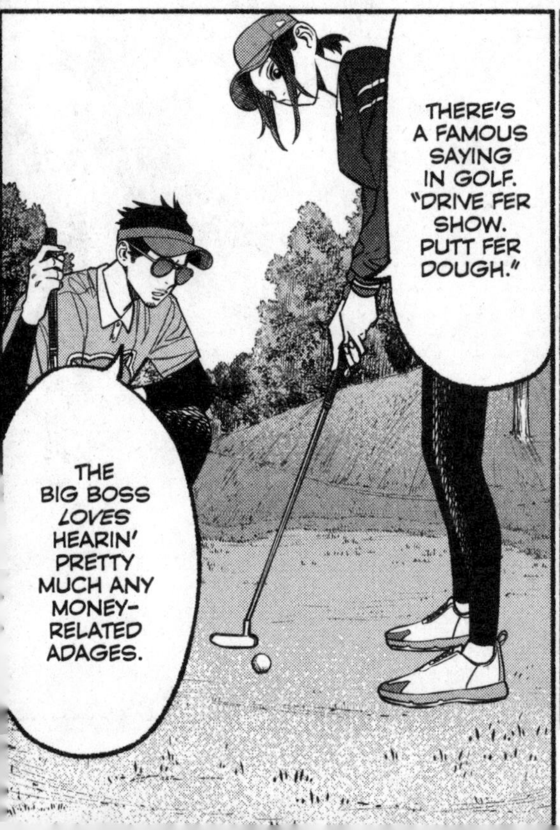
THERE'S A FAMOUS SAYING IN GOLF. "DRIVE FER SHOW. PUTT FER DOUGH."
THE BIG BOSS *LOVES* HEARIN' PRETTY MUCH ANY MONEY-RELATED ADAGES.

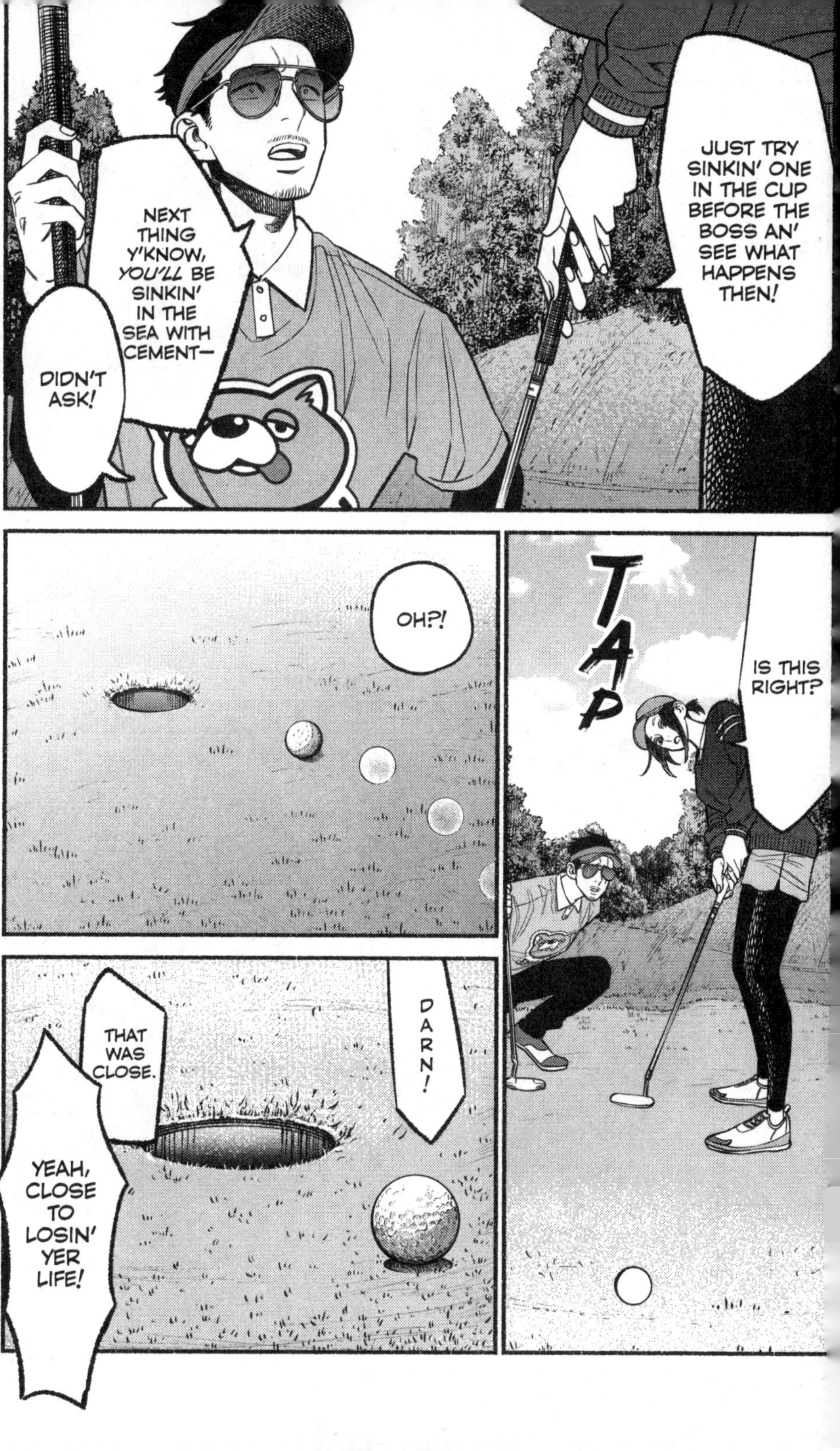
JUST TRY SINKIN' ONE IN THE CUP BEFORE THE BOSS AN' SEE WHAT HAPPENS THEN!
NEXT THING Y'KNOW, *YOU'LL* BE SINKIN' IN THE SEA WITH CEMENT—
DIDN'T ASK!
TAP TAP
IS THIS RIGHT?
OH?!
DARN!
THAT WAS CLOSE.
YEAH, CLOSE TO LOSIN' YER LIFE!

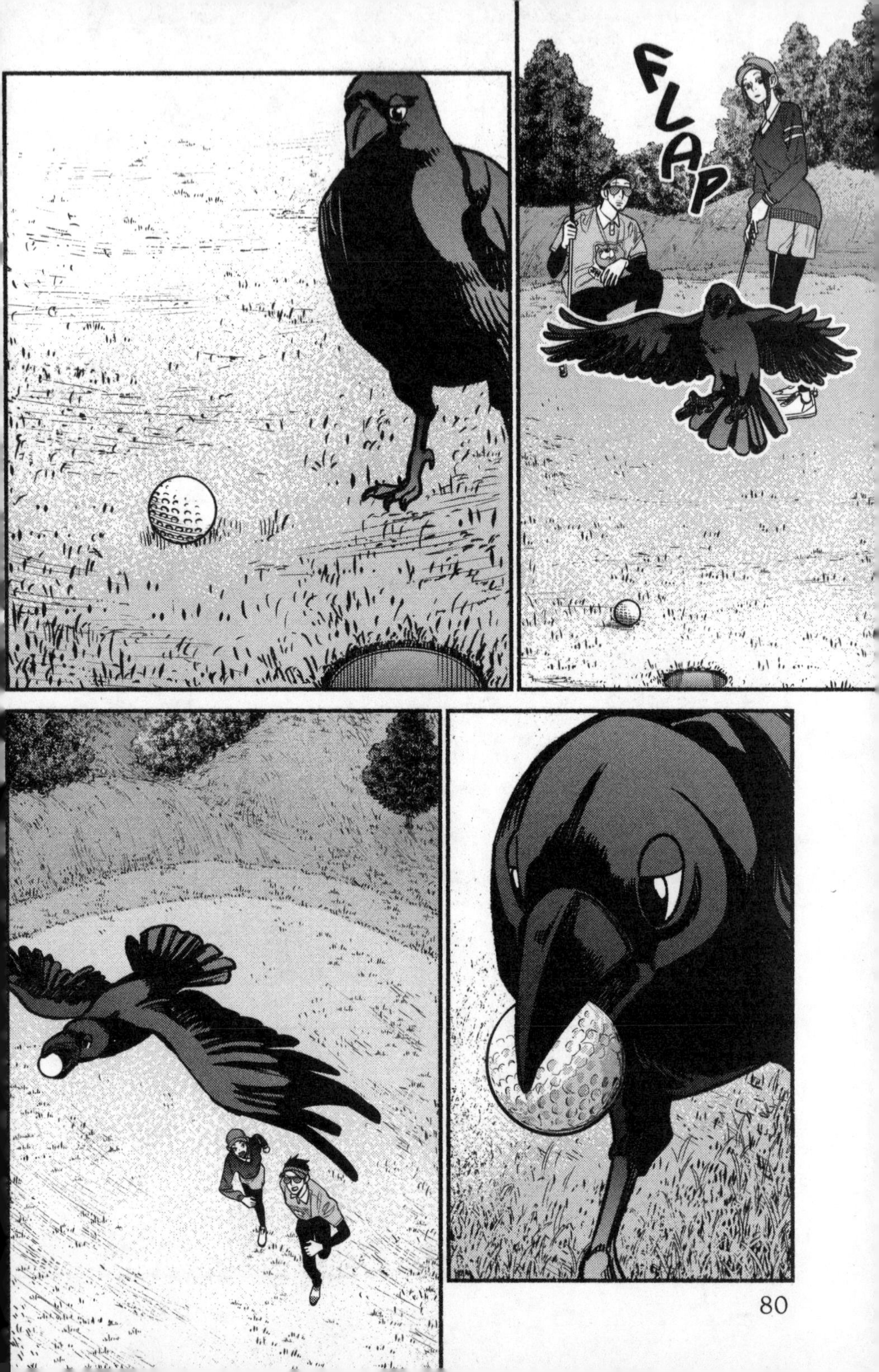
FLAP

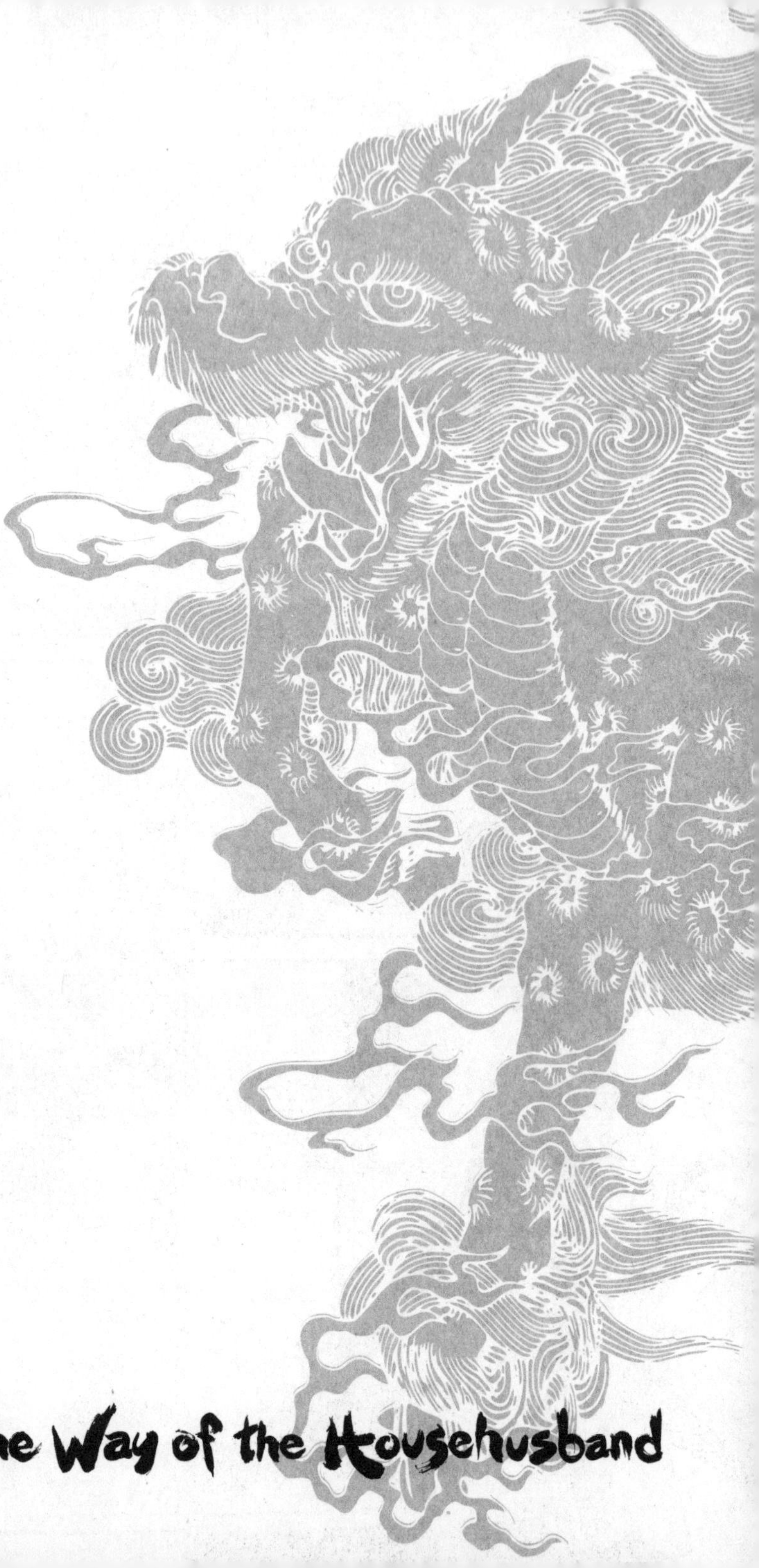

The Way of the Househusband

CHAPTER 69

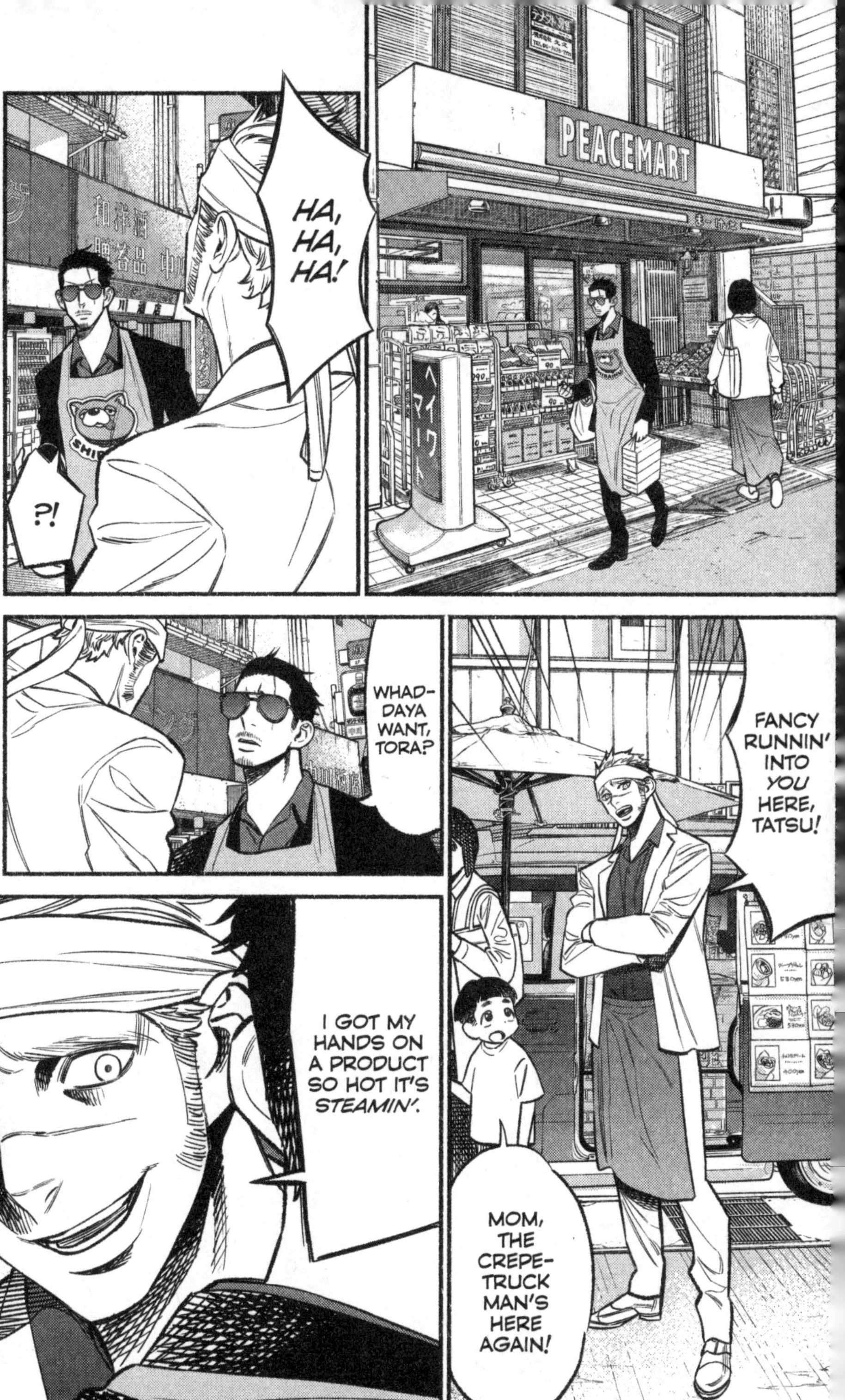
PEACEMART
HA, HA, HA!
?!
FANCY RUNNIN' INTO *YOU* HERE, TATSU!
MOM, THE CREPE-TRUCK MAN'S HERE AGAIN!
WHAD-DAYA WANT, TORA?
I GOT MY HANDS ON A PRODUCT SO HOT IT'S *STEAMIN'*.

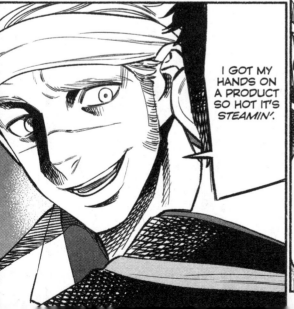

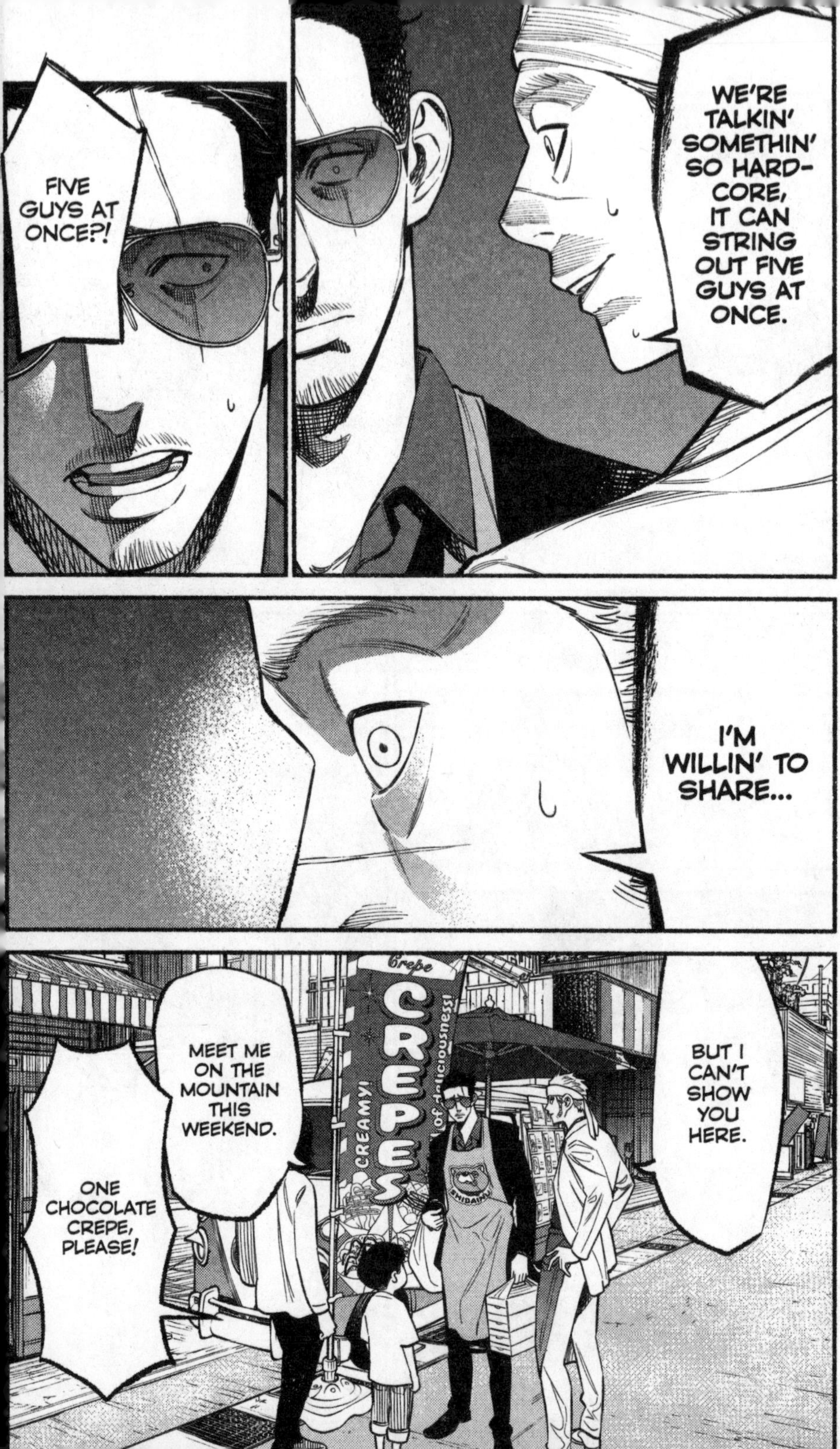
WE'RE TALKIN' SOMETHIN' SO HARD-CORE, IT CAN STRING OUT FIVE GUYS AT ONCE.
FIVE GUYS AT ONCE?!
I'M WILLIN' TO SHARE...
BUT I CAN'T SHOW YOU HERE.
MEET ME ON THE MOUNTAIN THIS WEEKEND.
Crepe
CREPES
CREAMY!
ONE CHOCOLATE CREPE, PLEASE!

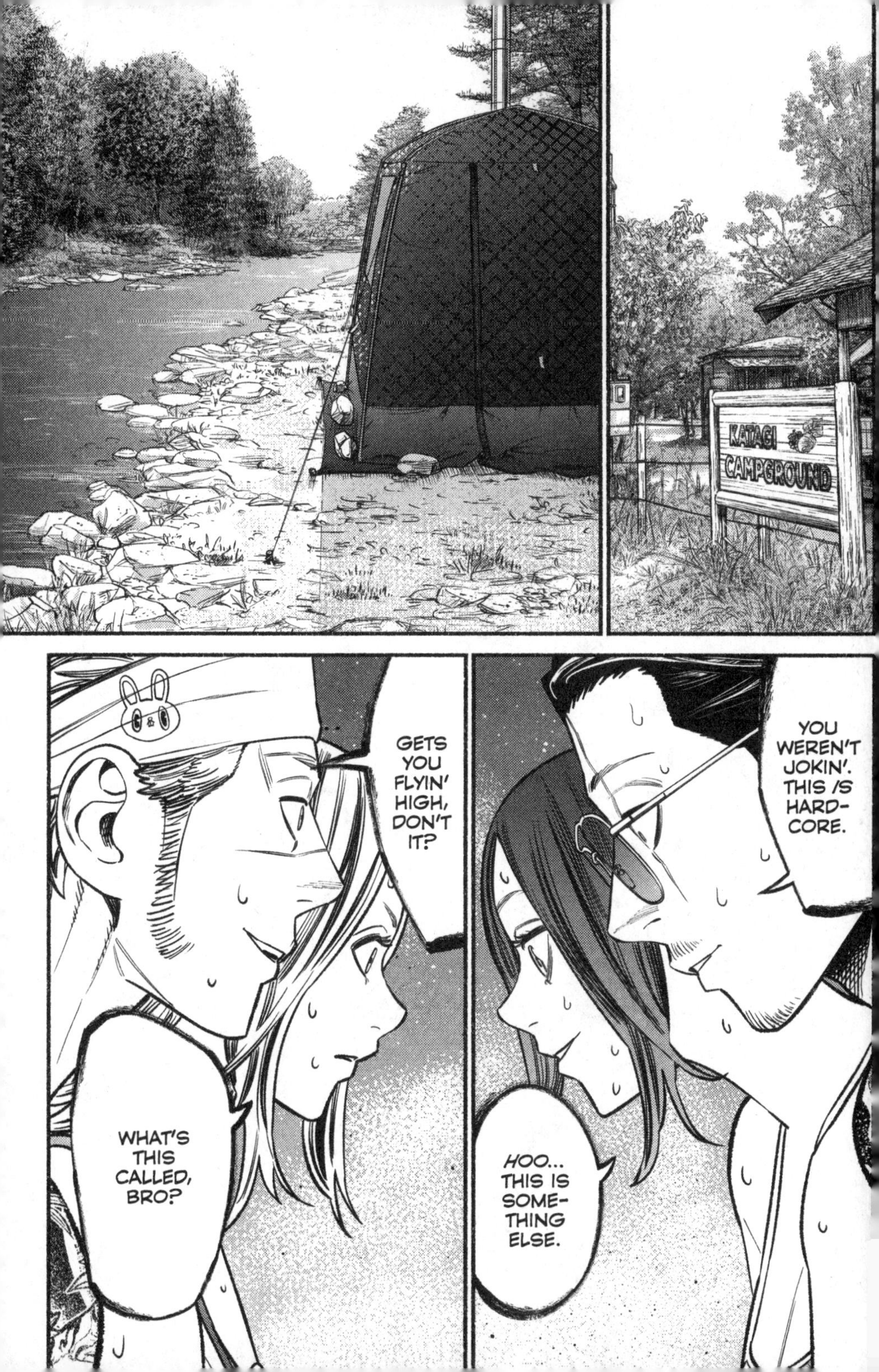
KATAGI CAMPGROUND
YOU WEREN'T JOKIN'. THIS IS HARD-CORE.
HOO... THIS IS SOME-THING ELSE.
GETS YOU FLYIN' HIGH, DON'T IT?
WHAT'S THIS CALLED, BRO?

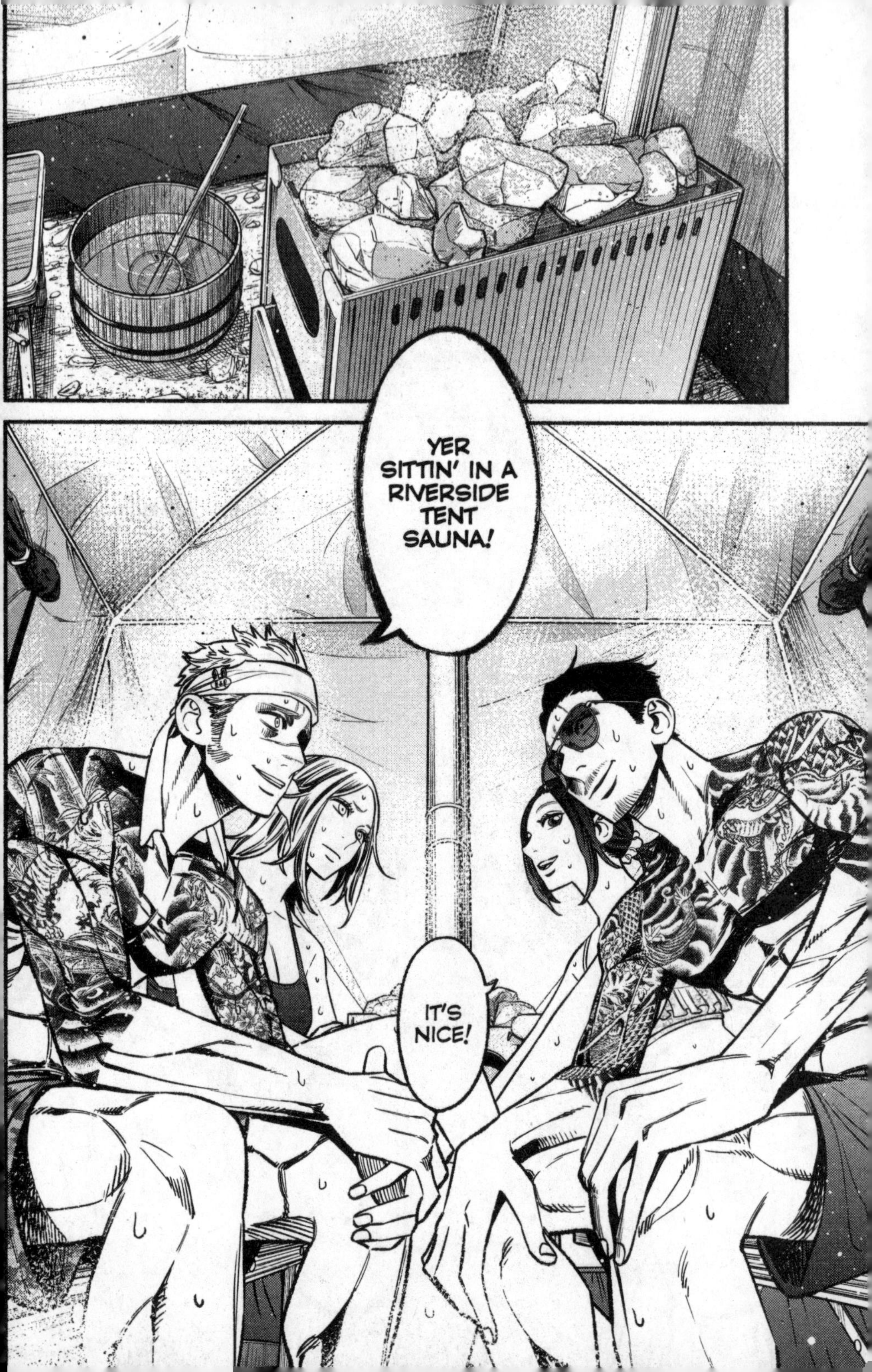
YER SITTIN' IN A RIVERSIDE TENT SAUNA!
IT'S NICE!

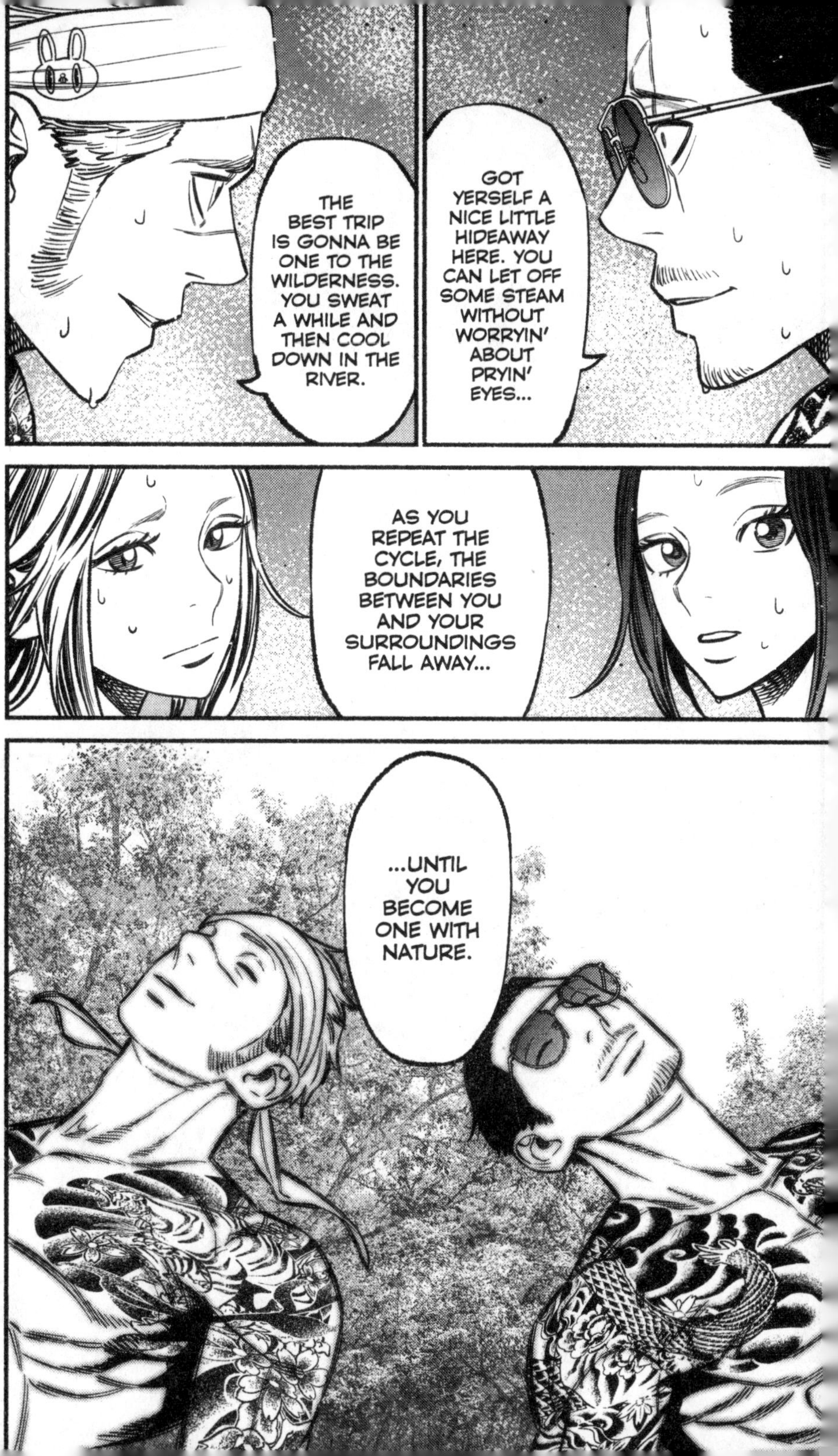
GOT YERSELF A NICE LITTLE HIDEAWAY HERE. YOU CAN LET OFF SOME STEAM WITHOUT WORRYIN' ABOUT PRYIN' EYES...
THE BEST TRIP IS GONNA BE ONE TO THE WILDERNESS. YOU SWEAT A WHILE AND THEN COOL DOWN IN THE RIVER.
AS YOU REPEAT THE CYCLE, THE BOUNDARIES BETWEEN YOU AND YOUR SURROUNDINGS FALL AWAY...
...UNTIL YOU BECOME ONE WITH NATURE.

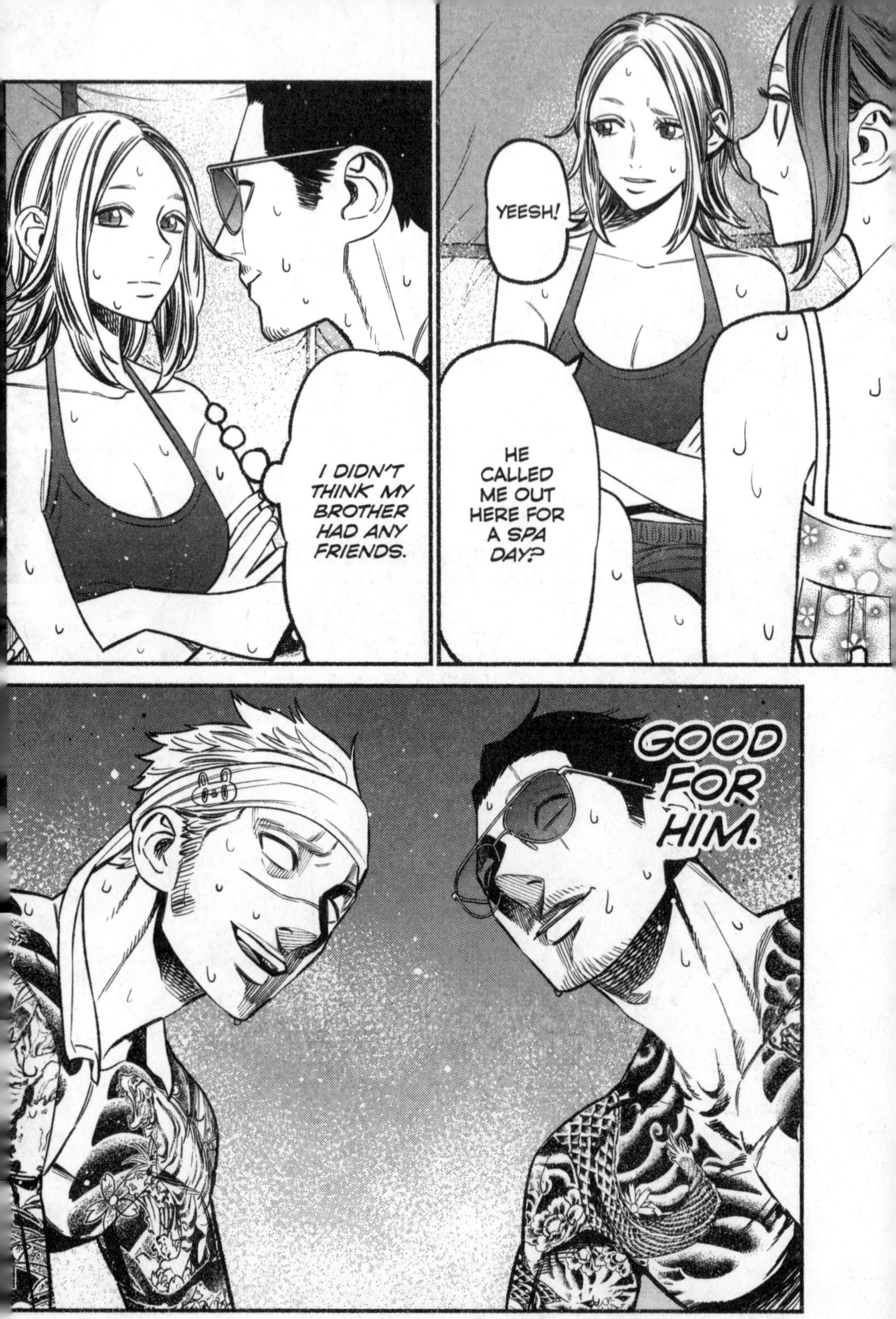
YEESH!
HE CALLED ME OUT HERE FOR A SPA DAY?
I DIDN'T THINK MY BROTHER HAD ANY FRIENDS.
GOOD FOR HIM.

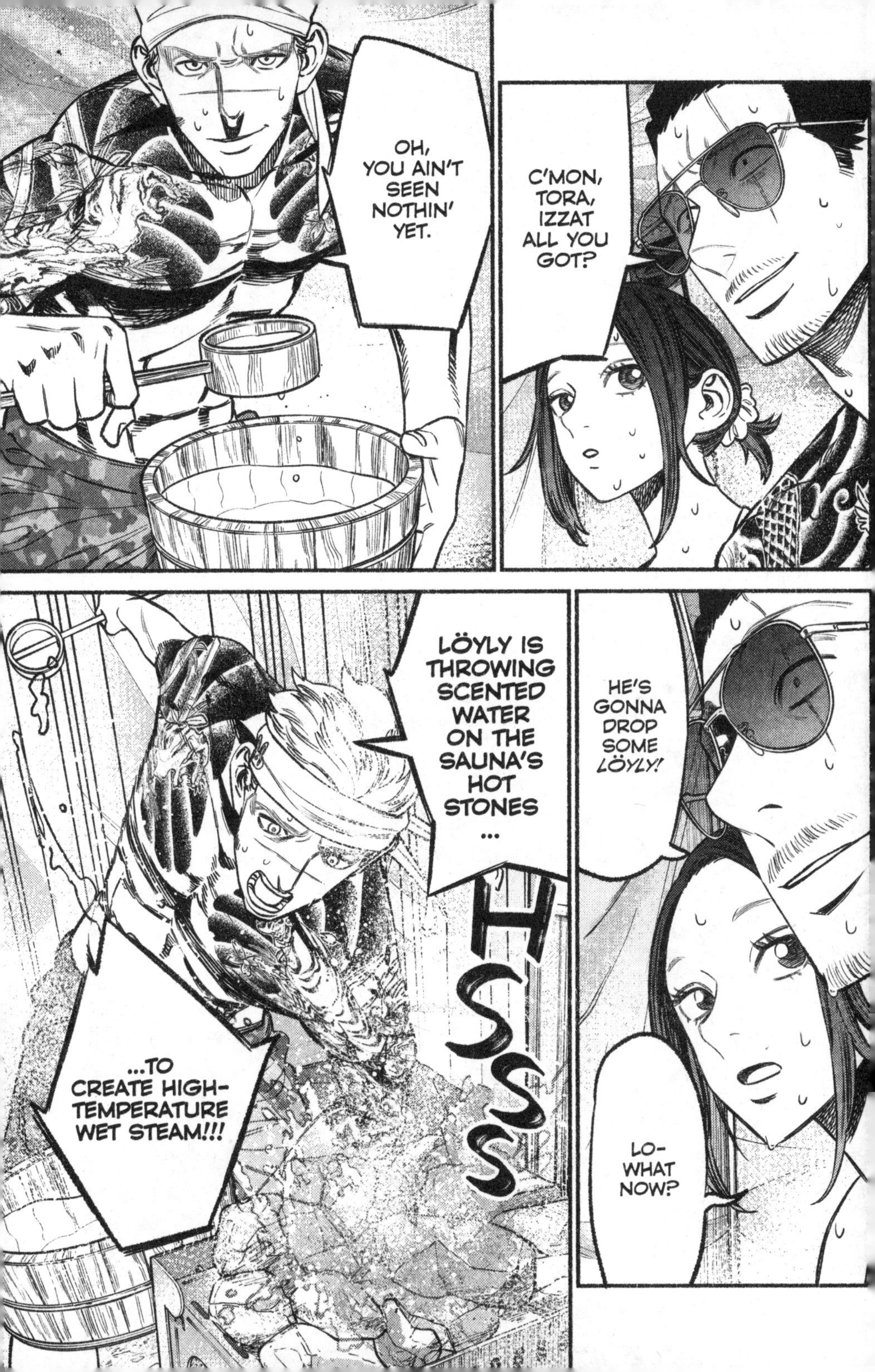
C'MON, TORA, IZZAT ALL YOU GOT?
OH, YOU AIN'T SEEN NOTHIN' YET.
HE'S GONNA DROP SOME *LÖYLY!*
LO-WHAT NOW?
LÖYLY IS THROWING SCENTED WATER ON THE SAUNA'S HOT STONES...
HISSS
...TO CREATE HIGH-TEMPERATURE WET STEAM!!!

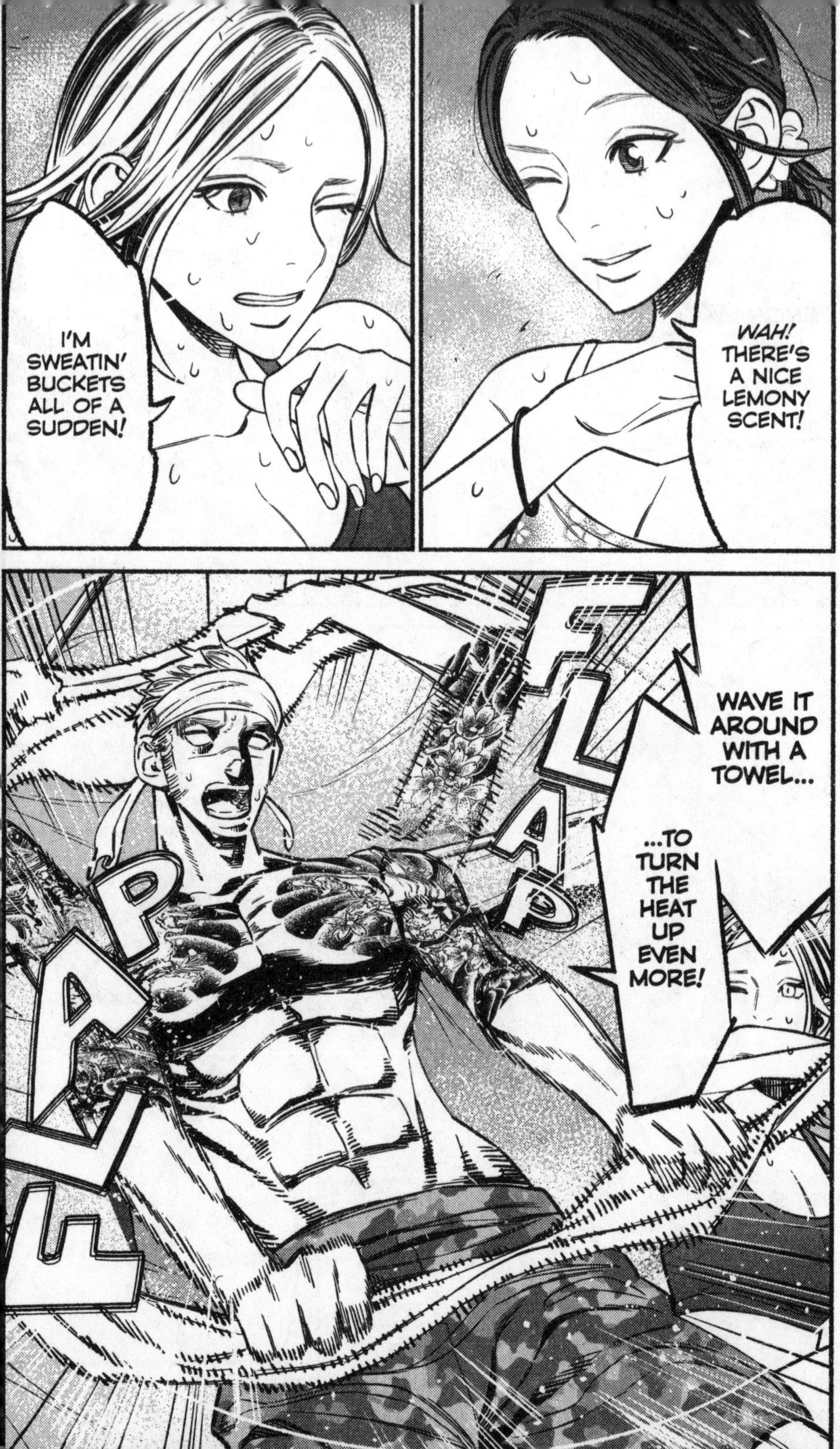
WAH! THERE'S A NICE LEMONY SCENT!
I'M SWEATIN' BUCKETS ALL OF A SUDDEN!
FLAP
WAVE IT AROUND WITH A TOWEL...
...TO TURN THE HEAT UP EVEN MORE!
FLAP

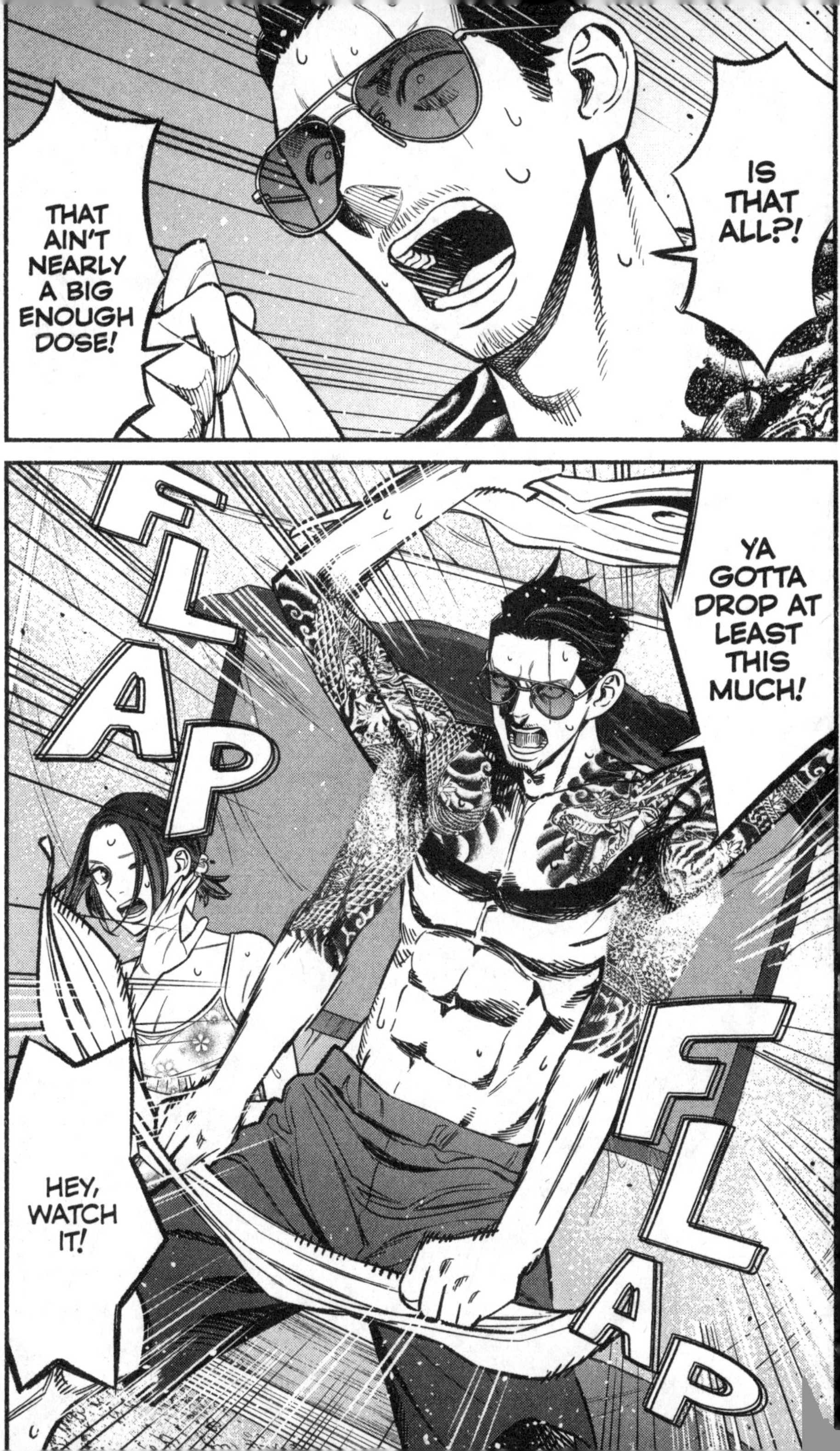
IS THAT ALL?!
THAT AIN'T NEARLY A BIG ENOUGH DOSE!
YA GOTTA DROP AT LEAST THIS MUCH!
FLAP
FLAP
HEY, WATCH IT!

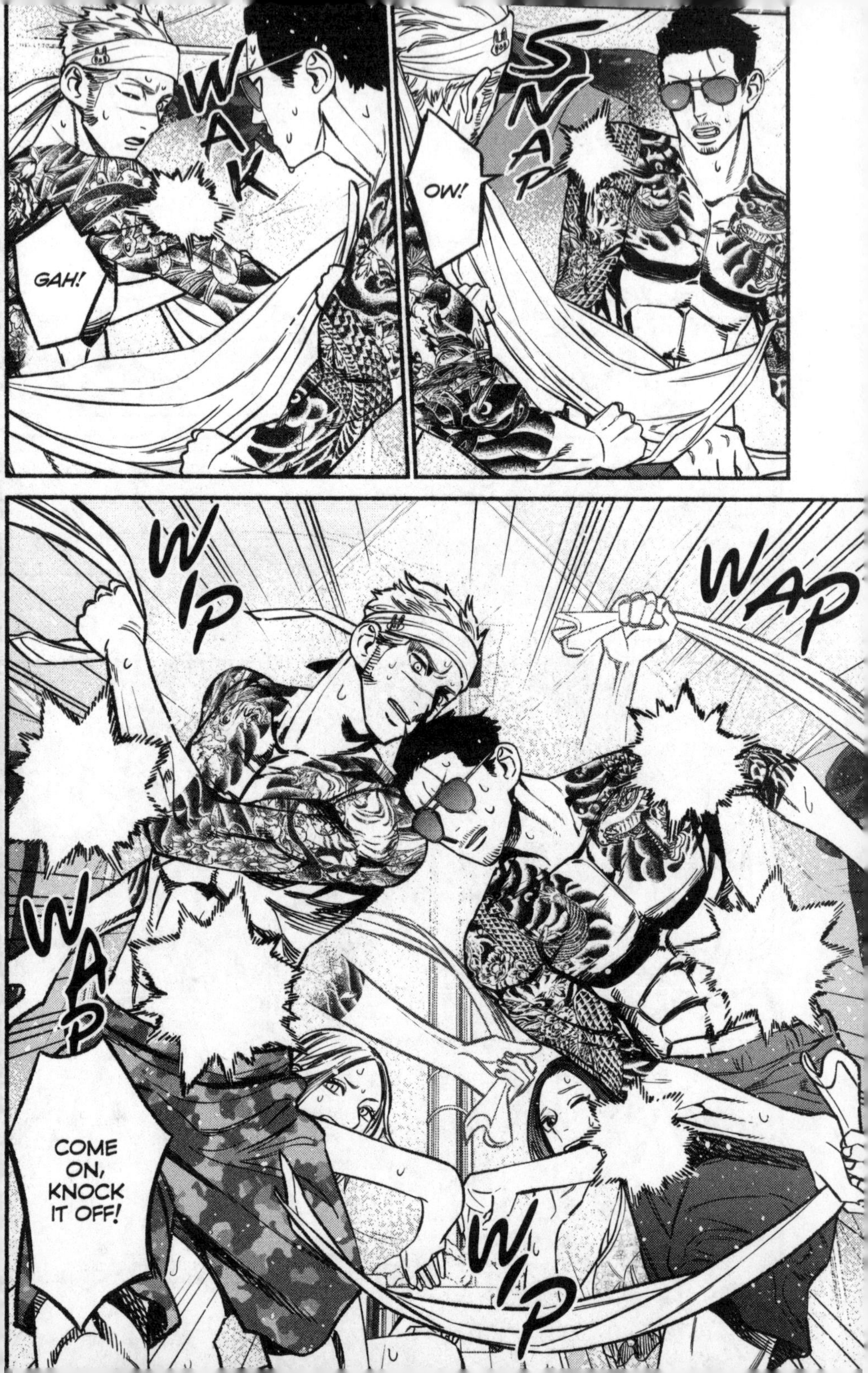
SNAP
OW!
WAK
GAH!
WAP
WIP
WAP
COME ON, KNOCK IT OFF!
WIP

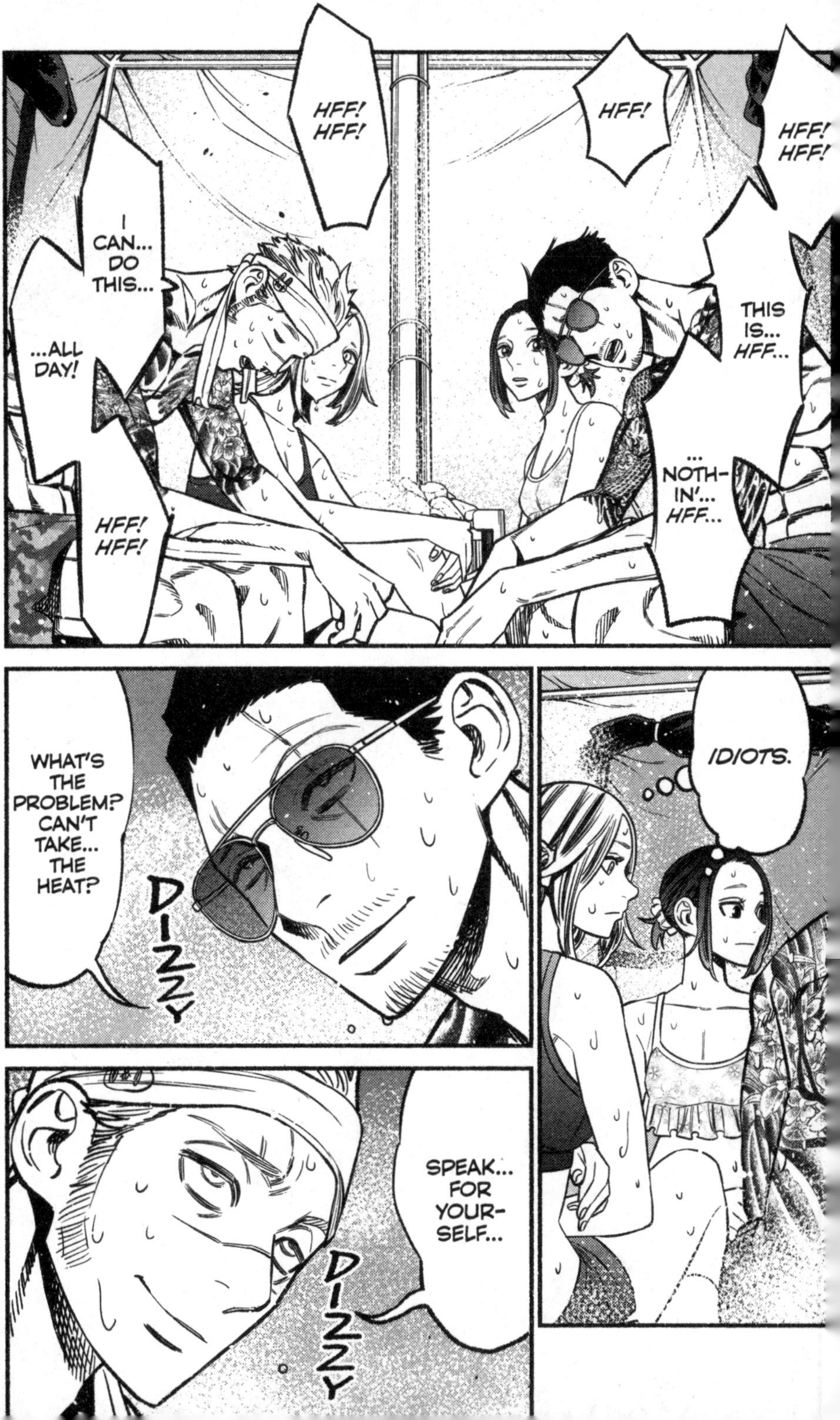
HFF! HFF!
HFF!
THIS IS... HFF...
... NOTHIN'... HFF...
HFF! HFF!
I CAN... DO THIS...
...ALL DAY!
HFF! HFF!
IDIOTS.
WHAT'S THE PROBLEM? CAN'T TAKE... THE HEAT?
DIZZY
SPEAK... FOR YOURSELF...
DIZZY

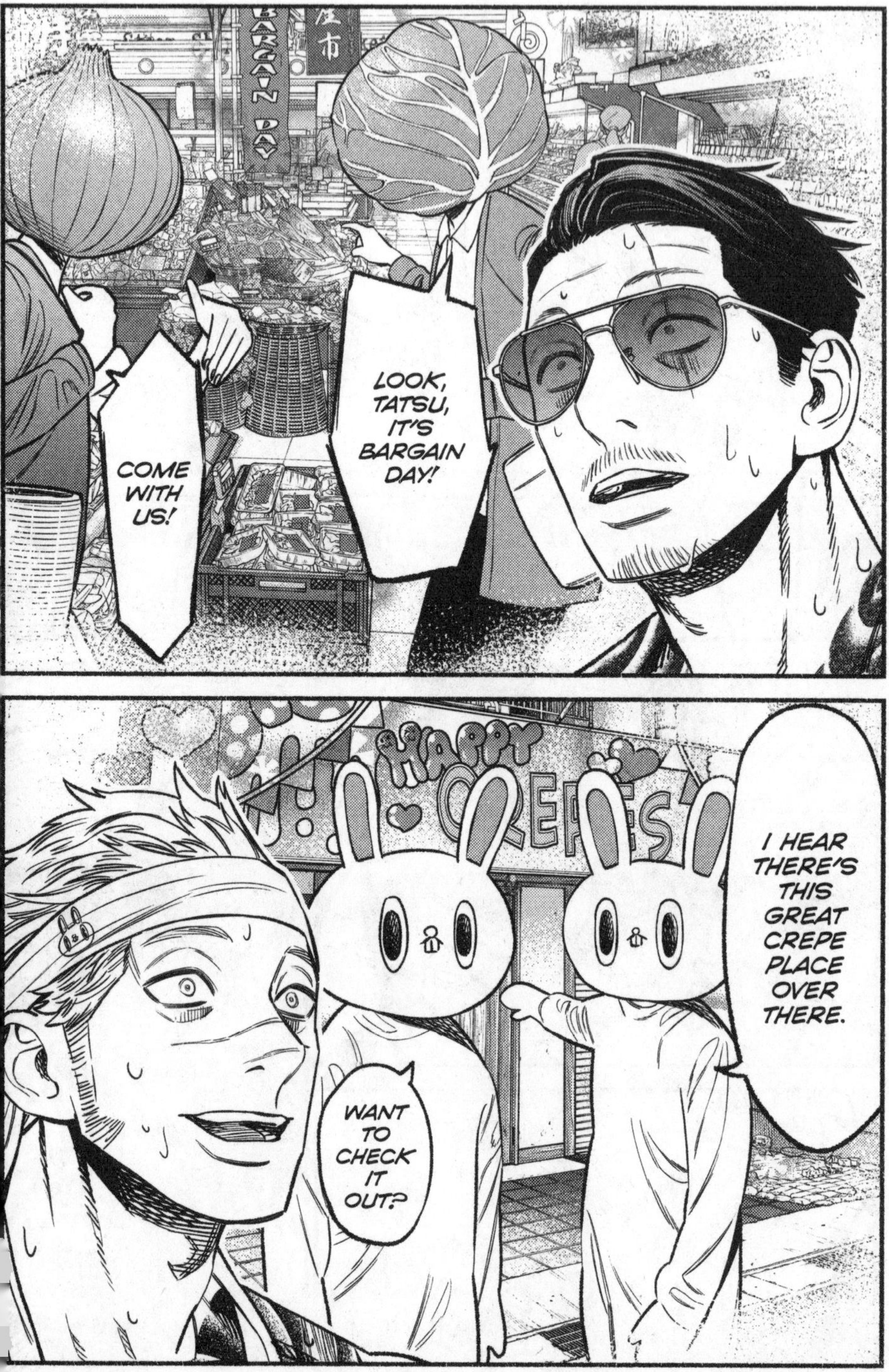
BARGAIN DAY
LOOK, TATSU, IT'S BARGAIN DAY!
COME WITH US!
HAPPY
I HEAR THERE'S THIS GREAT CREPE PLACE OVER THERE.
WANT TO CHECK IT OUT?

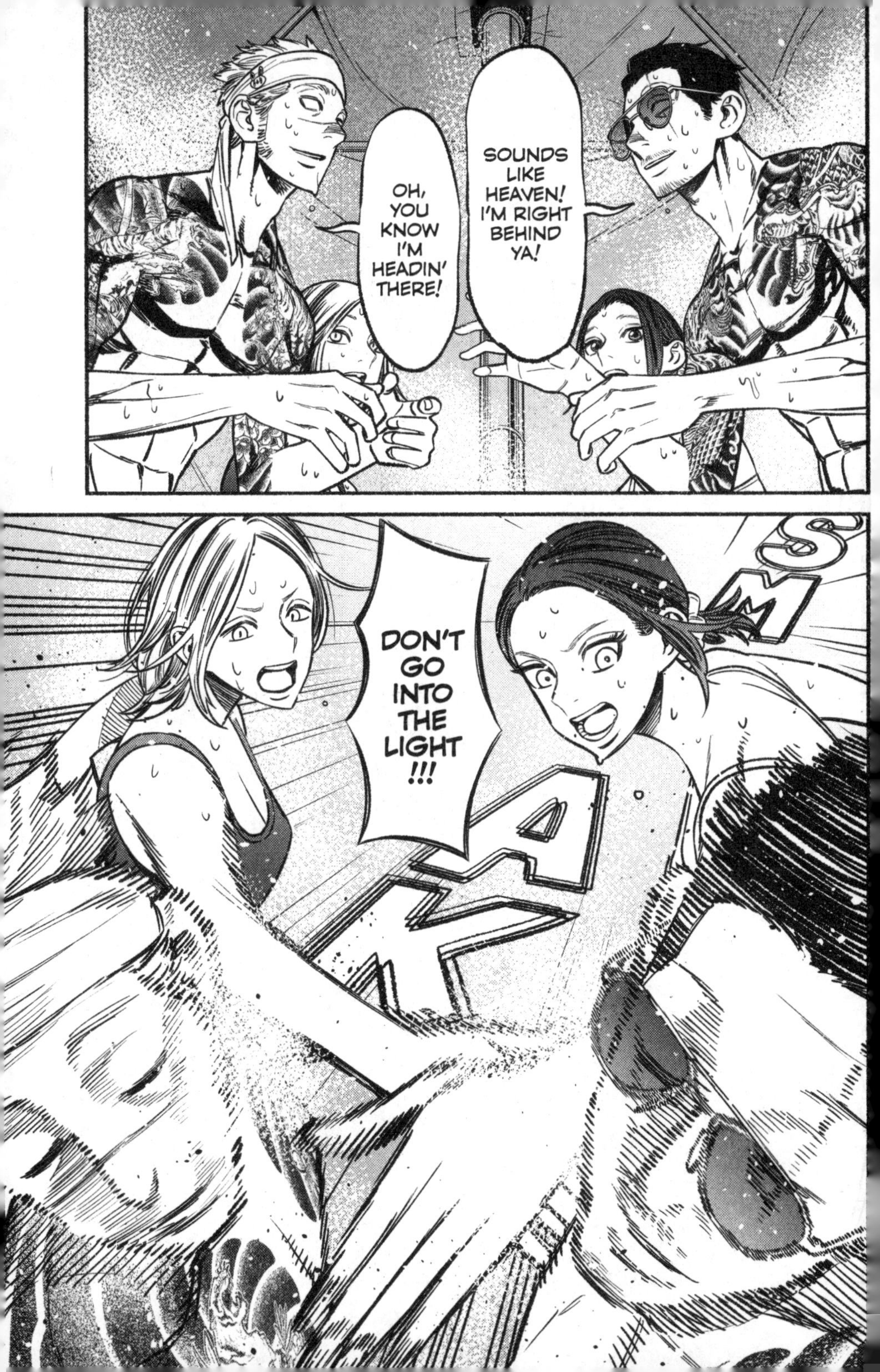
SOUNDS LIKE HEAVEN! I'M RIGHT BEHIND YA!
OH, YOU KNOW I'M HEADIN' THERE!
DON'T GO INTO THE LIGHT!!!

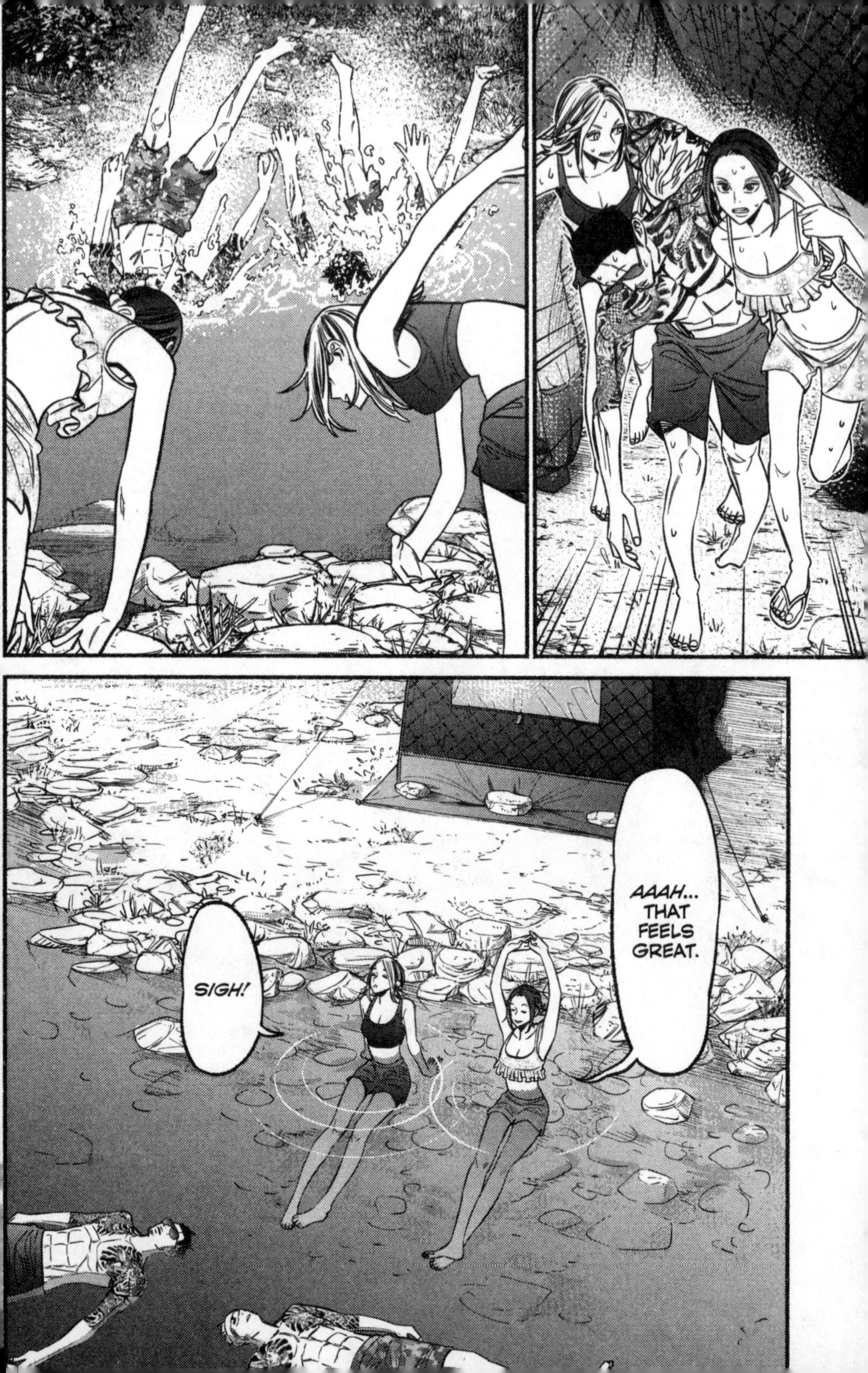
AAAH... THAT FEELS GREAT.
SIGH!

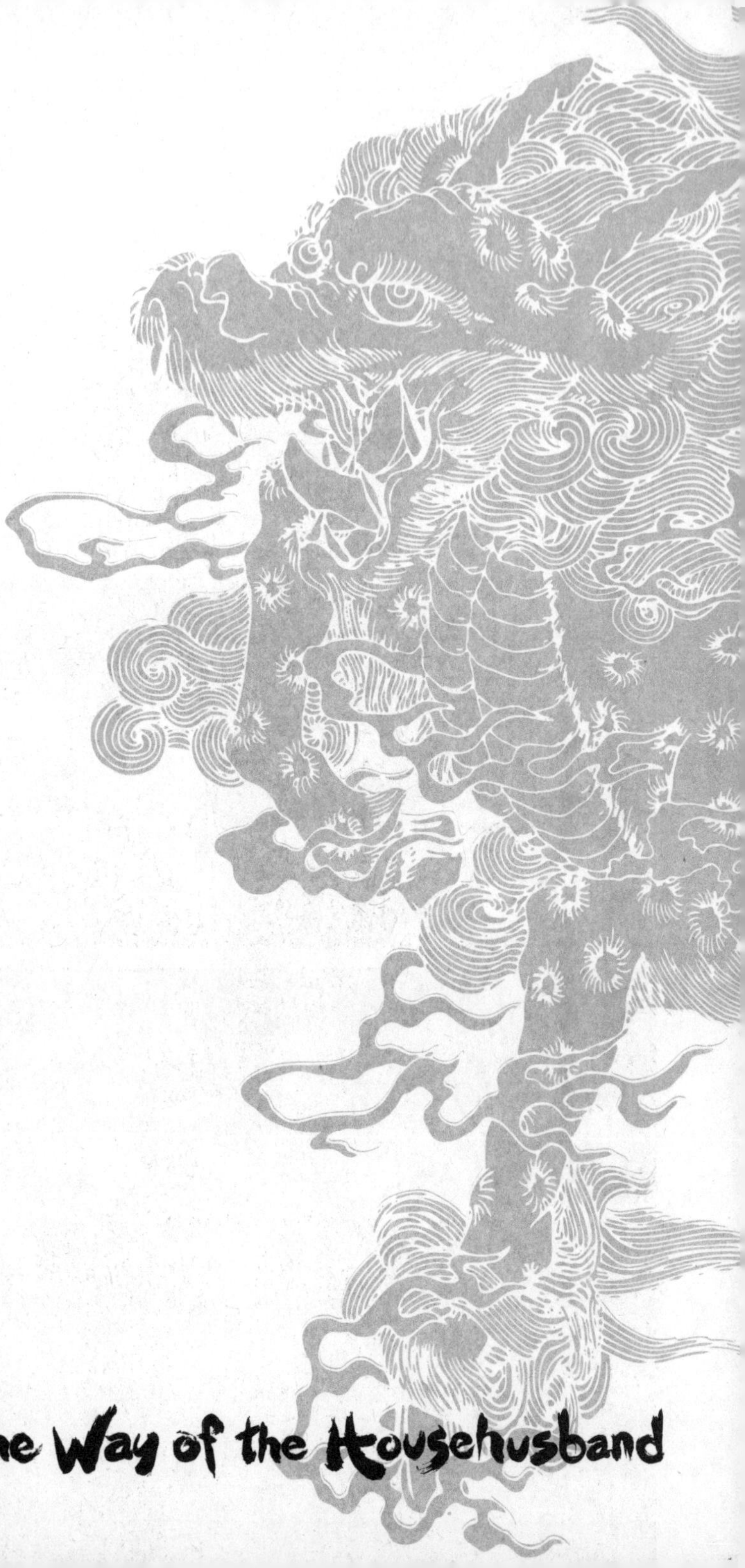

The Way of the Househusband

CHAPTER 70

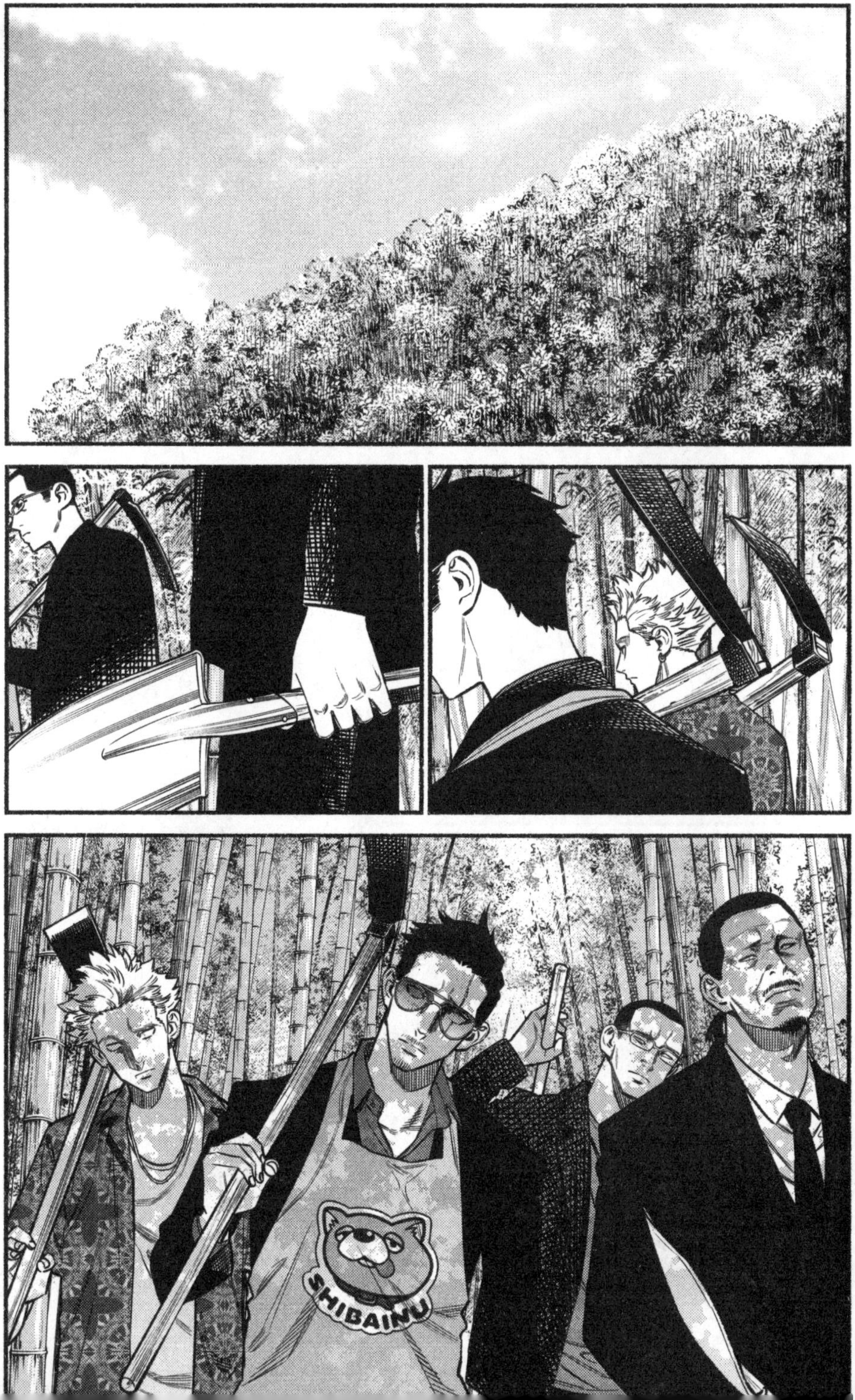
SHIBAINU

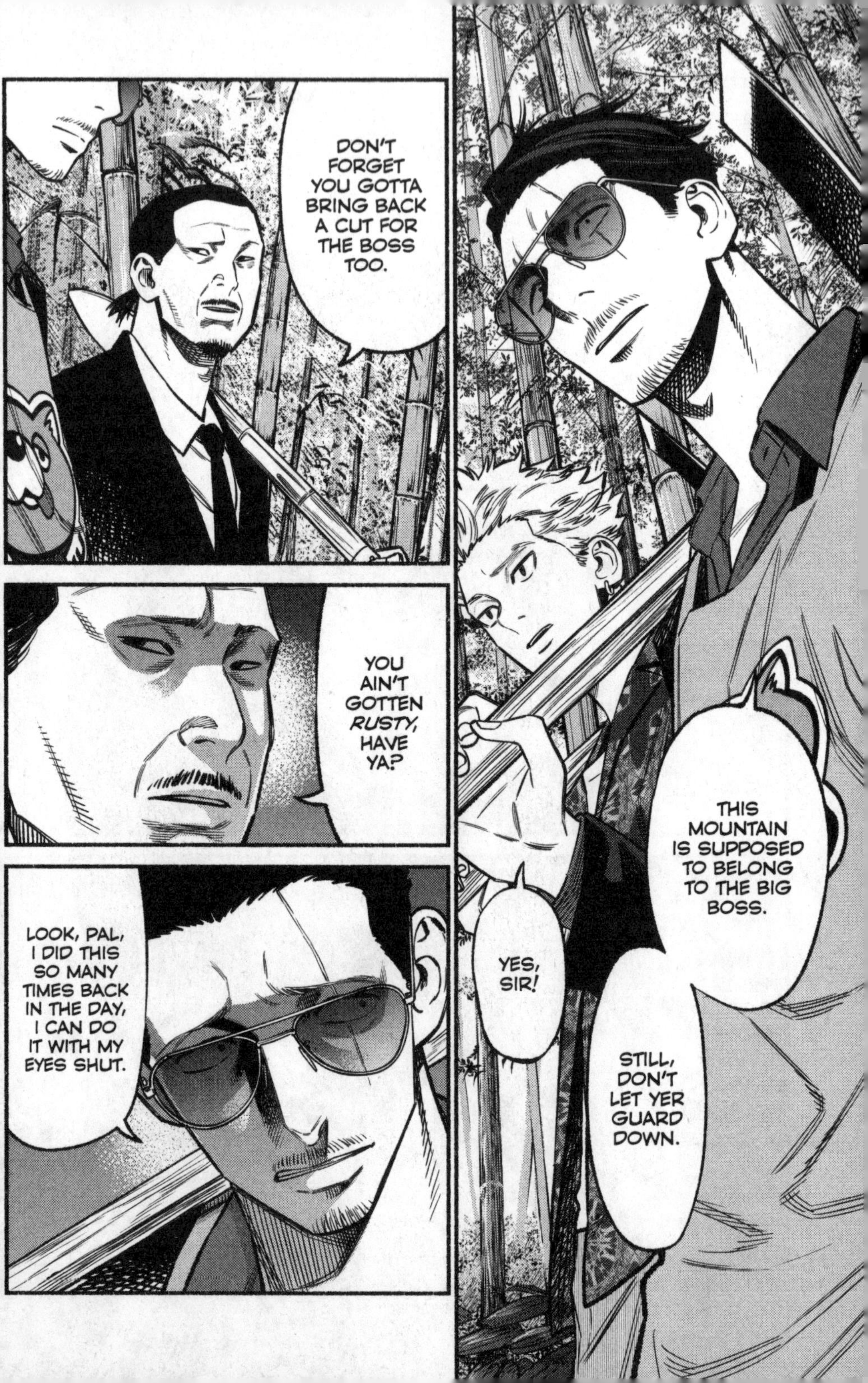
THIS MOUNTAIN IS SUPPOSED TO BELONG TO THE BIG BOSS.
STILL, DON'T LET YER GUARD DOWN.
YES, SIR!
DON'T FORGET YOU GOTTA BRING BACK A CUT FOR THE BOSS TOO.
YOU AIN'T GOTTEN *RUSTY*, HAVE YA?
LOOK, PAL, I DID THIS SO MANY TIMES BACK IN THE DAY, I CAN DO IT WITH MY EYES SHUT.

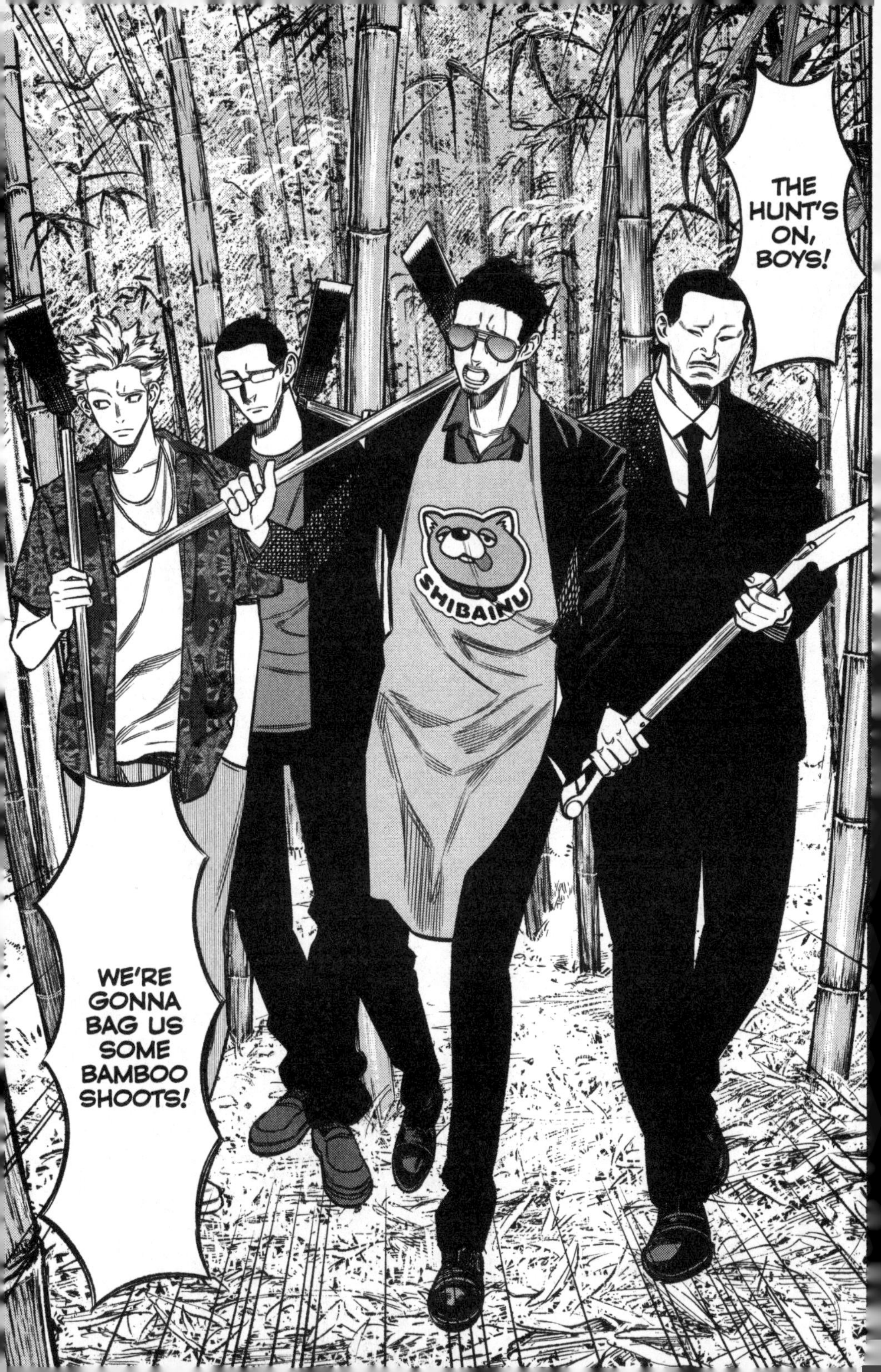
THE HUNT'S ON, BOYS!
SHIBAINU
WE'RE GONNA BAG US SOME BAMBOO SHOOTS!

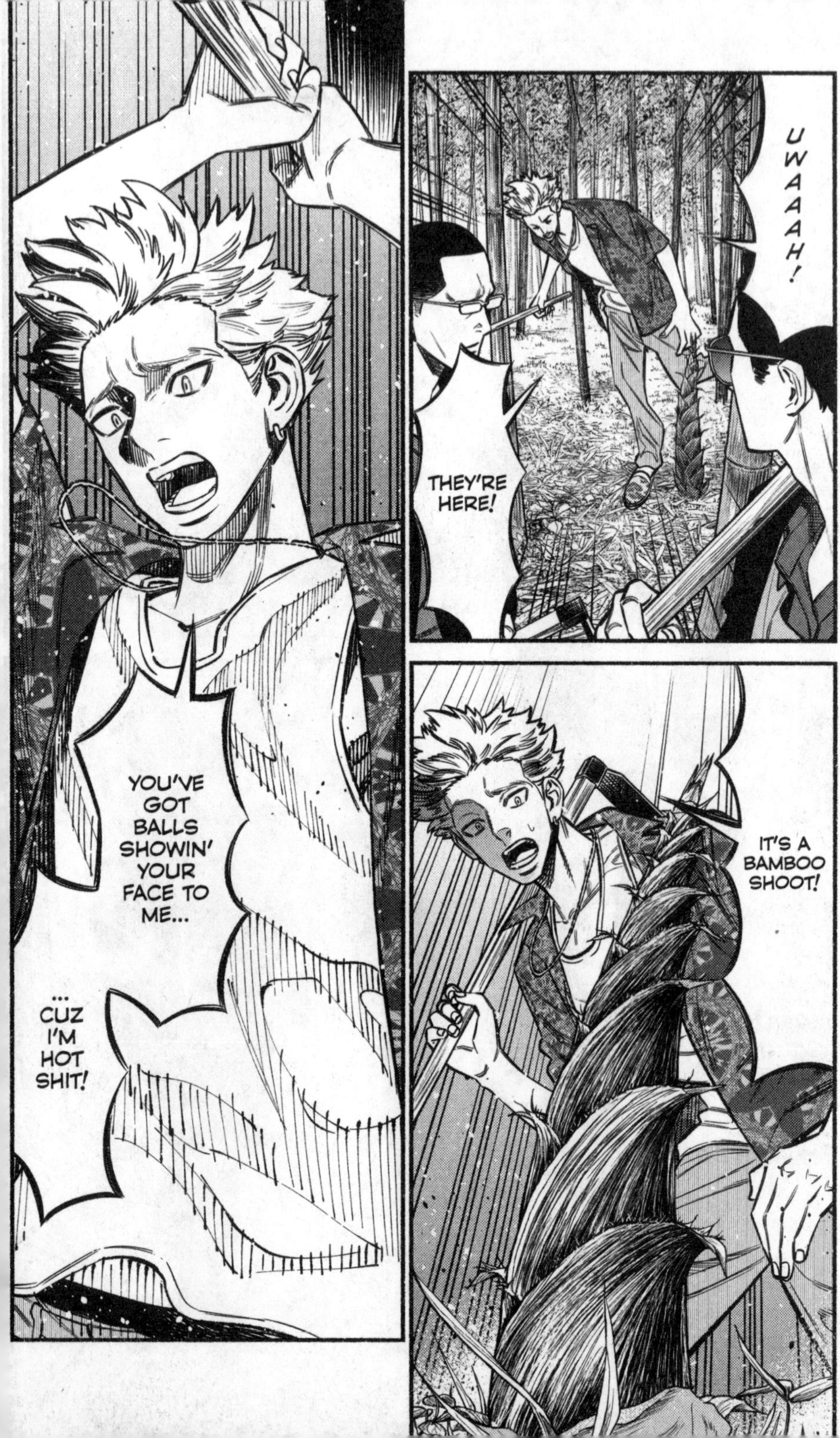
UWAAAAH!
THEY'RE HERE!
IT'S A BAMBOO SHOOT!
YOU'VE GOT BALLS SHOWIN' YOUR FACE TO ME...
...CUZ I'M HOT SHIT!

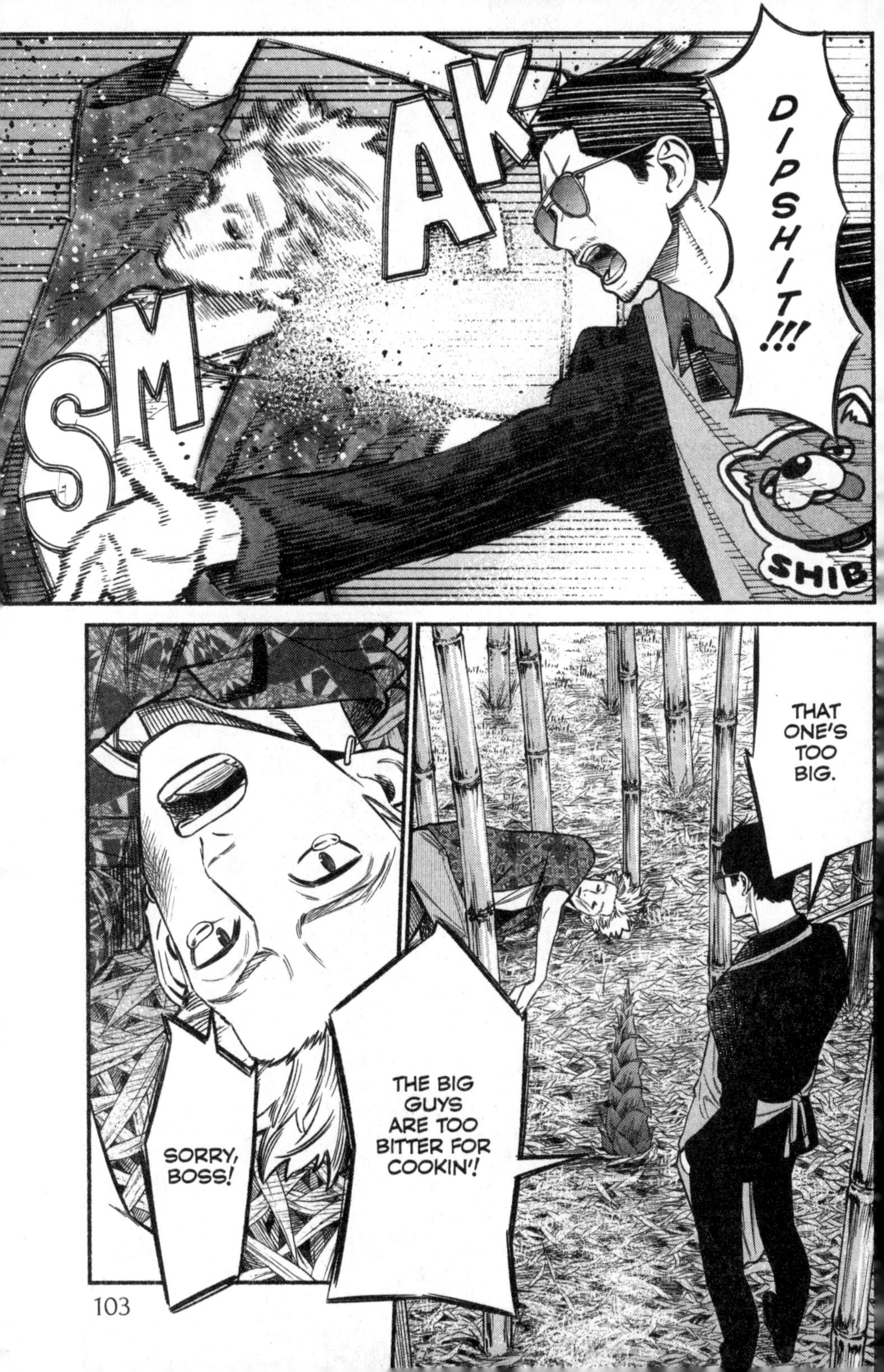
DIPSHIT!!!
SMAK
SHIB
THAT ONE'S TOO BIG.
THE BIG GUYS ARE TOO BITTER FOR COOKIN'!
SORRY, BOSS!

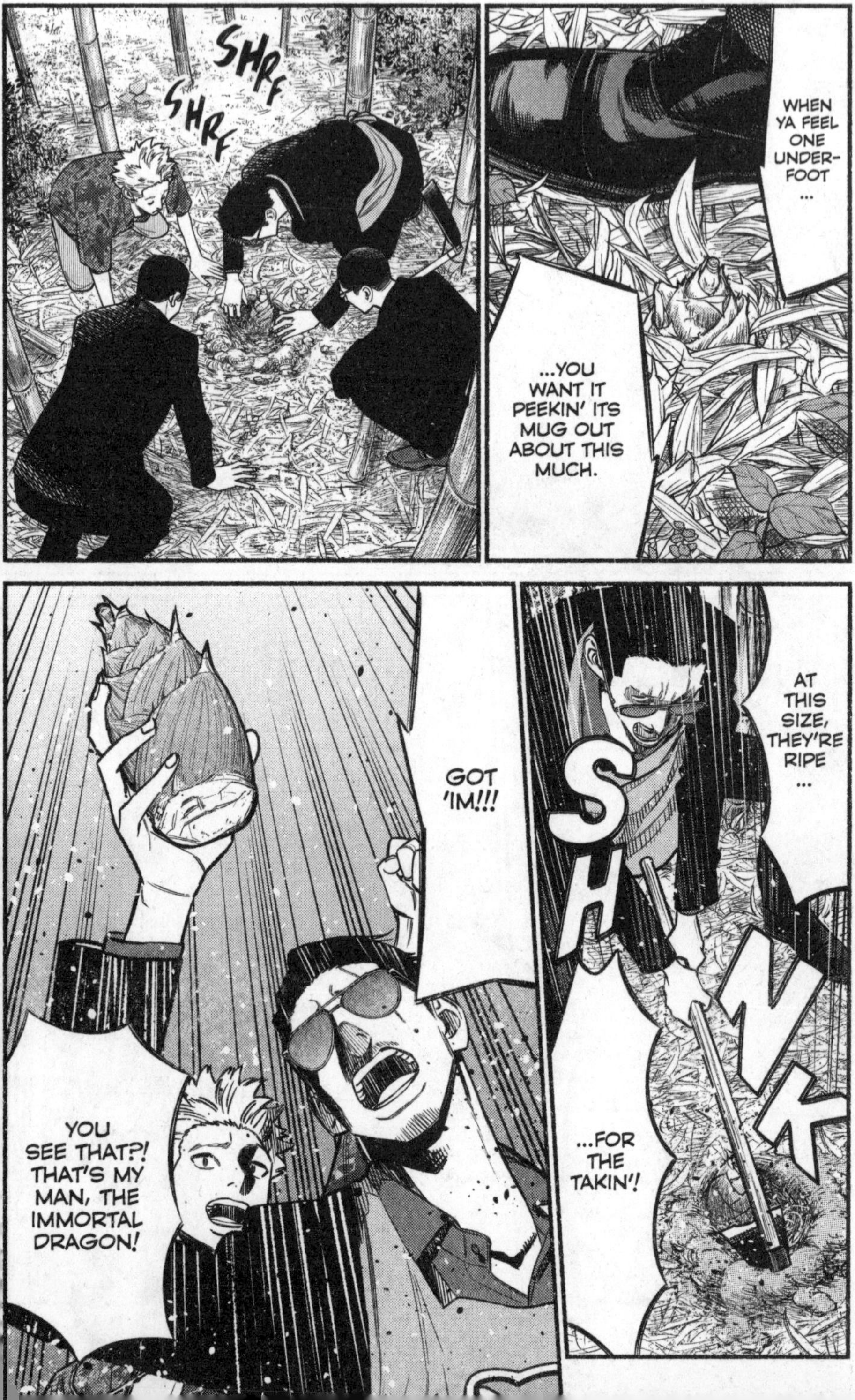
WHEN YA FEEL ONE UNDER-FOOT ...
...YOU WANT IT PEEKIN' ITS MUG OUT ABOUT THIS MUCH.
SHRF
SHRF
AT THIS SIZE, THEY'RE RIPE ...
SHNK
...FOR THE TAKIN'!
GOT 'IM!!!
YOU SEE THAT?! THAT'S MY MAN, THE IMMORTAL DRAGON!

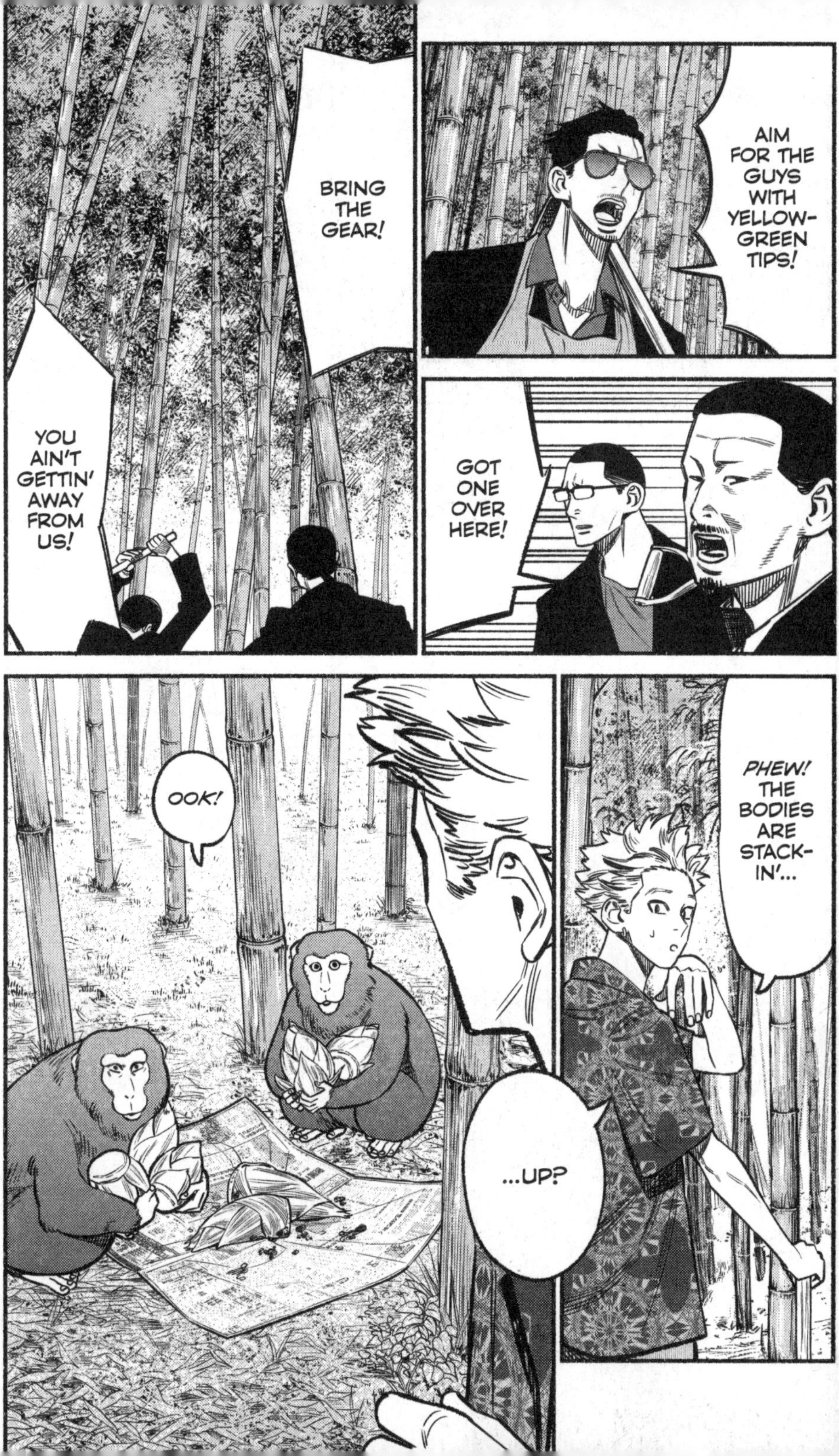
AIM FOR THE GUYS WITH YELLOW-GREEN TIPS!
GOT ONE OVER HERE!
BRING THE GEAR!
YOU AIN'T GETTIN' AWAY FROM US!
PHEW! THE BODIES ARE STACK-IN'...
OOK!
...UP?

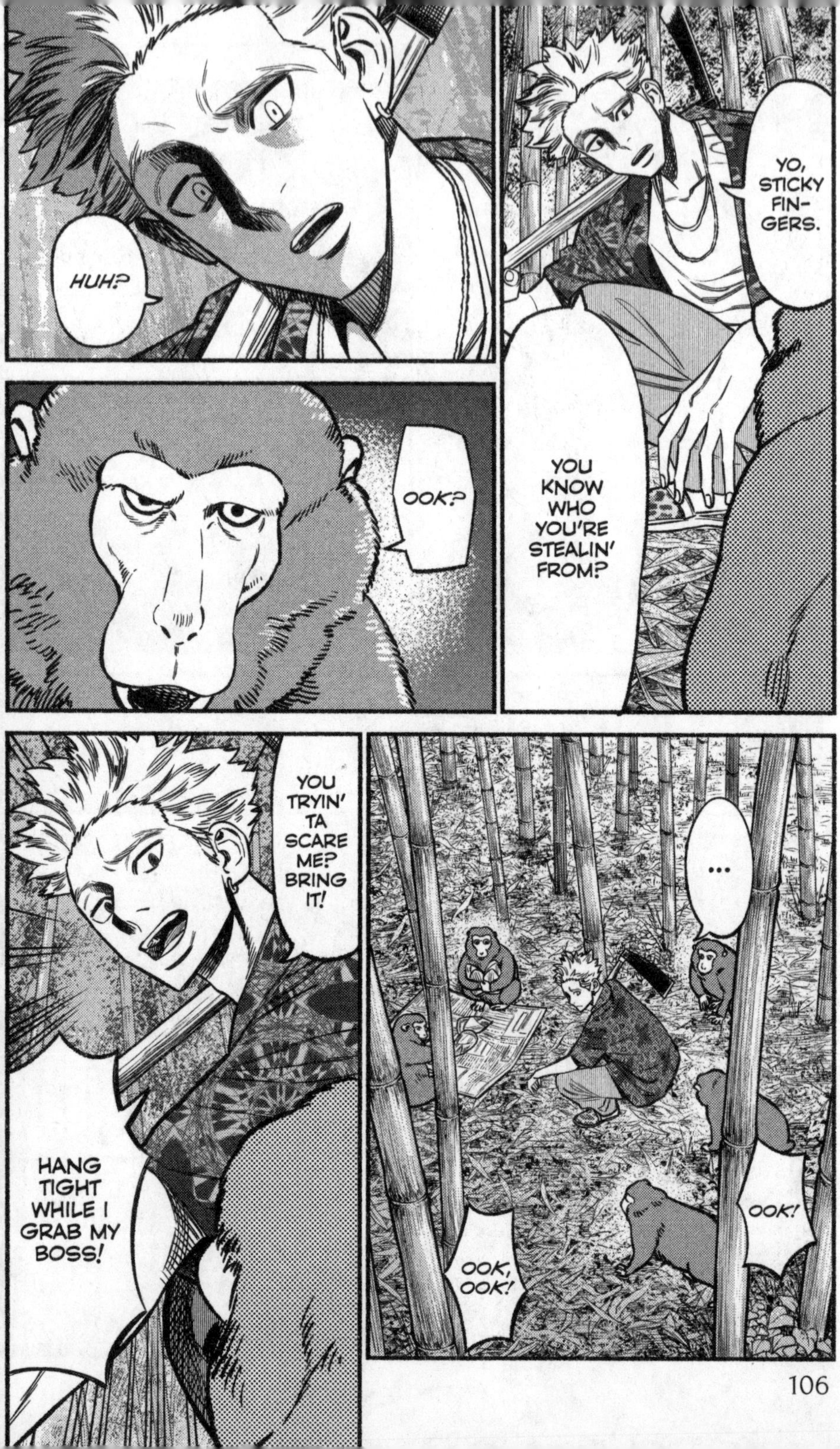
YO, STICKY FIN-GERS.
YOU KNOW WHO YOU'RE STEALIN' FROM?
HUH?
OOK?
...
OOK!
OOK, OOK!
YOU TRYIN' TA SCARE ME? BRING IT!
HANG TIGHT WHILE I GRAB MY BOSS!

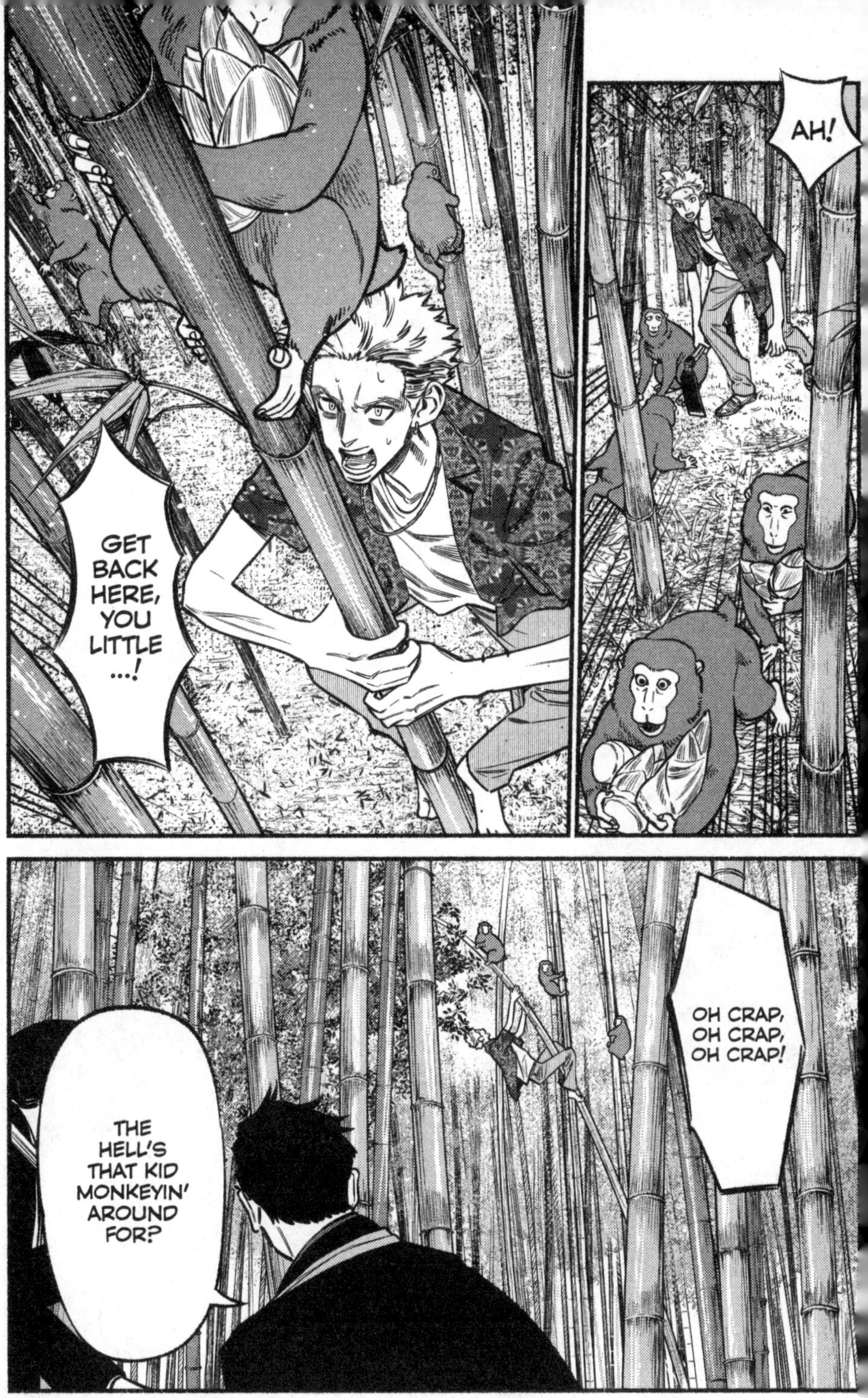
AH!
GET BACK HERE, YOU LITTLE ...!
OH CRAP, OH CRAP, OH CRAP!
THE HELL'S THAT KID MONKEYIN' AROUND FOR?

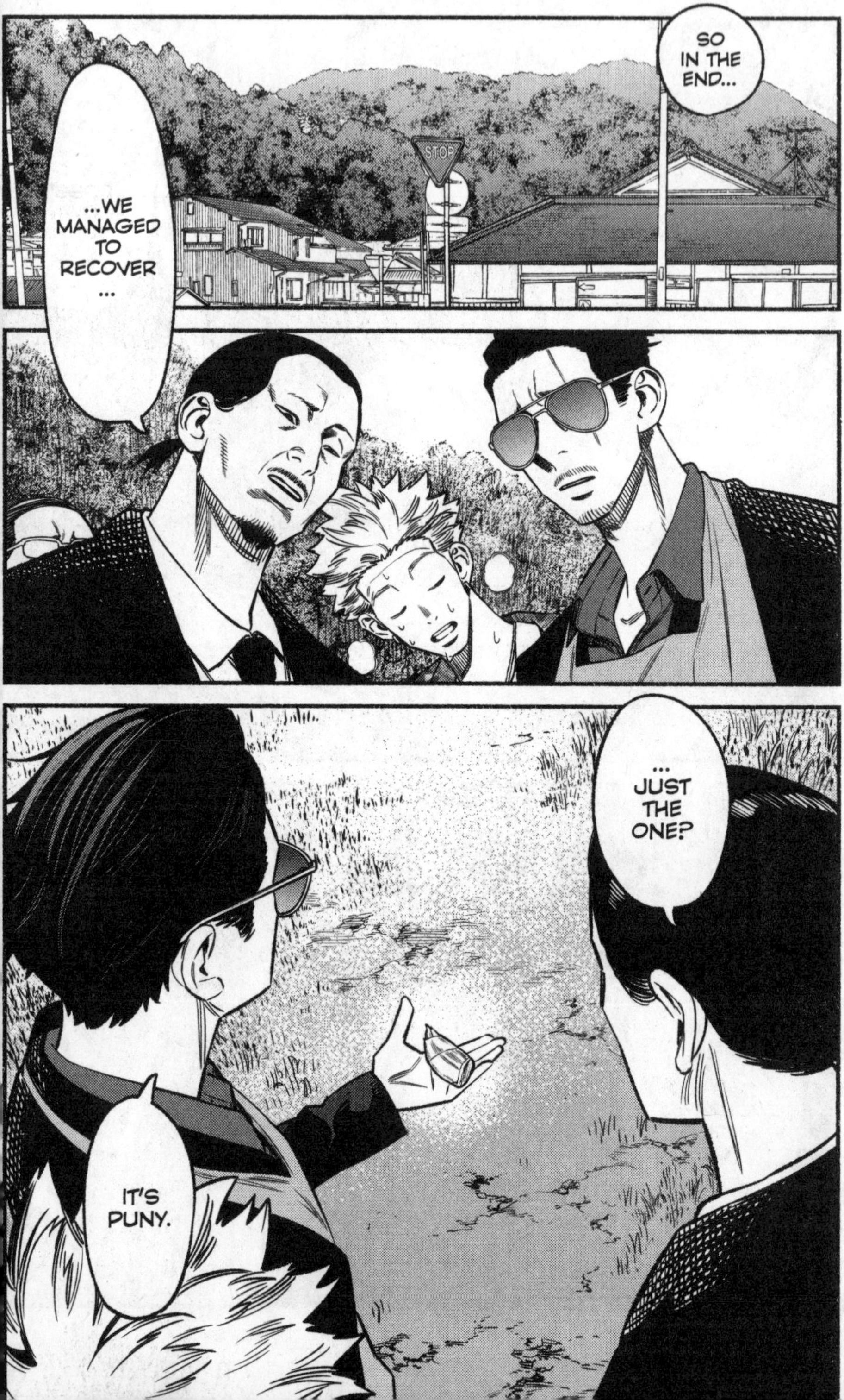
SO IN THE END...
...WE MANAGED TO RECOVER ...
STOP
...JUST THE ONE?
IT'S PUNY.

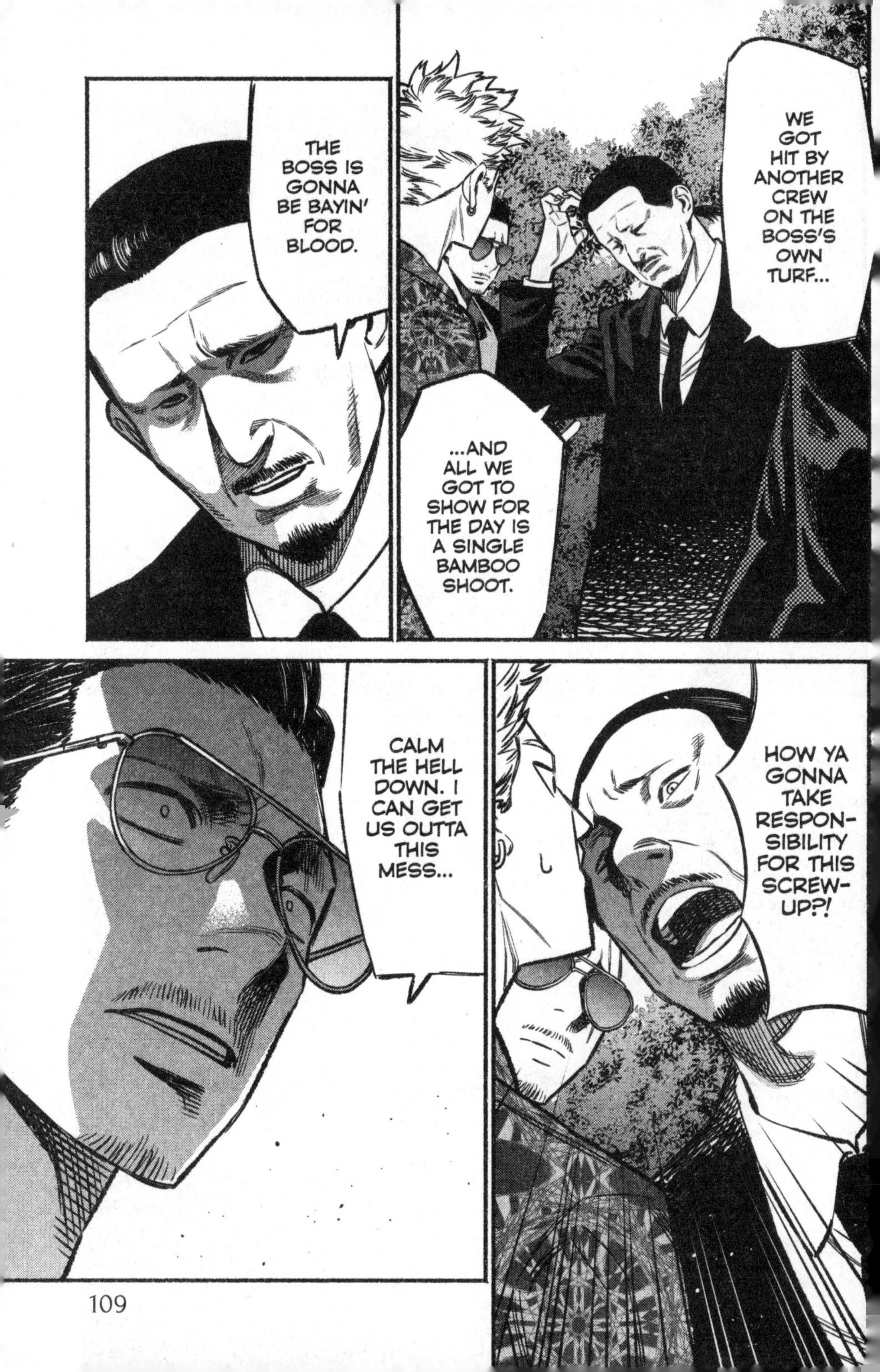
WE GOT HIT BY ANOTHER CREW ON THE BOSS'S OWN TURF...
...AND ALL WE GOT TO SHOW FOR THE DAY IS A SINGLE BAMBOO SHOOT.
THE BOSS IS GONNA BE BAYIN' FOR BLOOD.
HOW YA GONNA TAKE RESPON-SIBILITY FOR THIS SCREW-UP?!
CALM THE HELL DOWN. I CAN GET US OUTTA THIS MESS...

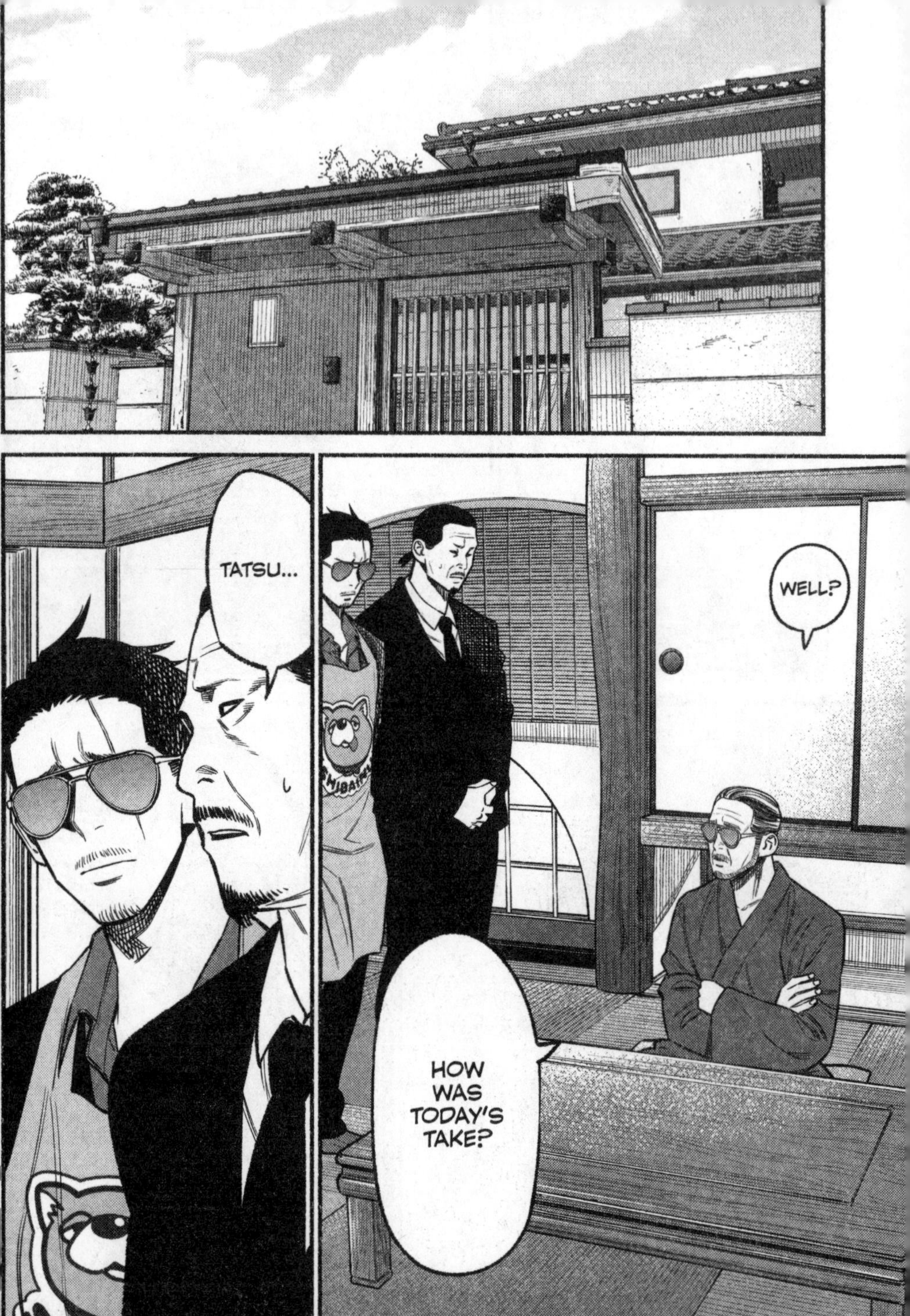
WELL?
HOW WAS TODAY'S TAKE?
TATSU...

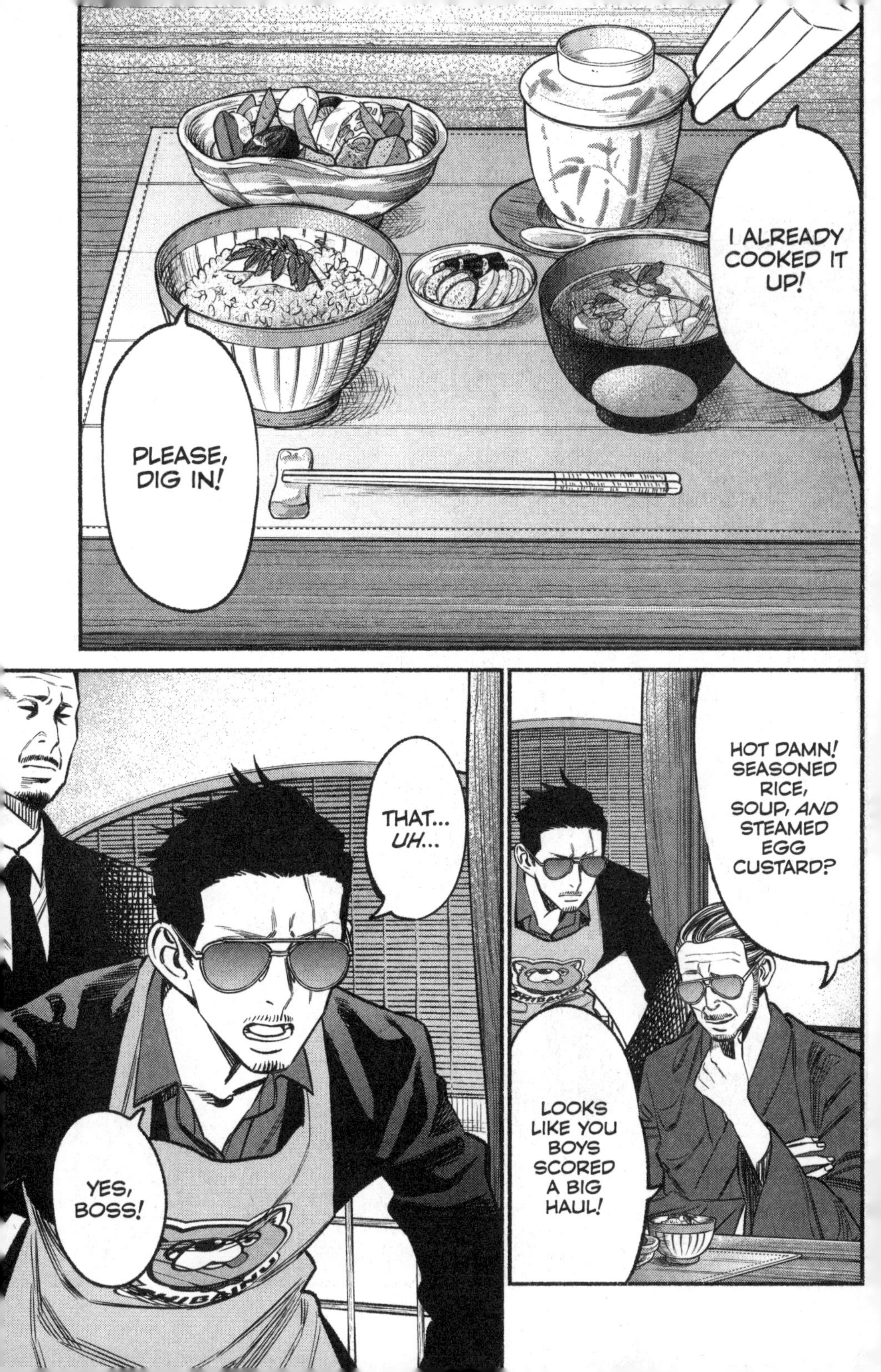
I ALREADY COOKED IT UP!
PLEASE, DIG IN!
HOT DAMN! SEASONED RICE, SOUP, *AND* STEAMED EGG CUSTARD?
LOOKS LIKE YOU BOYS SCORED A BIG HAUL!
THAT... *UH*...
YES, BOSS!

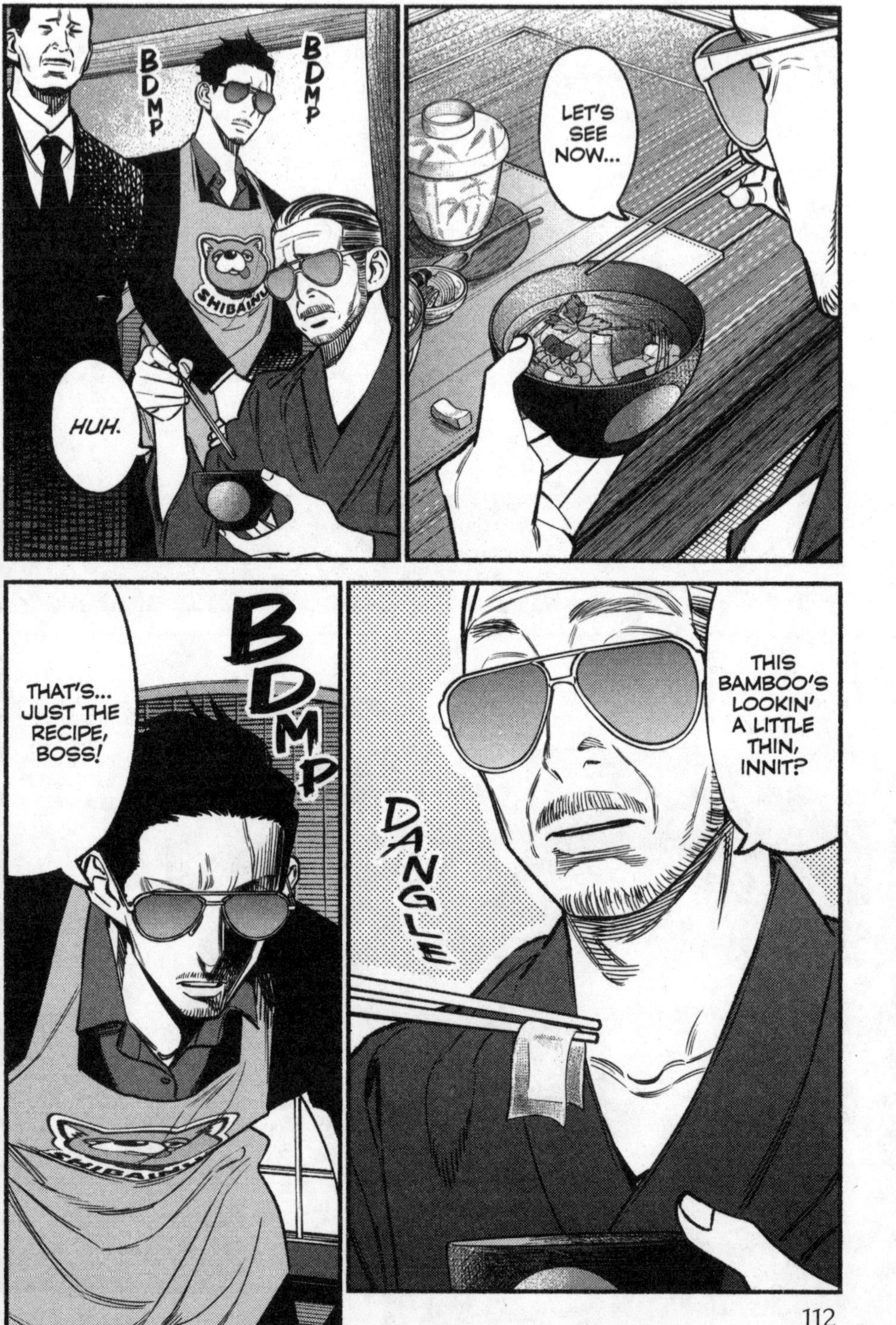
LET'S SEE NOW...
BDMP
BDMP
HUH.
THIS BAMBOO'S LOOKIN' A LITTLE THIN, INNIT?
DANGLE
BDMP
THAT'S... JUST THE RECIPE, BOSS!

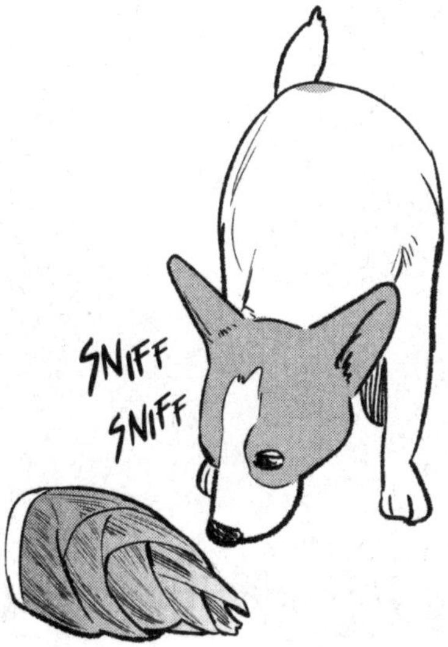
SNIFF
SNIFF

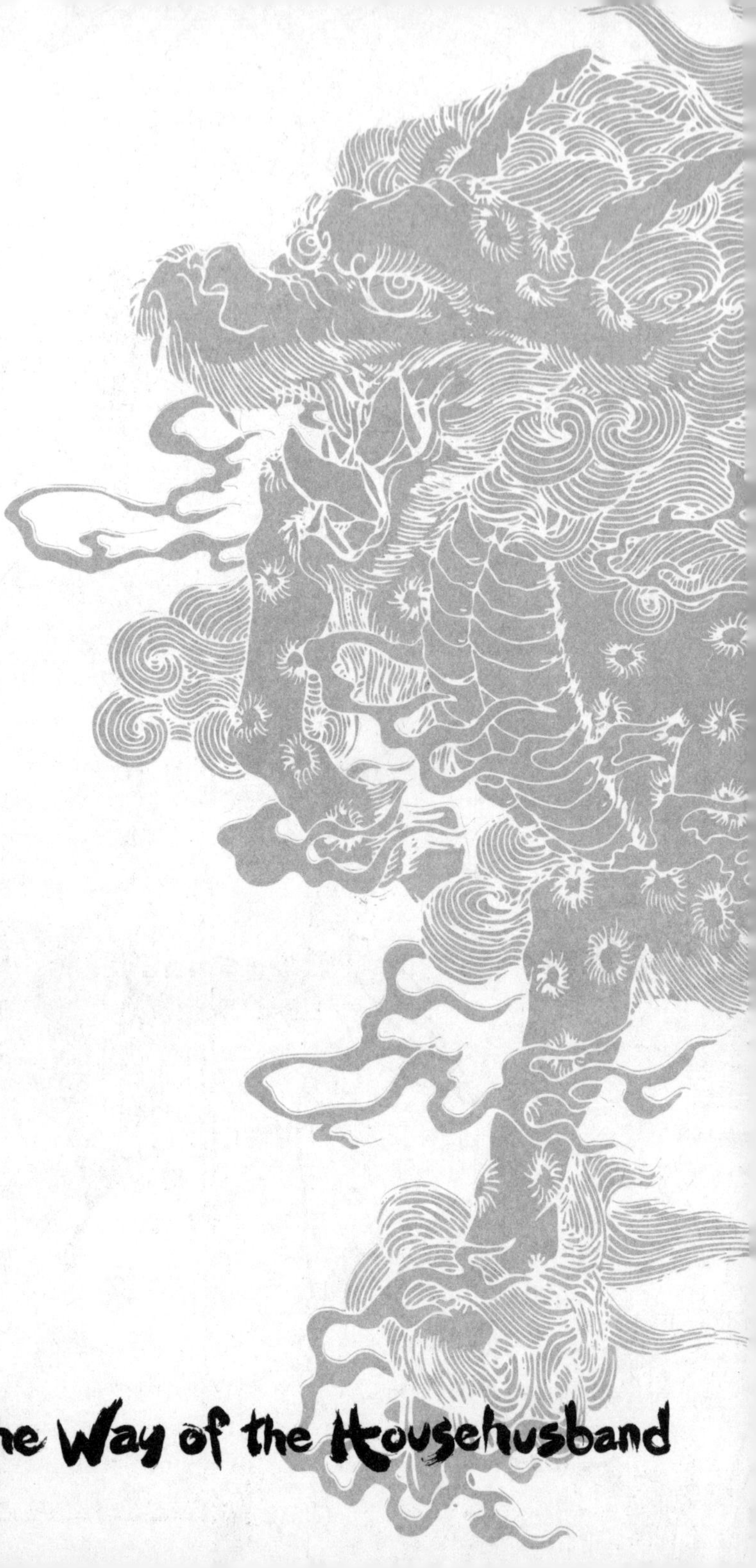

The Way of the Househusband

CHAPTER 71

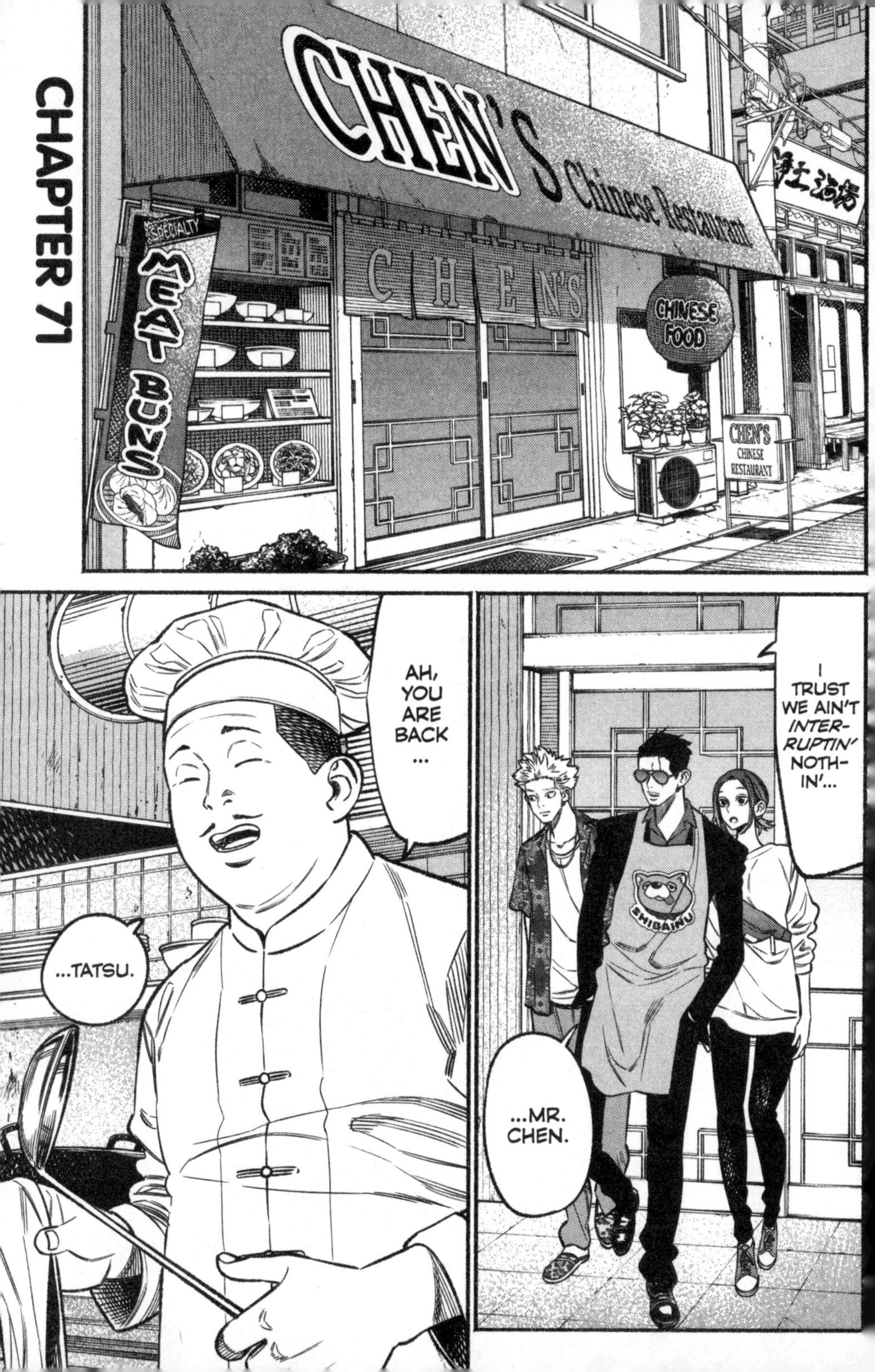
CHEN'S Chinese Restaurant
CHEN'S
SPECIALTY
MEAT BUNS
CHINESE FOOD
CHEN'S CHINESE RESTAURANT
I TRUST WE AIN'T *INTER-RUPTIN'* NOTH-IN'...
...MR. CHEN.
AH, YOU ARE BACK...
...TATSU.

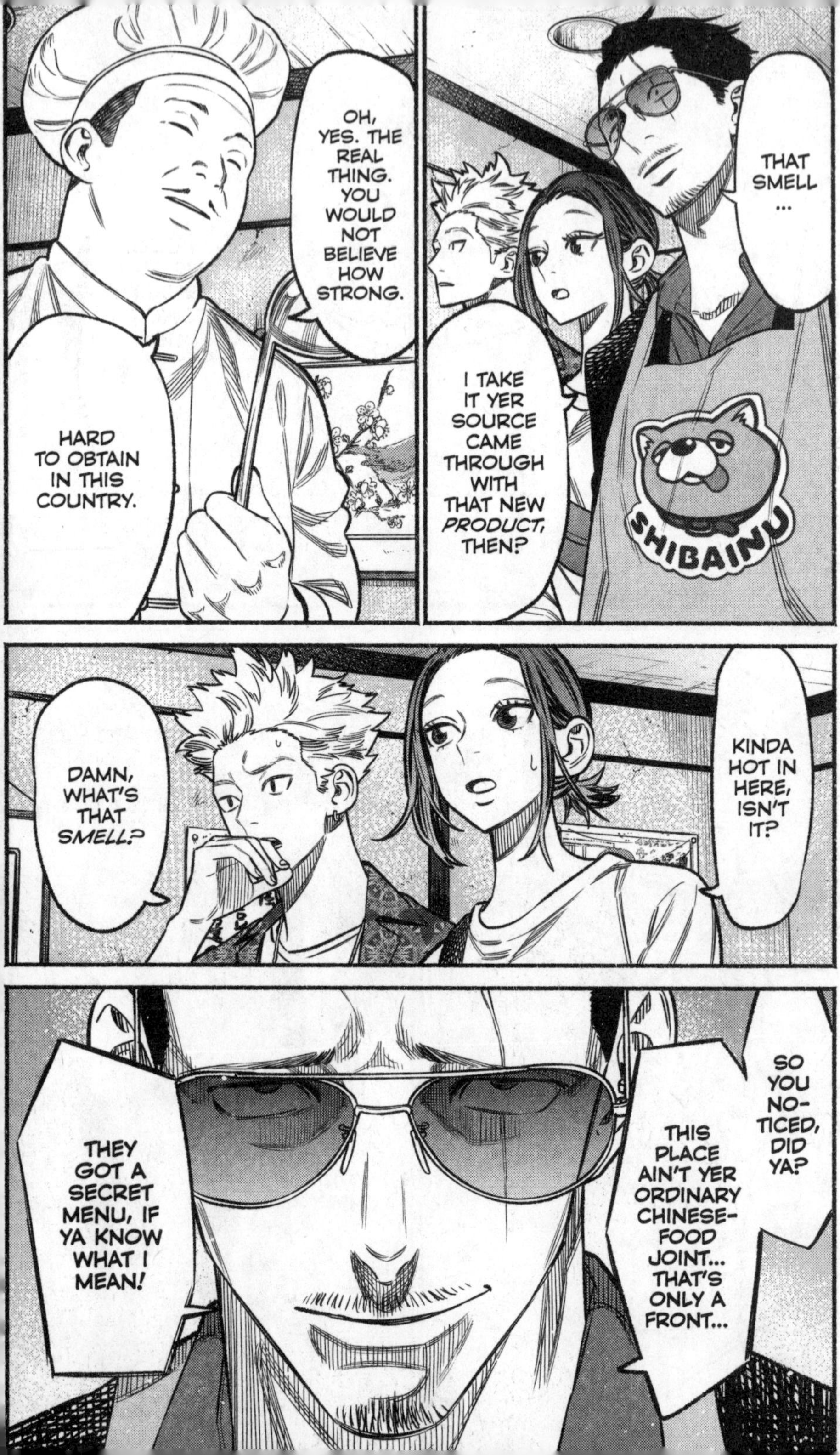
THAT SMELL ...
I TAKE IT YER SOURCE CAME THROUGH WITH THAT NEW *PRODUCT*, THEN?
OH, YES. THE REAL THING. YOU WOULD NOT BELIEVE HOW STRONG.
HARD TO OBTAIN IN THIS COUNTRY.
KINDA HOT IN HERE, ISN'T IT?
DAMN, WHAT'S THAT *SMELL?*
SO YOU NO-TICED, DID YA?
THIS PLACE AIN'T YER ORDINARY CHINESE-FOOD JOINT... THAT'S ONLY A FRONT...
THEY GOT A SECRET MENU, IF YA KNOW WHAT I MEAN!

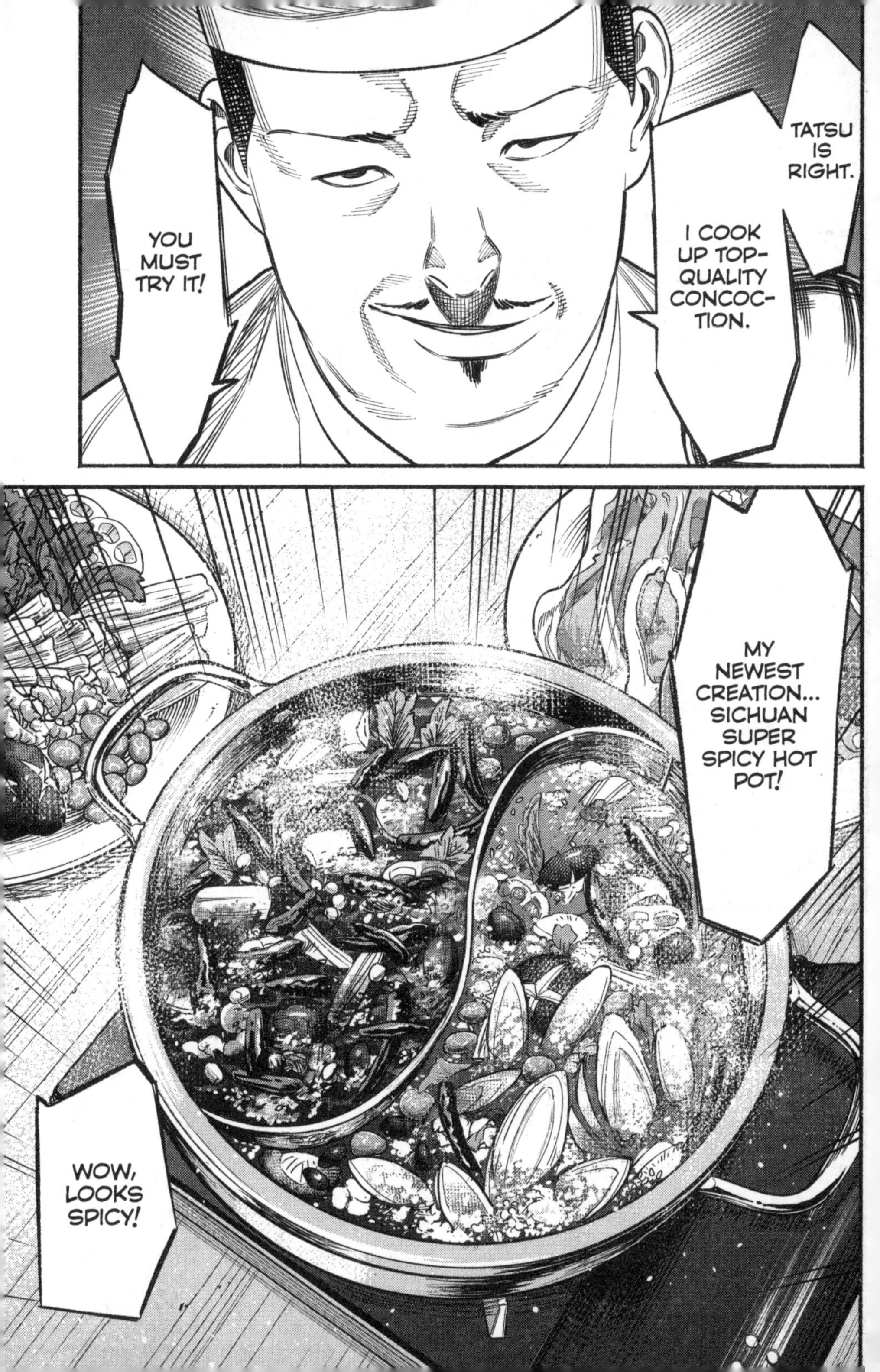
TATSU IS RIGHT.
I COOK UP TOP-QUALITY CONCOCTION.
YOU MUST TRY IT!
MY NEWEST CREATION... SICHUAN SUPER SPICY HOT POT!
WOW, LOOKS SPICY!

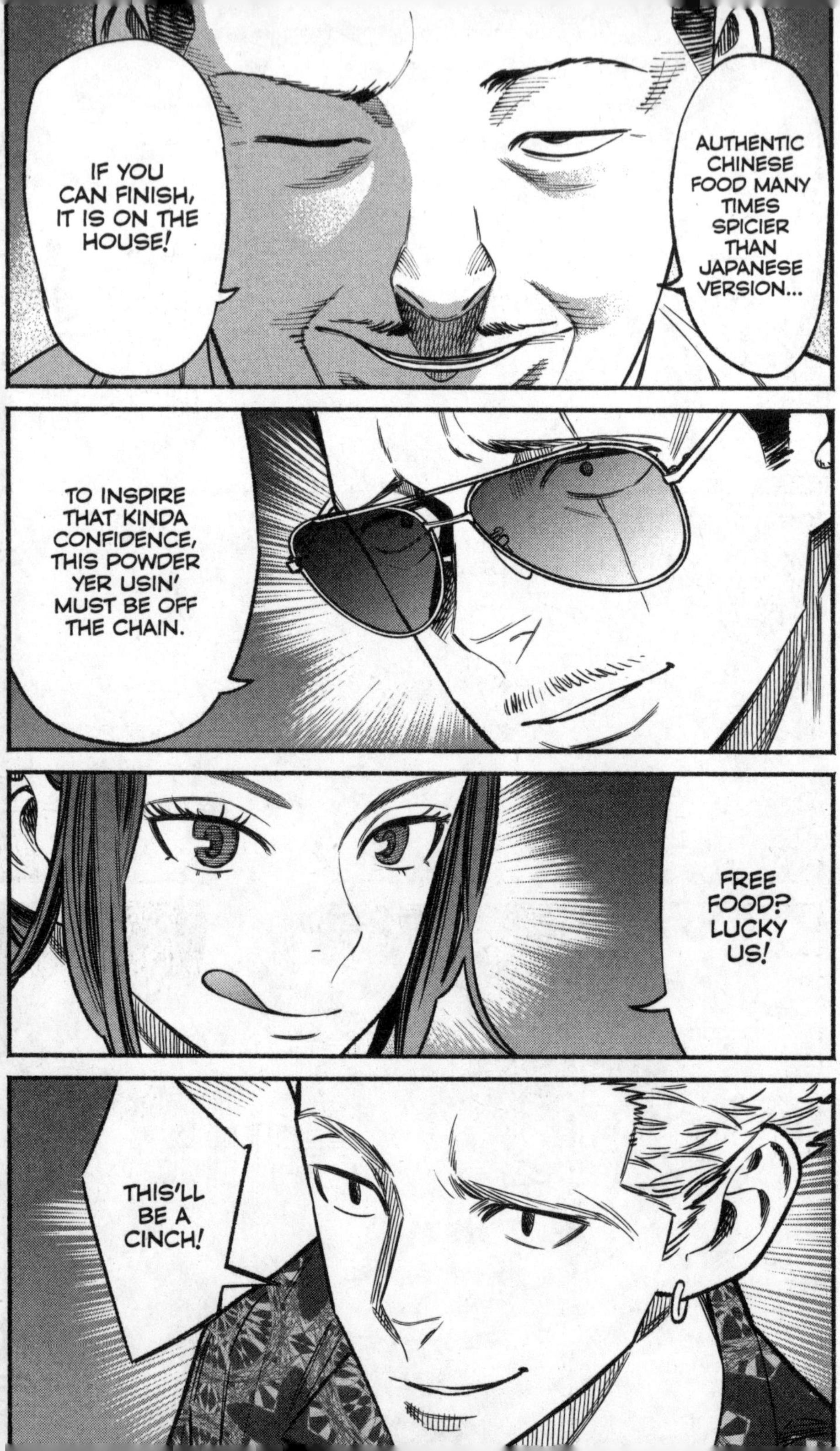
AUTHENTIC CHINESE FOOD MANY TIMES SPICIER THAN JAPANESE VERSION...
IF YOU CAN FINISH, IT IS ON THE HOUSE!
TO INSPIRE THAT KINDA CONFIDENCE, THIS POWDER YER USIN' MUST BE OFF THE CHAIN.
FREE FOOD? LUCKY US!
THIS'LL BE A CINCH!

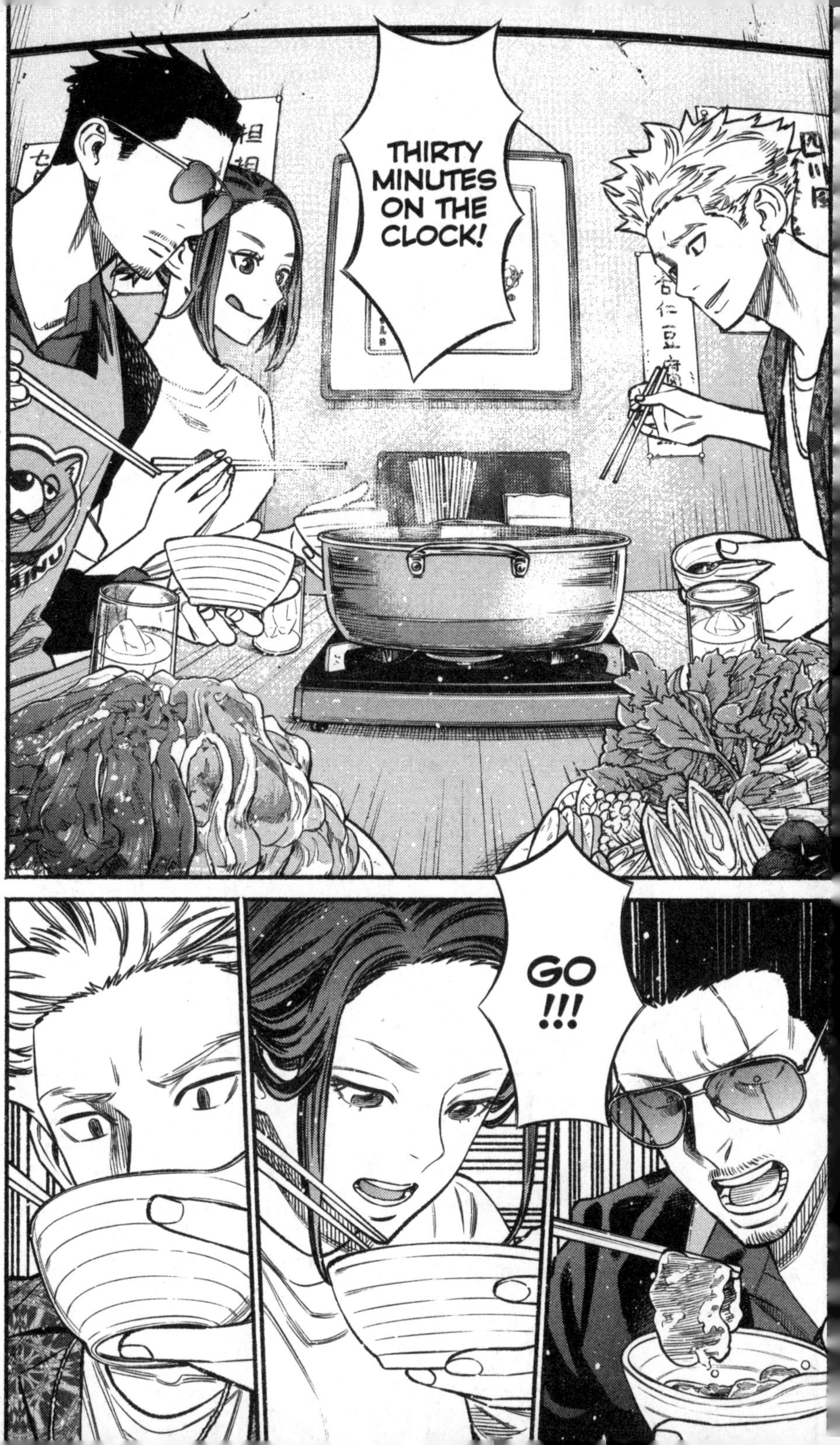
THIRTY MINUTES ON THE CLOCK!
GO !!!

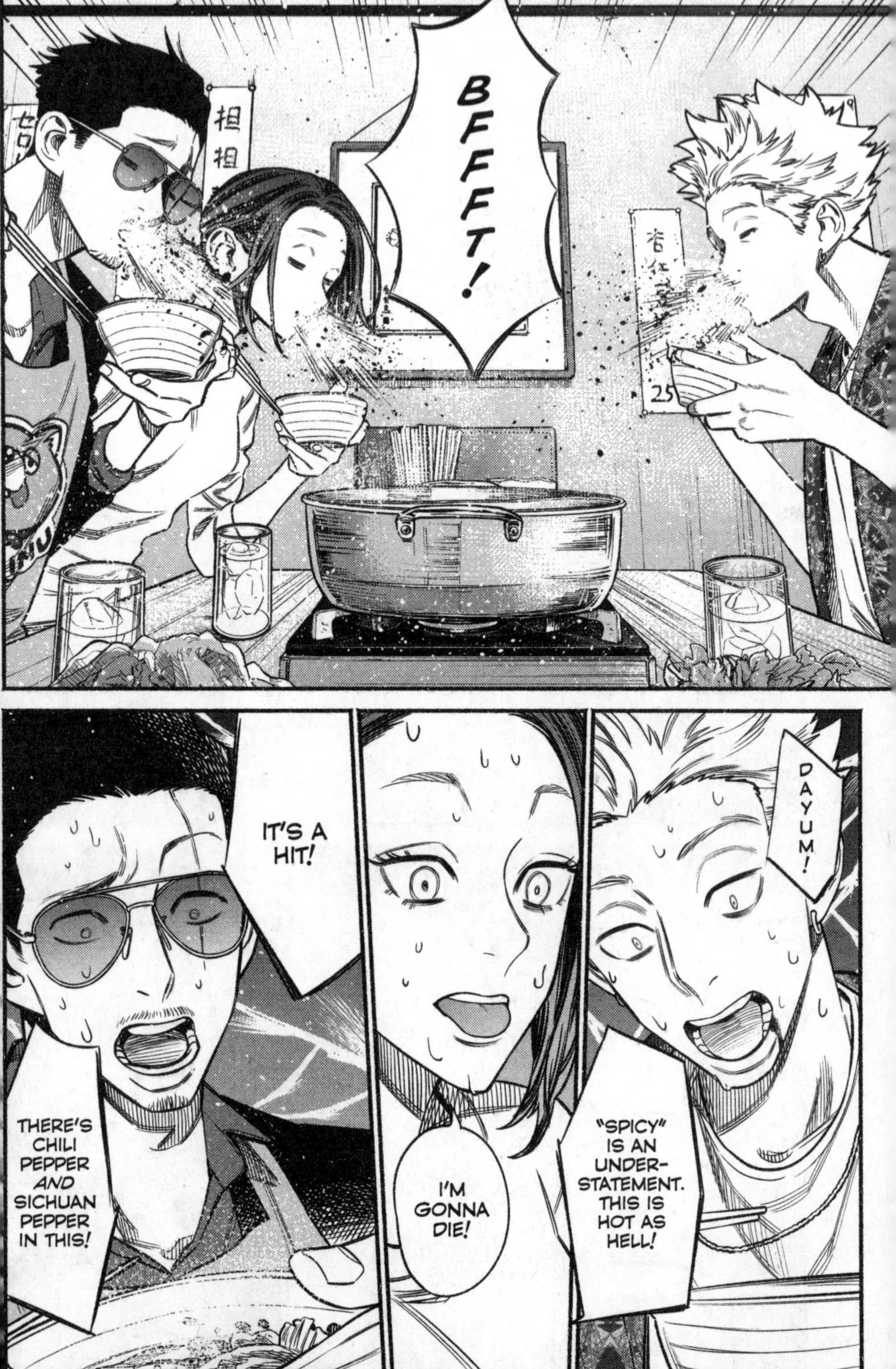
BFFFFT!
DAYUM!
"SPICY" IS AN UNDER-STATEMENT. THIS IS HOT AS HELL!
I'M GONNA DIE!
IT'S A HIT!
THERE'S CHILI PEPPER AND SICHUAN PEPPER IN THIS!

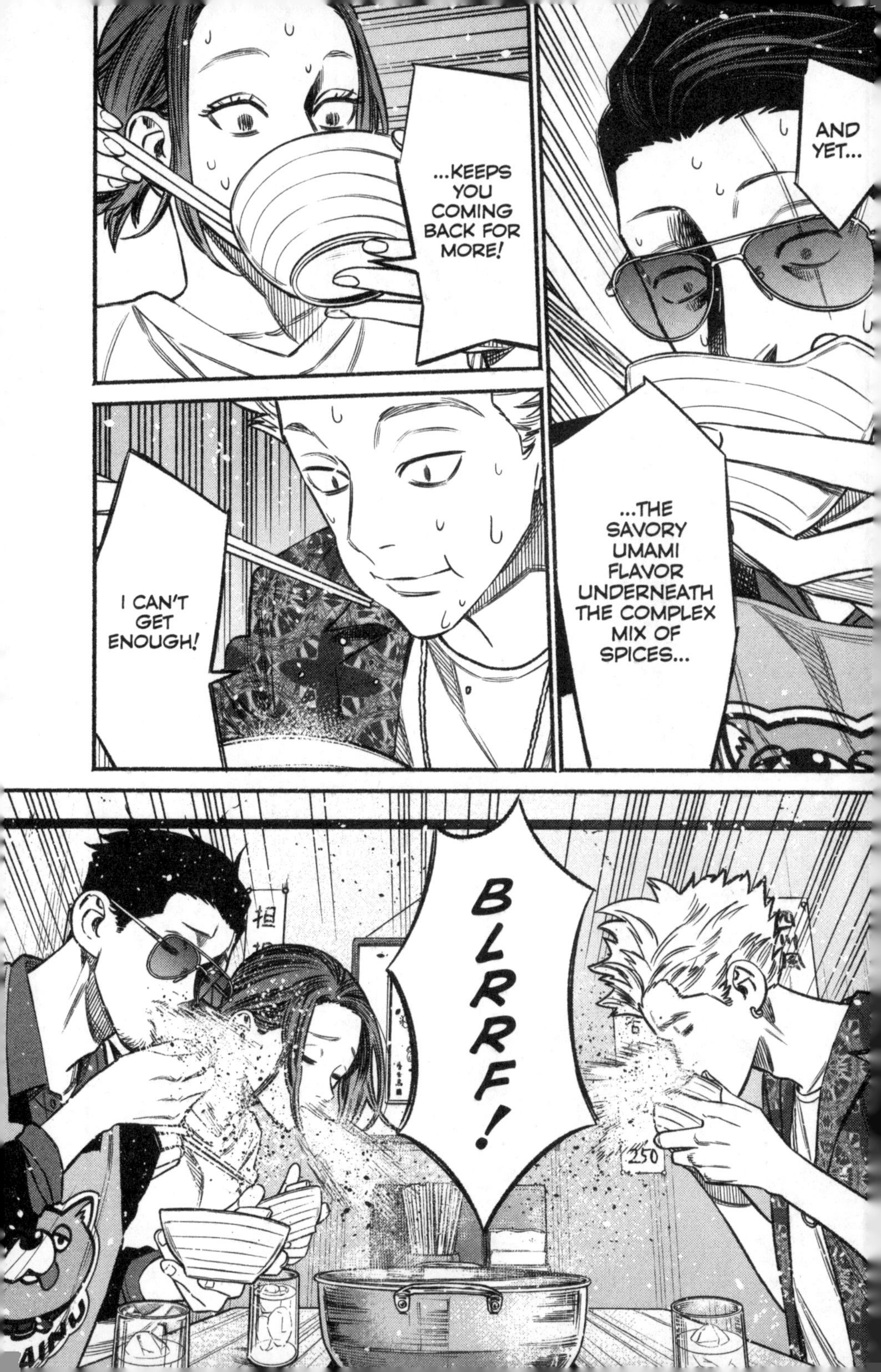
AND YET...
...THE SAVORY UMAMI FLAVOR UNDERNEATH THE COMPLEX MIX OF SPICES...
...KEEPS YOU COMING BACK FOR MORE!
I CAN'T GET ENOUGH!
BLRRF!

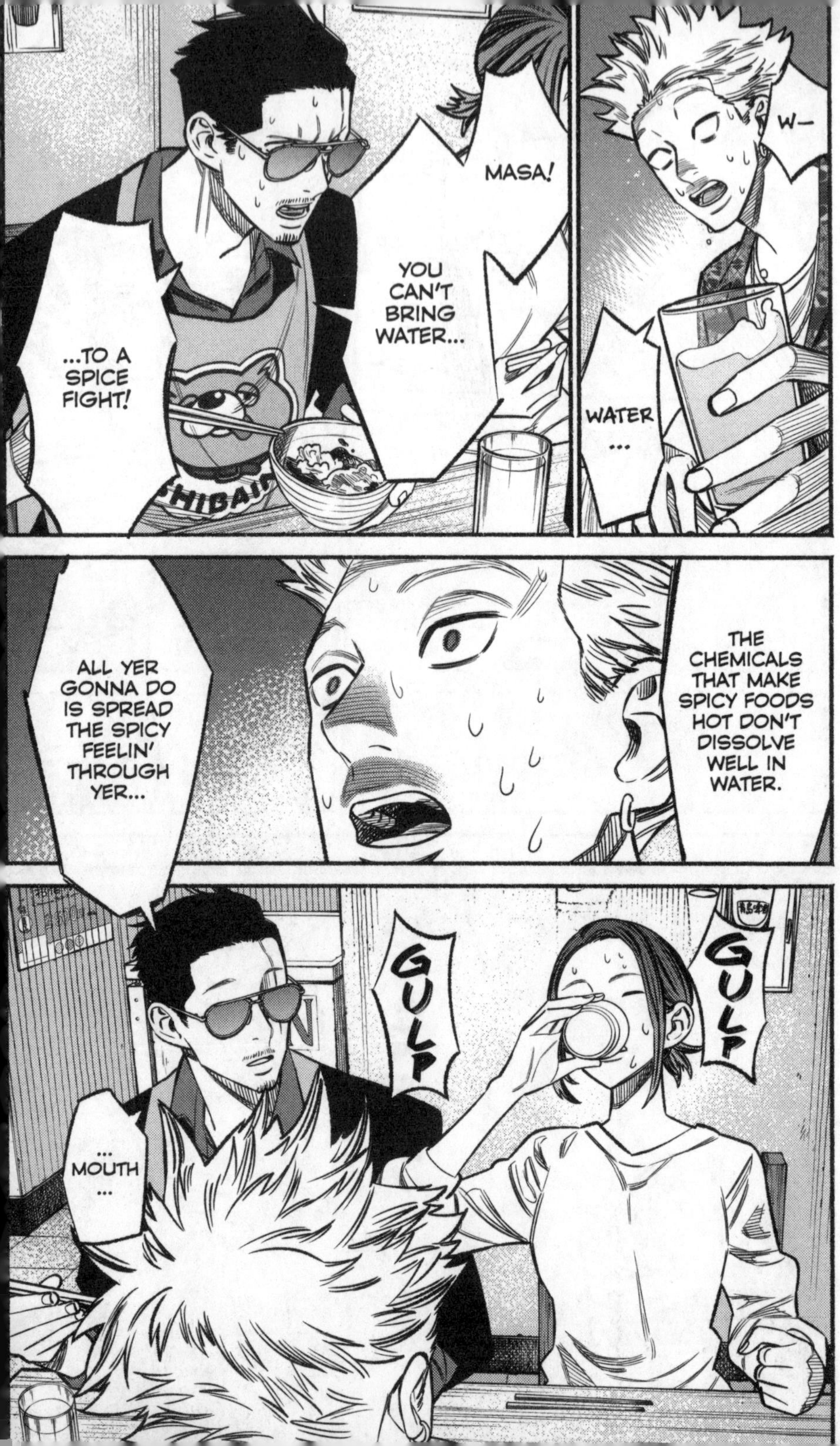
W—
WATER ...
MASA!
YOU CAN'T BRING WATER...
...TO A SPICE FIGHT!
THE CHEMICALS THAT MAKE SPICY FOODS HOT DON'T DISSOLVE WELL IN WATER.
ALL YER GONNA DO IS SPREAD THE SPICY FEELIN' THROUGH YER...
GULP
GULP
... MOUTH ...

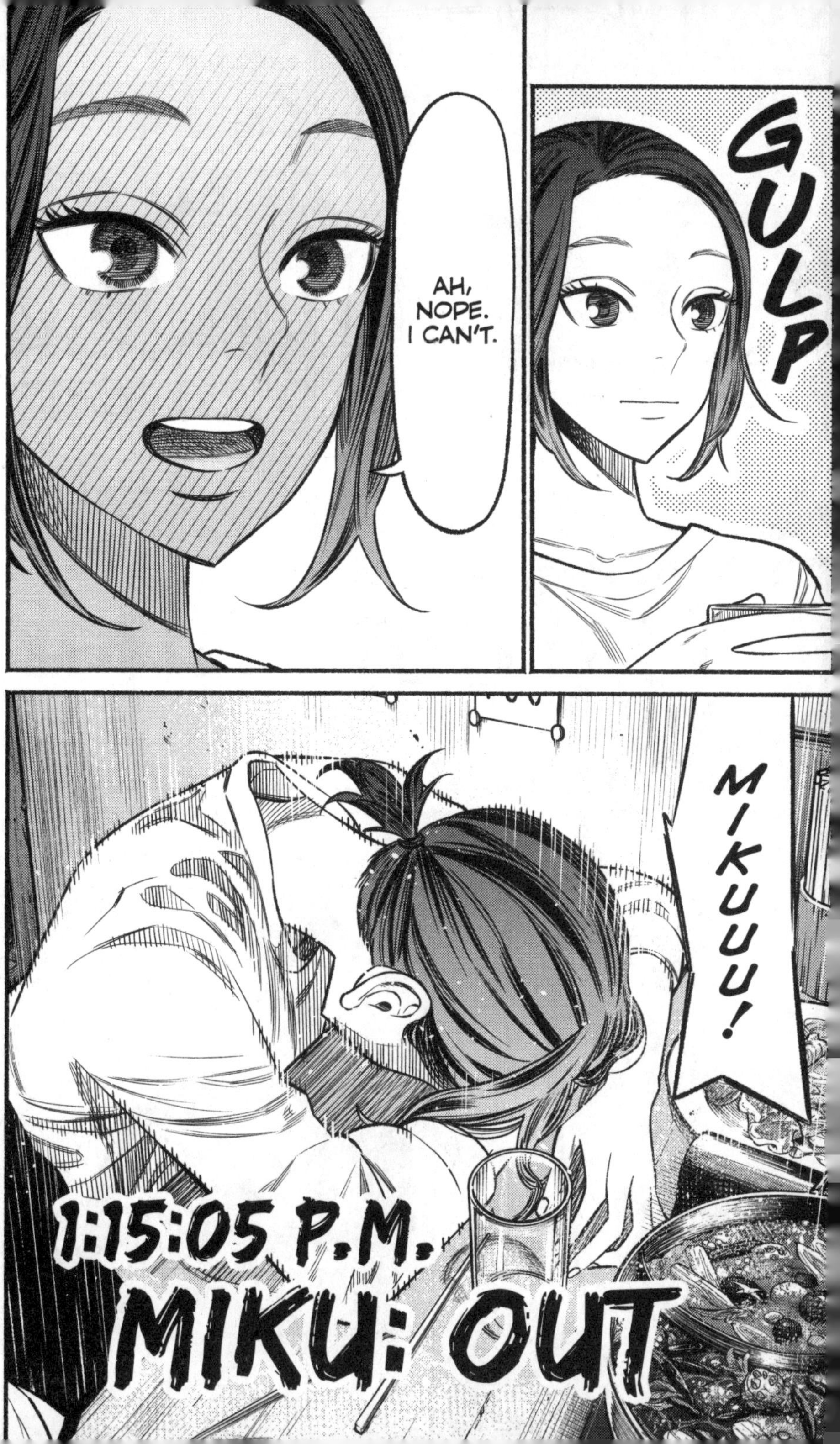
GULP
AH, NOPE. I CAN'T.
MIKUUUU!
1:15:05 P.M.
MIKU: OUT

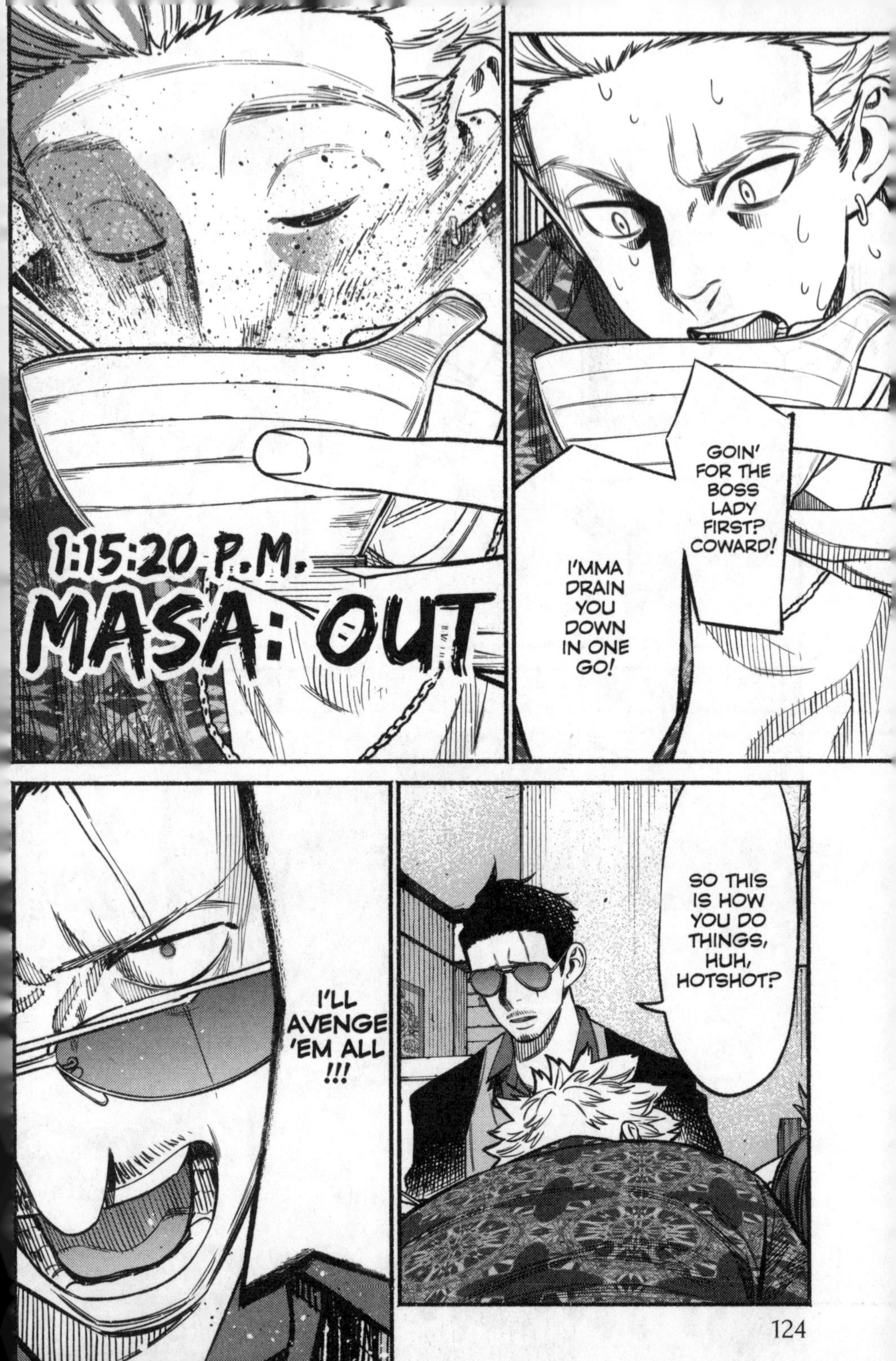
GOIN' FOR THE BOSS LADY FIRST? COWARD!
I'MMA DRAIN YOU DOWN IN ONE GO!
1:15:20 P.M.
MASA: OUT
SO THIS IS HOW YOU DO THINGS, HUH, HOTSHOT?
I'LL AVENGE 'EM ALL!!!

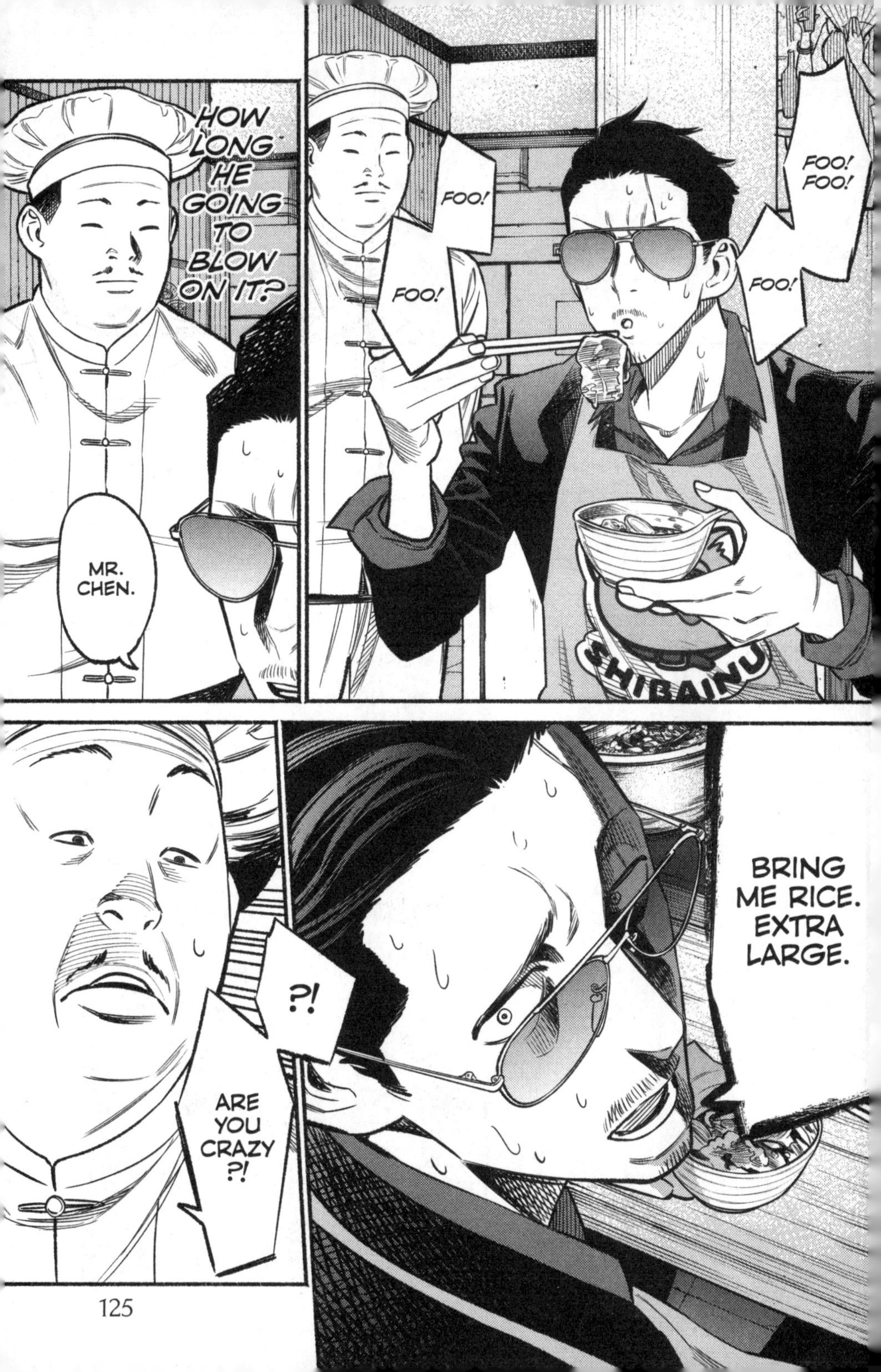
FOO! FOO!
FOO!
FOO!
FOO!
SHIBAINU
HOW LONG HE GOING TO BLOW ON IT?
MR. CHEN.
BRING ME RICE. EXTRA LARGE.
?!
ARE YOU CRAZY ?!

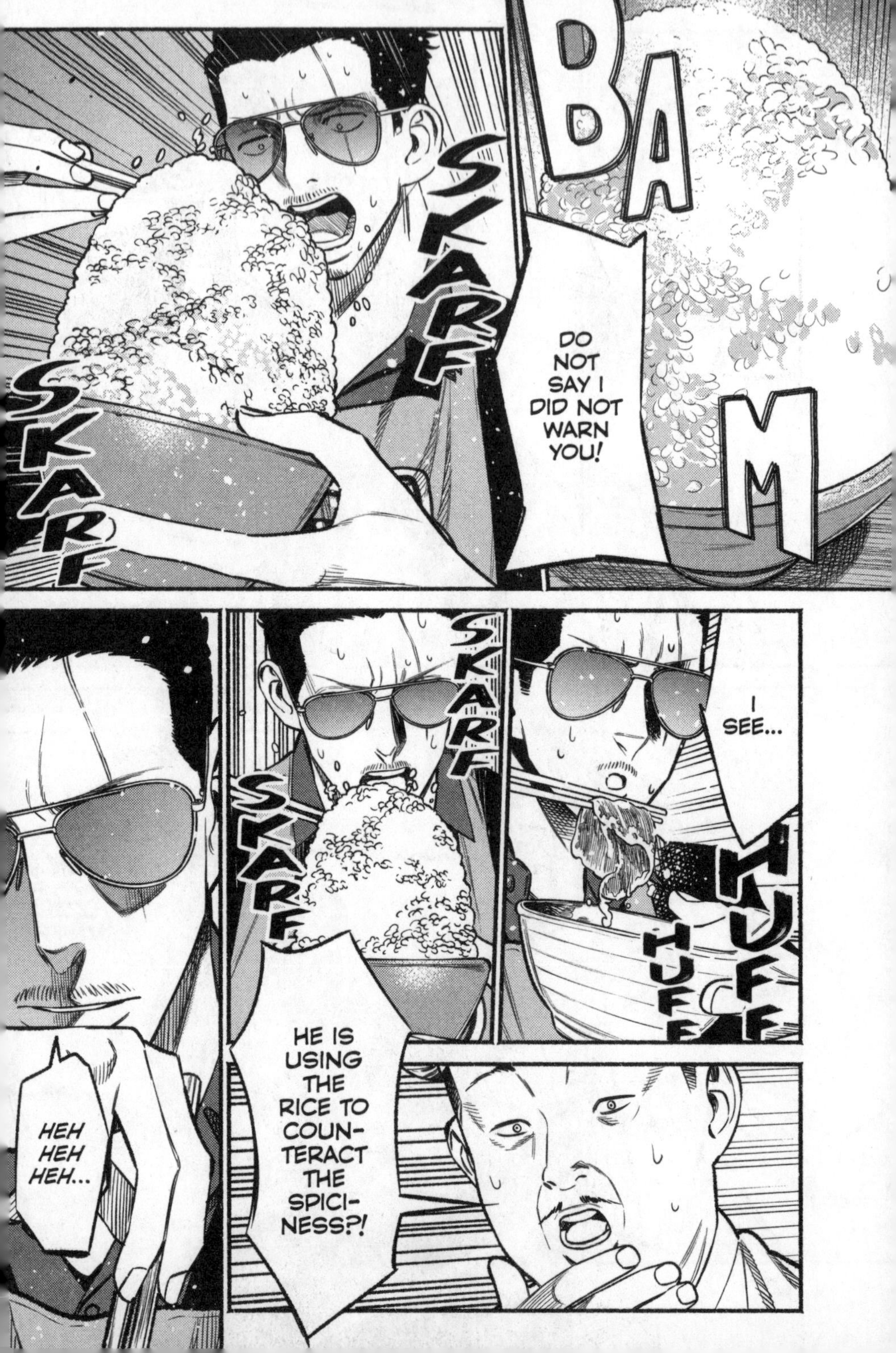
BAM
DO NOT SAY I DID NOT WARN YOU!
SKARF
SKARF
I SEE...
HUFF
HUFF
SKARF
SKARF
HE IS USING THE RICE TO COUNTERACT THE SPICINESS?!
HEH HEH HEH...

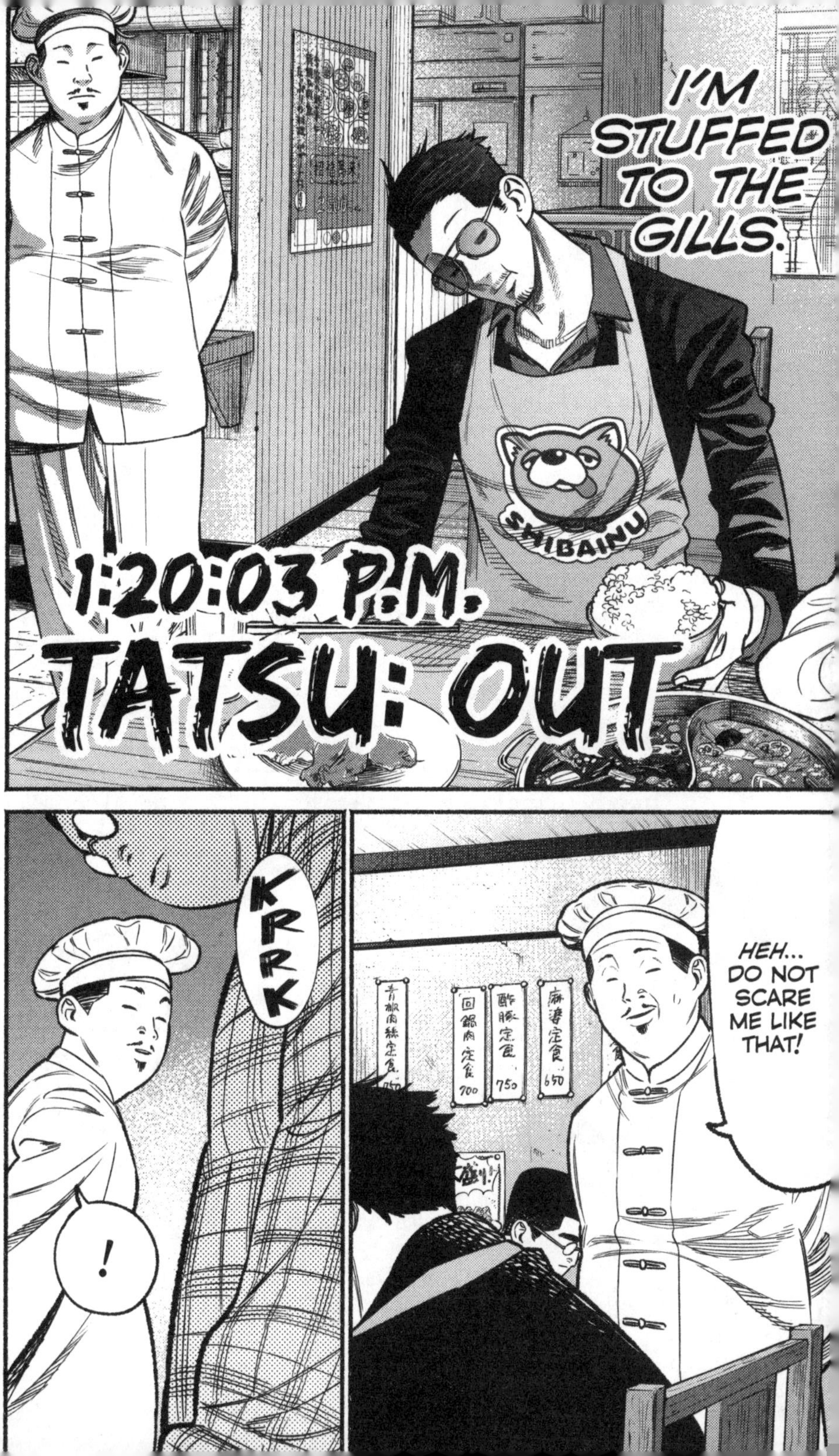
I'M STUFFED TO THE GILLS.
SHIBAINU
1:20:03 P.M.
TATSU: OUT
HEH... DO NOT SCARE ME LIKE THAT!
麻婆定食 650
酢豚定食 750
回鍋肉定食 700
青椒肉絲定食 750
KRRK
!

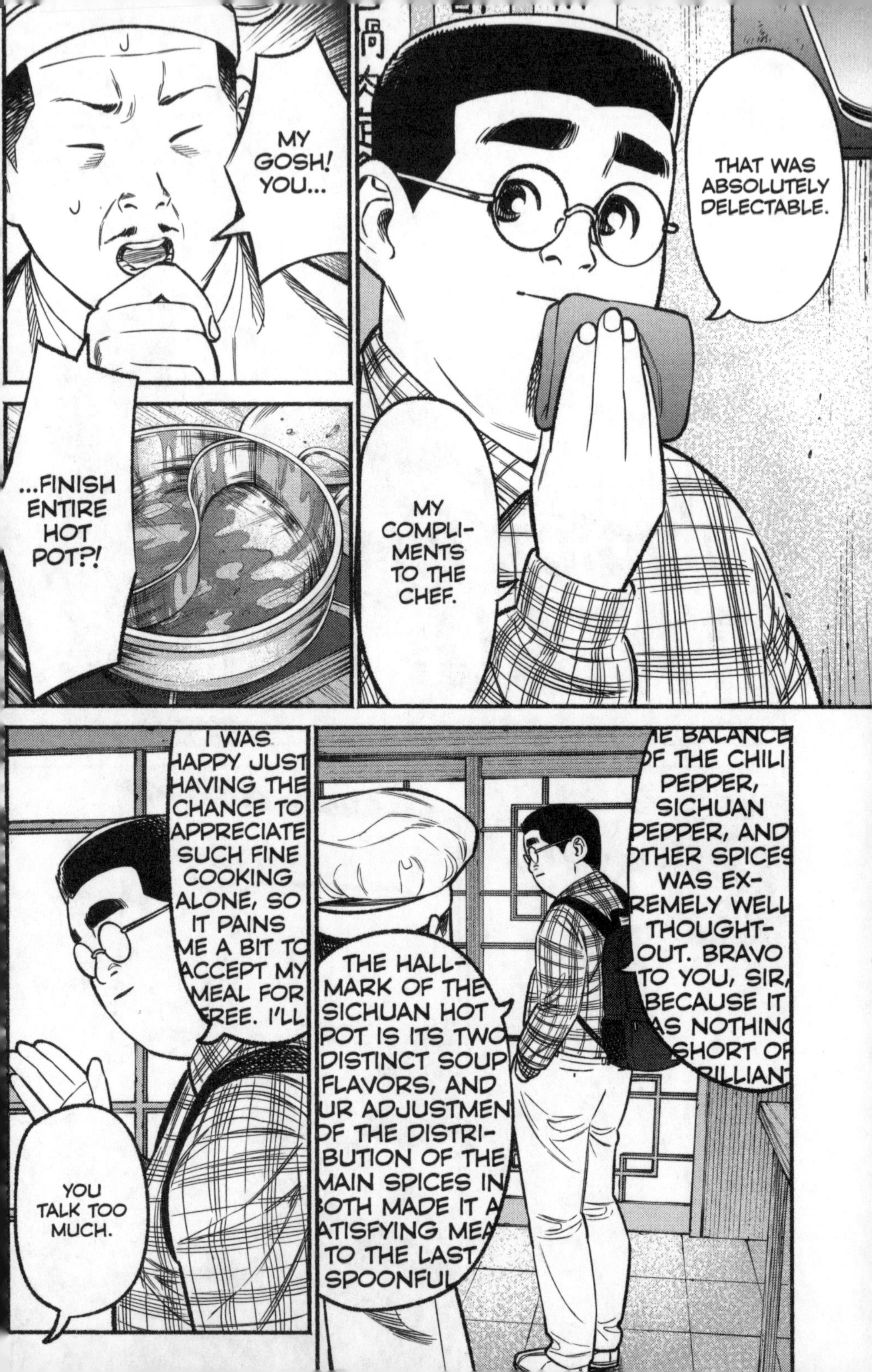
THAT WAS ABSOLUTELY DELECTABLE.
MY COMPLIMENTS TO THE CHEF.
MY GOSH! YOU...
...FINISH ENTIRE HOT POT?!
IE BALANCE OF THE CHILI PEPPER, SICHUAN PEPPER, AND OTHER SPICES WAS EX- REMELY WELL THOUGHT- OUT. BRAVO TO YOU, SIR, BECAUSE IT AS NOTHING SHORT OF ILLIANT
THE HALL- MARK OF THE SICHUAN HOT POT IS ITS TWO DISTINCT SOUP FLAVORS, AND UR ADJUSTMEN OF THE DISTRI- BUTION OF THE MAIN SPICES IN OTH MADE IT A ATISFYING MEA TO THE LAST SPOONFUL
I WAS HAPPY JUST HAVING THE CHANCE TO APPRECIATE SUCH FINE COOKING ALONE, SO IT PAINS ME A BIT TO ACCEPT MY MEAL FOR EE. I'LL
YOU TALK TOO MUCH.

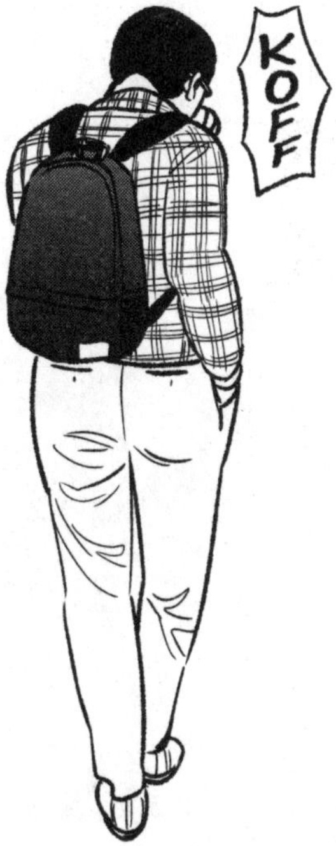
KOFF

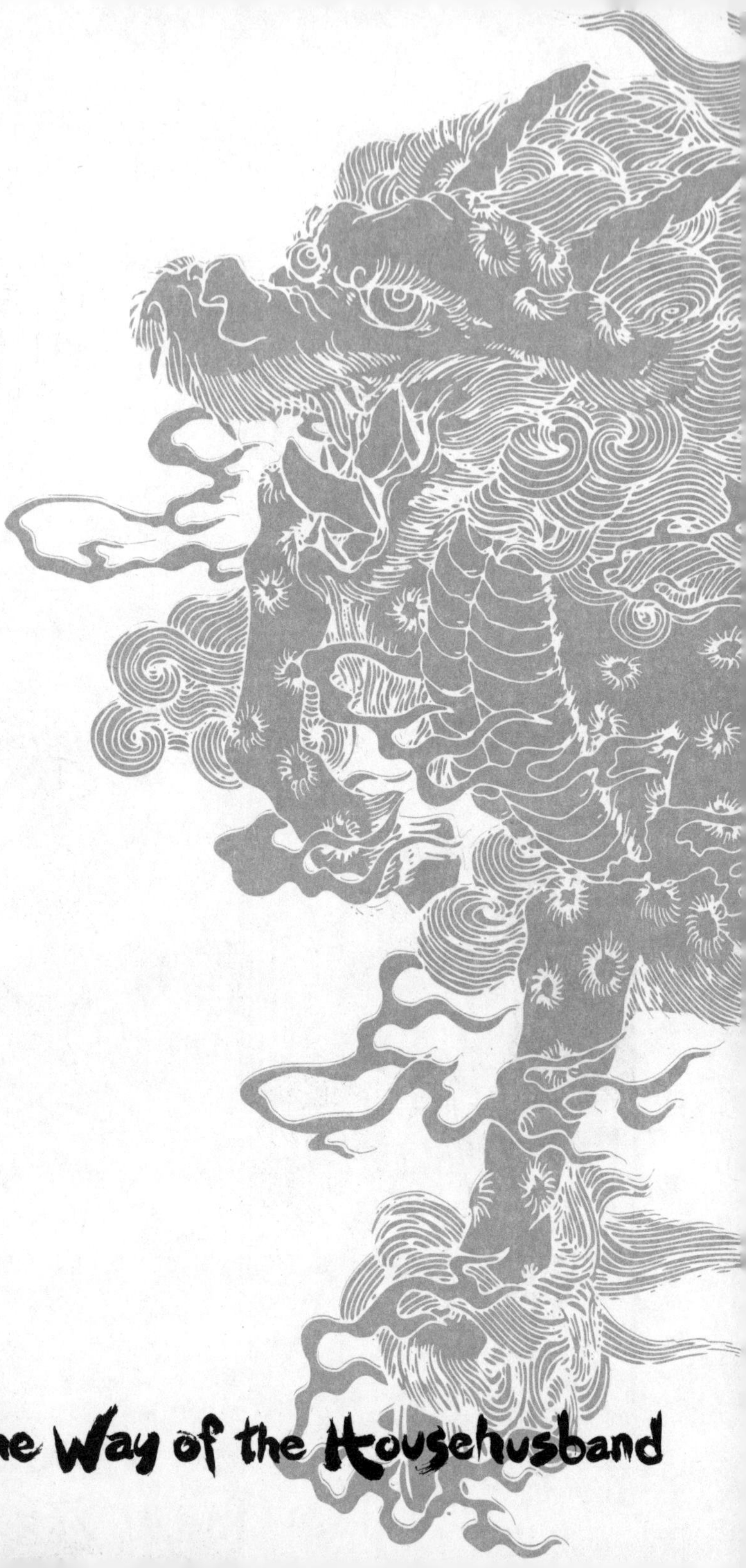

The Way of the Househusband

CHAPTER 72

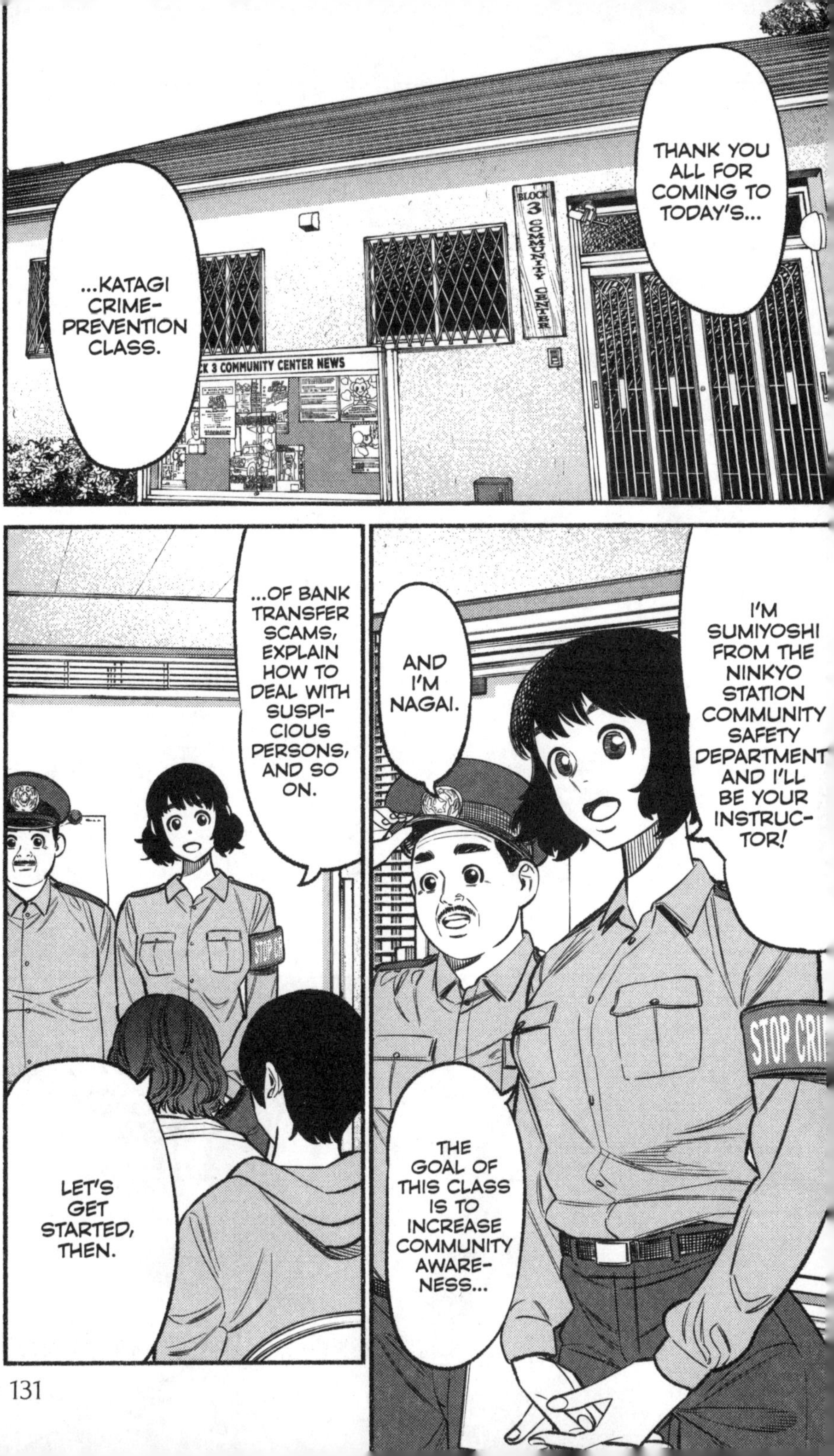

THANK YOU ALL FOR COMING TO TODAY'S...
BLOCK 3 COMMUNITY CENTER
...KATAGI CRIME-PREVENTION CLASS.
CK 3 COMMUNITY CENTER NEWS
I'M SUMIYOSHI FROM THE NINKYO STATION COMMUNITY SAFETY DEPARTMENT AND I'LL BE YOUR INSTRUCTOR!
AND I'M NAGAI.
STOP CRI
THE GOAL OF THIS CLASS IS TO INCREASE COMMUNITY AWARENESS...
...OF BANK TRANSFER SCAMS, EXPLAIN HOW TO DEAL WITH SUSPICIOUS PERSONS, AND SO ON.
LET'S GET STARTED, THEN.

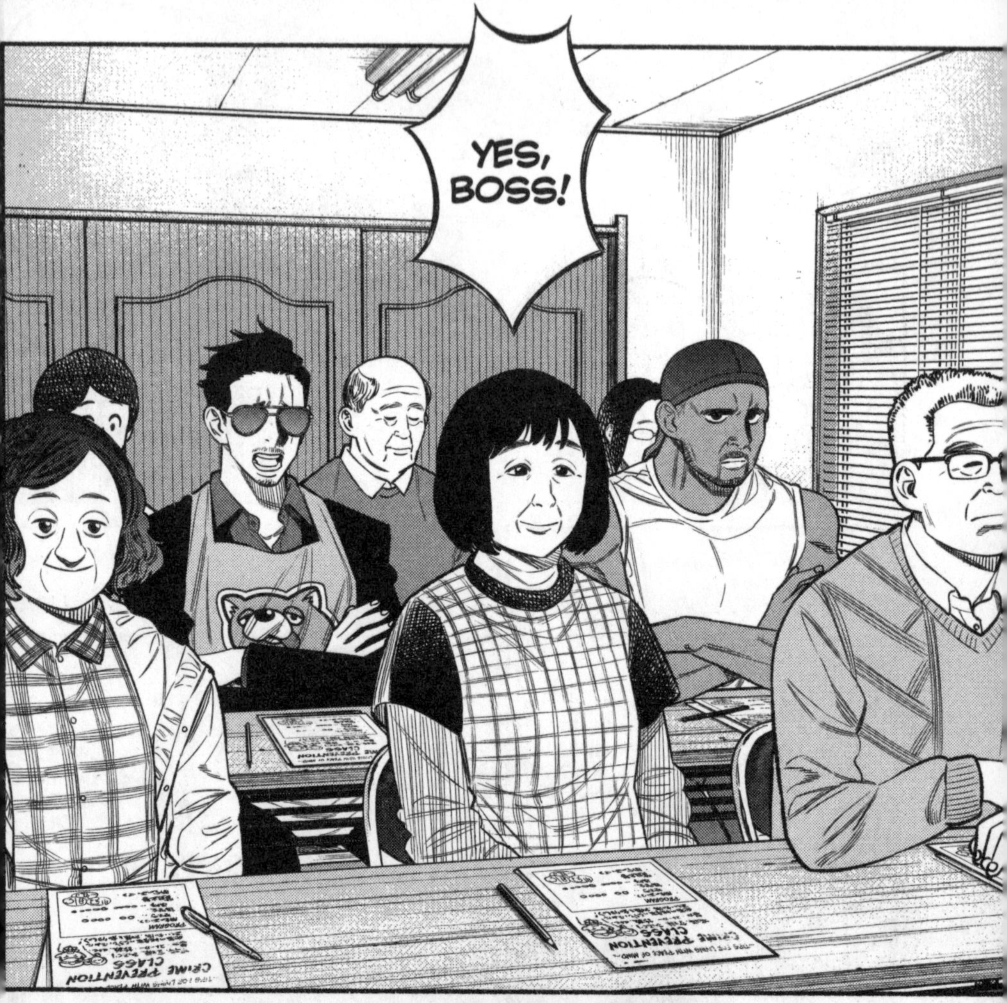
YES, BOSS!

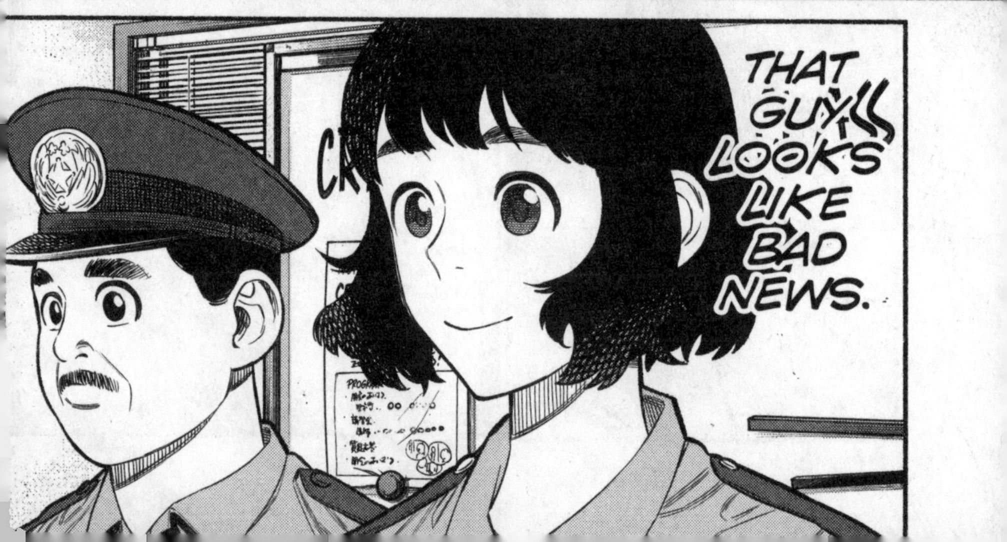
THAT GUY LOOKS LIKE BAD NEWS.

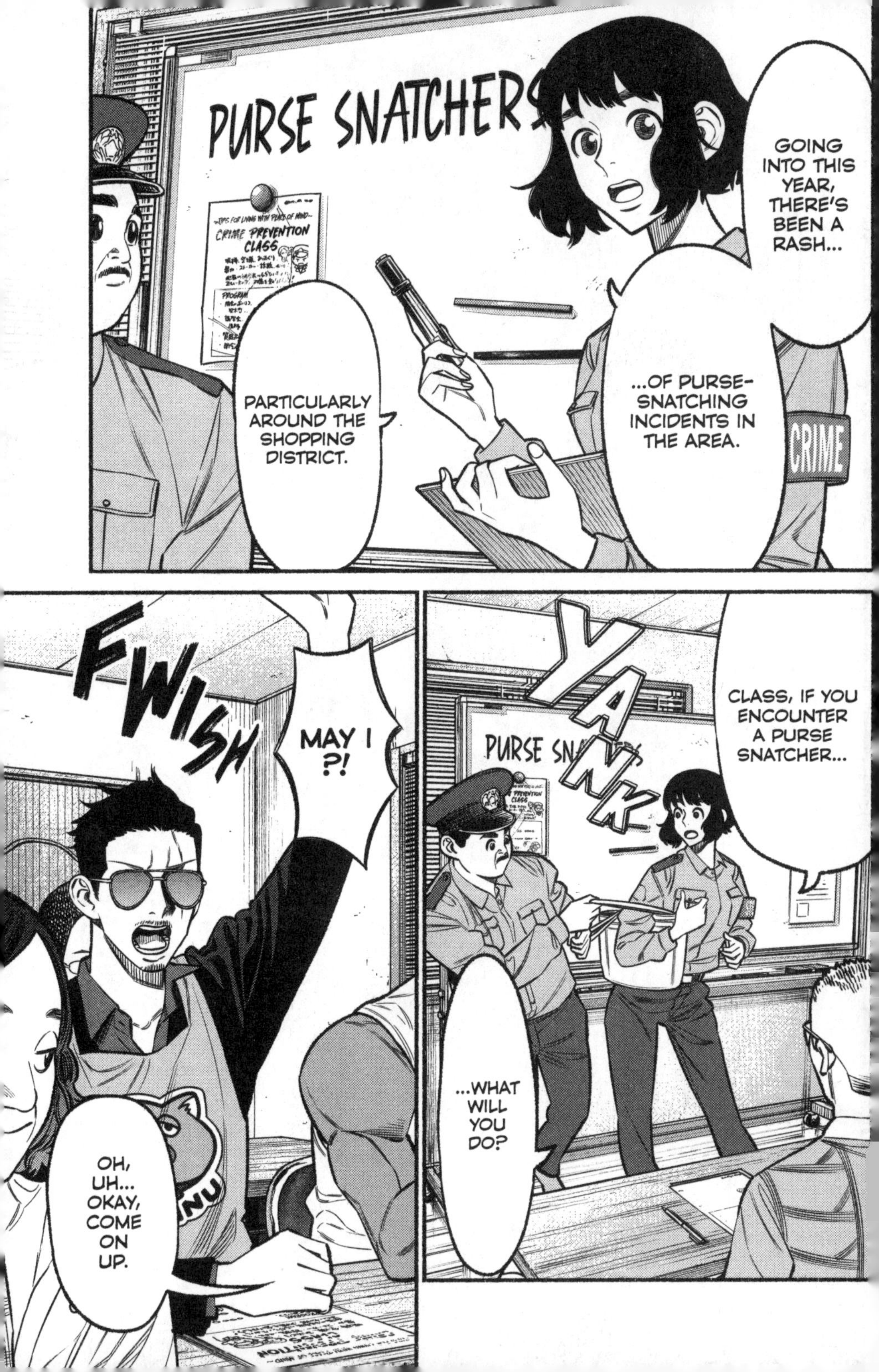
PURSE SNATCHERS
CRIME PREVENTION CLASS
GOING INTO THIS YEAR, THERE'S BEEN A RASH...
...OF PURSE-SNATCHING INCIDENTS IN THE AREA.
CRIME
PARTICULARLY AROUND THE SHOPPING DISTRICT.
CLASS, IF YOU ENCOUNTER A PURSE SNATCHER...
YANK
...WHAT WILL YOU DO?
MAY I ?!
FWISH
OH, UH... OKAY, COME ON UP.

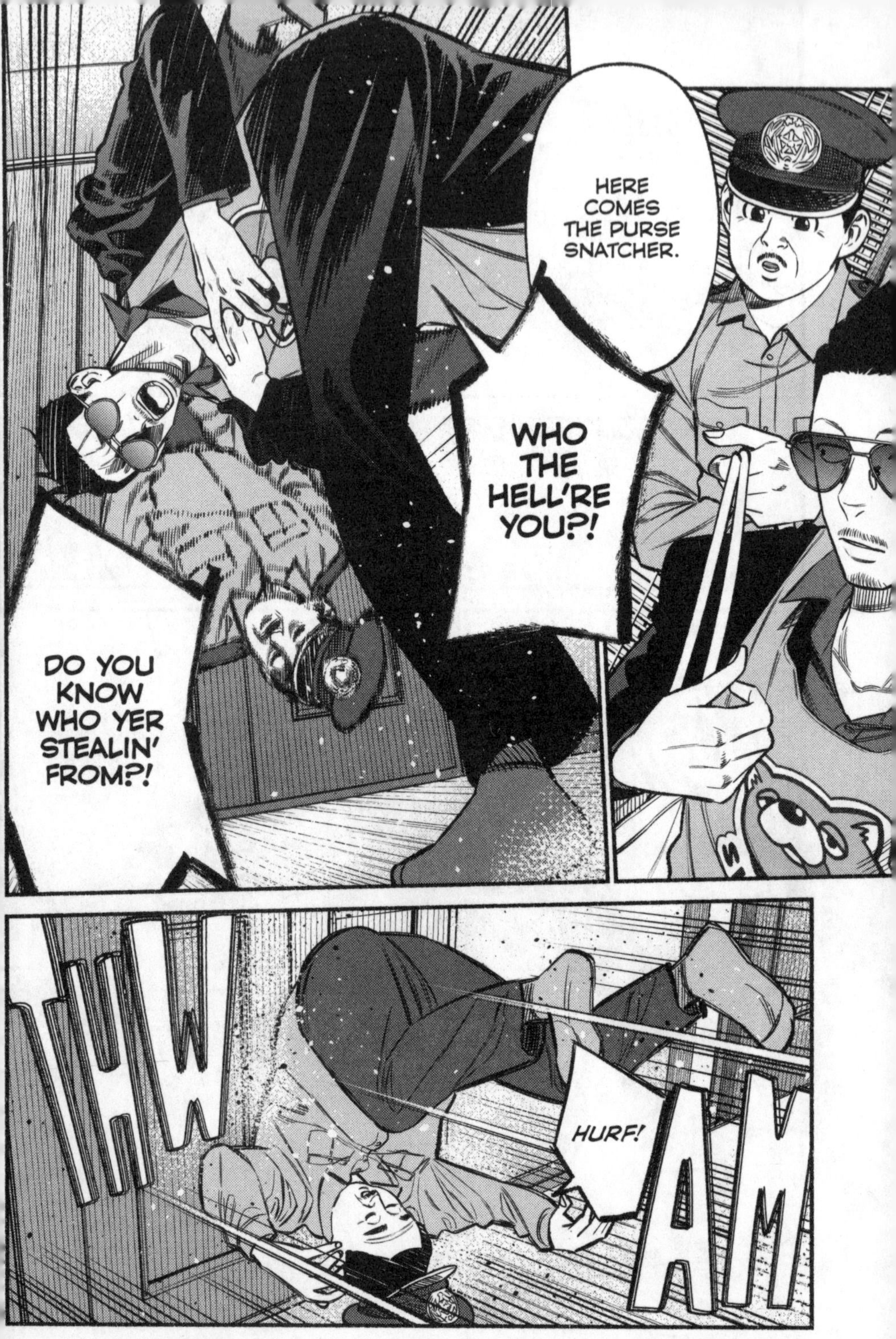
HERE COMES THE PURSE SNATCHER.
WHO THE HELL'RE YOU?!
DO YOU KNOW WHO YER STEALIN' FROM?!
HURF!
THWAM

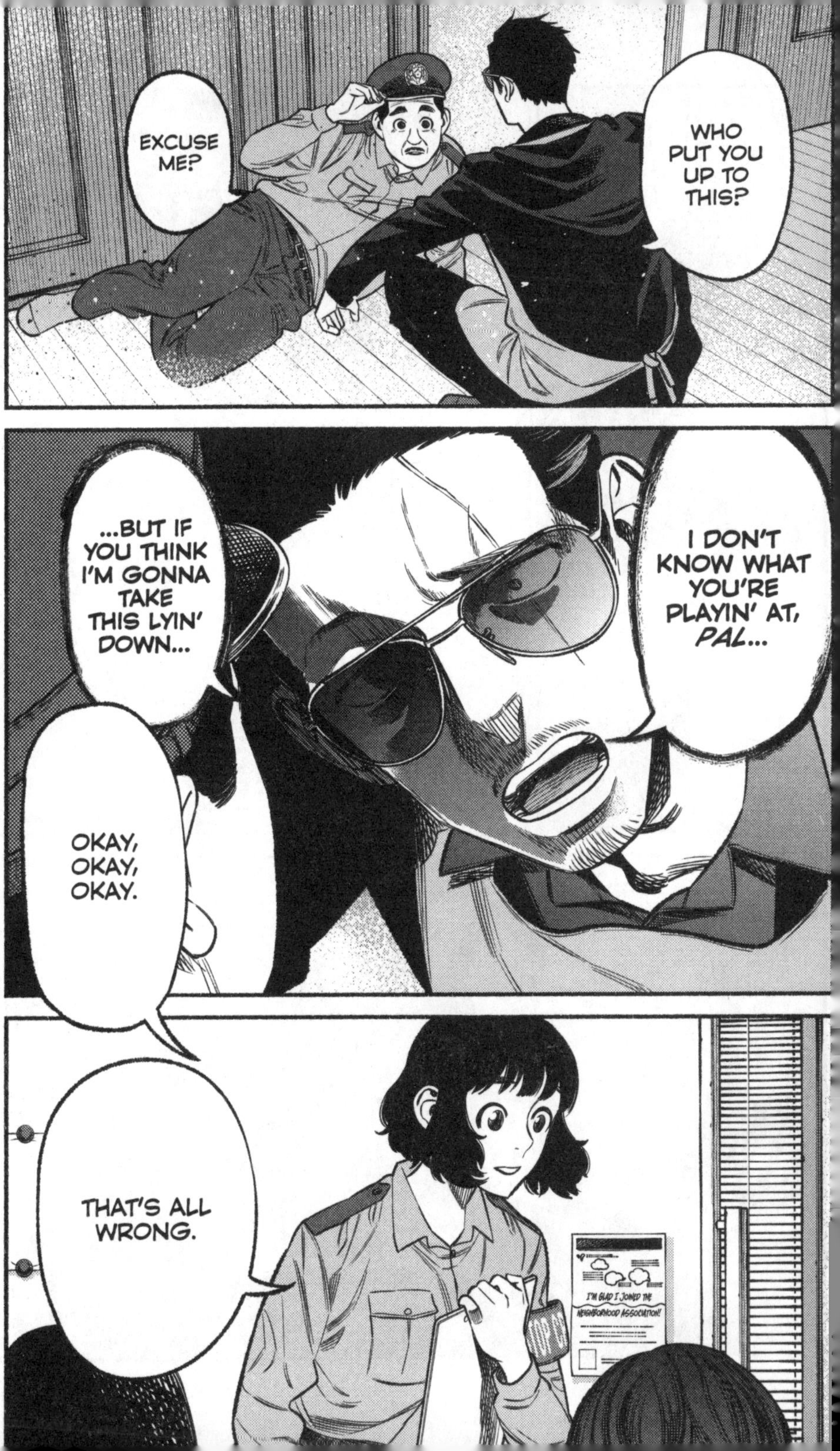
WHO PUT YOU UP TO THIS?
EXCUSE ME?
I DON'T KNOW WHAT YOU'RE PLAYIN' AT, *PAL*...
...BUT IF YOU THINK I'M GONNA TAKE THIS LYIN' DOWN...
OKAY, OKAY, OKAY.
THAT'S ALL WRONG.
I'M GLAD I JOINED THE NEIGHBORHOOD ASSOCIATION!

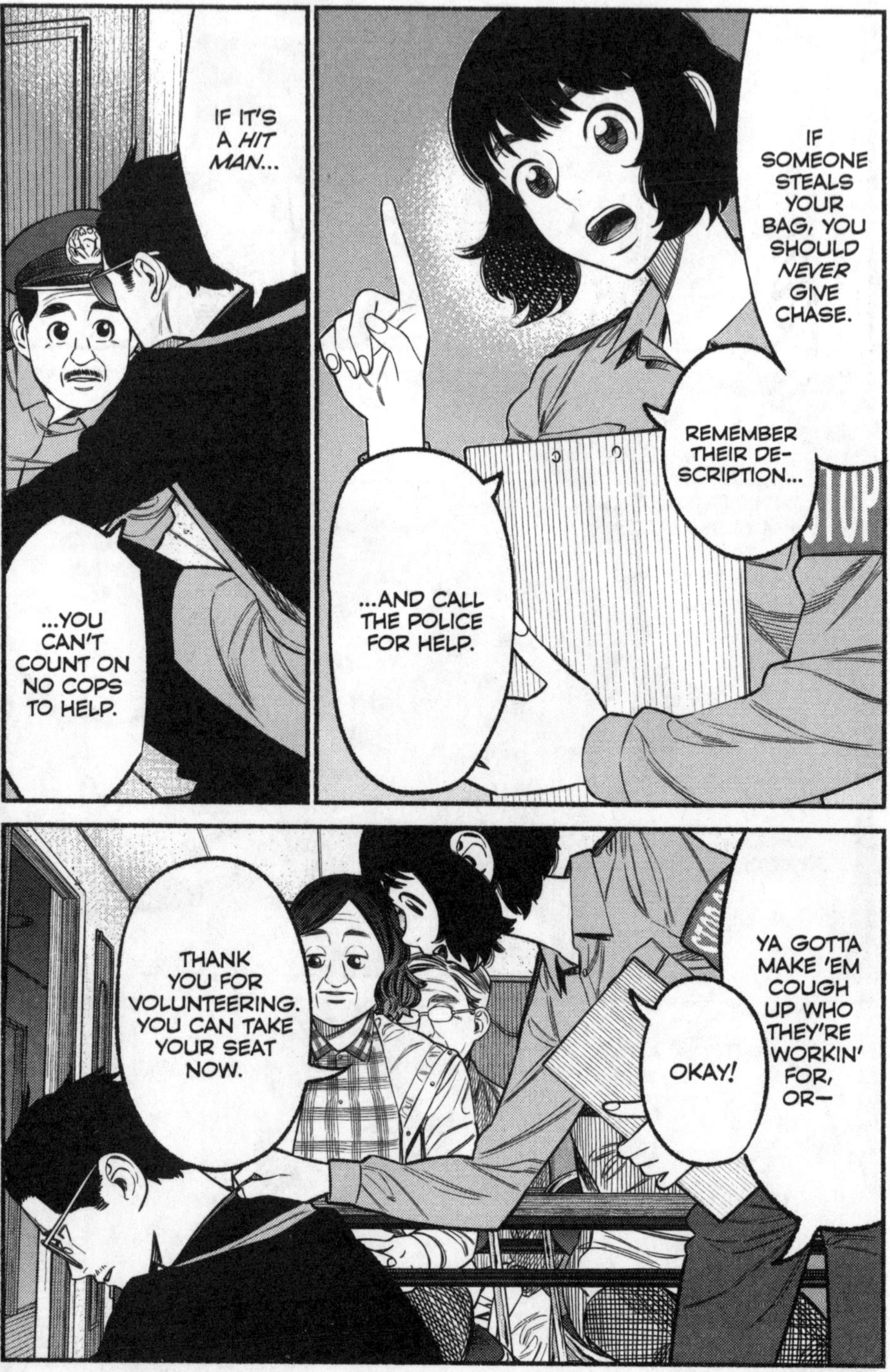
IF SOMEONE STEALS YOUR BAG, YOU SHOULD *NEVER* GIVE CHASE.
REMEMBER THEIR DE-SCRIPTION...
...AND CALL THE POLICE FOR HELP.
IF IT'S A *HIT MAN*...
...YOU CAN'T COUNT ON NO COPS TO HELP.
STOP
YA GOTTA MAKE 'EM COUGH UP WHO THEY'RE WORKIN' FOR, OR—
OKAY!
THANK YOU FOR VOLUNTEERING. YOU CAN TAKE YOUR SEAT NOW.

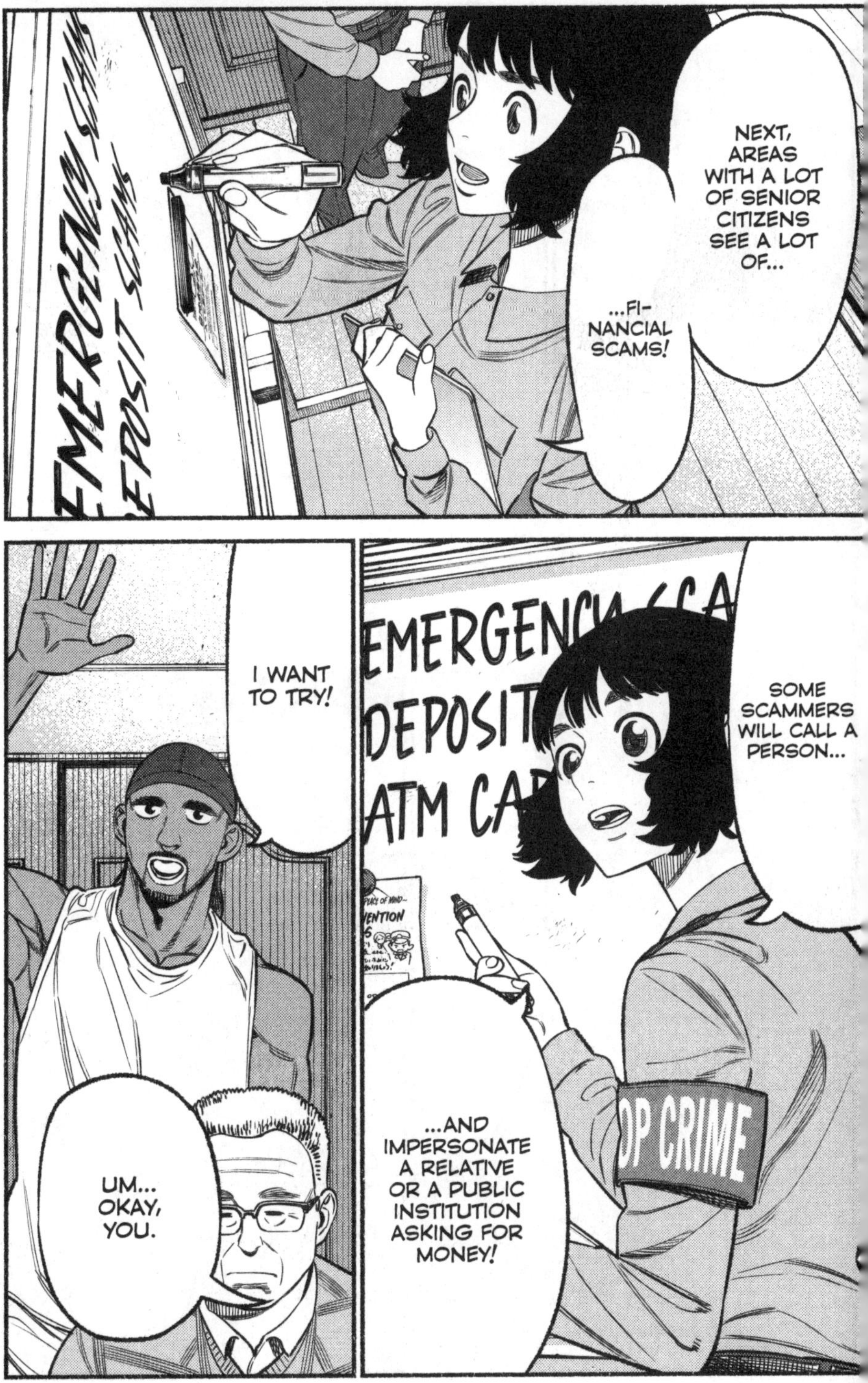
NEXT, AREAS WITH A LOT OF SENIOR CITIZENS SEE A LOT OF...
...FI-NANCIAL SCAMS!
SOME SCAMMERS WILL CALL A PERSON...
...AND IMPERSONATE A RELATIVE OR A PUBLIC INSTITUTION ASKING FOR MONEY!
I WANT TO TRY!
UM... OKAY, YOU.

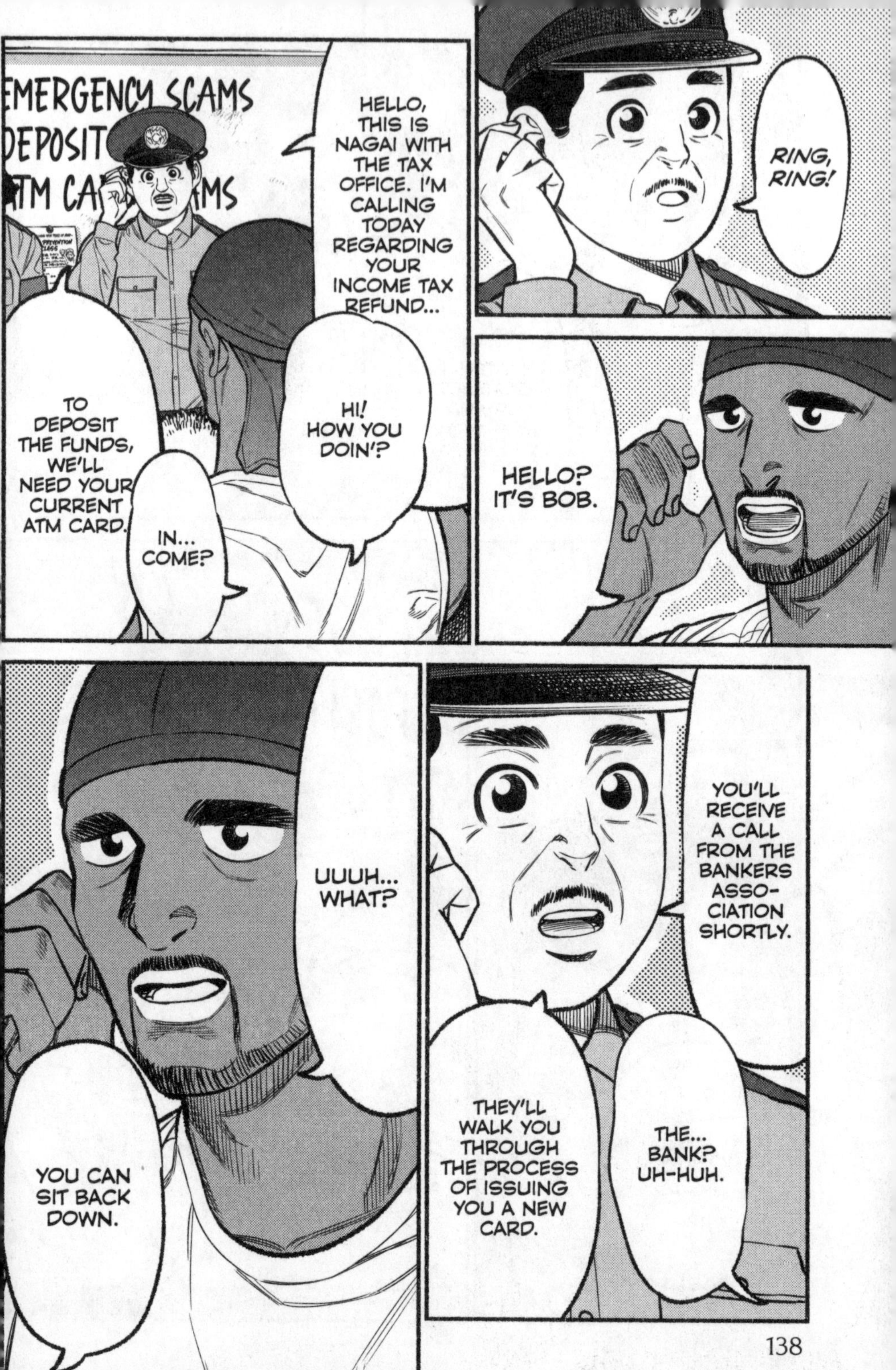
RING, RING!
HELLO? IT'S BOB.
EMERGENCY SCAMS
DEPOSIT
HELLO, THIS IS NAGAI WITH THE TAX OFFICE. I'M CALLING TODAY REGARDING YOUR INCOME TAX REFUND...
HI! HOW YOU DOIN'?
TO DEPOSIT THE FUNDS, WE'LL NEED YOUR CURRENT ATM CARD.
IN... COME?
YOU'LL RECEIVE A CALL FROM THE BANKERS ASSO-CIATION SHORTLY.
THE... BANK? UH-HUH.
THEY'LL WALK YOU THROUGH THE PROCESS OF ISSUING YOU A NEW CARD.
UUUH... WHAT?
YOU CAN SIT BACK DOWN.

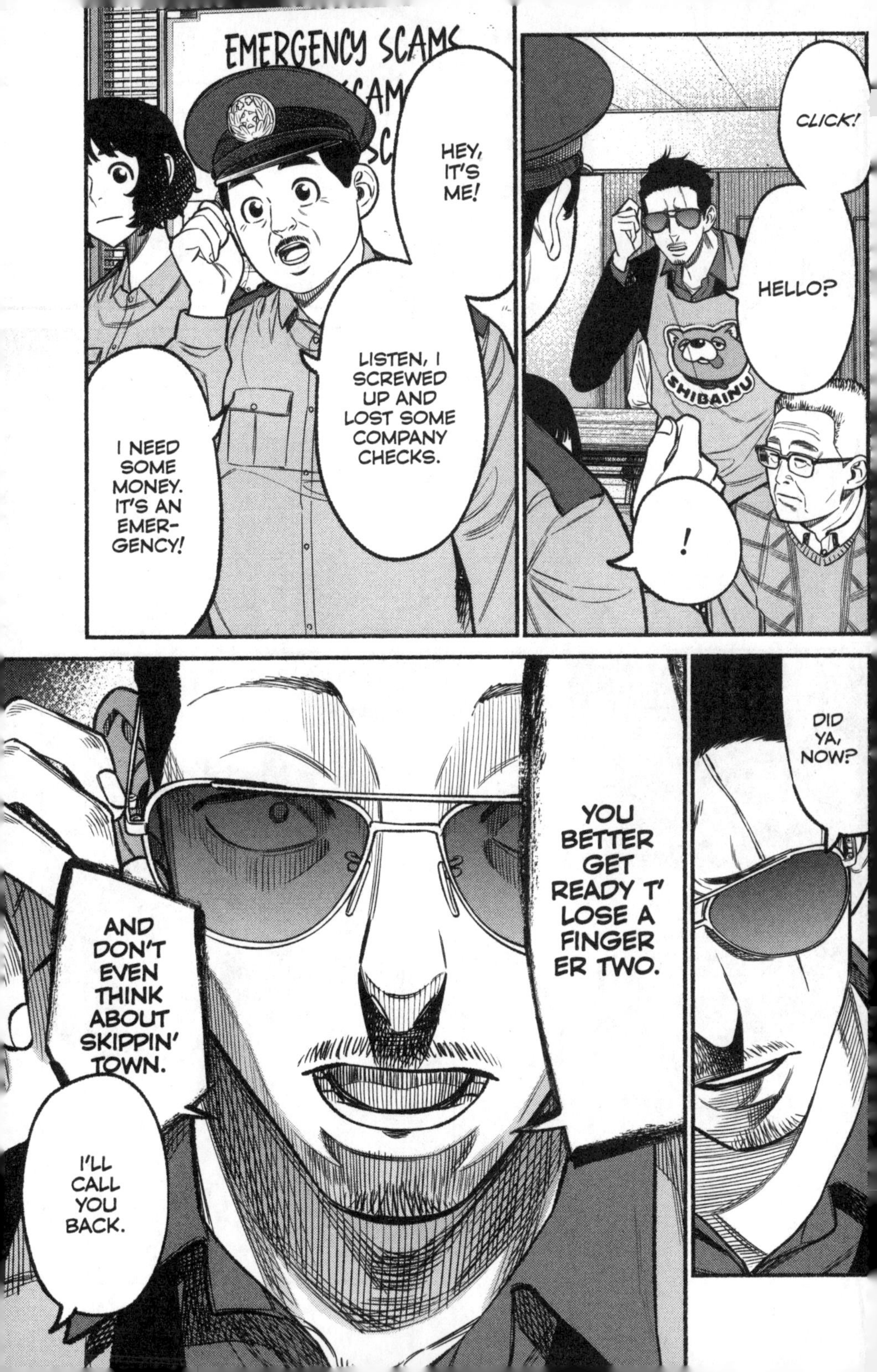
CLICK!
HELLO?
!
EMERGENCY SCAMS
HEY, IT'S ME!
LISTEN, I SCREWED UP AND LOST SOME COMPANY CHECKS.
I NEED SOME MONEY. IT'S AN EMER-GENCY!
DID YA, NOW?
YOU BETTER GET READY T' LOSE A FINGER ER TWO.
AND DON'T EVEN THINK ABOUT SKIPPIN' TOWN.
I'LL CALL YOU BACK.

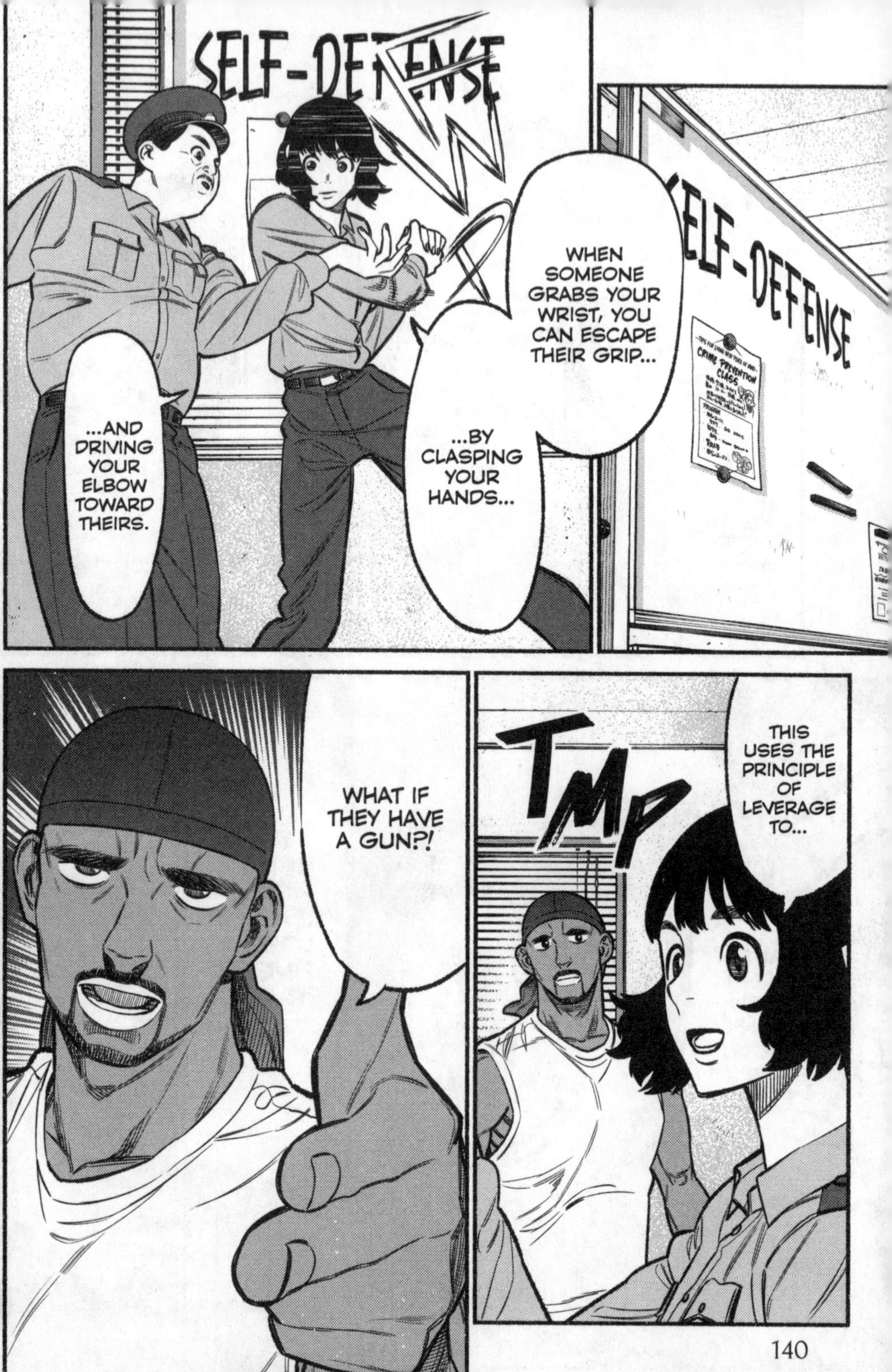
SELF-DEFENSE
CRIME PREVENTION CLASS
WHEN SOMEONE GRABS YOUR WRIST, YOU CAN ESCAPE THEIR GRIP...
SELF-DEFENSE
...BY CLASPING YOUR HANDS...
...AND DRIVING YOUR ELBOW TOWARD THEIRS.
THIS USES THE PRINCIPLE OF LEVERAGE TO...
TMP
WHAT IF THEY HAVE A GUN?!

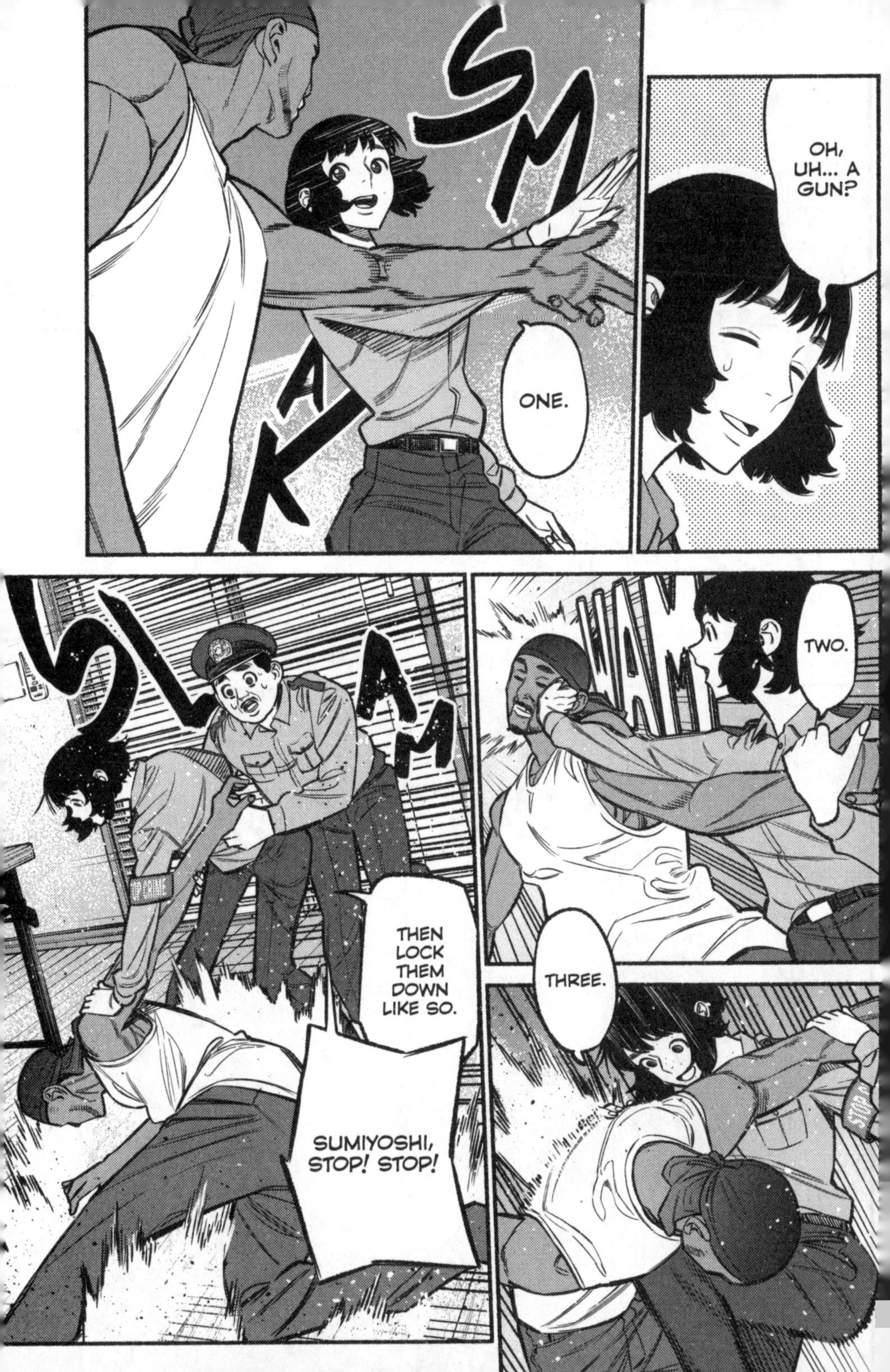
OH, UH... A GUN?
SMAK
ONE.
WAM
TWO.
THREE.
SLAM
THEN LOCK THEM DOWN LIKE SO.
SUMIYOSHI, STOP! STOP!

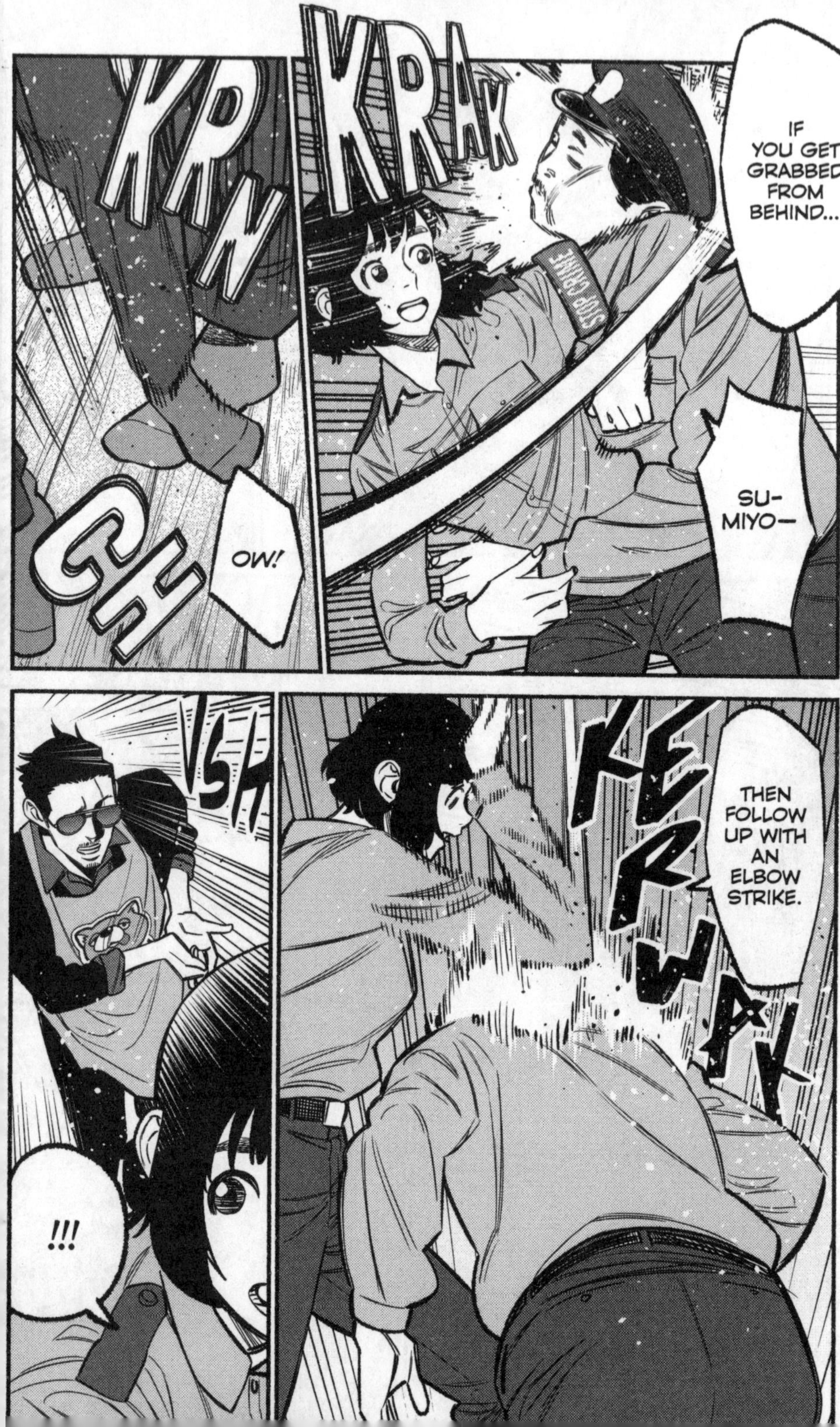
KRAK
IF YOU GET GRABBED FROM BEHIND...
SU-MIYO—
OW!
THEN FOLLOW UP WITH AN ELBOW STRIKE.
!!!

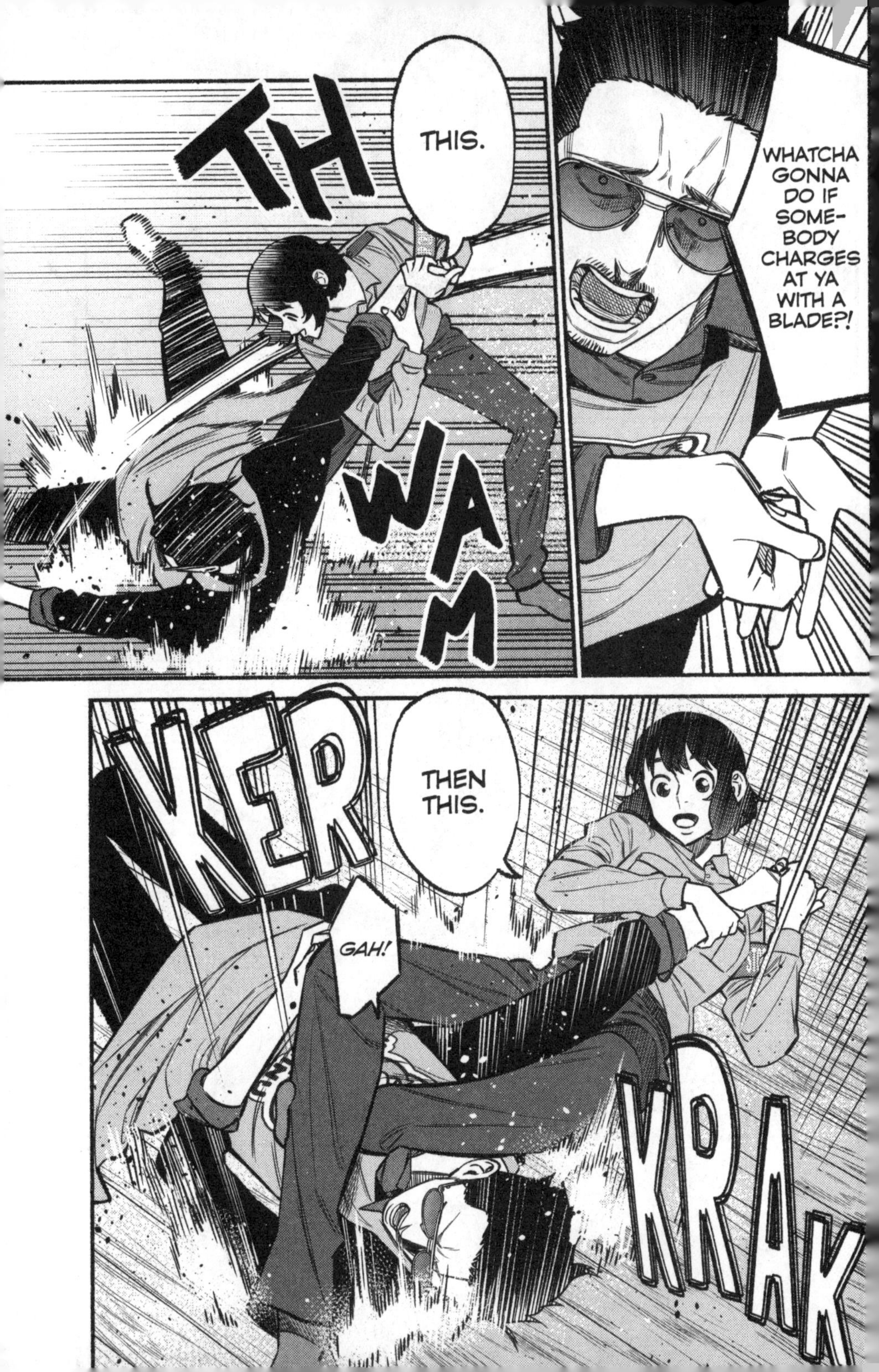
WHATCHA GONNA DO IF SOME-BODY CHARGES AT YA WITH A BLADE?!
THIS.
TH
WAM
THEN THIS.
KER
GAH!
KRAK

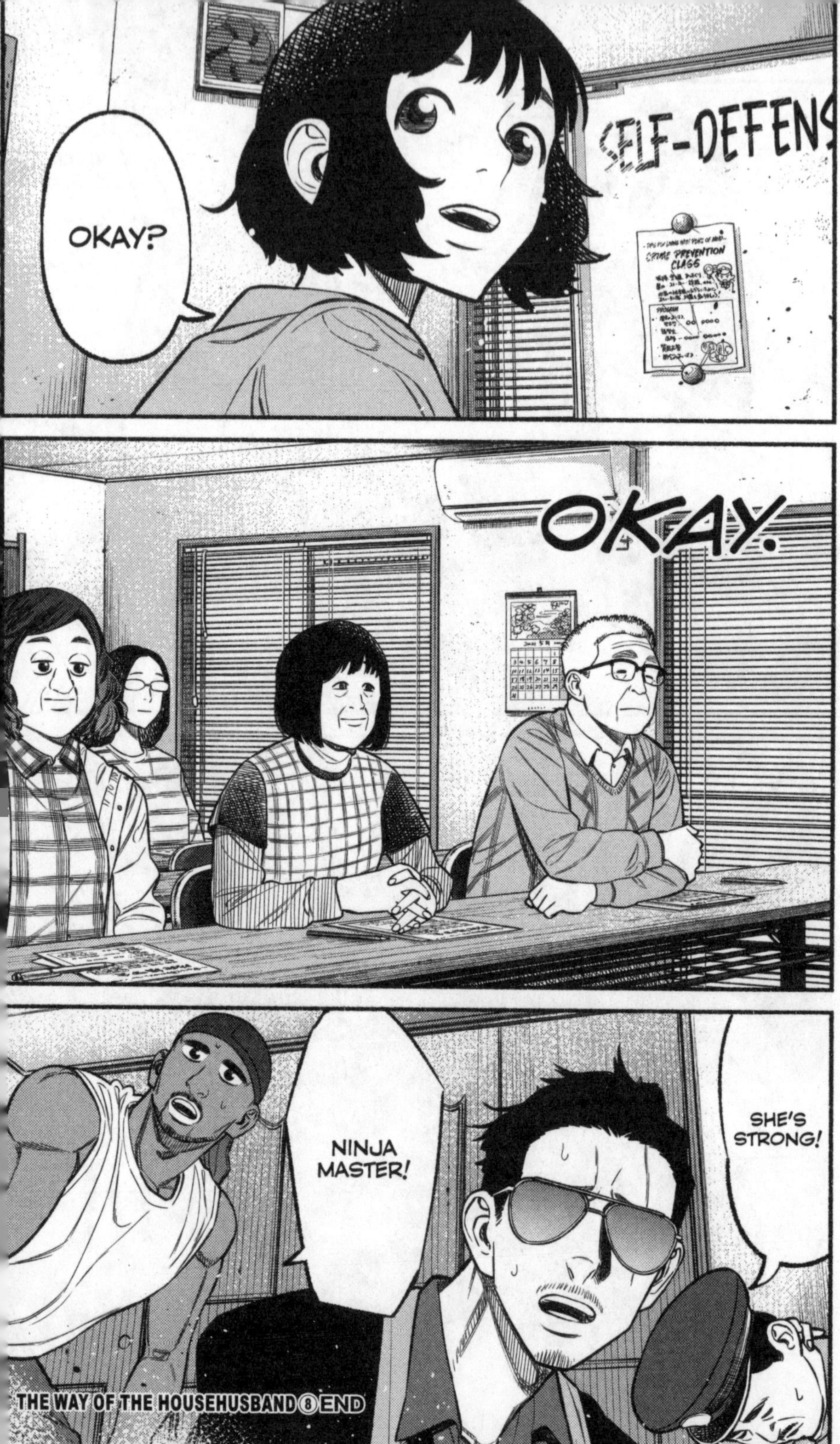
SELF-DEFENS
CRIME PREVENTION CLASS
OKAY?
OKAY.
SHE'S STRONG!
NINJA MASTER!
THE WAY OF THE HOUSEHUSBAND 8 END

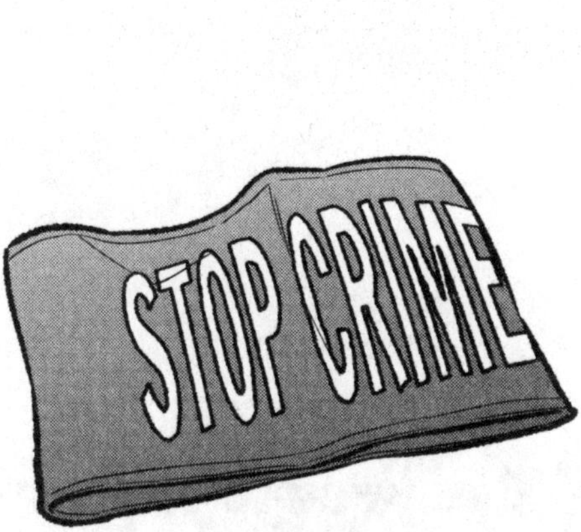
STOP CRIME

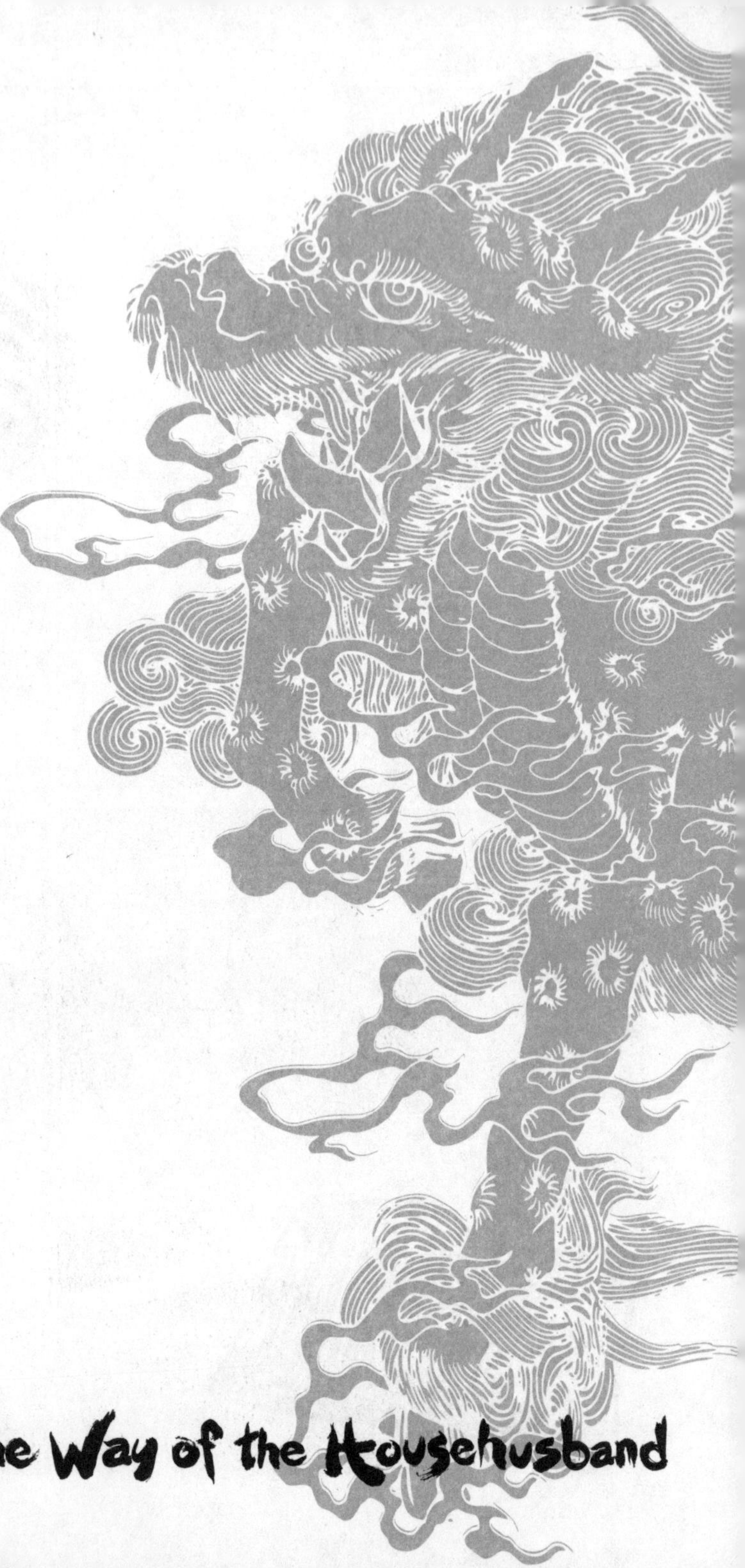

The Way of the Househusband

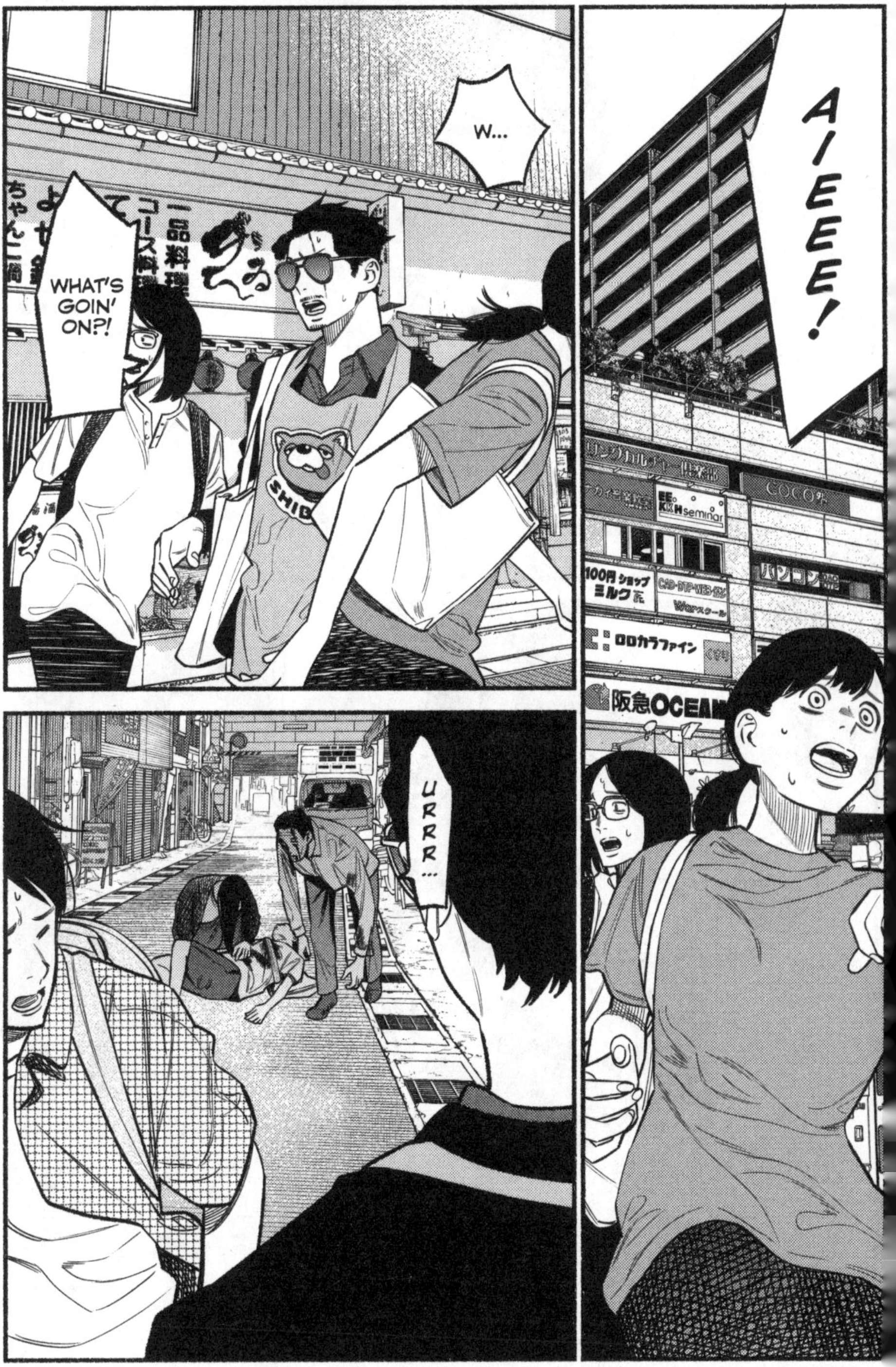
AIEEE!
COCO
KKH seminar
100円ショップ
ミルク
ロロカラファイン
阪急OCEAN
W...
WHAT'S GOIN' ON?!
一品料理
コース料理
URRR...

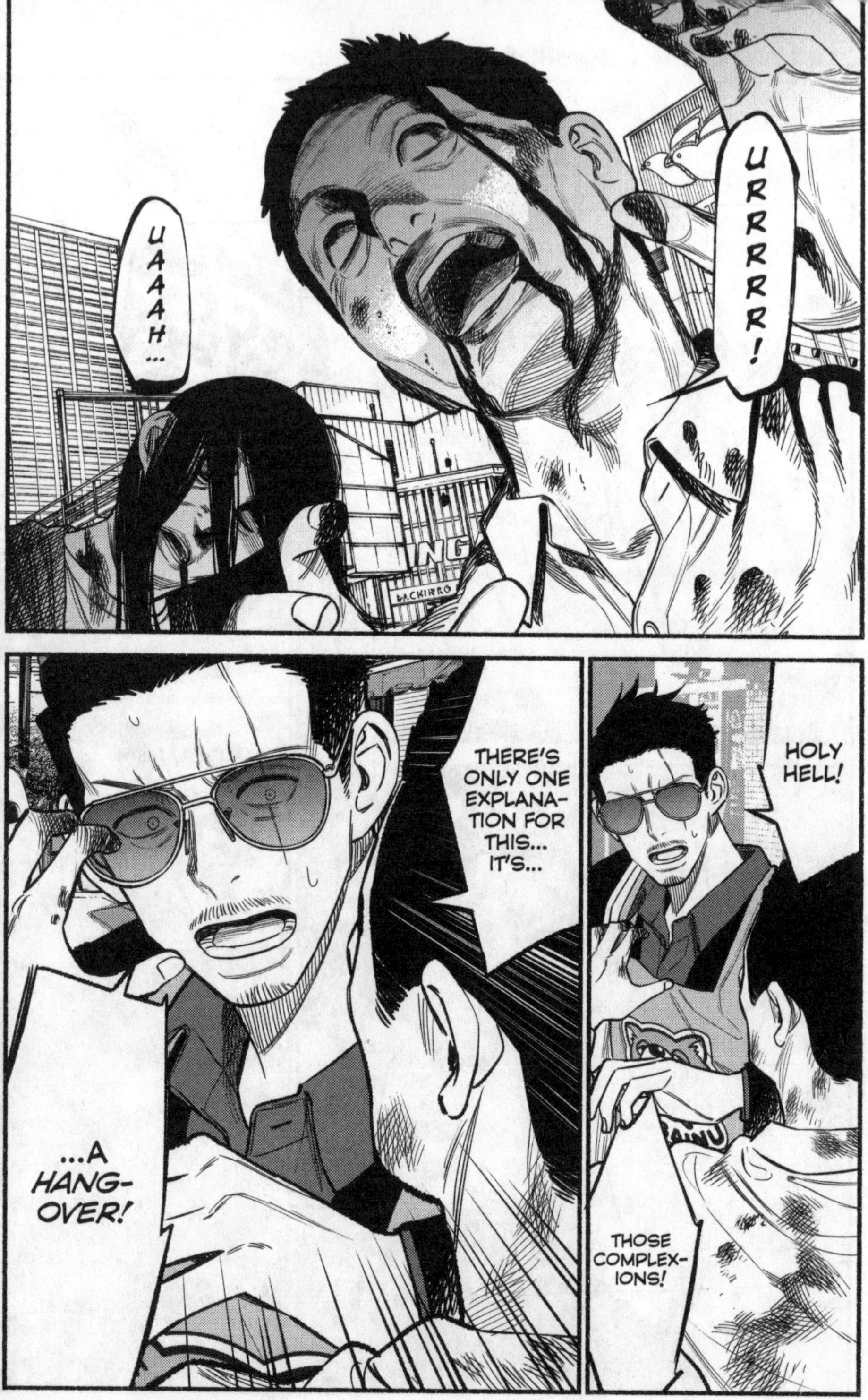
URRRRR!
UAAAH...
HOLY HELL!
THOSE COMPLEXIONS!
THERE'S ONLY ONE EXPLANATION FOR THIS... IT'S...
...A HANGOVER!

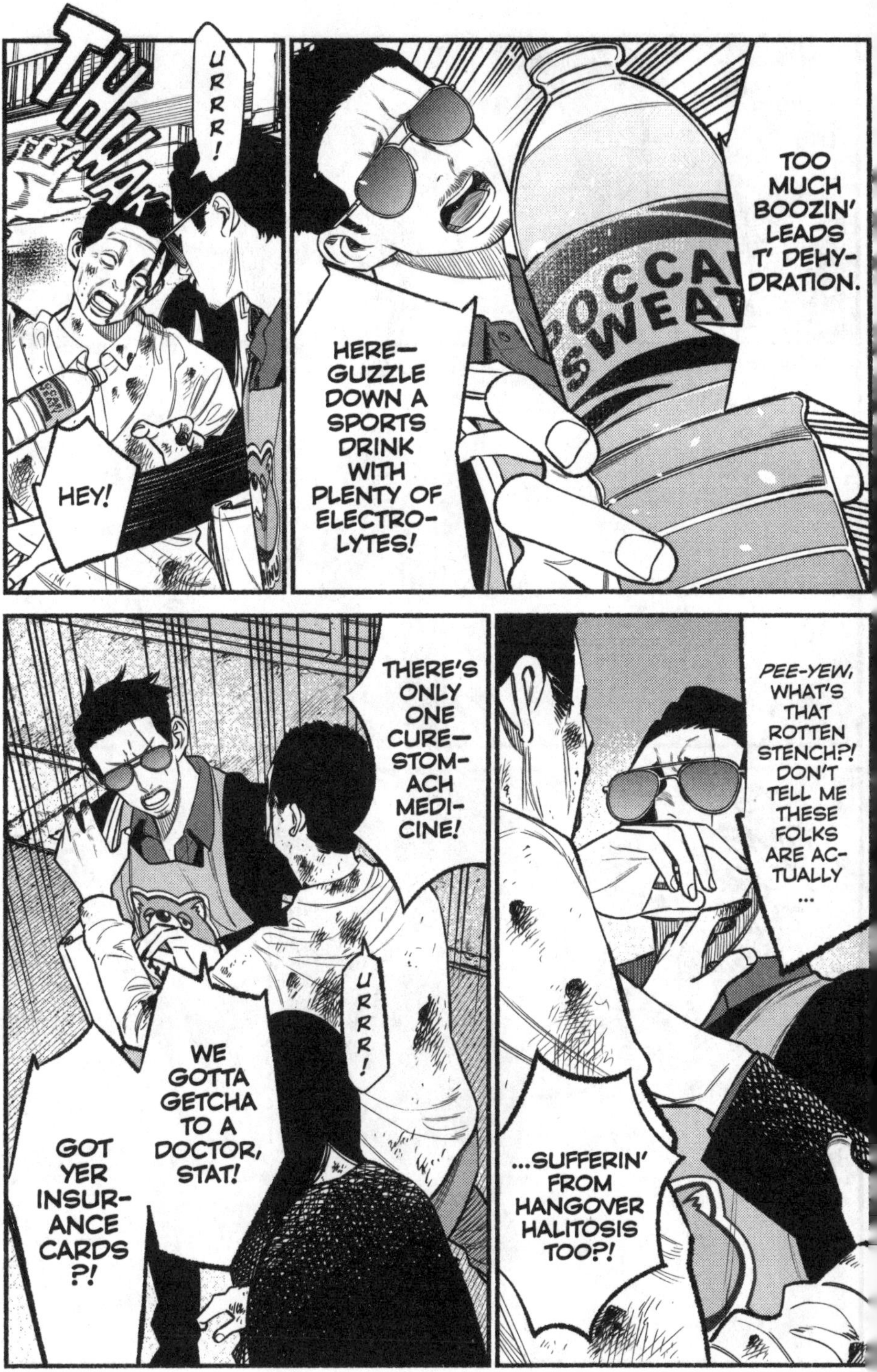
TOO MUCH BOOZIN' LEADS T' DEHY-DRATION.
HERE—GUZZLE DOWN A SPORTS DRINK WITH PLENTY OF ELECTRO-LYTES!
POCCARI SWEAT
URRR!
THWAK
HEY!
PEE-YEW, WHAT'S THAT ROTTEN STENCH?! DON'T TELL ME THESE FOLKS ARE AC-TUALLY ...
...SUFFERIN' FROM HANGOVER HALITOSIS TOO?!
THERE'S ONLY ONE CURE—STOM-ACH MEDI-CINE!
URRR!
WE GOTTA GETCHA TO A DOCTOR, STAT!
GOT YER INSURANCE CARDS?!

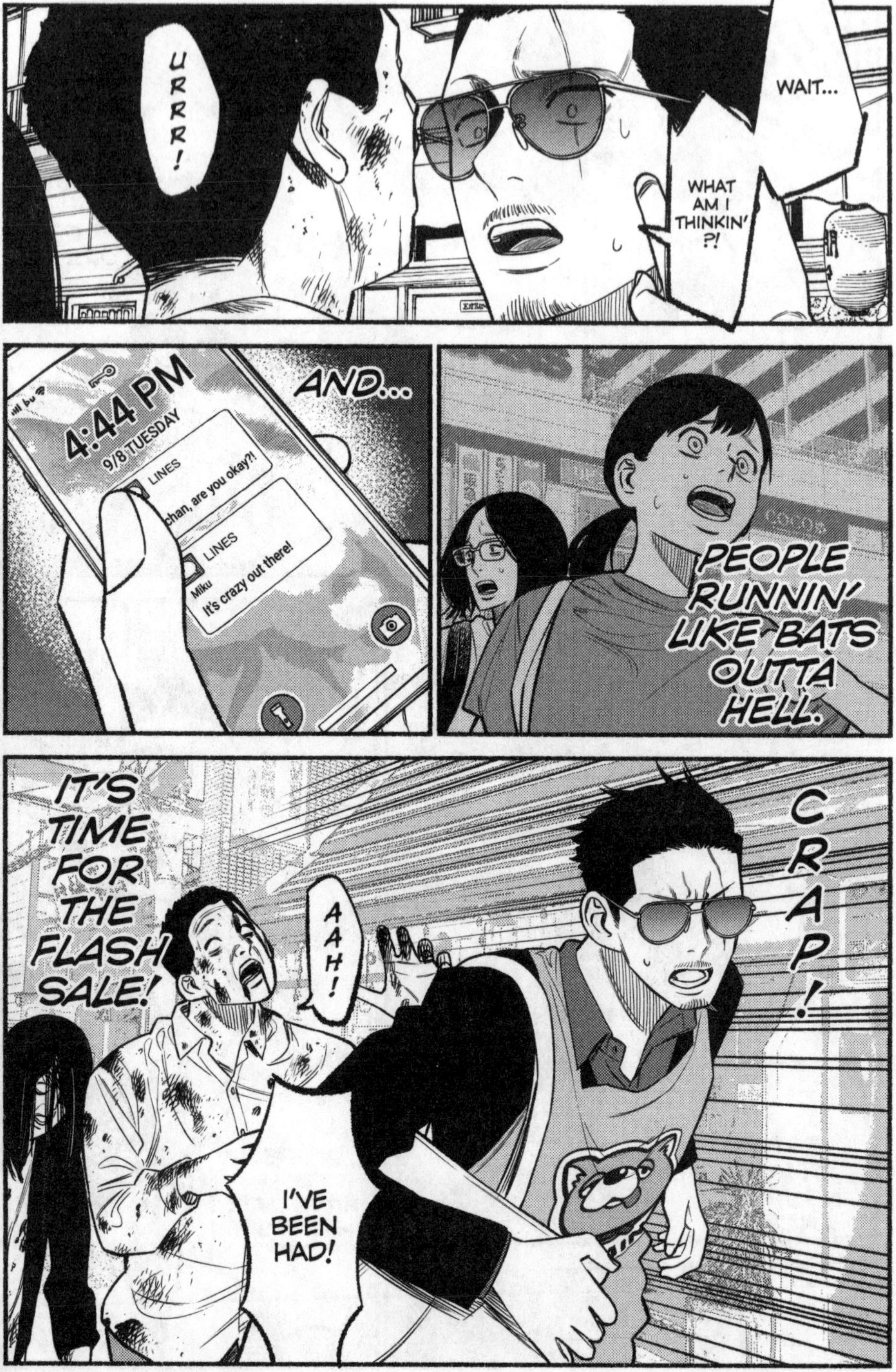
WAIT...
WHAT AM I THINKIN'?!
URRR!
PEOPLE RUNNIN' LIKE BATS OUTTA HELL.
AND...
4:44 PM
9/8 TUESDAY
LINES
chan, are you okay?!
LINES
Miku
It's crazy out there!
CRAP!
AAH!
IT'S TIME FOR THE FLASH SALE!
I'VE BEEN HAD!

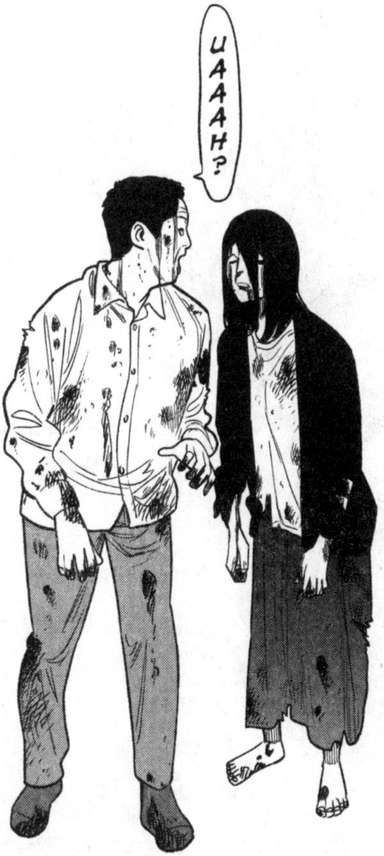
UAAAAH?

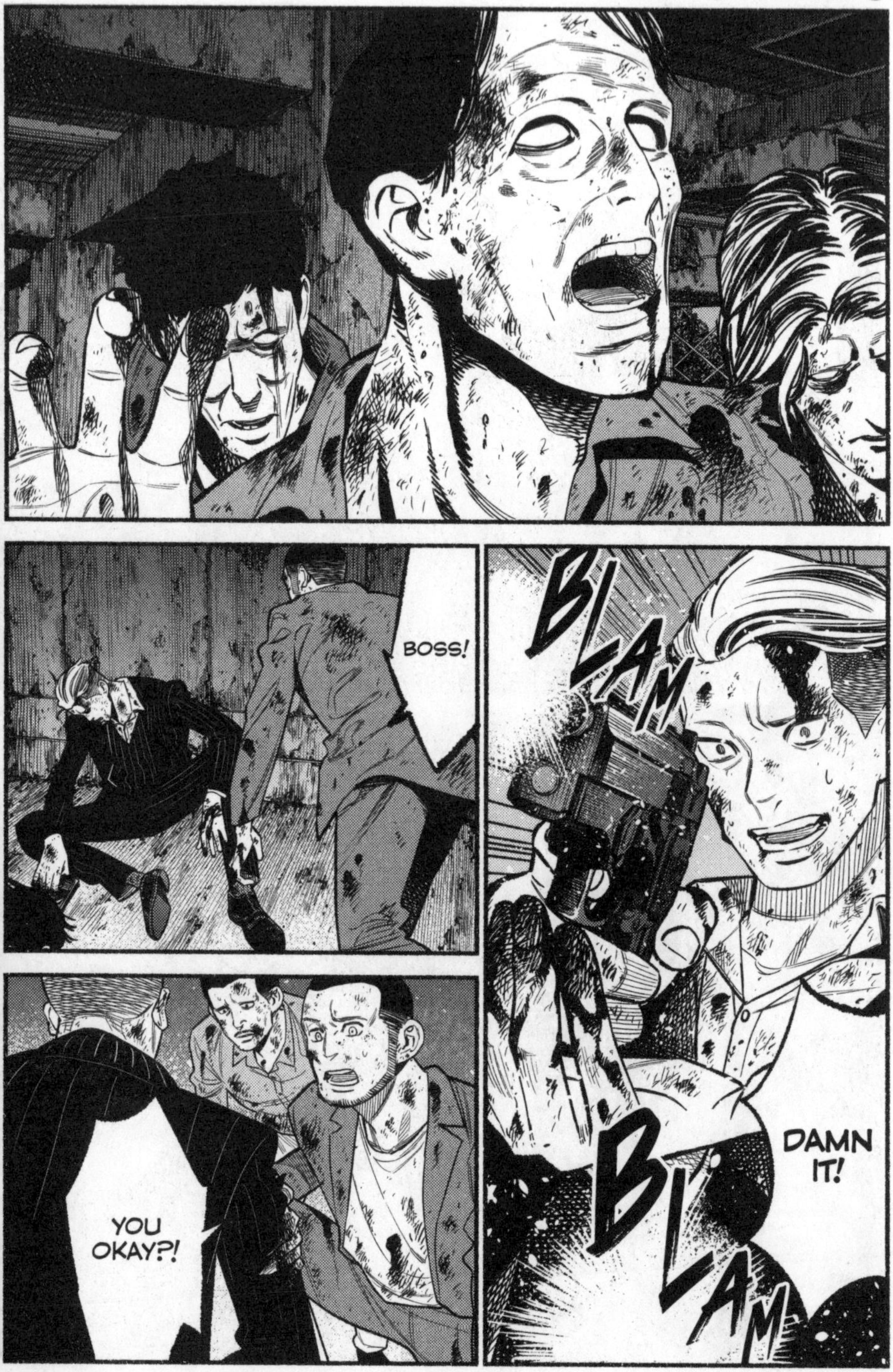
BLAM
DAMN IT!
BLAM
BOSS!
YOU OKAY?!

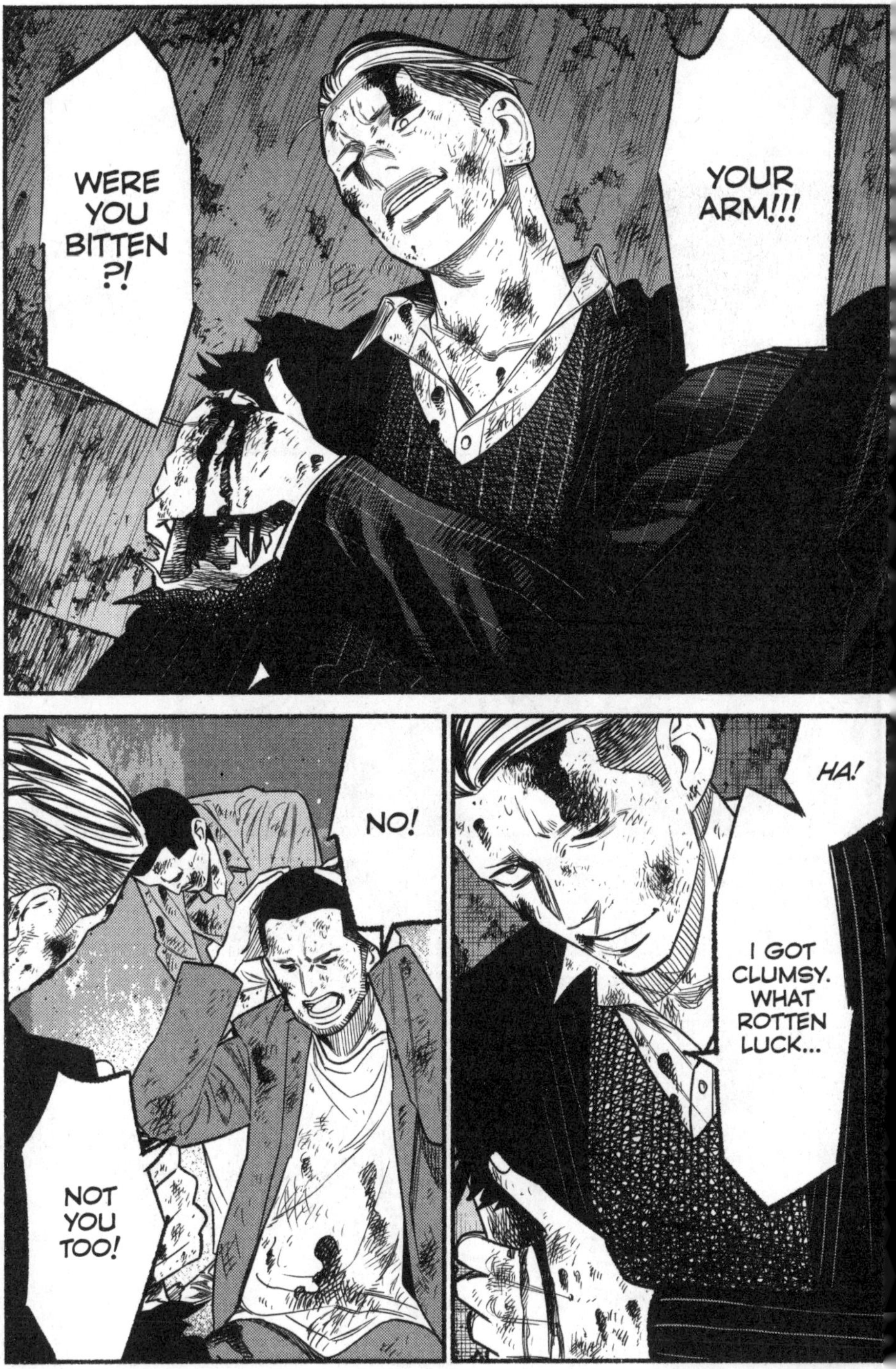
YOUR ARM!!!
WERE YOU BITTEN ?!
HA!
I GOT CLUMSY. WHAT ROTTEN LUCK...
NO!
NOT YOU TOO!

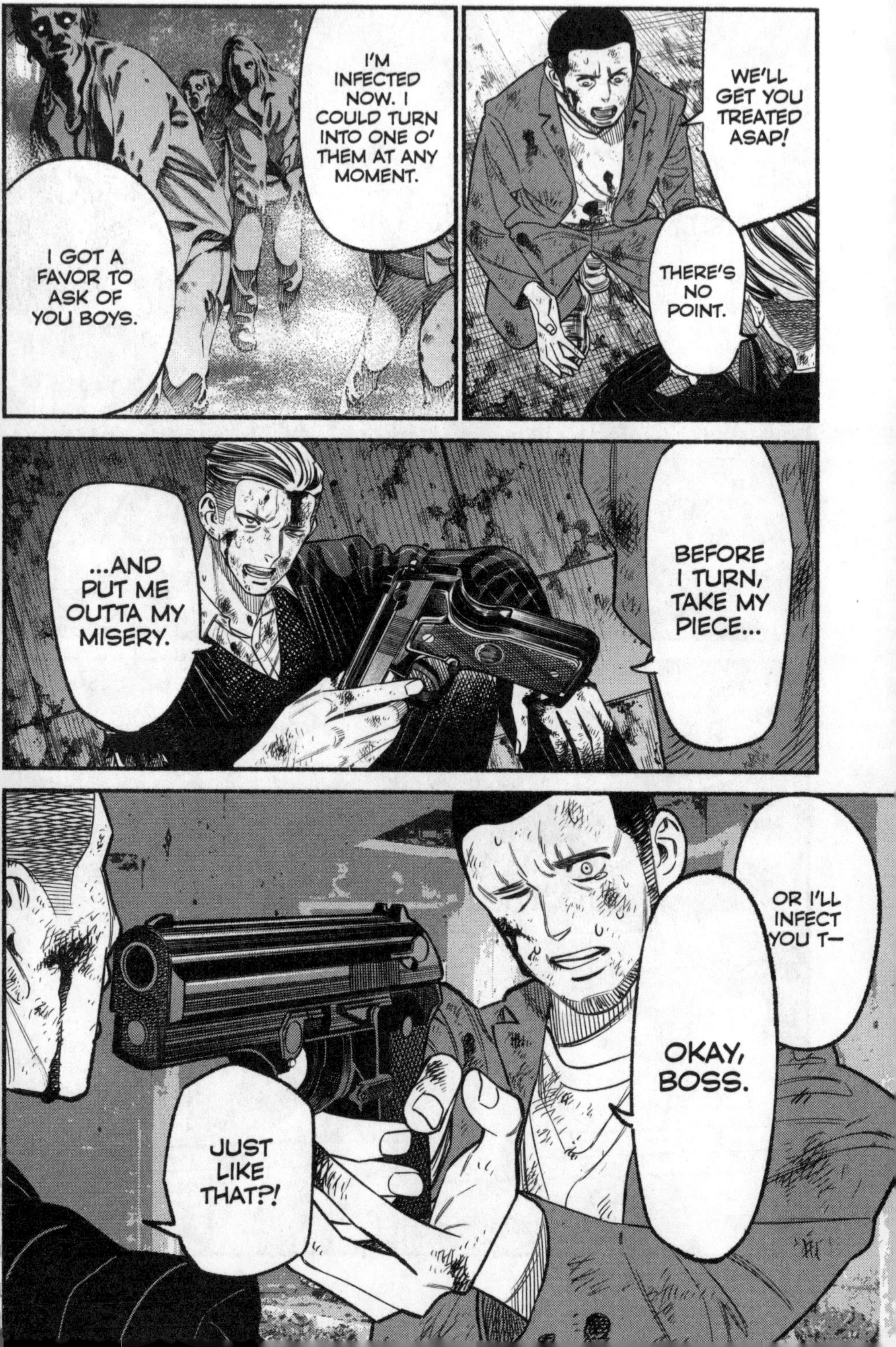
WE'LL GET YOU TREATED ASAP!
THERE'S NO POINT.
I'M INFECTED NOW. I COULD TURN INTO ONE O' THEM AT ANY MOMENT.
I GOT A FAVOR TO ASK OF YOU BOYS.
BEFORE I TURN, TAKE MY PIECE...
...AND PUT ME OUTTA MY MISERY.
OR I'LL INFECT YOU T—
OKAY, BOSS.
JUST LIKE THAT?!

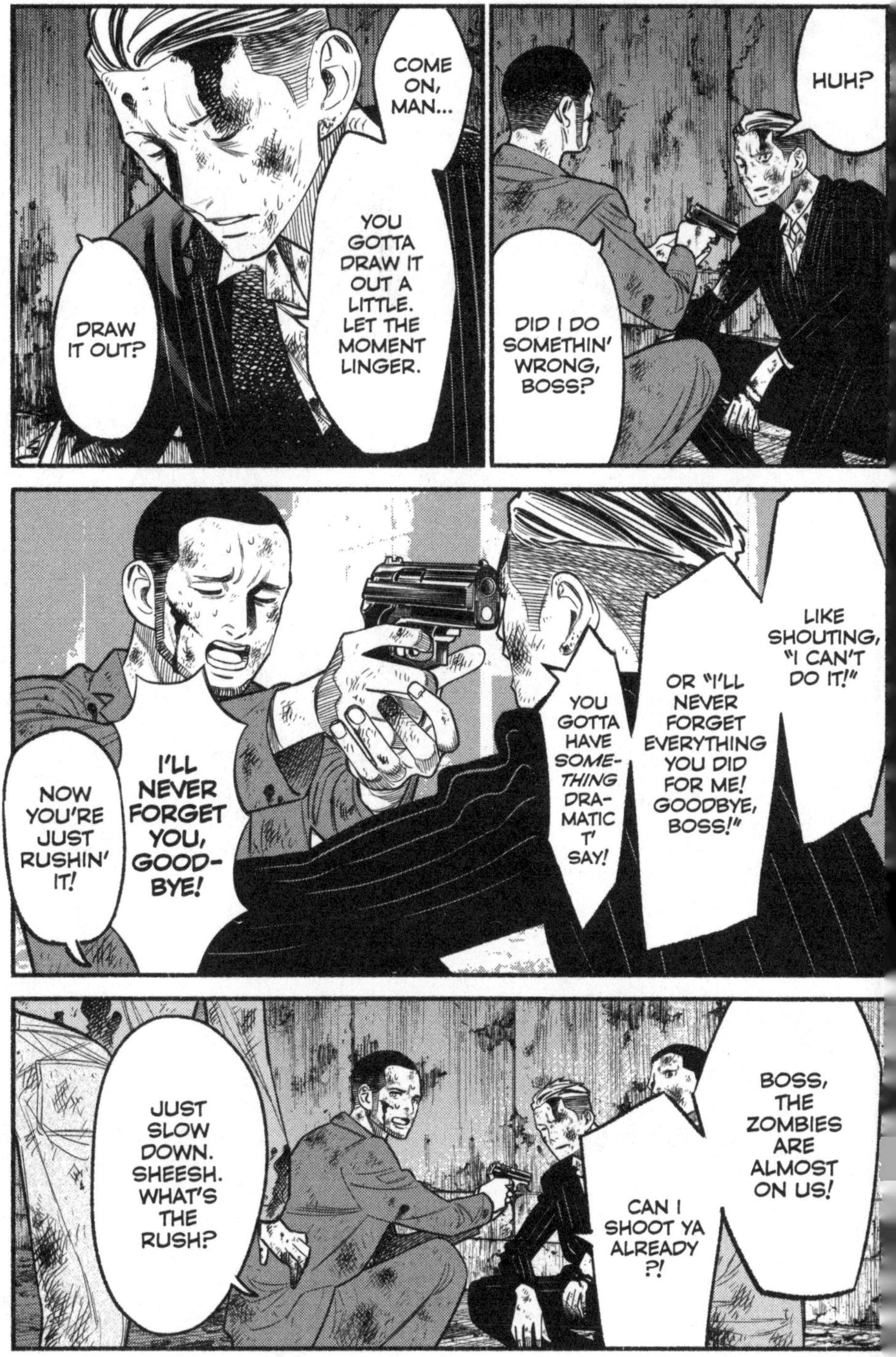
HUH?
DID I DO SOMETHIN' WRONG, BOSS?
COME ON, MAN...
YOU GOTTA DRAW IT OUT A LITTLE. LET THE MOMENT LINGER.
DRAW IT OUT?
LIKE SHOUTING, "I CAN'T DO IT!"
OR "I'LL NEVER FORGET EVERYTHING YOU DID FOR ME! GOODBYE, BOSS!"
YOU GOTTA HAVE *SOMETHING* DRAMATIC T' SAY!
I'LL NEVER FORGET YOU, GOODBYE!
NOW YOU'RE JUST RUSHIN' IT!
BOSS, THE ZOMBIES ARE ALMOST ON US!
CAN I SHOOT YA ALREADY?!
JUST SLOW DOWN. SHEESH. WHAT'S THE RUSH?

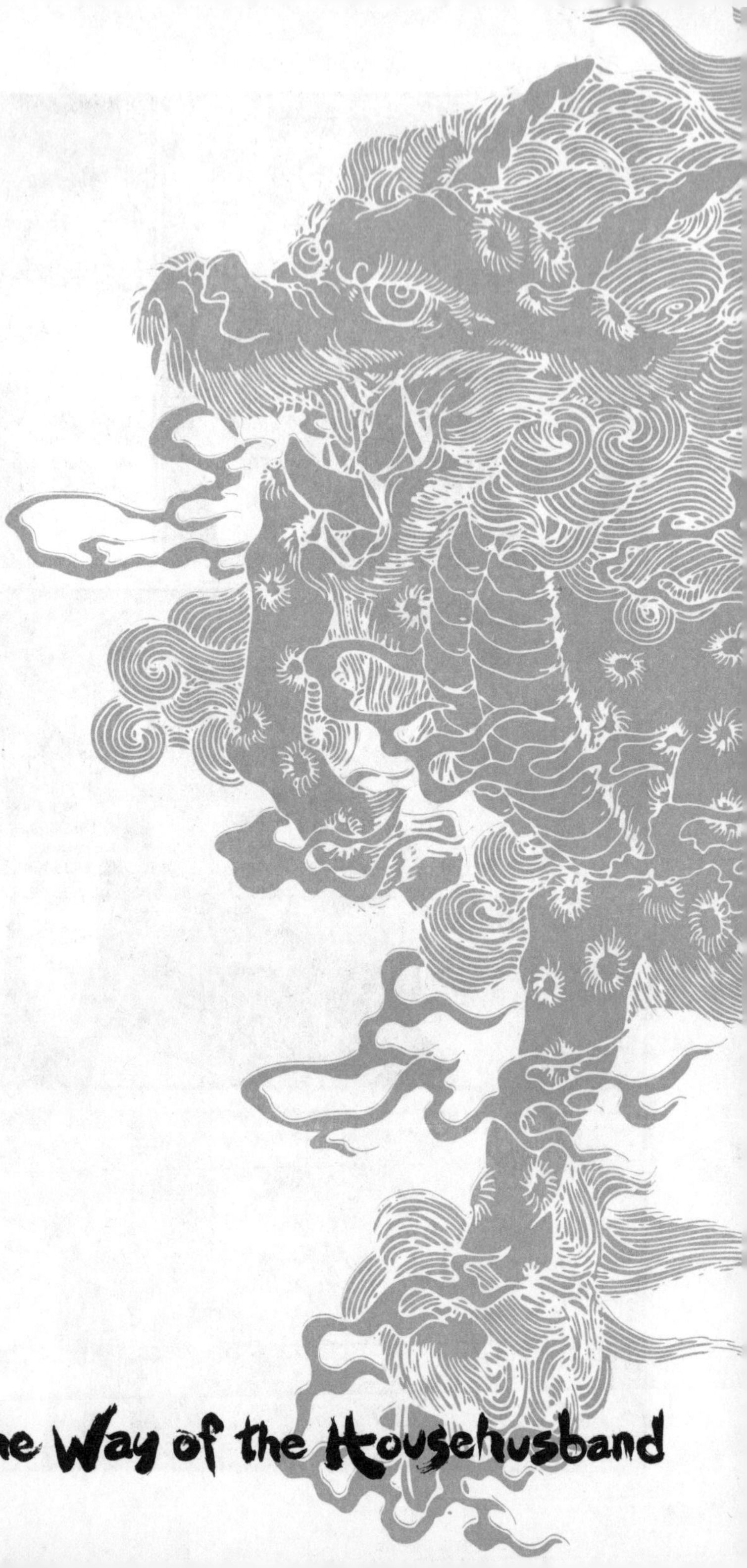

The Way of the Househusband

BONUS MANGA ③ MAMETARO

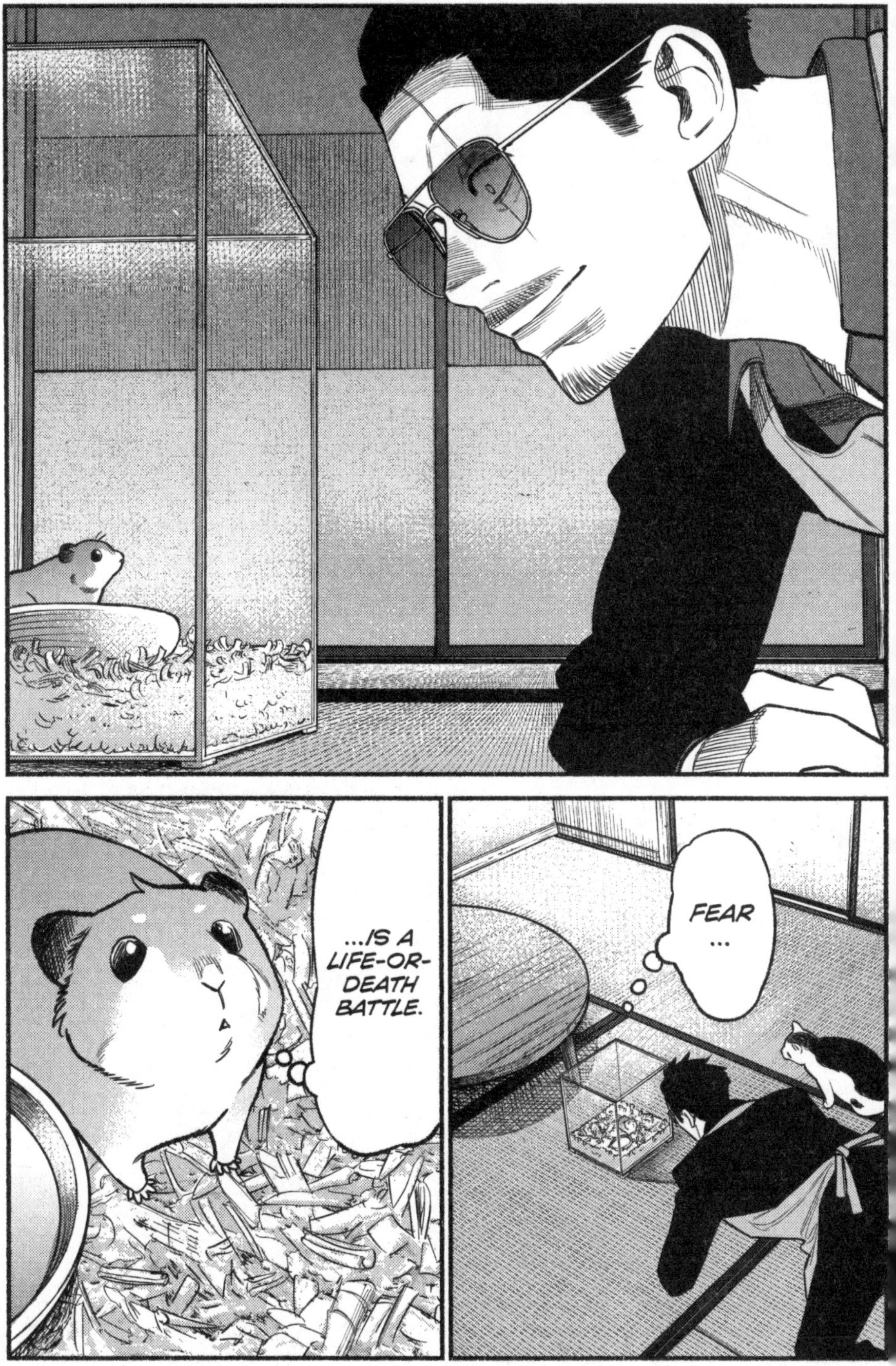
FEAR …
…IS A LIFE-OR-DEATH BATTLE.

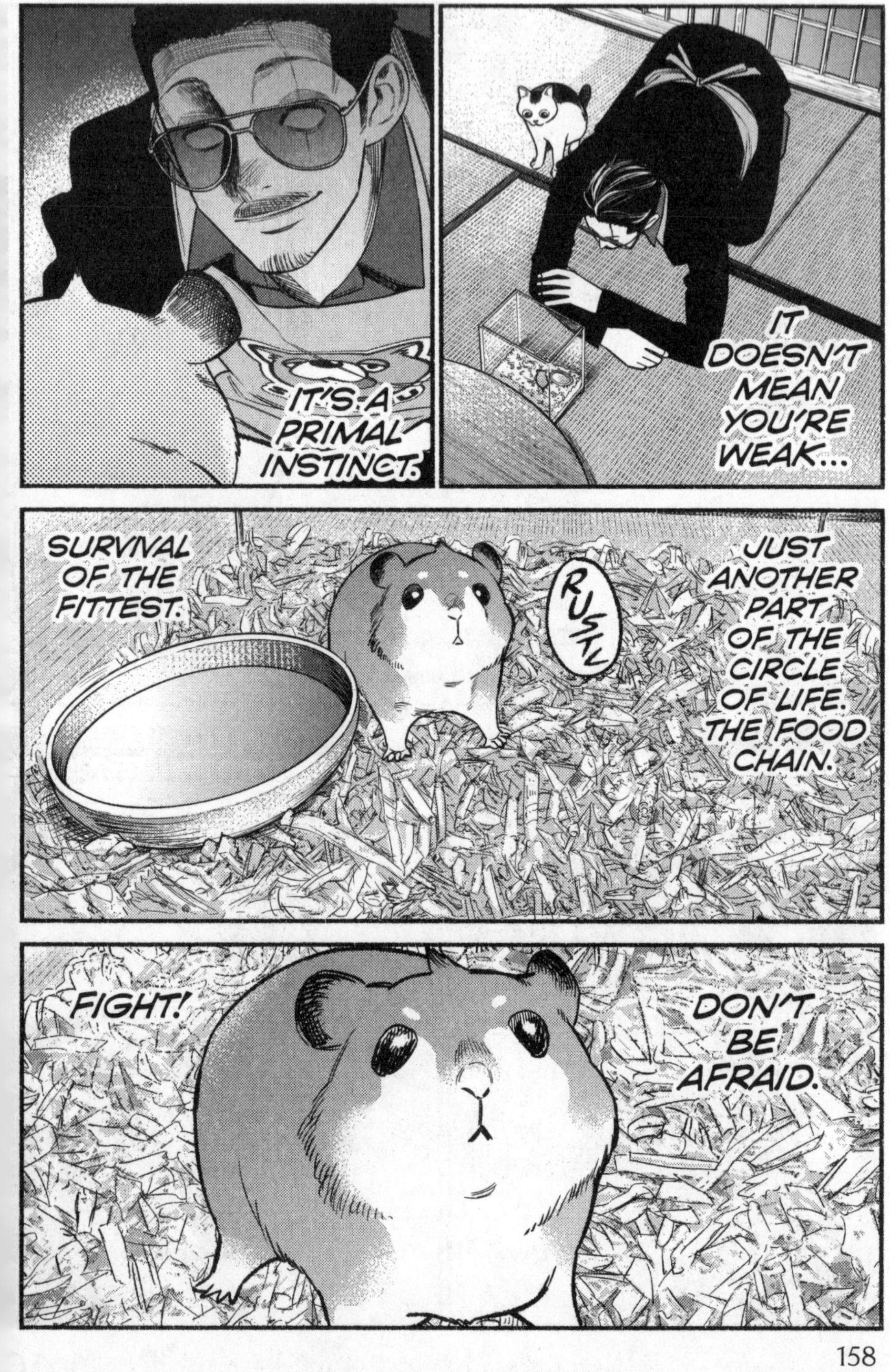
IT DOESN'T MEAN YOU'RE WEAK...
IT'S A PRIMAL INSTINCT.
JUST ANOTHER PART OF THE CIRCLE OF LIFE. THE FOOD CHAIN.
RUSTL
SURVIVAL OF THE FITTEST.
DON'T BE AFRAID.
FIGHT!

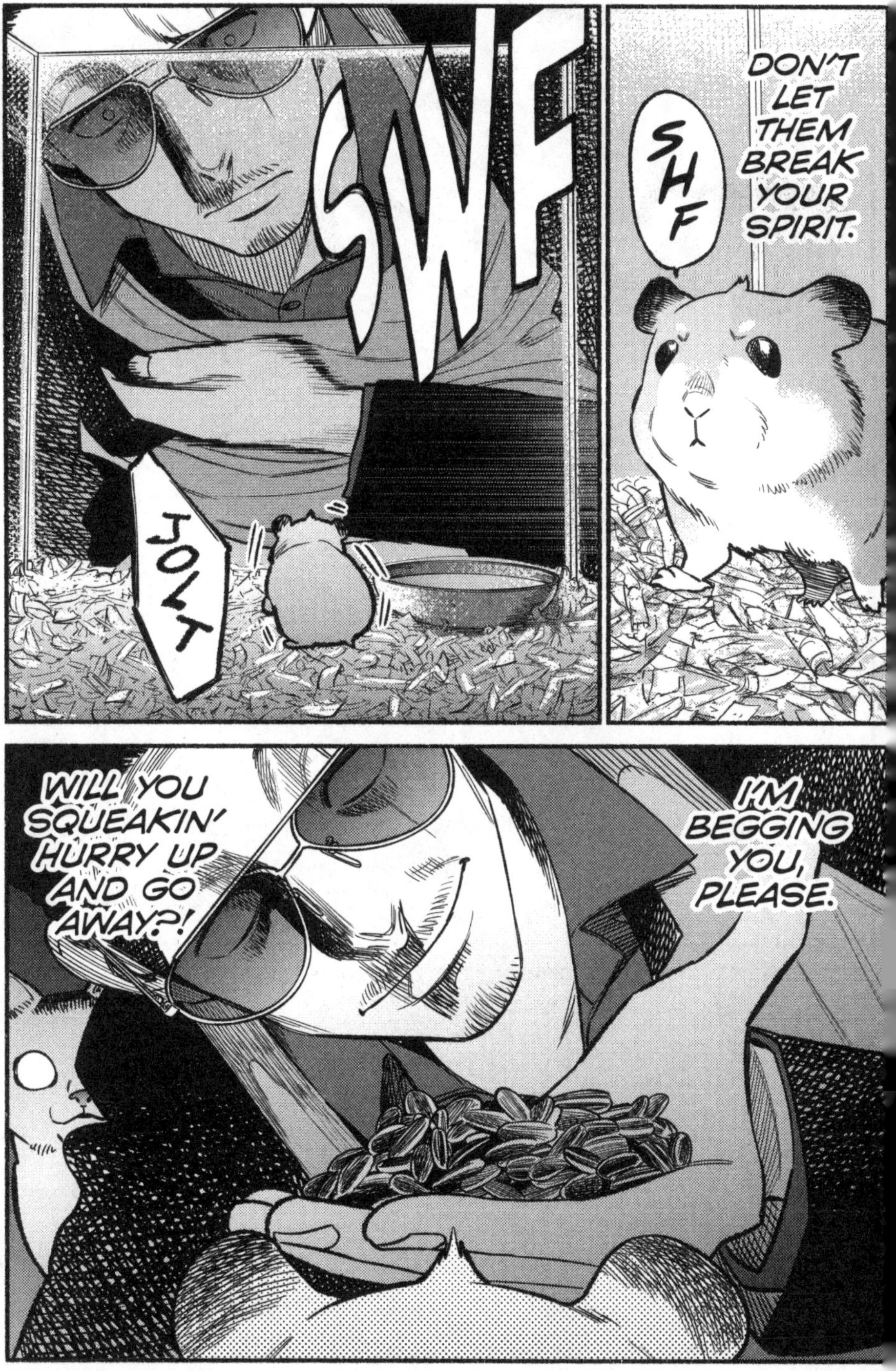
DON'T LET THEM BREAK YOUR SPIRIT.
SHF
SWF
JOLT
I'M BEGGING YOU, PLEASE.
WILL YOU SQUEAKIN' HURRY UP AND GO AWAY?!

DON'T GIVE UP, MAMETARO! THIS IS YOUR LAST STAND. DON'T MISS VOLUME 9!

STAFF-MIDORINO. KZK HELP-YOSHIDA. KIMURA. moac

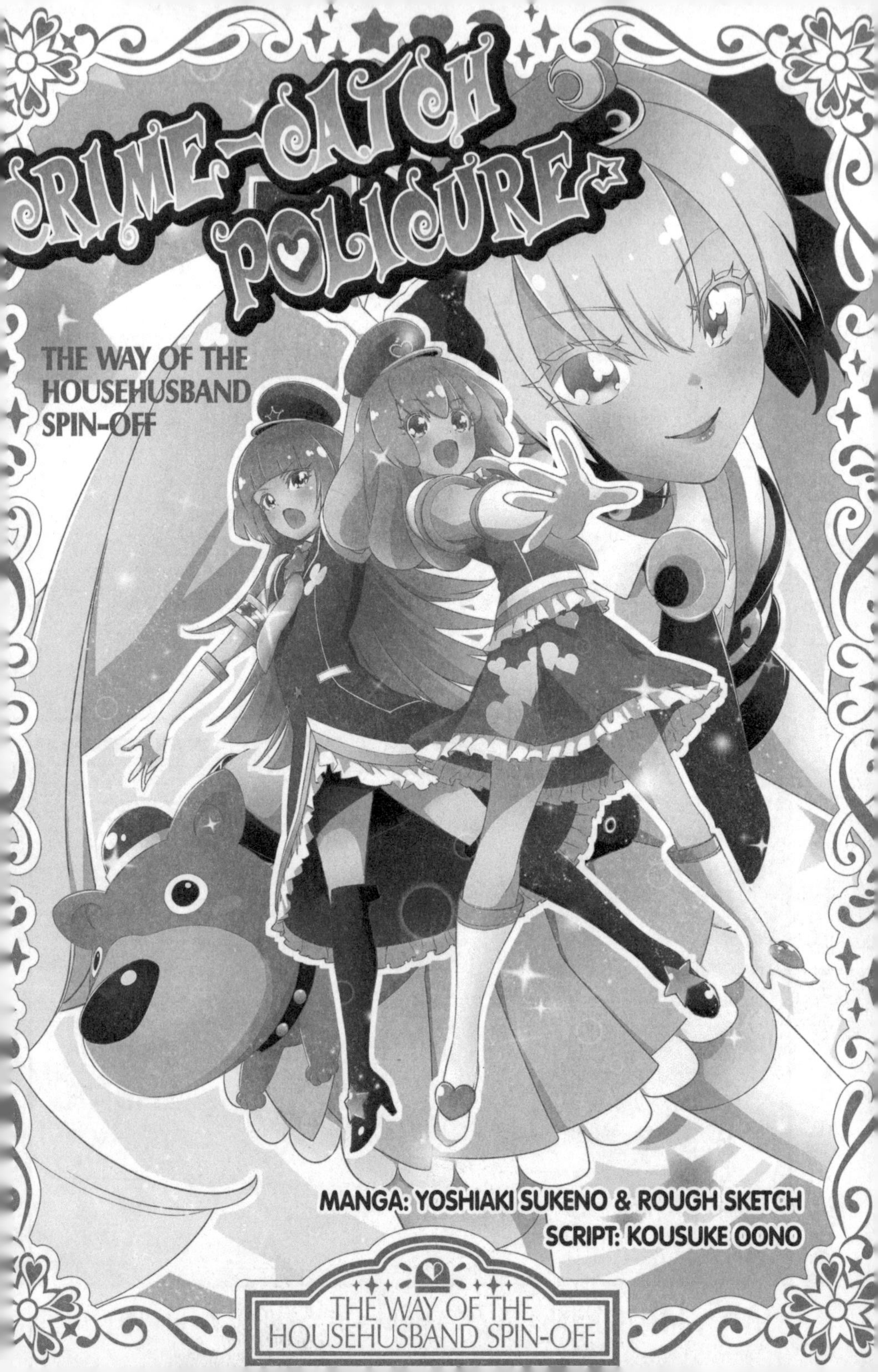
CRIME-CATCH POLICURE
THE WAY OF THE HOUSEHUSBAND SPIN-OFF
MANGA: YOSHIAKI SUKENO & ROUGH SKETCH
SCRIPT: KOUSUKE OONO
THE WAY OF THE HOUSEHUSBAND SPIN-OFF

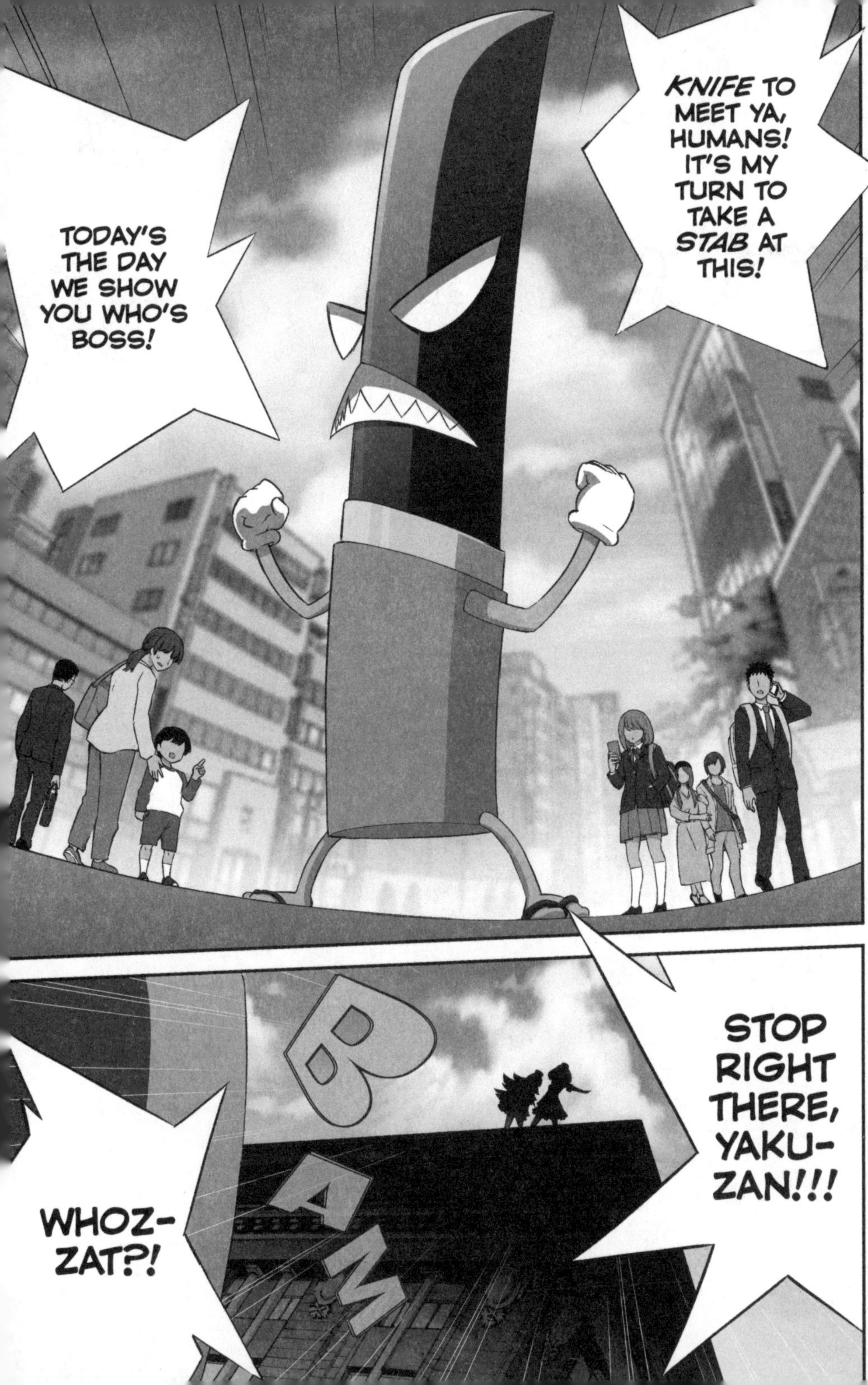
KNIFE TO MEET YA, HUMANS! IT'S MY TURN TO TAKE A STAB AT THIS!
TODAY'S THE DAY WE SHOW YOU WHO'S BOSS!
STOP RIGHT THERE, YAKU-ZAN!!!
BAM
WHOZ-ZAT?!

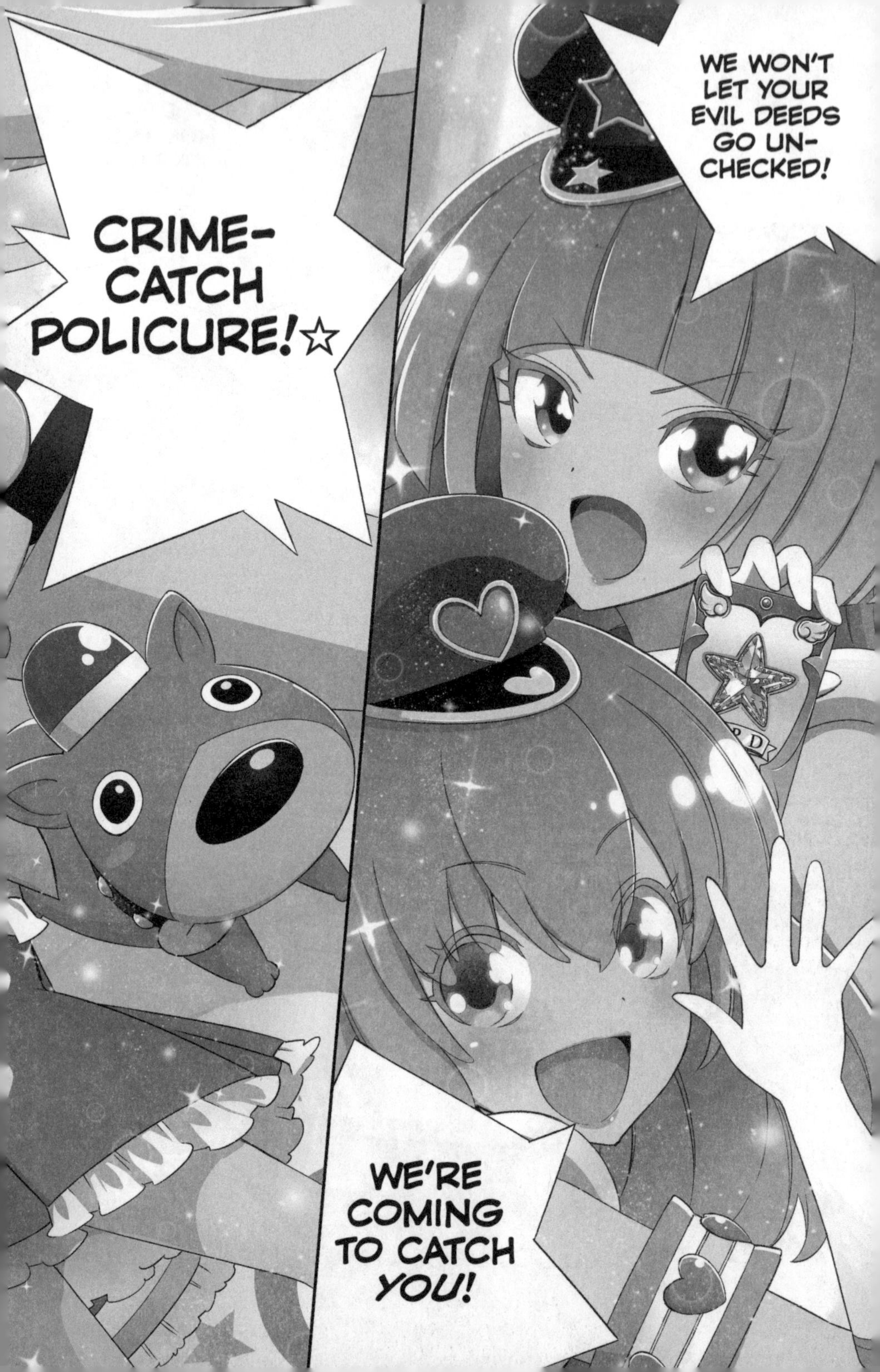
WE WON'T LET YOUR EVIL DEEDS GO UN-CHECKED!
WE'RE COMING TO CATCH YOU!
CRIME-CATCH POLICURE!☆

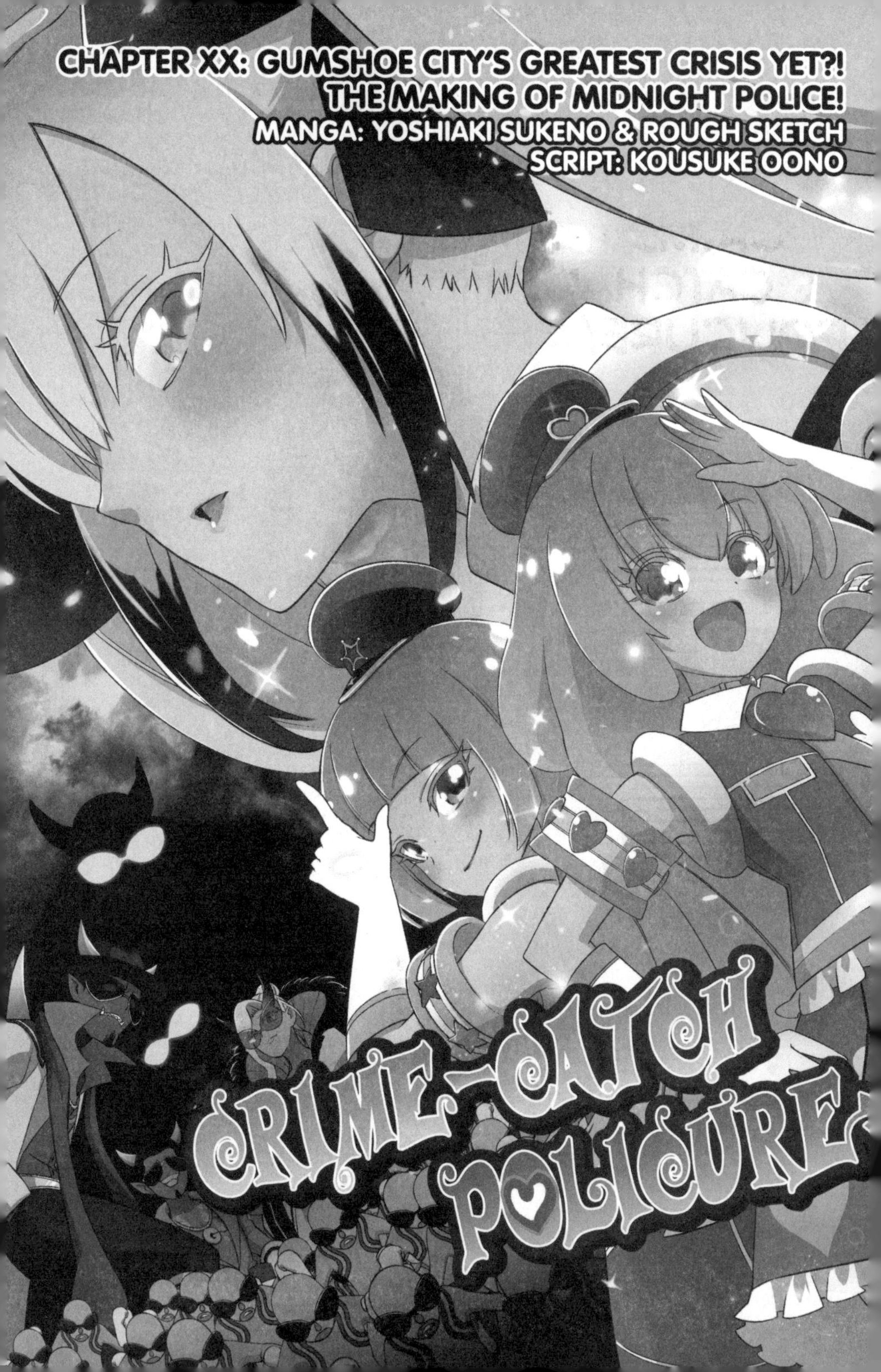
CHAPTER XX: GUMSHOE CITY'S GREATEST CRISIS YET?!
THE MAKING OF MIDNIGHT POLICE!
MANGA: YOSHIAKI SUKENO & ROUGH SKETCH
SCRIPT: KOUSUKE OONO
CRIME-CATCH POLICURE!

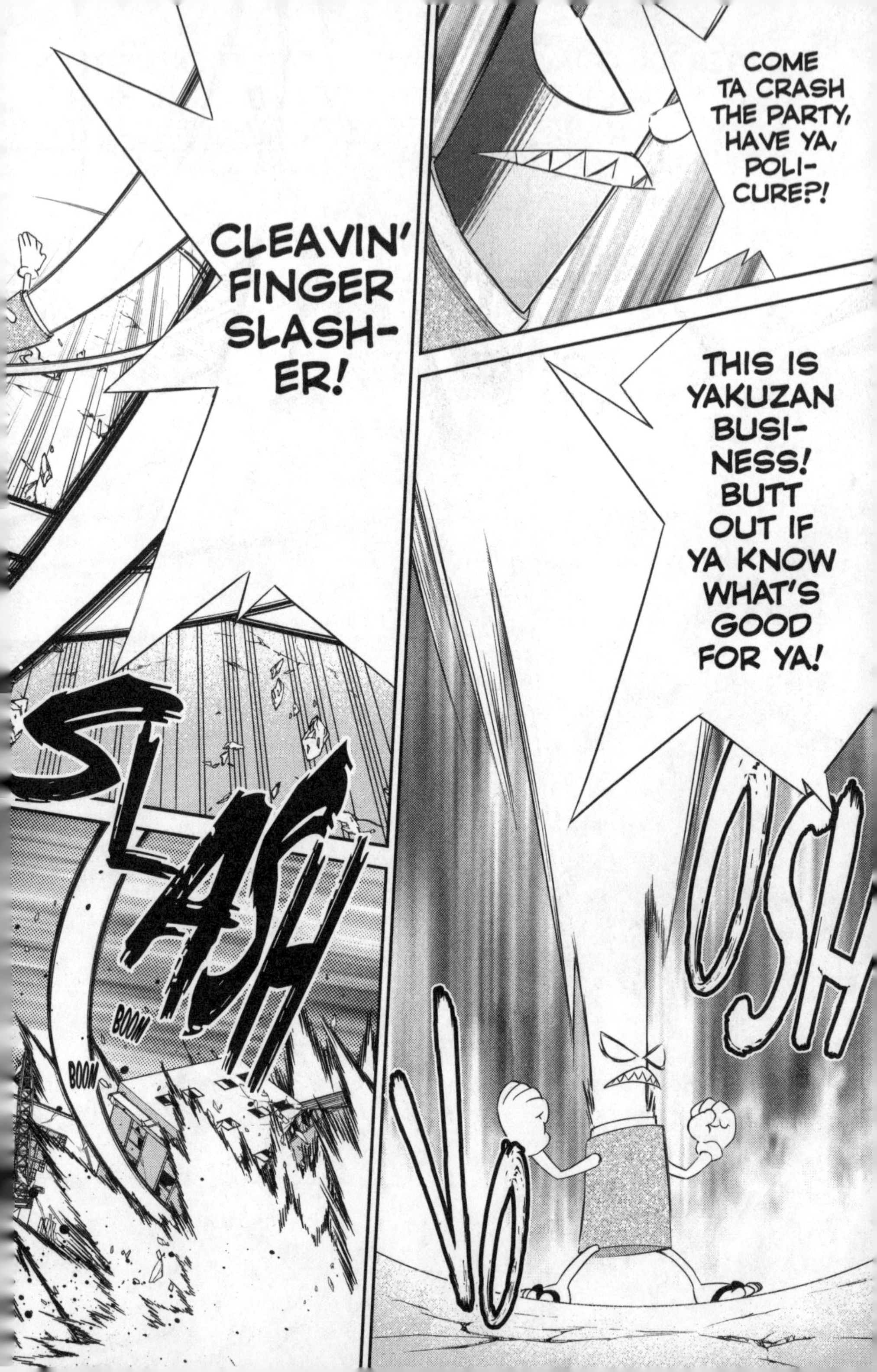
COME TA CRASH THE PARTY, HAVE YA, POLI-CURE?!
THIS IS YAKUZAN BUSI-NESS! BUTT OUT IF YA KNOW WHAT'S GOOD FOR YA!
VOOSH
CLEAVIN' FINGER SLASH-ER!
SLASH
BOOM
BOOM

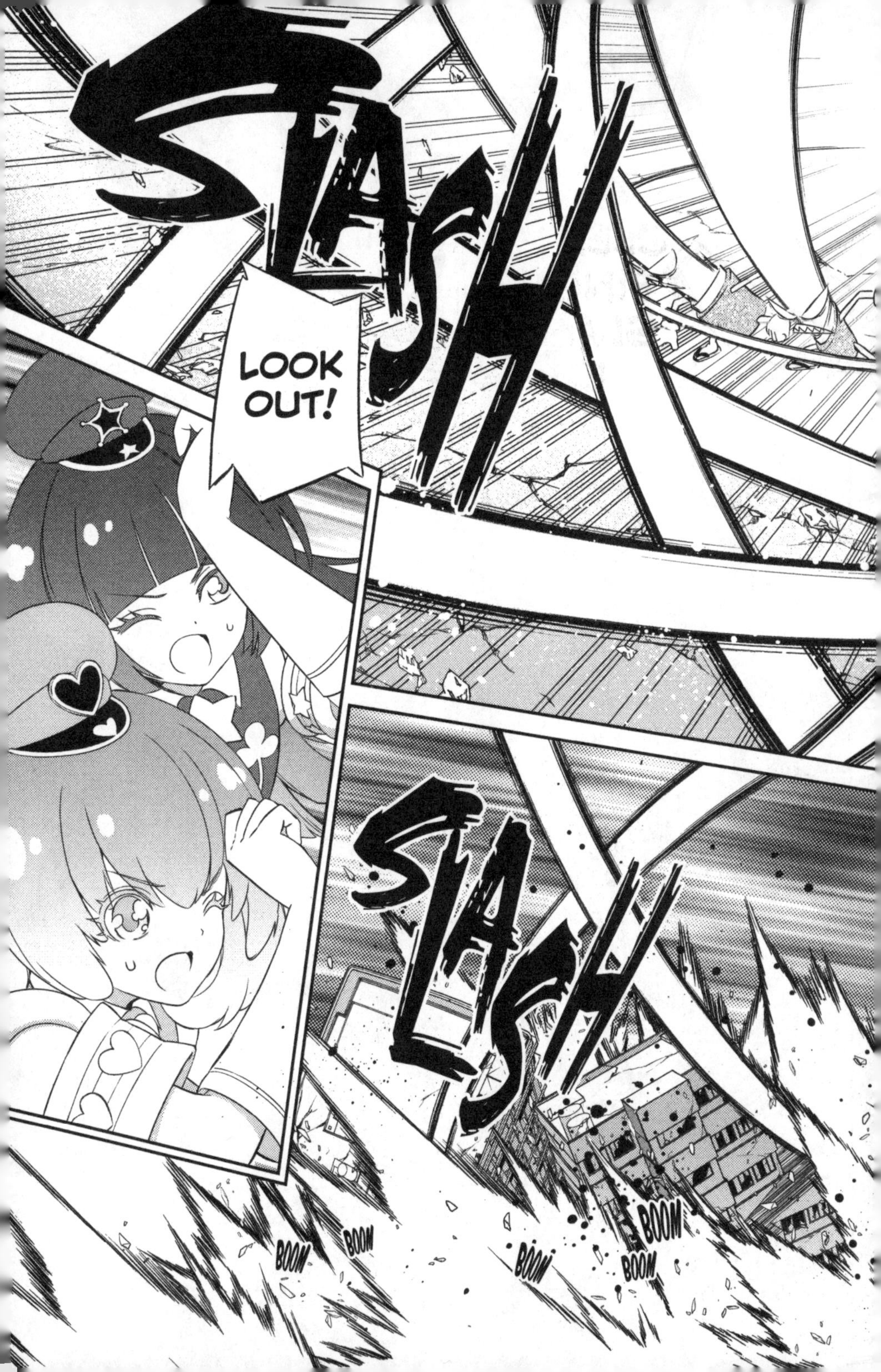
SLASH
LOOK OUT!
SLASH
BOOM
BOOM
BOOM
BOOM
BOOM

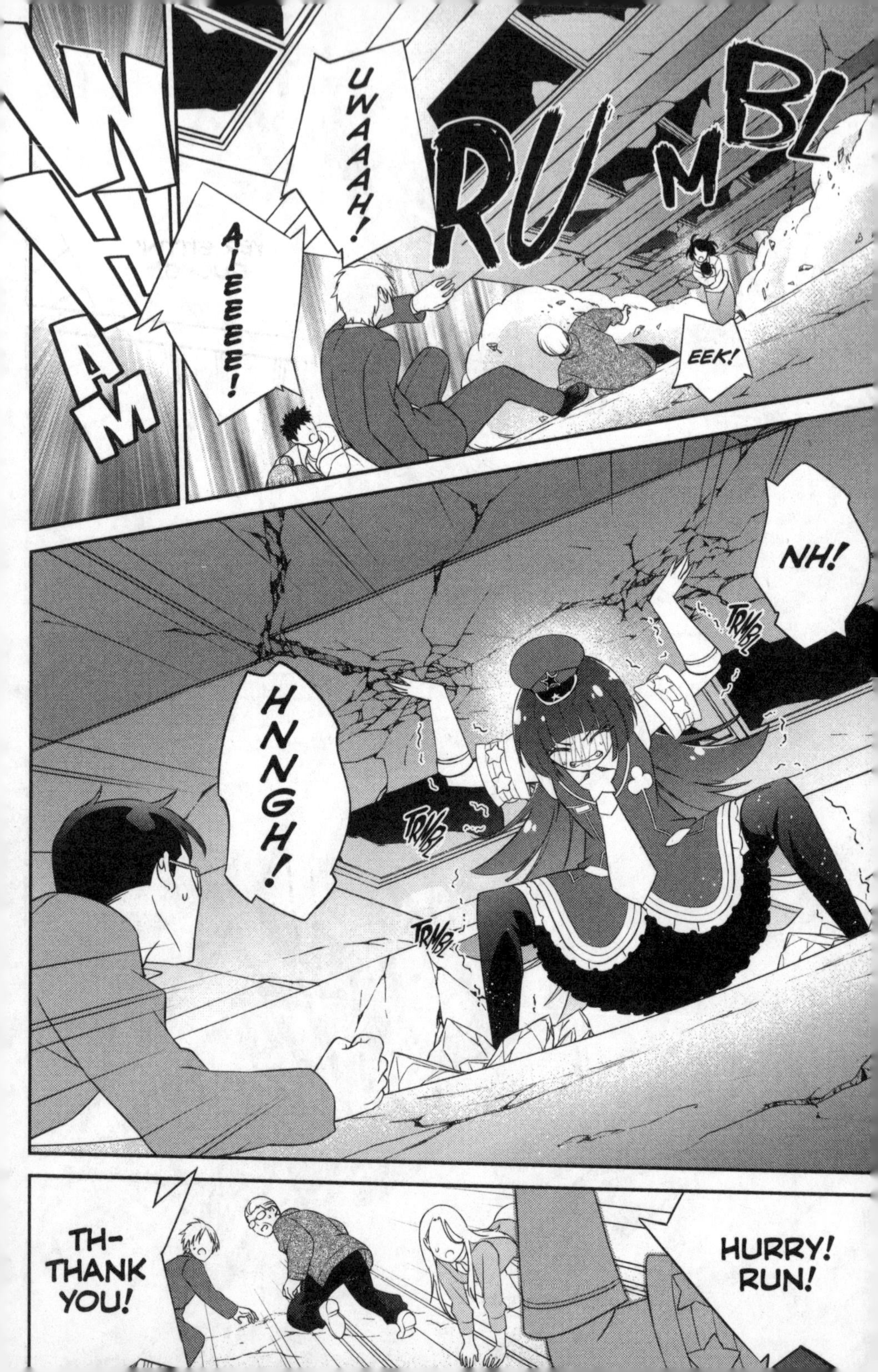
RUMBL
UWAAAH!
EEK!
AIEEEEE!
WHAM
NH!
TRMBL
HNNGH!
TRMBL
TRMBL
HURRY! RUN!
TH-THANK YOU!

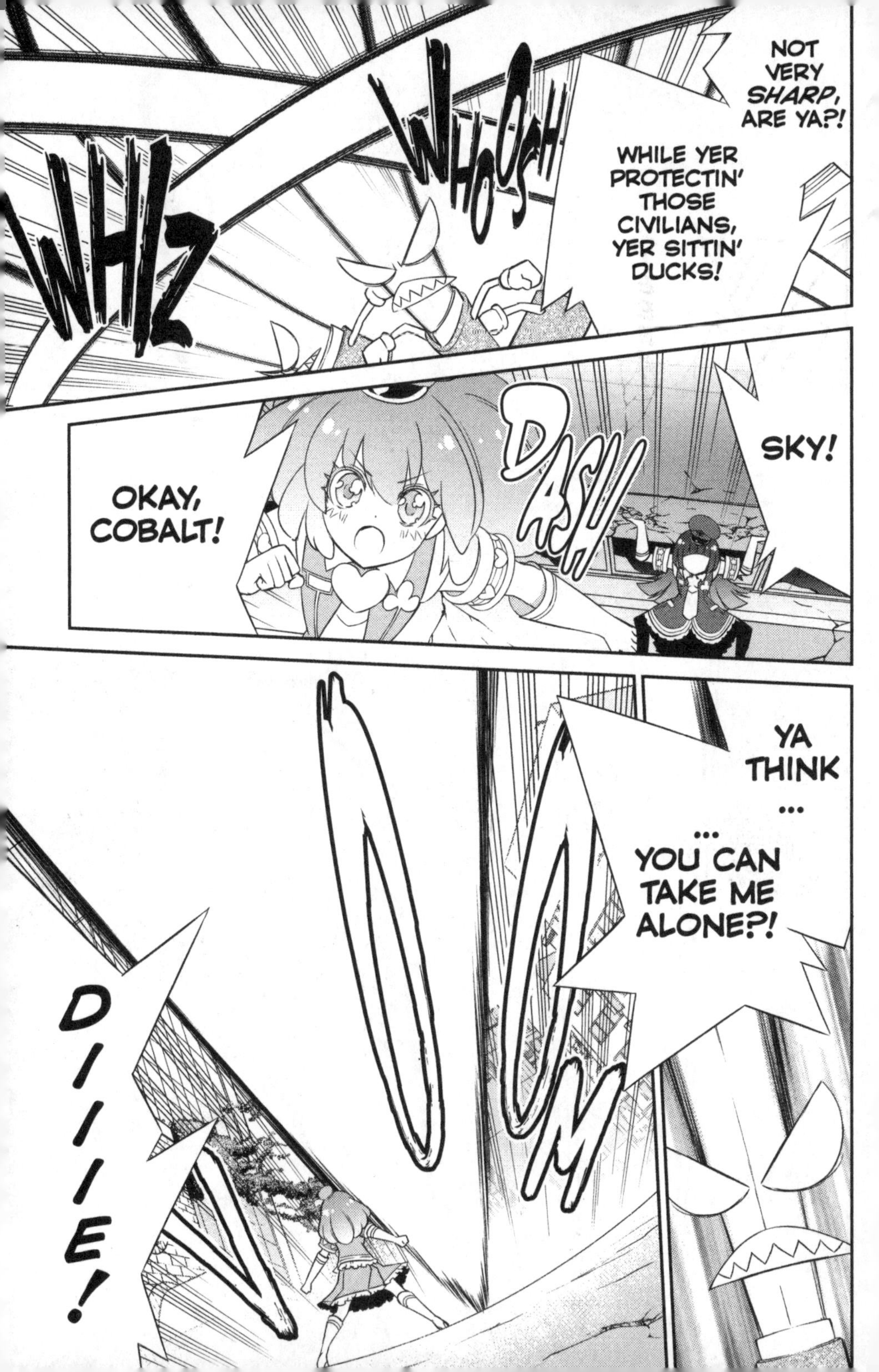
NOT VERY SHARP, ARE YA?!
WHILE YER PROTECTIN' THOSE CIVILIANS, YER SITTIN' DUCKS!
WHOOSH
WHIZ
SKY!
DASH
OKAY, COBALT!
YA THINK...
...YOU CAN TAKE ME ALONE?!
DIIIE!

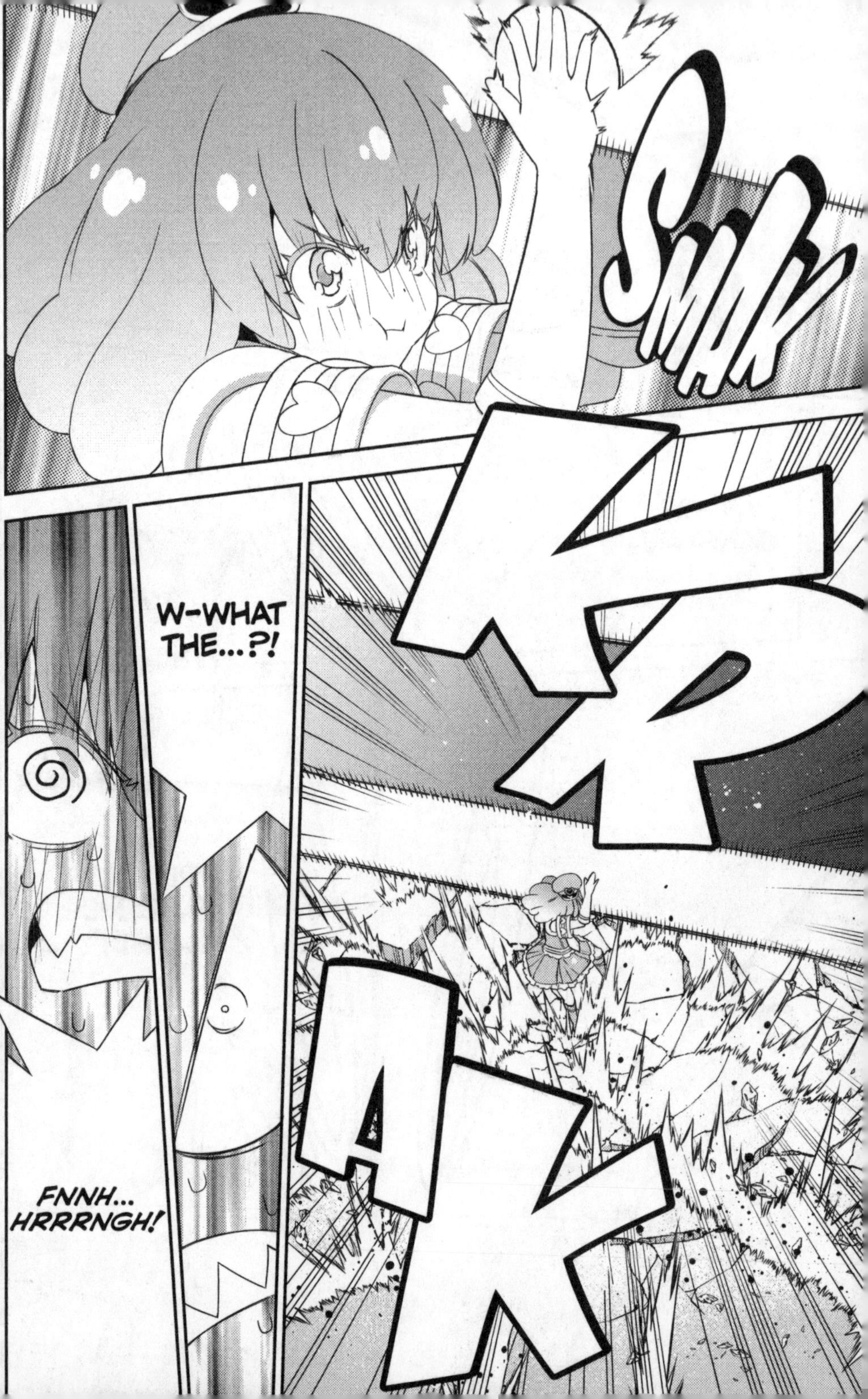
SMAK
KRAK
W-WHAT THE...?!
FNNH... HRRRNGH!

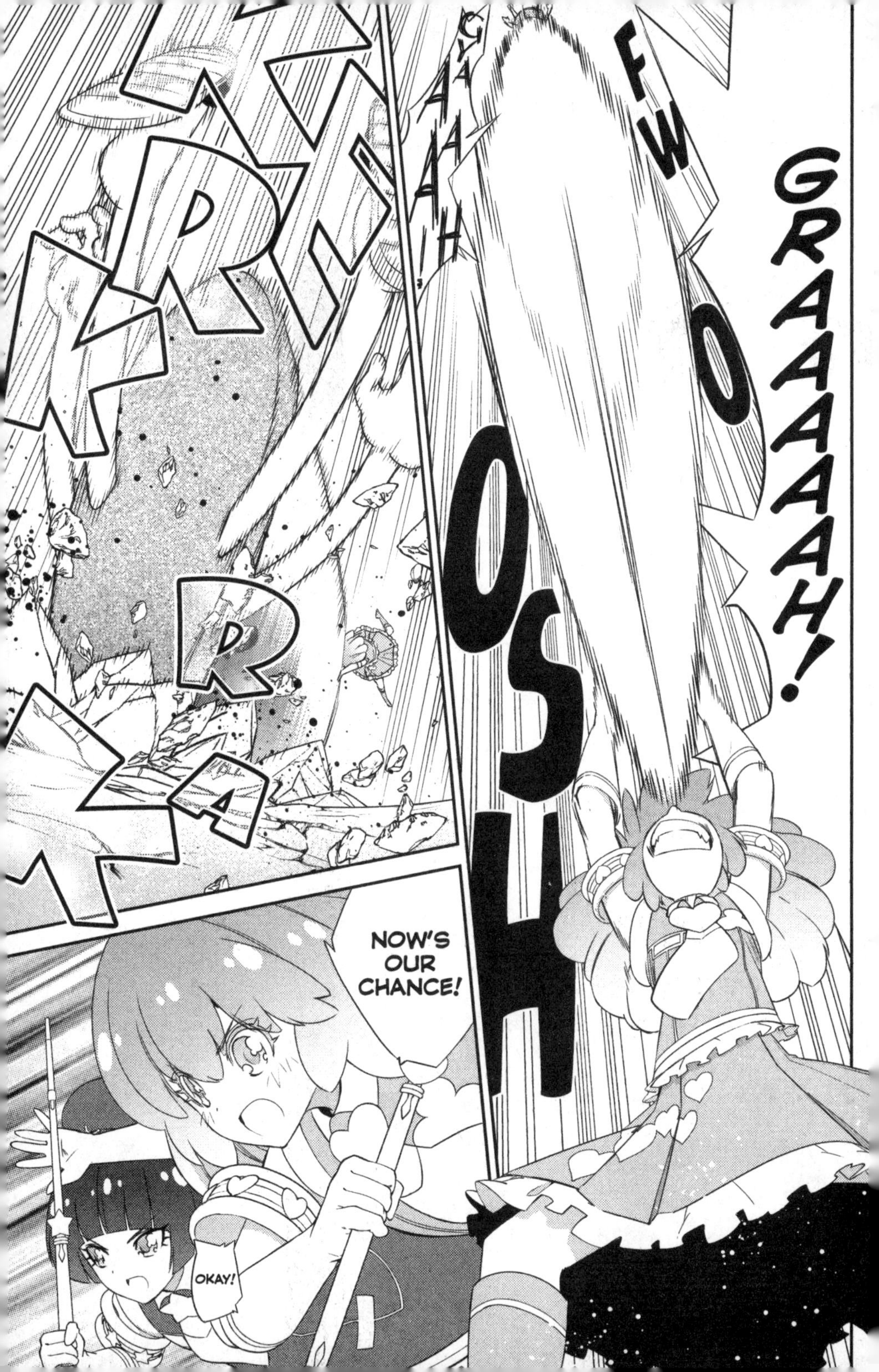
GRAAAAAH!
FWOOSH
GYAAAAH!
NOW'S OUR CHANCE!
OKAY!

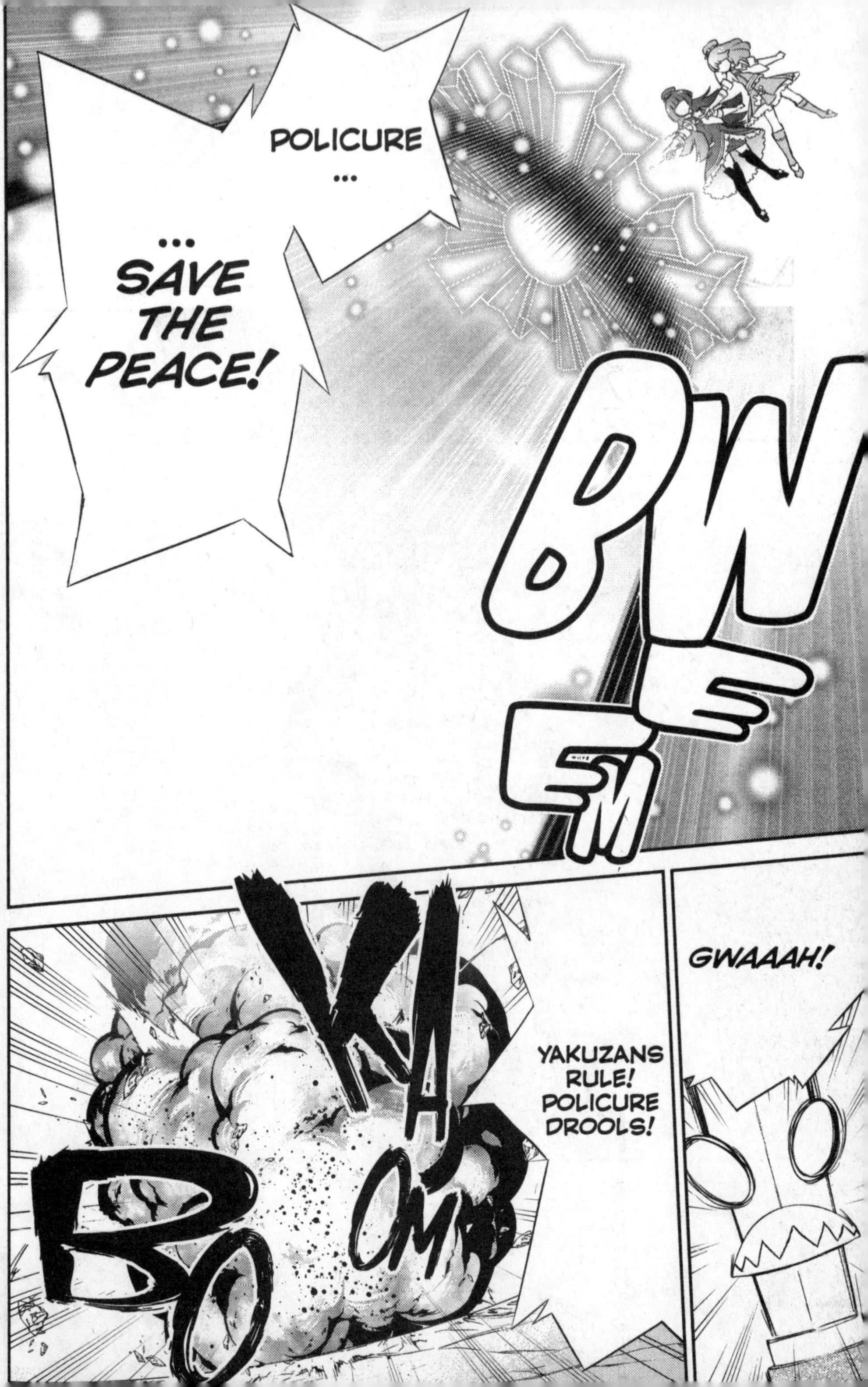
POLICURE
...
... SAVE THE PEACE!
GWAAAH!
YAKUZANS RULE! POLICURE DROOLS!
KABOOM

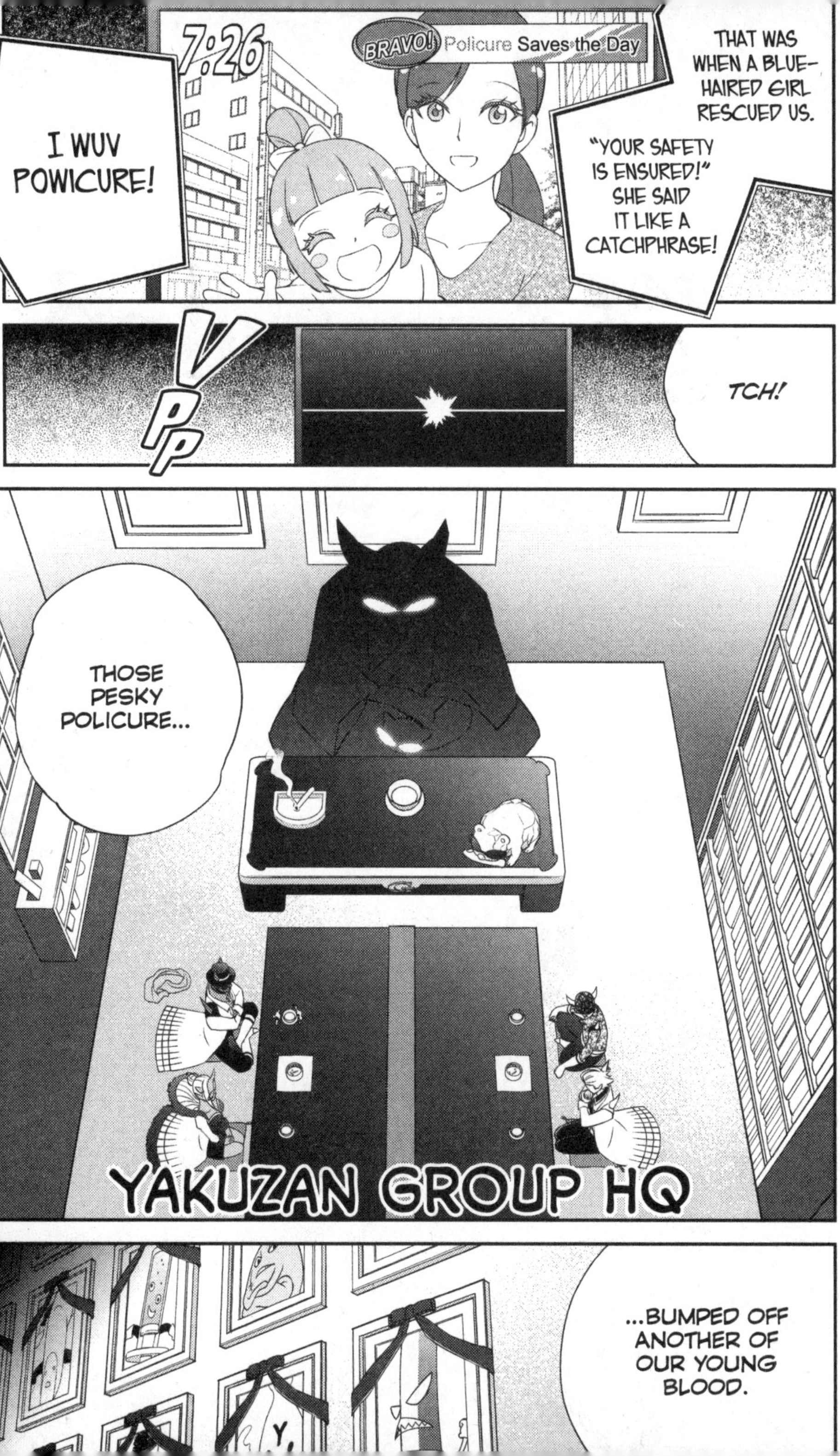
THAT WAS WHEN A BLUE-HAIRED GIRL RESCUED US.
"YOUR SAFETY IS ENSURED!" SHE SAID IT LIKE A CATCHPHRASE!
BRAVO! Policure Saves the Day
7:26
I WUV POWICURE!
TCH!
VPP
THOSE PESKY POLICURE...
YAKUZAN GROUP HQ
...BUMPED OFF ANOTHER OF OUR YOUNG BLOOD.

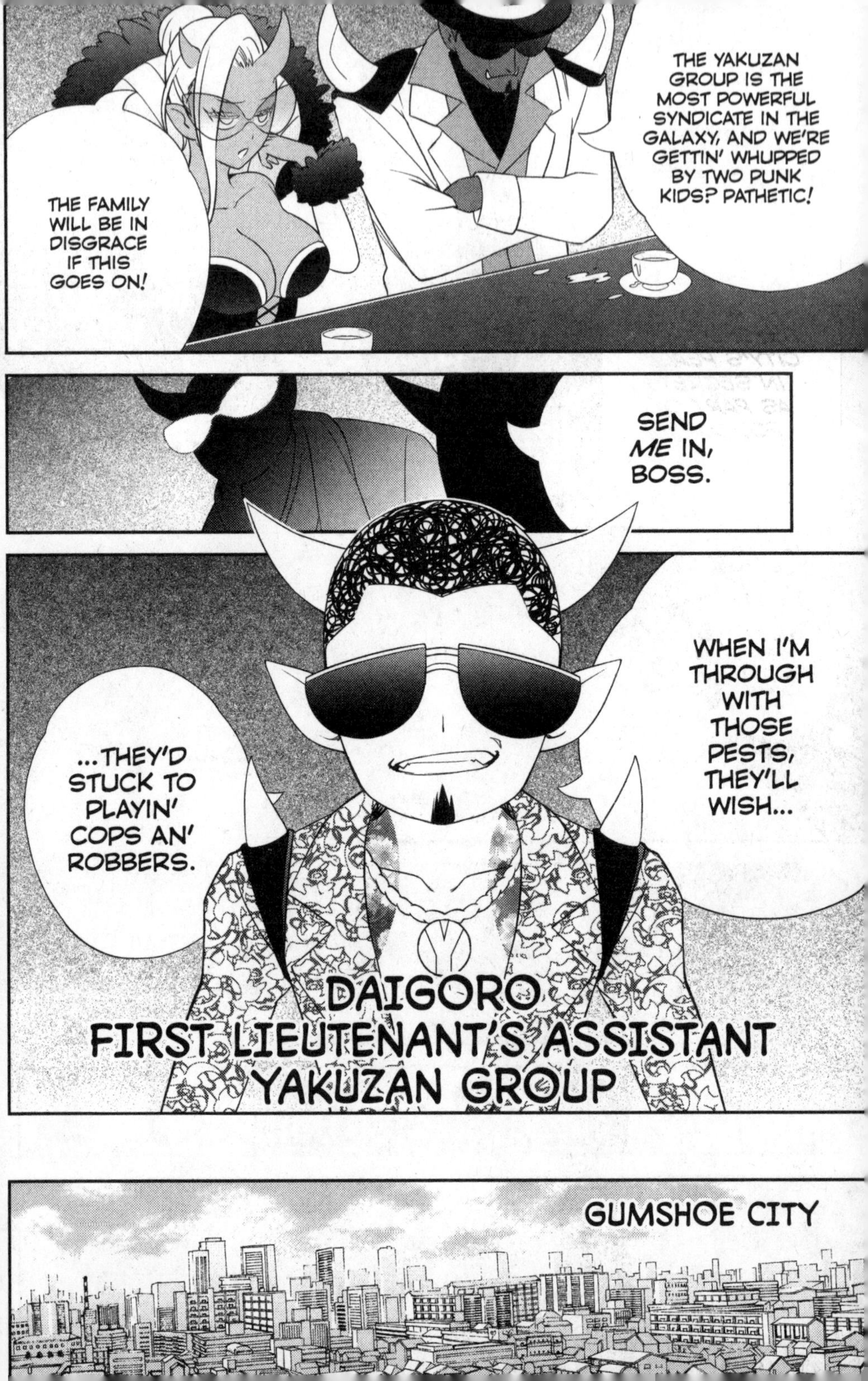
THE YAKUZAN GROUP IS THE MOST POWERFUL SYNDICATE IN THE GALAXY, AND WE'RE GETTIN' WHUPPED BY TWO PUNK KIDS? PATHETIC!
THE FAMILY WILL BE IN DISGRACE IF THIS GOES ON!
SEND *ME* IN, BOSS.
WHEN I'M THROUGH WITH THOSE PESTS, THEY'LL WISH...
...THEY'D STUCK TO PLAYIN' COPS AN' ROBBERS.
DAIGORO
FIRST LIEUTENANT'S ASSISTANT
YAKUZAN GROUP
GUMSHOE CITY

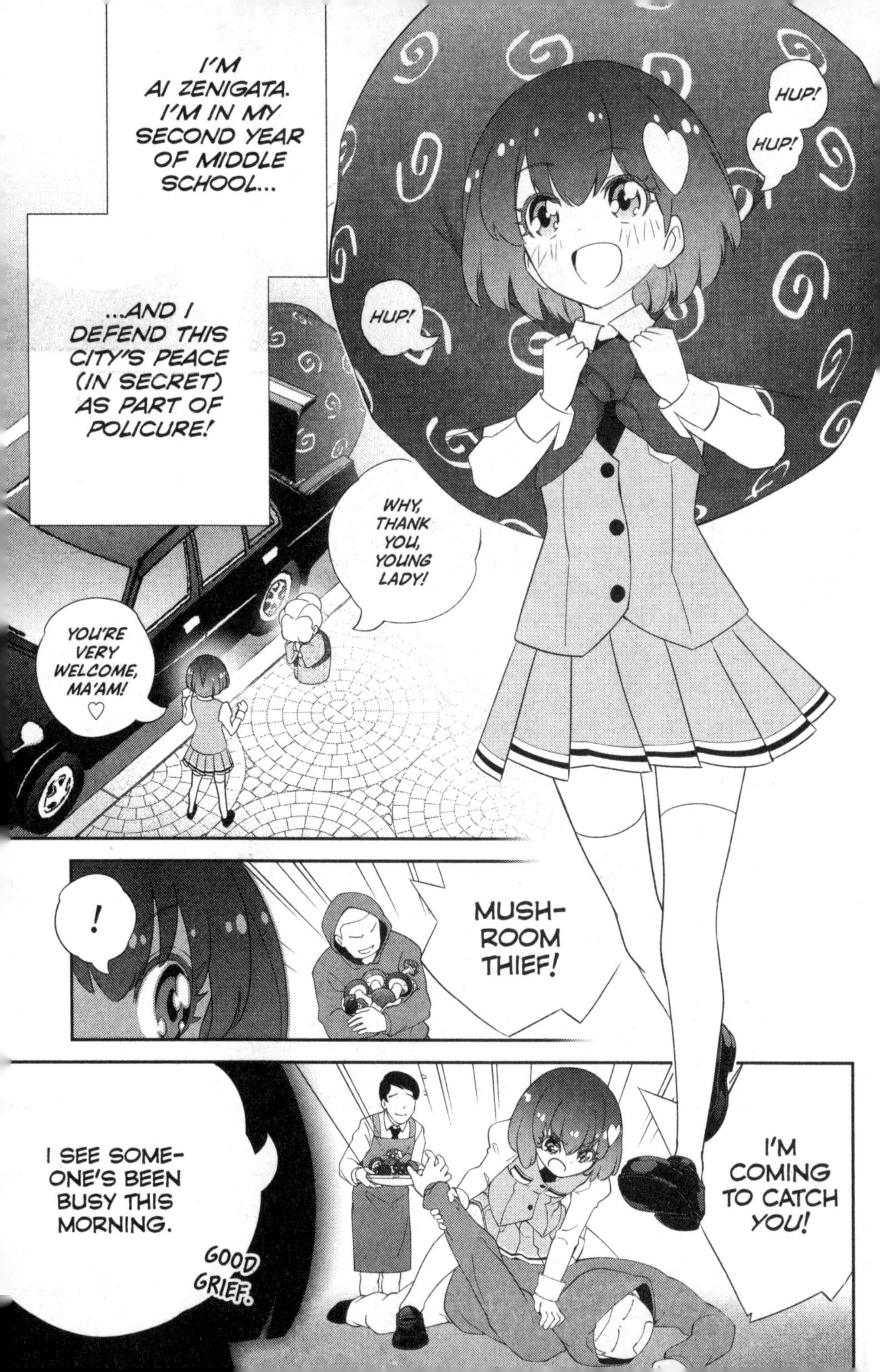

HUP!
HUP!
I'M AI ZENIGATA. I'M IN MY SECOND YEAR OF MIDDLE SCHOOL...
HUP!
...AND I DEFEND THIS CITY'S PEACE (IN SECRET) AS PART OF POLICURE!
WHY, THANK YOU, YOUNG LADY!
YOU'RE VERY WELCOME, MA'AM! ♡
MUSH-ROOM THIEF!
!
I'M COMING TO CATCH YOU!
I SEE SOME-ONE'S BEEN BUSY THIS MORNING.
GOOD GRIEF.

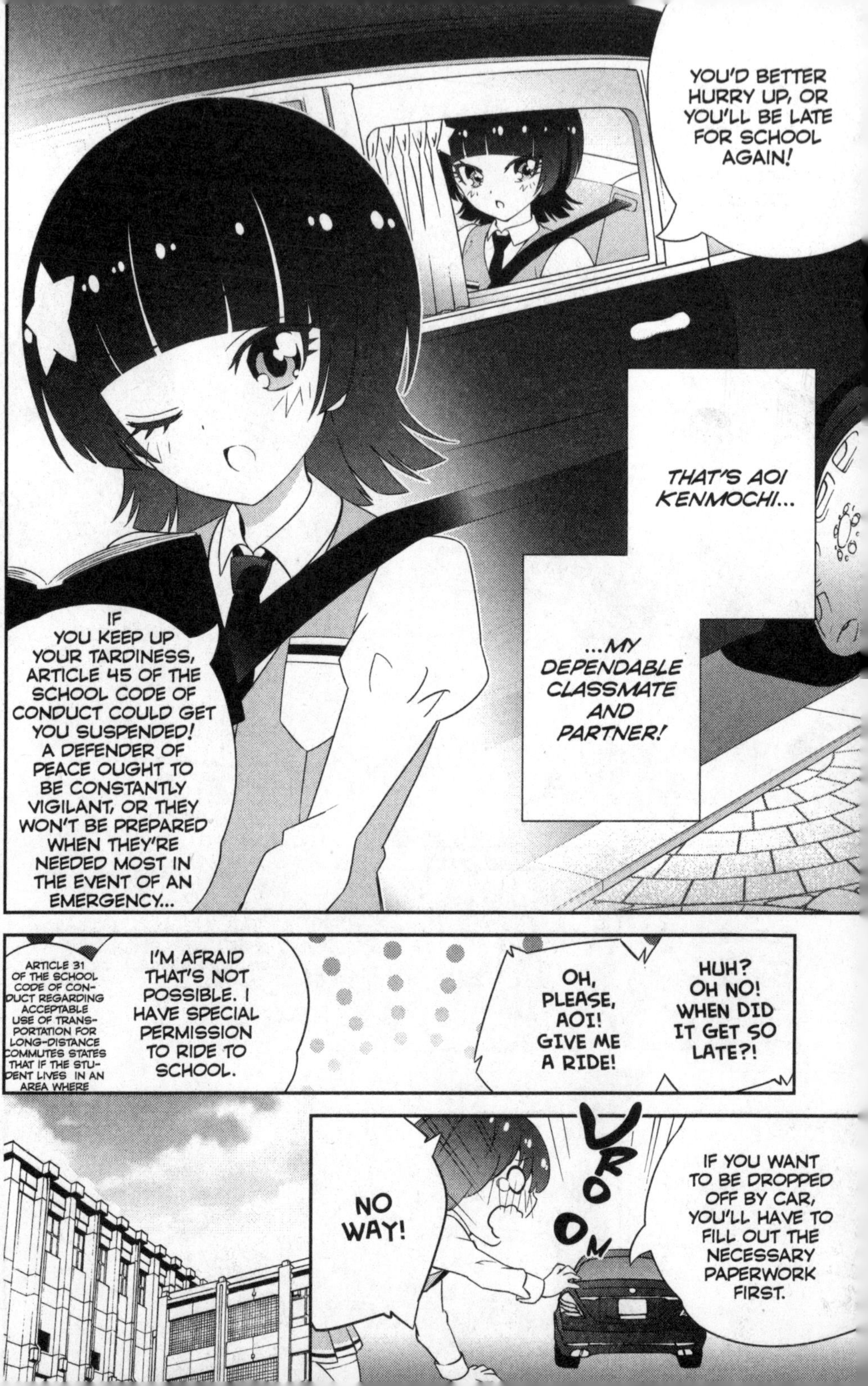
YOU'D BETTER HURRY UP, OR YOU'LL BE LATE FOR SCHOOL AGAIN!
THAT'S AOI KENMOCHI...
...MY DEPENDABLE CLASSMATE AND PARTNER!
IF YOU KEEP UP YOUR TARDINESS, ARTICLE 45 OF THE SCHOOL CODE OF CONDUCT COULD GET YOU SUSPENDED! A DEFENDER OF PEACE OUGHT TO BE CONSTANTLY VIGILANT, OR THEY WON'T BE PREPARED WHEN THEY'RE NEEDED MOST IN THE EVENT OF AN EMERGENCY...
HUH? OH NO! WHEN DID IT GET SO LATE?!
OH, PLEASE, AOI! GIVE ME A RIDE!
I'M AFRAID THAT'S NOT POSSIBLE. I HAVE SPECIAL PERMISSION TO RIDE TO SCHOOL.
ARTICLE 31 OF THE SCHOOL CODE OF CONDUCT REGARDING ACCEPTABLE USE OF TRANSPORTATION FOR LONG-DISTANCE COMMUTES STATES THAT IF THE STUDENT LIVES IN AN AREA WHERE
IF YOU WANT TO BE DROPPED OFF BY CAR, YOU'LL HAVE TO FILL OUT THE NECESSARY PAPERWORK FIRST.
VROOM
NO WAY!

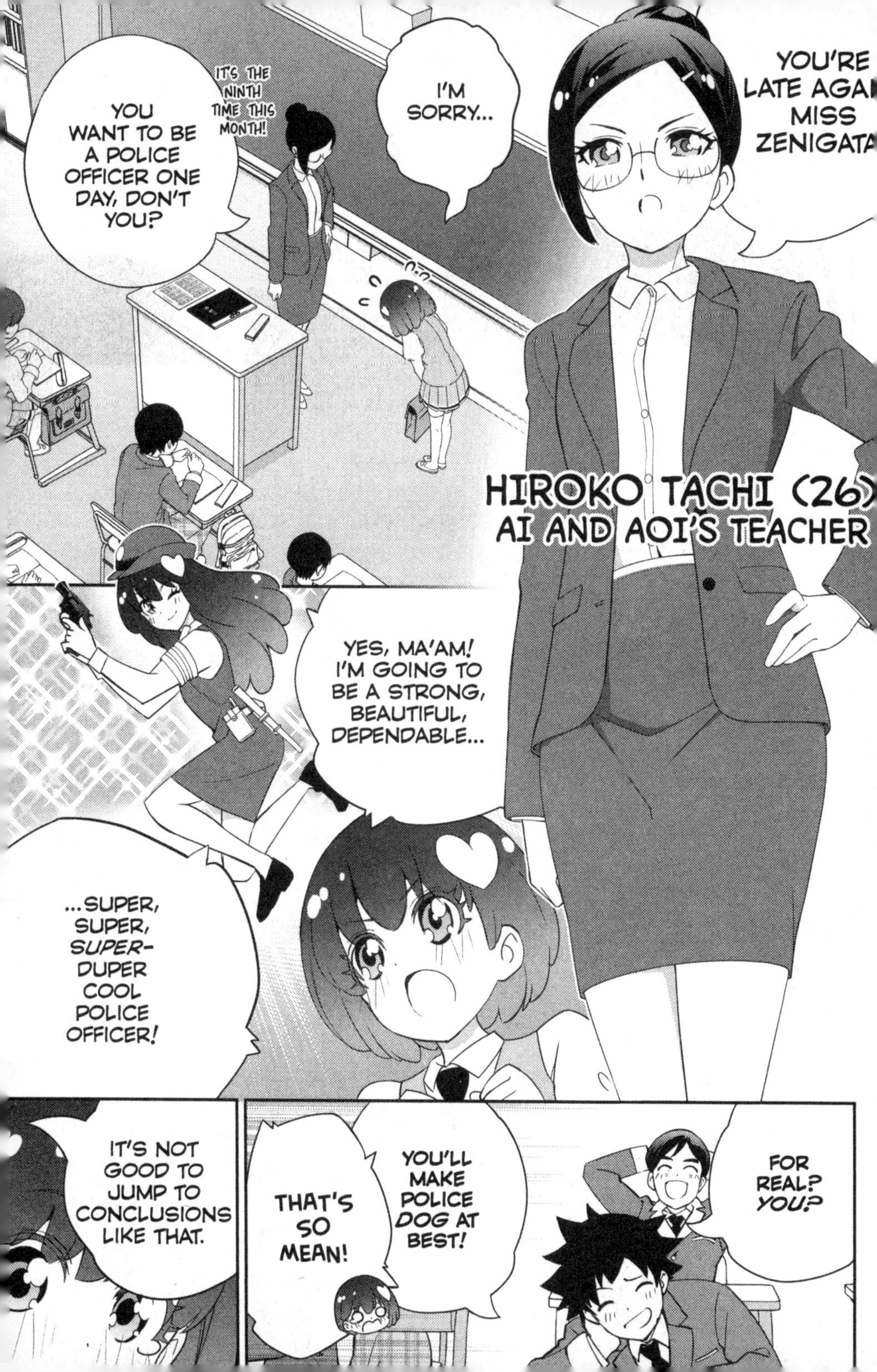
YOU'RE LATE AGAI MISS ZENIGATA
HIROKO TACHI (26)
AI AND AOI'S TEACHER
I'M SORRY...
IT'S THE NINTH TIME THIS MONTH!
YOU WANT TO BE A POLICE OFFICER ONE DAY, DON'T YOU?
YES, MA'AM! I'M GOING TO BE A STRONG, BEAUTIFUL, DEPENDABLE...
...SUPER, SUPER, *SUPER*-DUPER COOL POLICE OFFICER!
FOR REAL? *YOU?*
YOU'LL MAKE POLICE *DOG* AT BEST!
THAT'S SO MEAN!
IT'S NOT GOOD TO JUMP TO CONCLUSIONS LIKE THAT.

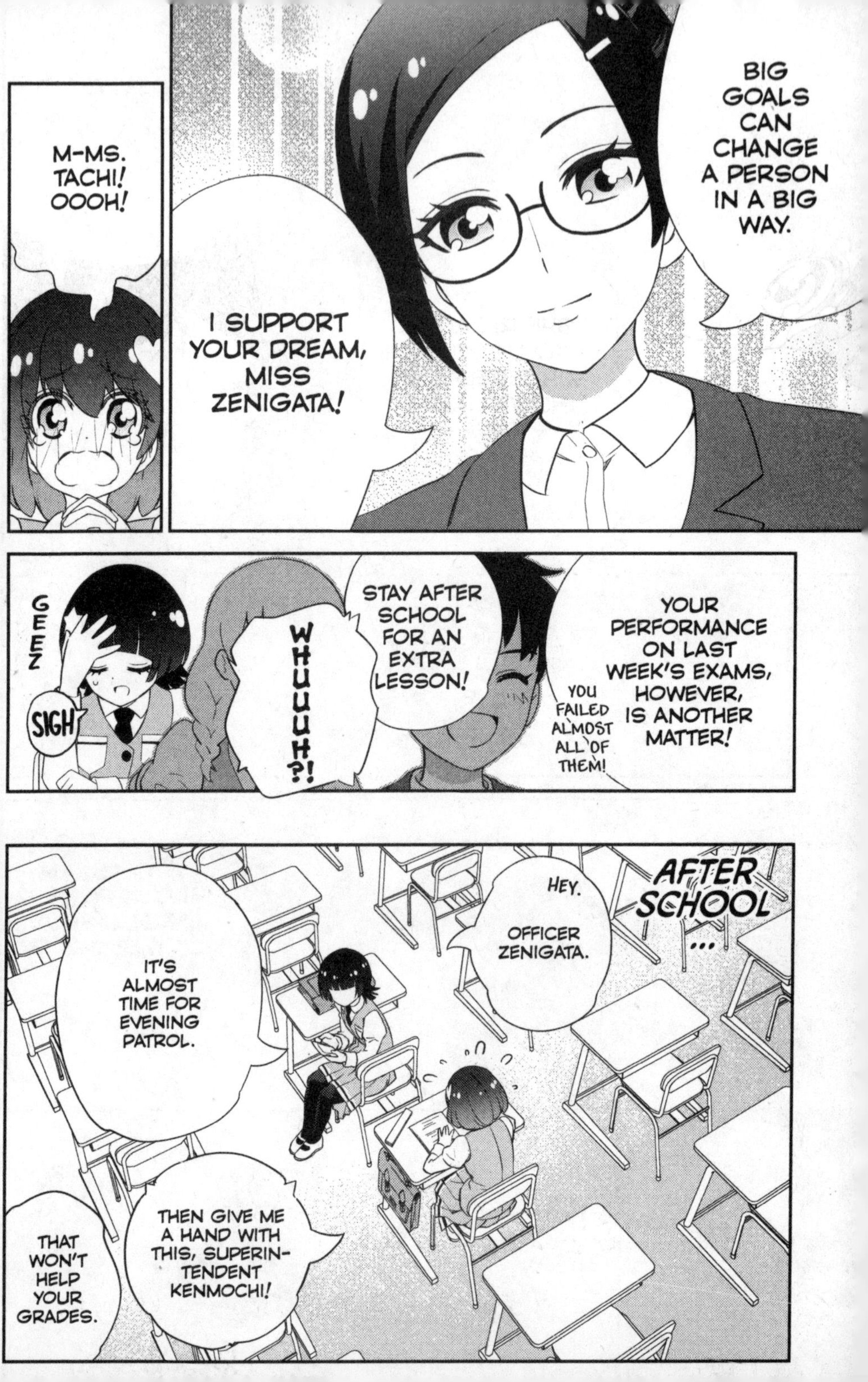
BIG GOALS CAN CHANGE A PERSON IN A BIG WAY.
I SUPPORT YOUR DREAM, MISS ZENIGATA!
M-MS. TACHI! OOOH!
YOUR PERFORMANCE ON LAST WEEK'S EXAMS, HOWEVER, IS ANOTHER MATTER!
YOU FAILED ALMOST ALL OF THEM!
STAY AFTER SCHOOL FOR AN EXTRA LESSON!
WHUUUUH?!
GEEZ
SIGH
AFTER SCHOOL...
HEY.
OFFICER ZENIGATA.
IT'S ALMOST TIME FOR EVENING PATROL.
THEN GIVE ME A HAND WITH THIS, SUPERINTENDENT KENMOCHI!
THAT WON'T HELP YOUR GRADES.

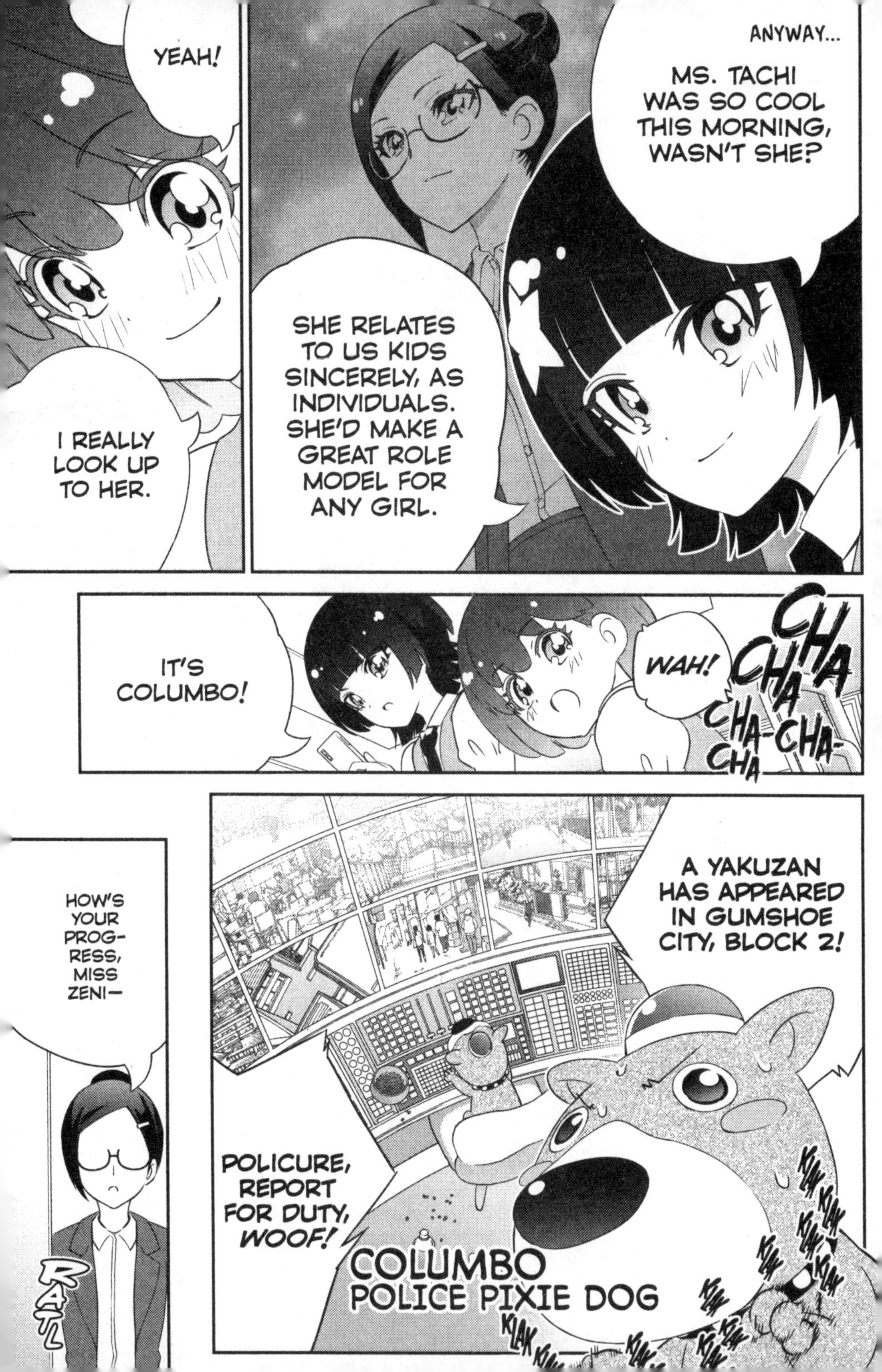
ANYWAY...
MS. TACHI WAS SO COOL THIS MORNING, WASN'T SHE?
SHE RELATES TO US KIDS SINCERELY, AS INDIVIDUALS. SHE'D MAKE A GREAT ROLE MODEL FOR ANY GIRL.
YEAH!
I REALLY LOOK UP TO HER.
CHA CHA CHA-CHA-CHA-CHA
WAH!
IT'S COLUMBO!
A YAKUZAN HAS APPEARED IN GUMSHOE CITY, BLOCK 2!
KLAK KLAK KLAK KLAK KLAK KLAK KLAK KLAK KLAK KLAK KLAK KLAK
POLICURE, REPORT FOR DUTY, WOOF!
COLUMBO POLICE PIXIE DOG
HOW'S YOUR PROG-RESS, MISS ZENI—
RATL

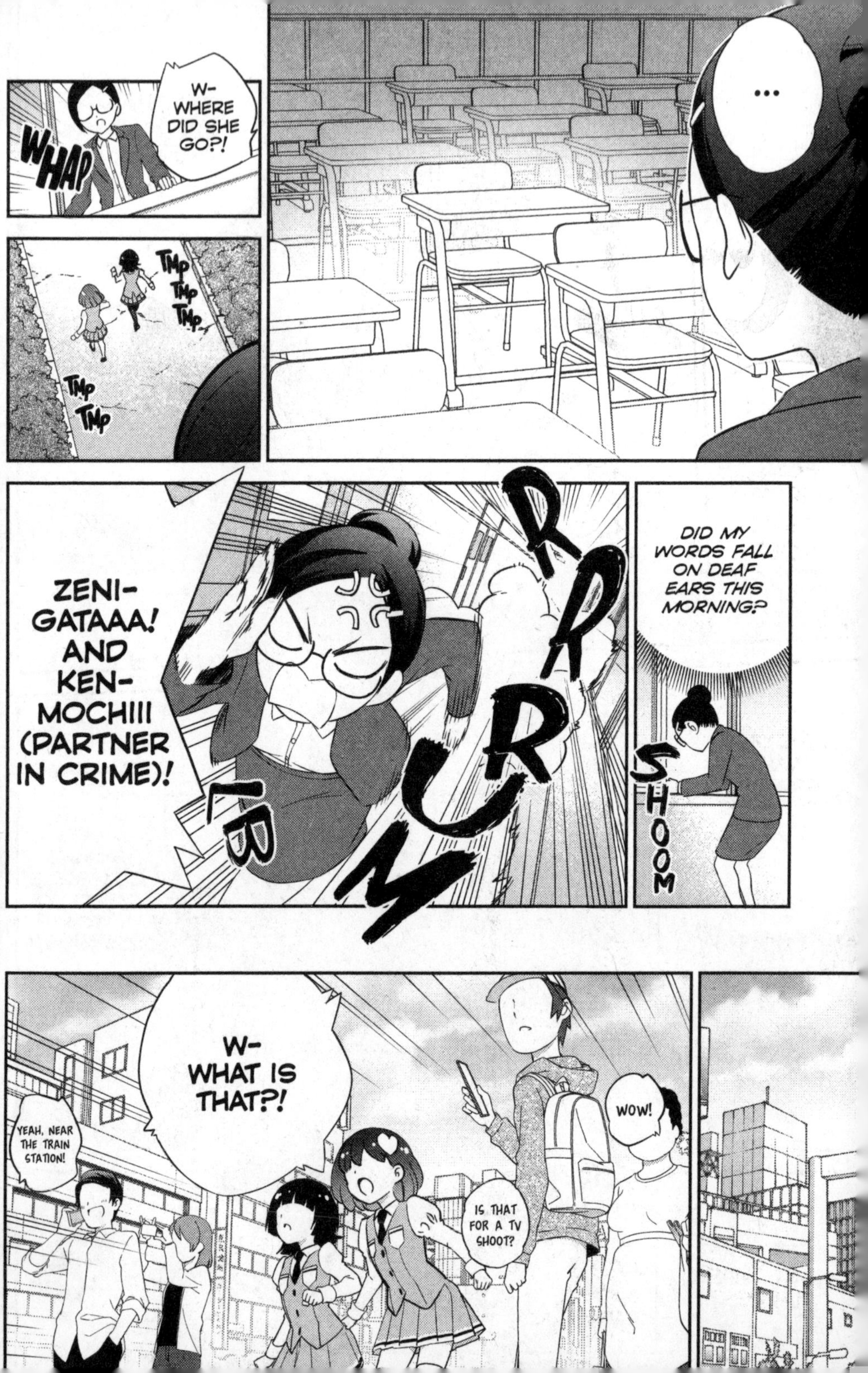
...
WHAP
W- WHERE DID SHE GO?!
TMP TMP TMP
TMP TMP
DID MY WORDS FALL ON DEAF EARS THIS MORNING?
SHOOM
RRRUMBL
ZENI-GATAAA! AND KEN-MOCHIII (PARTNER IN CRIME)!
W- WHAT IS THAT?!
WOW!
IS THAT FOR A TV SHOOT?
YEAH, NEAR THE TRAIN STATION!

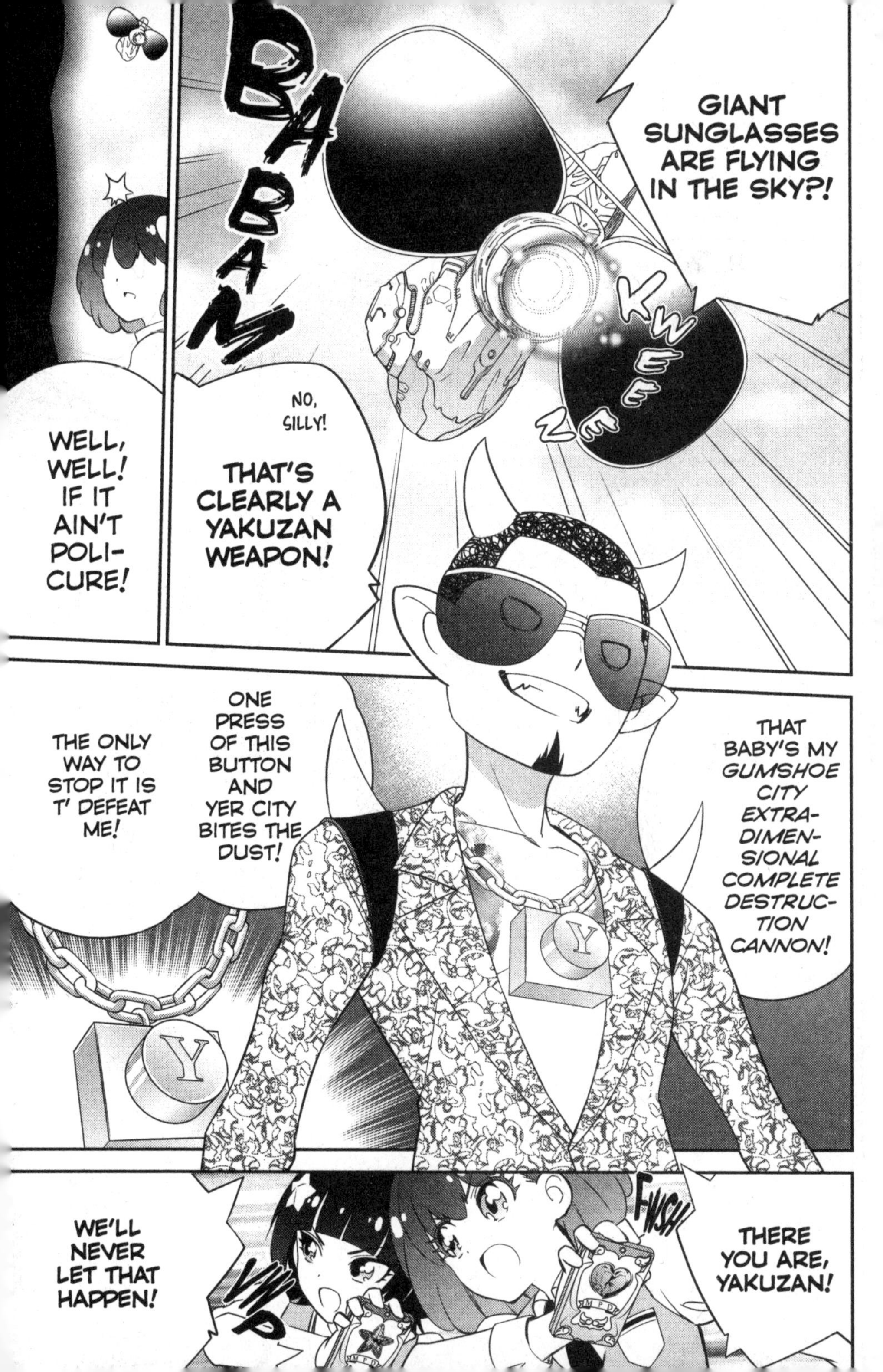
GIANT SUNGLASSES ARE FLYING IN THE SKY?!
KWEEE
BABAM
NO, SILLY!
THAT'S CLEARLY A YAKUZAN WEAPON!
WELL, WELL! IF IT AIN'T POLI-CURE!
THAT BABY'S MY GUMSHOE CITY EXTRA-DIMEN-SIONAL COMPLETE DESTRUC-TION CANNON!
ONE PRESS OF THIS BUTTON AND YER CITY BITES THE DUST!
THE ONLY WAY TO STOP IT IS T' DEFEAT ME!
FWSH
THERE YOU ARE, YAKUZAN!
VMP
WE'LL NEVER LET THAT HAPPEN!

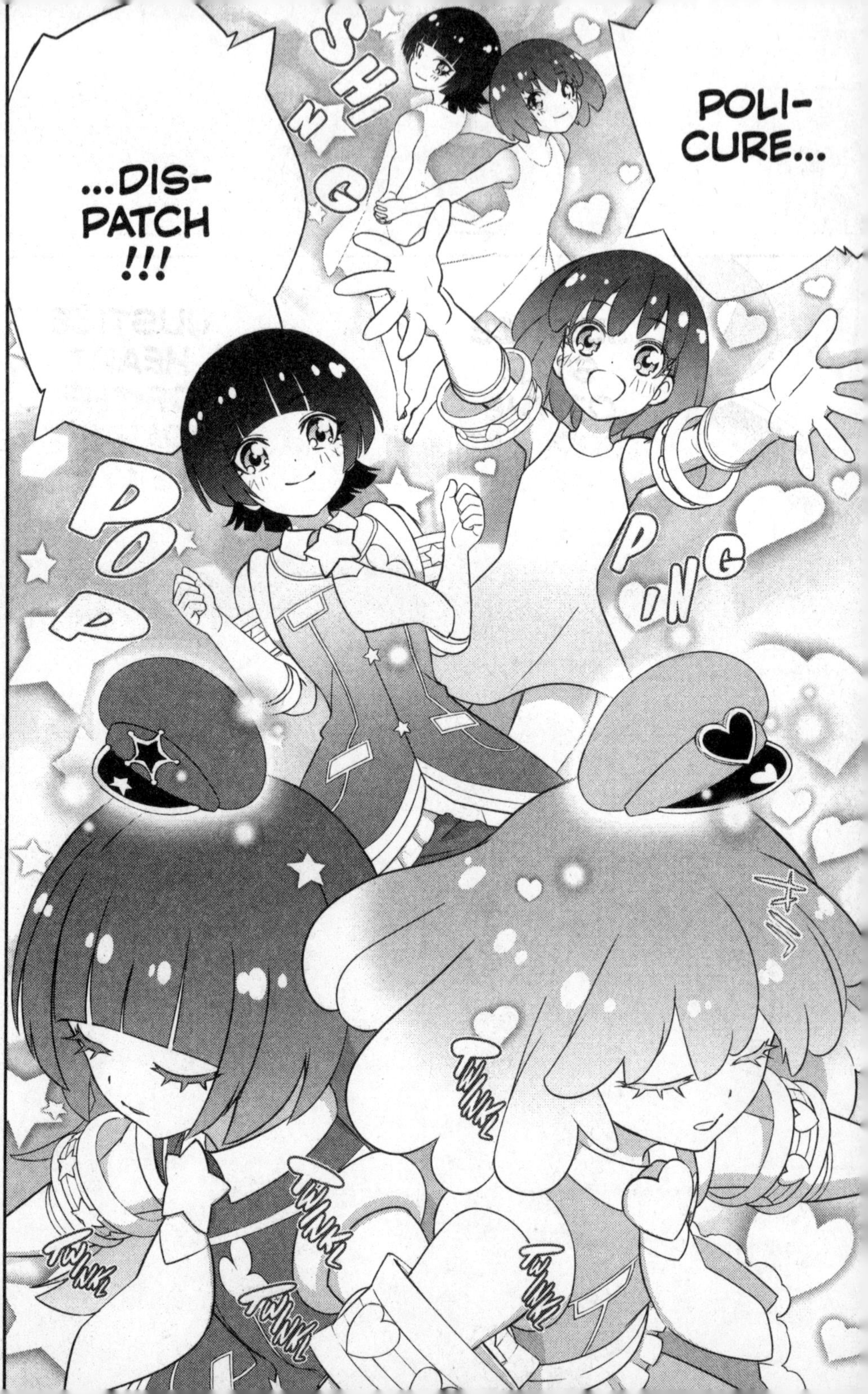
POLI-CURE...
SHING
...DIS-PATCH!!!
PING
POP
TWINKL
TWINKL
TWINKL
TWINKL
TWINKL

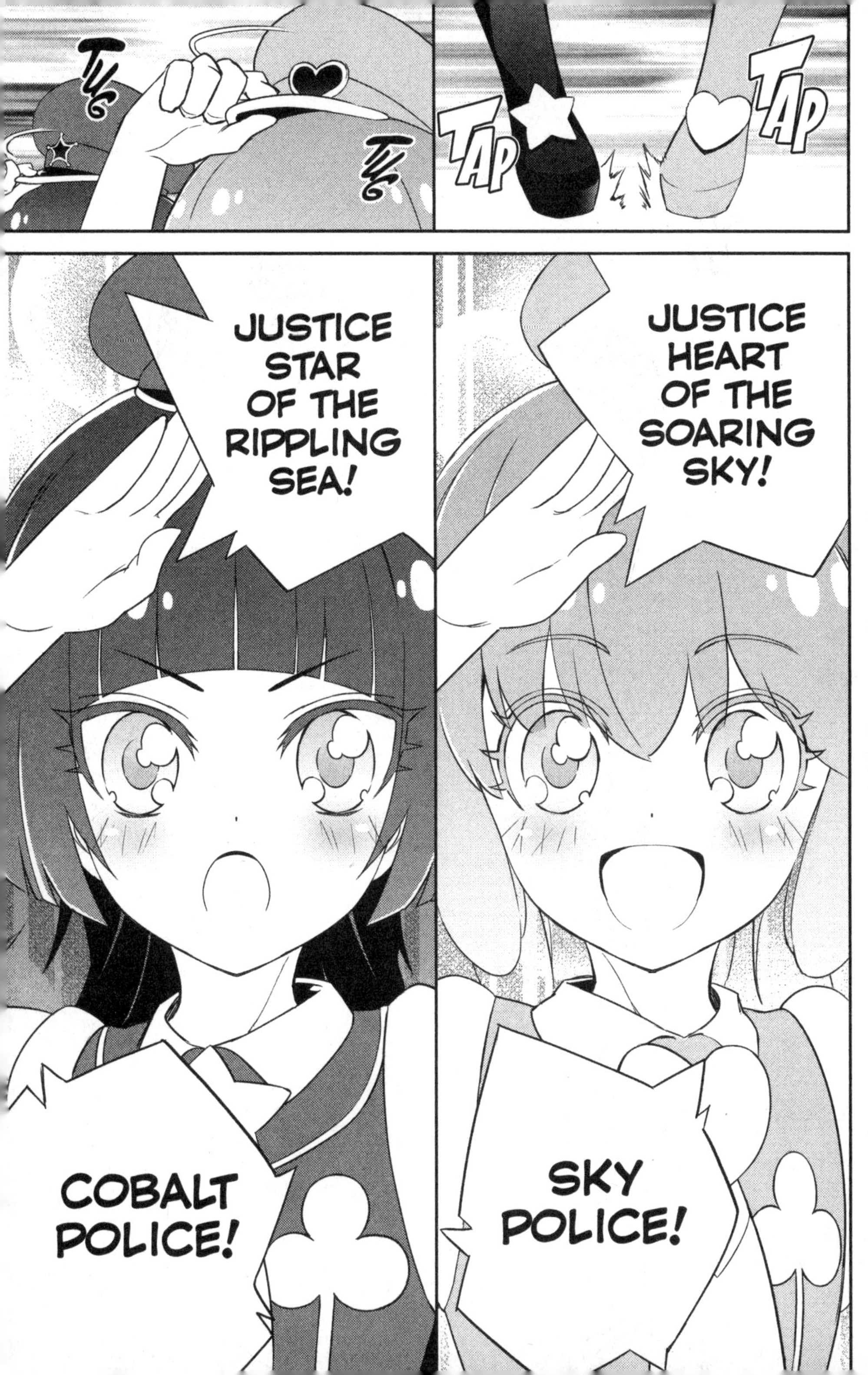
TAP
TAP
TUG
TUG
JUSTICE HEART OF THE SOARING SKY!
SKY POLICE!
JUSTICE STAR OF THE RIPPLING SEA!
COBALT POLICE!

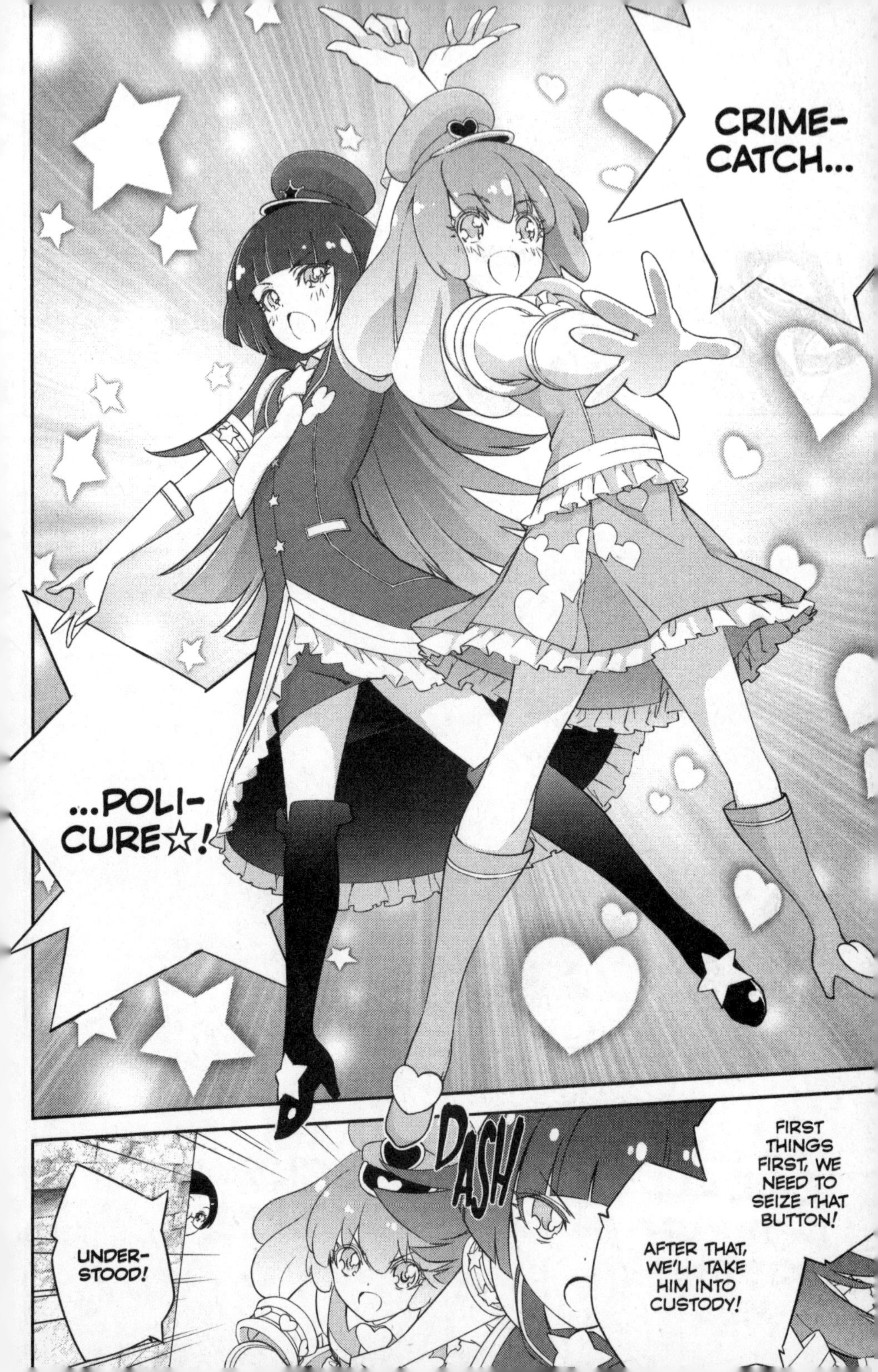
CRIME-CATCH...
...POLI-CURE☆!
FIRST THINGS FIRST, WE NEED TO SEIZE THAT BUTTON!
AFTER THAT, WE'LL TAKE HIM INTO CUSTODY!
DASH
UNDER-STOOD!

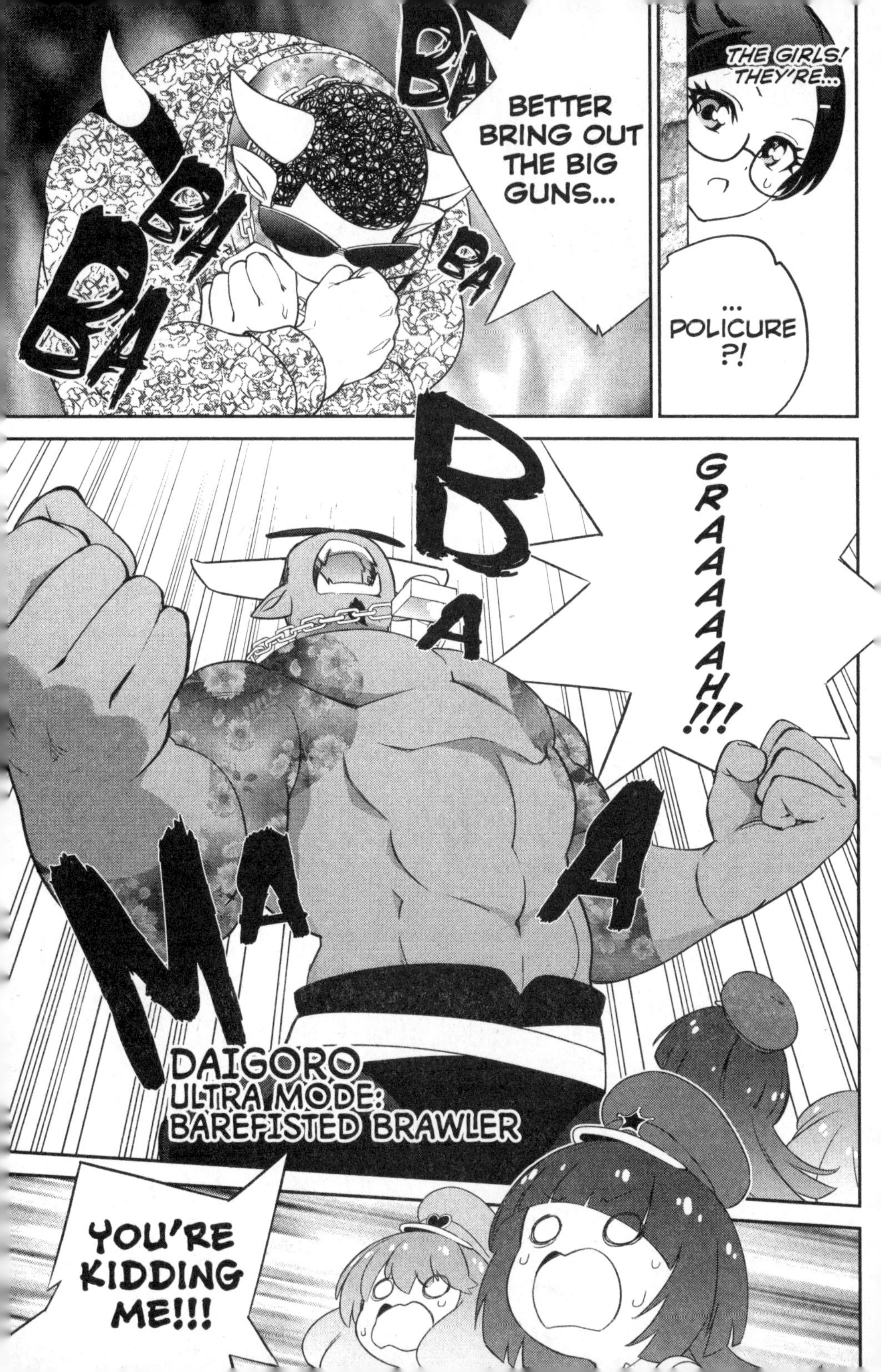
THE GIRLS! THEY'RE...
... POLICURE ?!
BETTER BRING OUT THE BIG GUNS...
BA BA BA BA BA BA
GRAAAAAAH!!!
BAAMAA
DAIGORO ULTRA MODE: BAREFISTED BRAWLER
YOU'RE KIDDING ME!!!

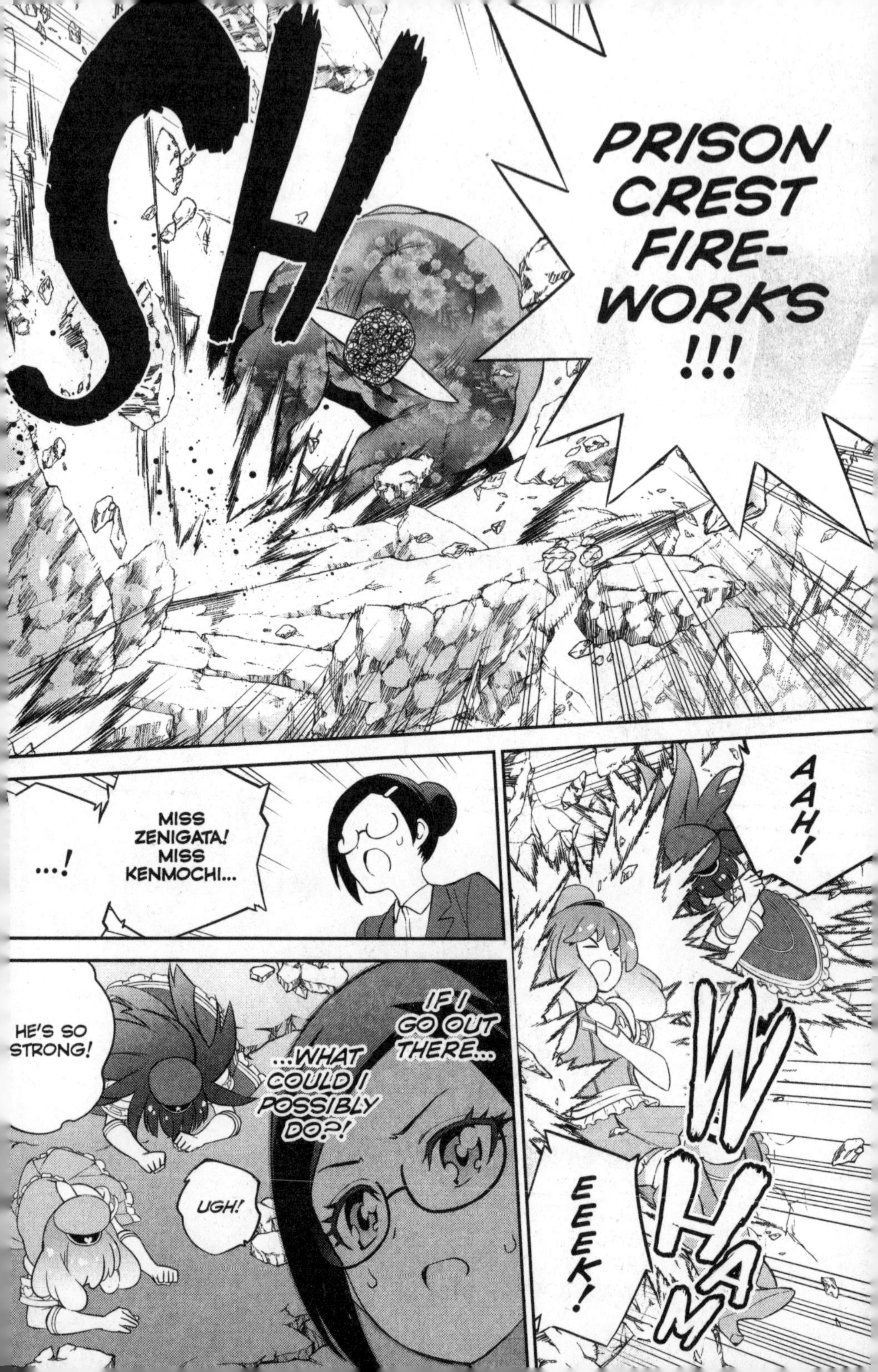
PRISON CREST FIRE-WORKS !!!
SH
AAH!
WHAM
EEEK!
MISS ZENIGATA! MISS KENMOCHI...
...!
IF I GO OUT THERE...
...WHAT COULD I POSSIBLY DO?!
HE'S SO STRONG!
UGH!

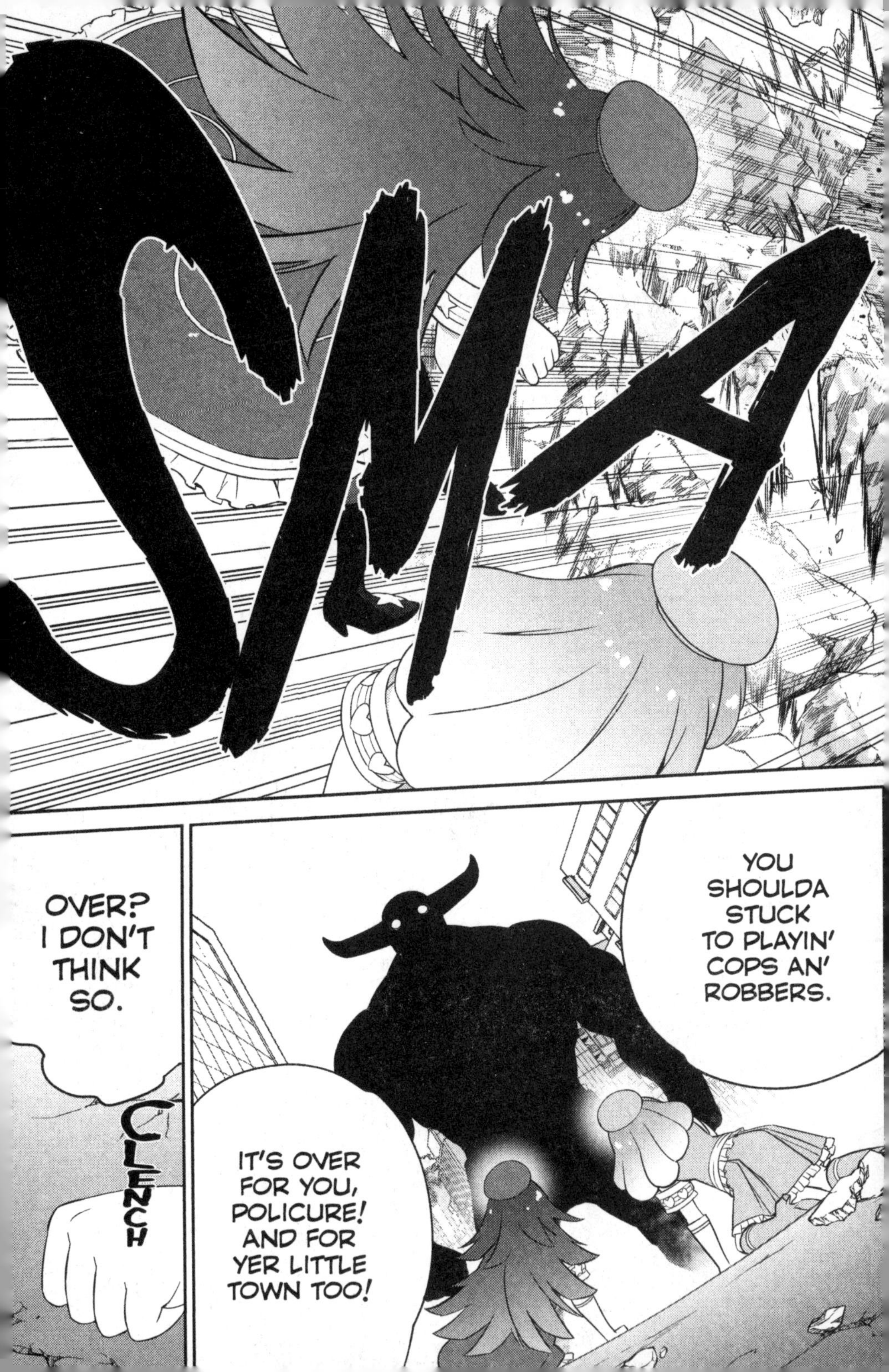
SMA
YOU SHOULDA STUCK TO PLAYIN' COPS AN' ROBBERS.
IT'S OVER FOR YOU, POLICURE! AND FOR YER LITTLE TOWN TOO!
OVER? I DON'T THINK SO.
CLENCH

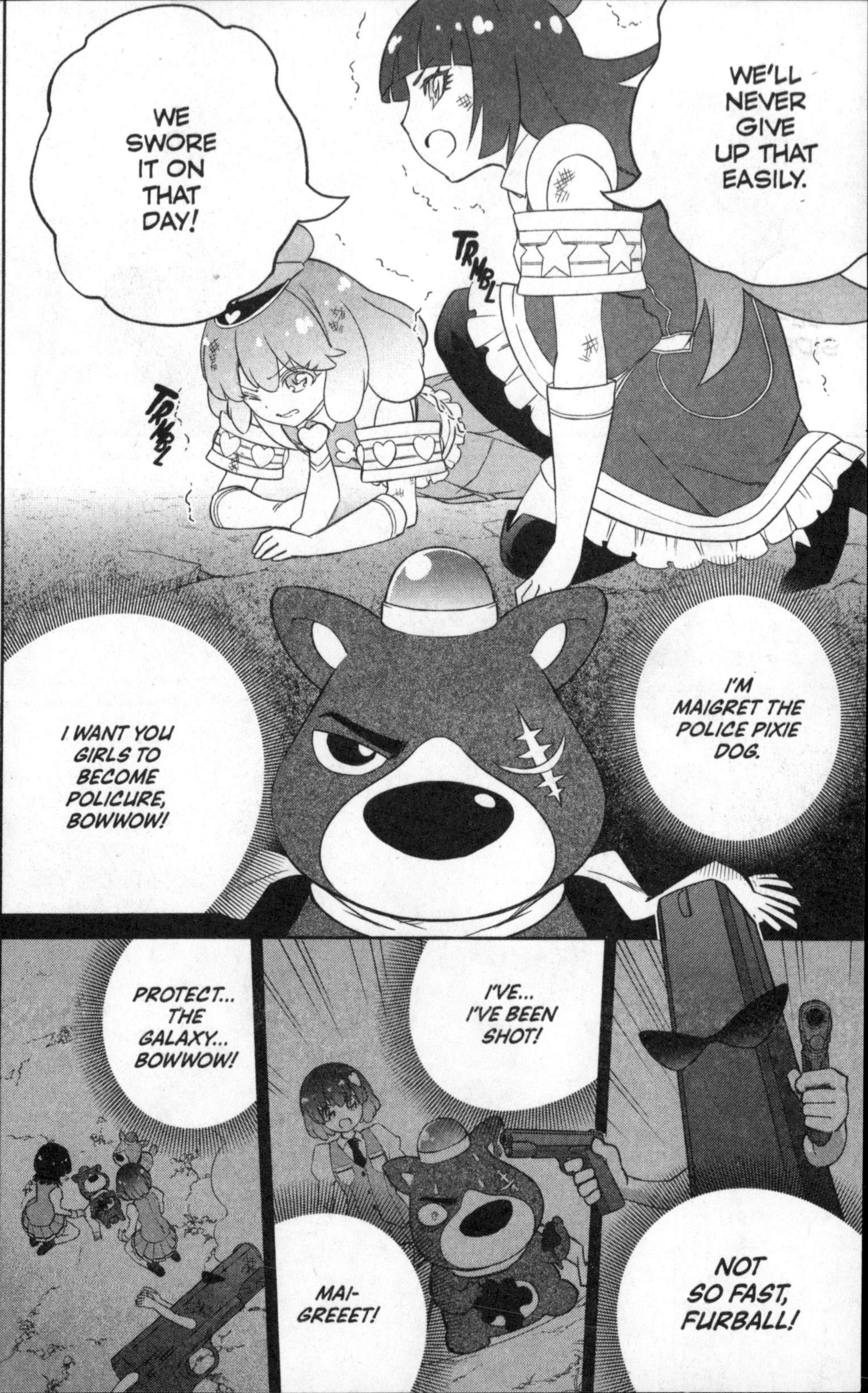
WE'LL NEVER GIVE UP THAT EASILY.
WE SWORE IT ON THAT DAY!
TRMBL
TRMBL
I'M MAIGRET THE POLICE PIXIE DOG.
I WANT YOU GIRLS TO BECOME POLICURE, BOWWOW!
NOT SO FAST, FURBALL!
I'VE... I'VE BEEN SHOT!
MAI-GREEET!
PROTECT... THE GALAXY... BOWWOW!

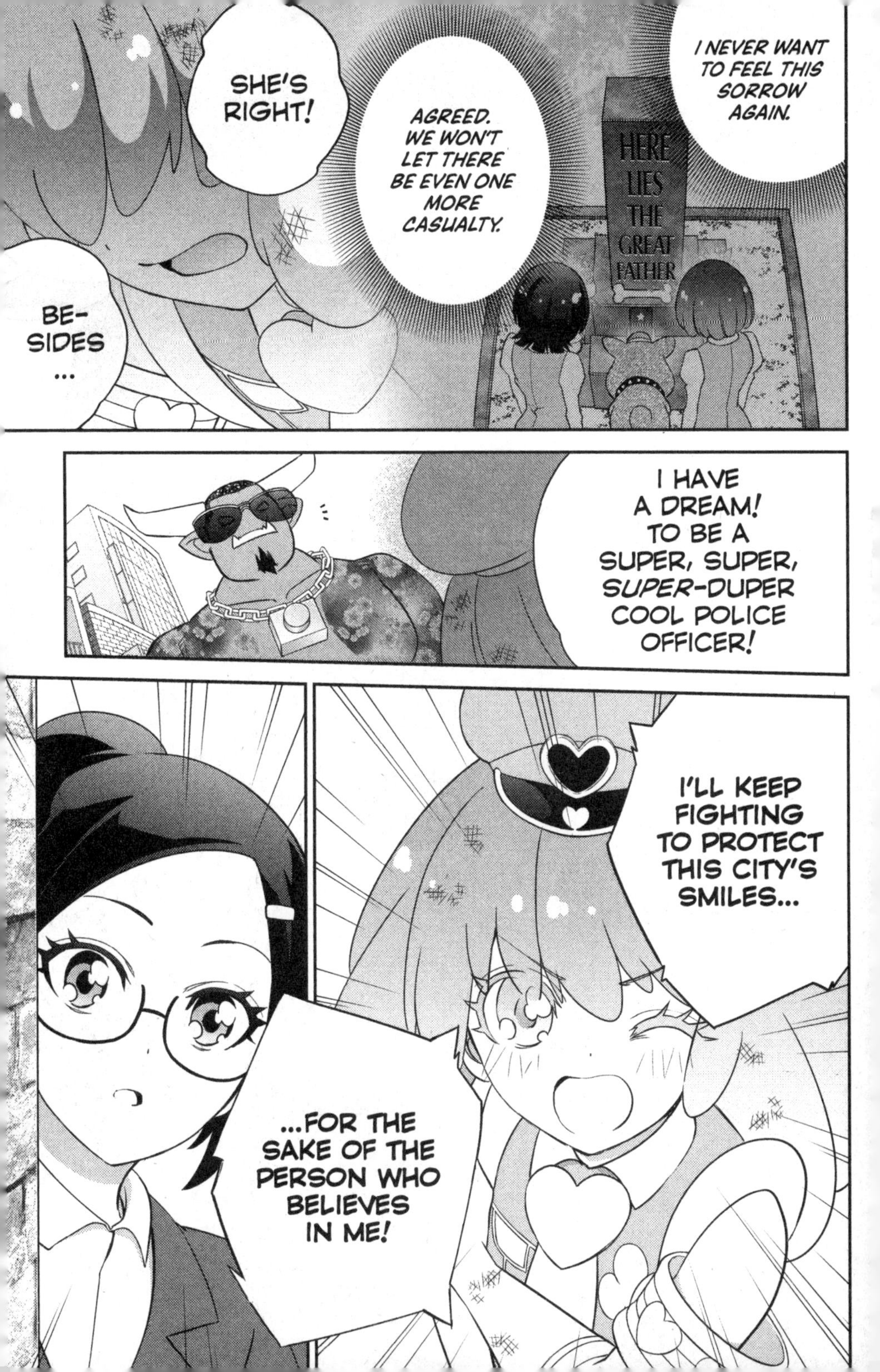
I NEVER WANT TO FEEL THIS SORROW AGAIN.
AGREED. WE WON'T LET THERE BE EVEN ONE MORE CASUALTY.
SHE'S RIGHT!
HERE LIES THE GREAT FATHER
BE-SIDES ...
I HAVE A DREAM! TO BE A SUPER, SUPER, *SUPER*-DUPER COOL POLICE OFFICER!
I'LL KEEP FIGHTING TO PROTECT THIS CITY'S SMILES...
...FOR THE SAKE OF THE PERSON WHO BELIEVES IN ME!

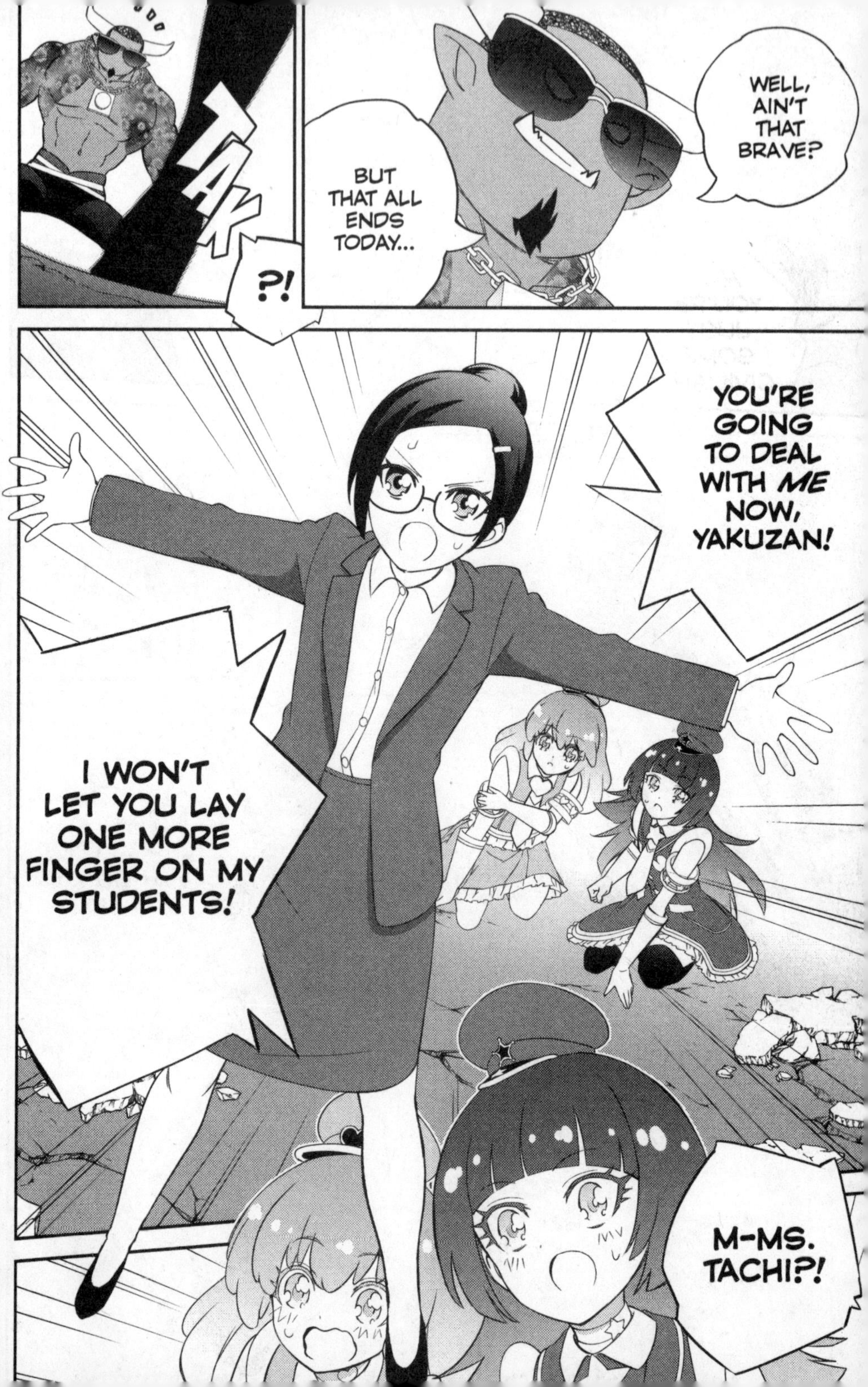
WELL, AIN'T THAT BRAVE?
BUT THAT ALL ENDS TODAY...
TAK
?!
YOU'RE GOING TO DEAL WITH *ME* NOW, YAKUZAN!
I WON'T LET YOU LAY ONE MORE FINGER ON MY STUDENTS!
M-MS. TACHI?!

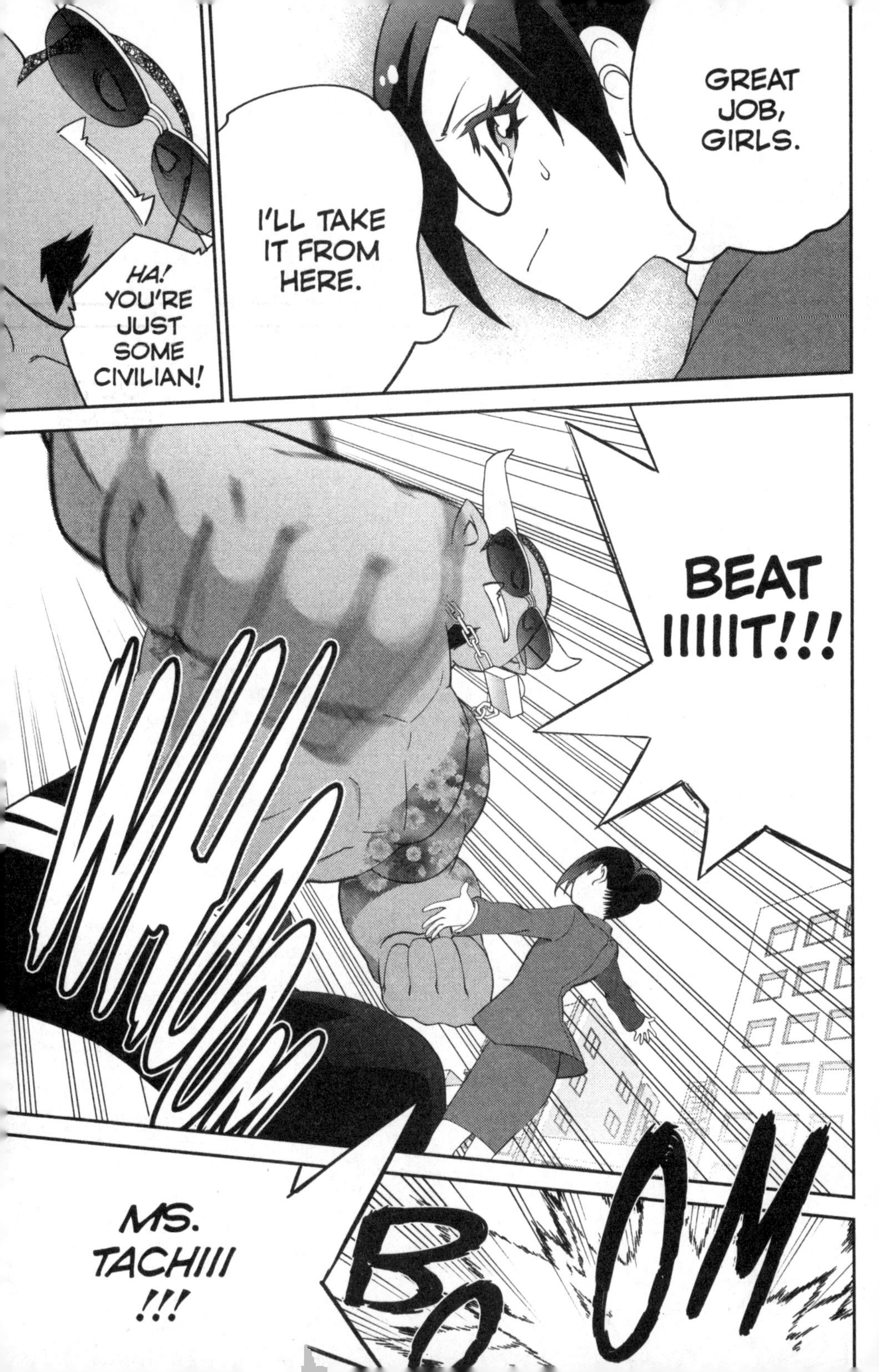
GREAT JOB, GIRLS.
I'LL TAKE IT FROM HERE.
HA! YOU'RE JUST SOME CIVILIAN!
BEAT IIIIIT!!!
MS. TACHIIII!!!
BOOM

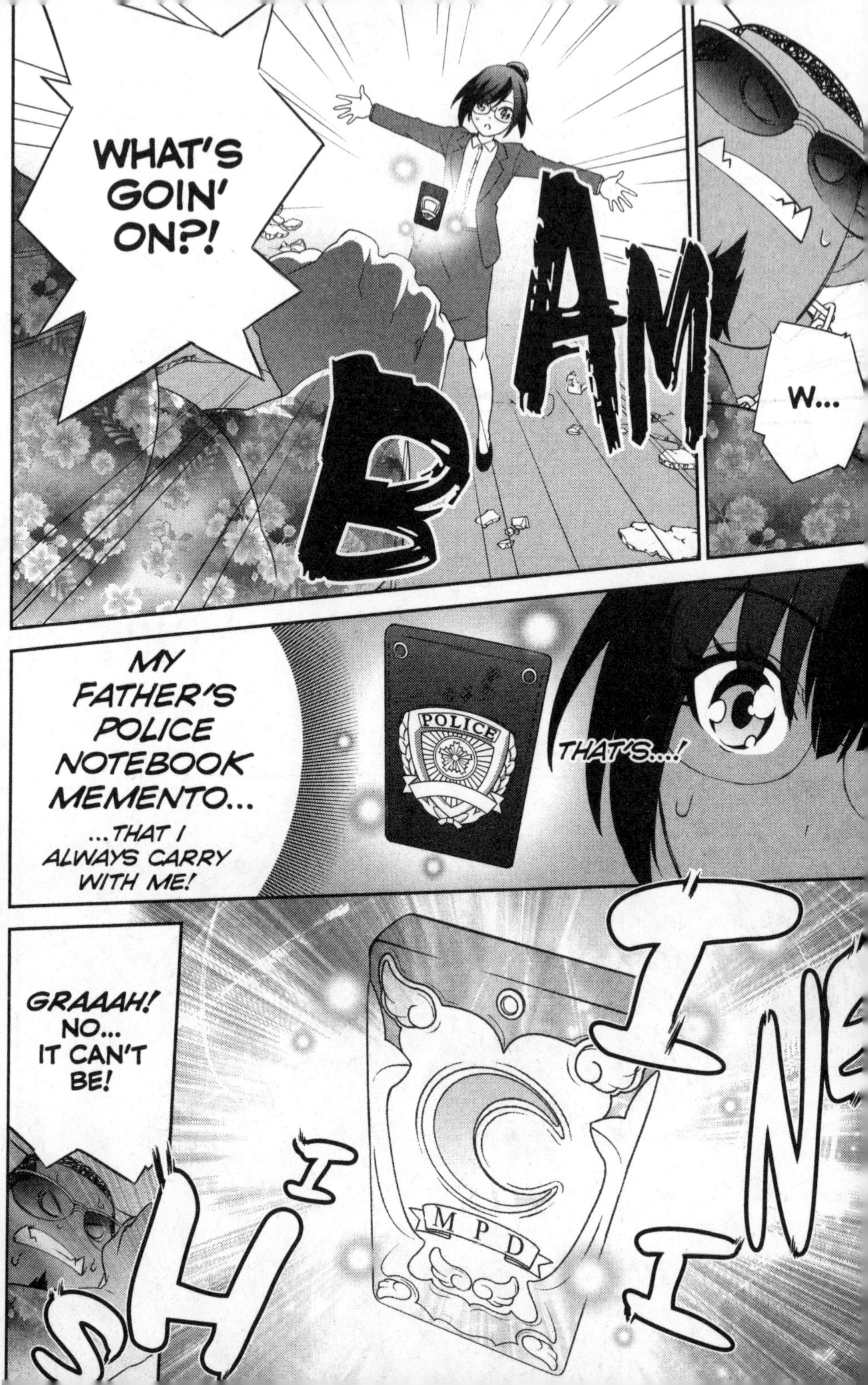
W...
WHAT'S GOIN' ON?!
BAM
THAT'S...!
POLICE
MY FATHER'S POLICE NOTEBOOK MEMENTO...
...THAT I ALWAYS CARRY WITH ME!
SHIIINE
M P D
GRAAAH! NO... IT CAN'T BE!

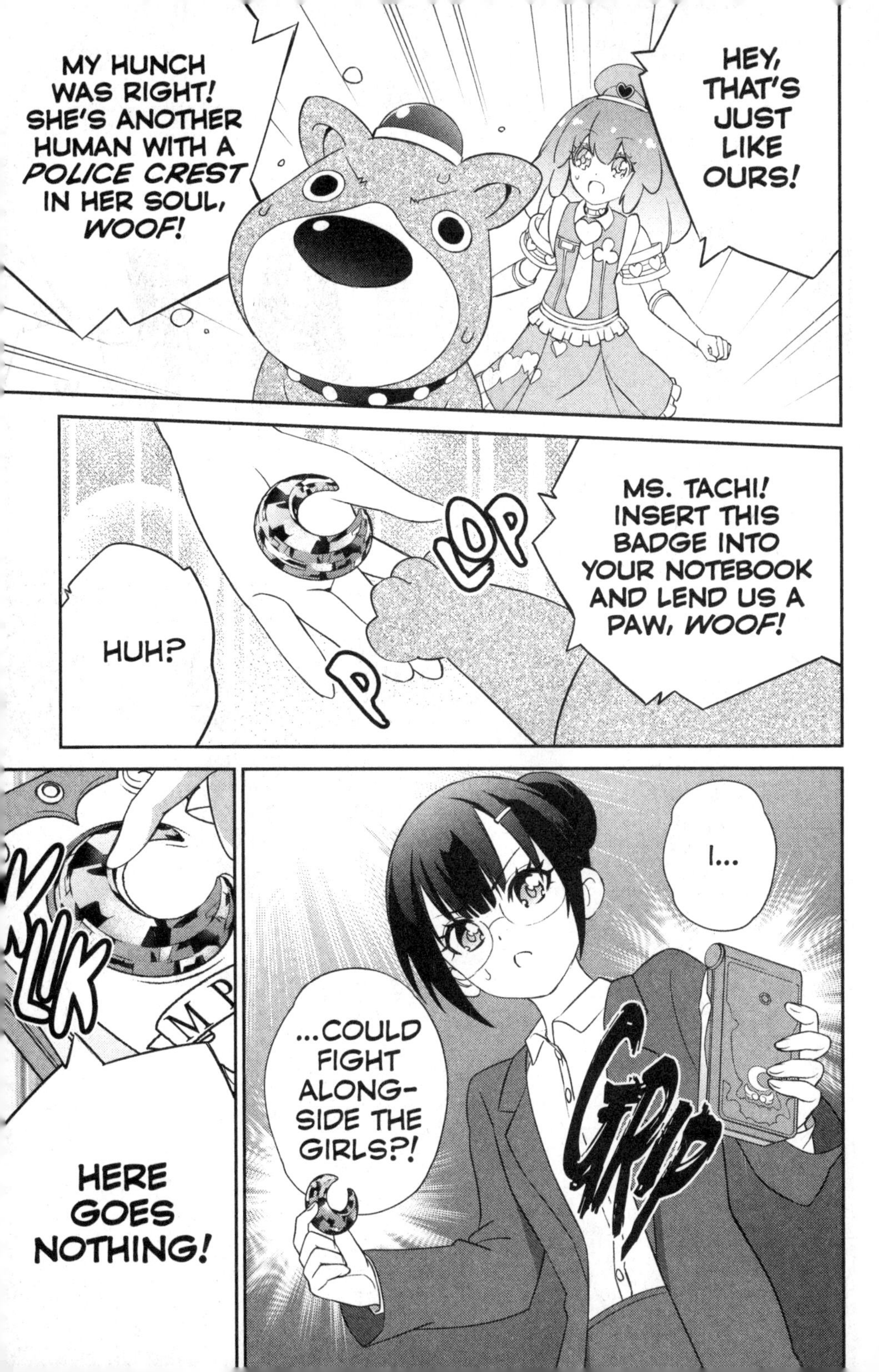
HEY, THAT'S JUST LIKE OURS!
MY HUNCH WAS RIGHT! SHE'S ANOTHER HUMAN WITH A *POLICE CREST* IN HER SOUL, *WOOF!*
MS. TACHI! INSERT THIS BADGE INTO YOUR NOTEBOOK AND LEND US A PAW, *WOOF!*
PLOP
HUH?
I...
...COULD FIGHT ALONG-SIDE THE GIRLS?!
GRIP
KLIK
HERE GOES NOTHING!

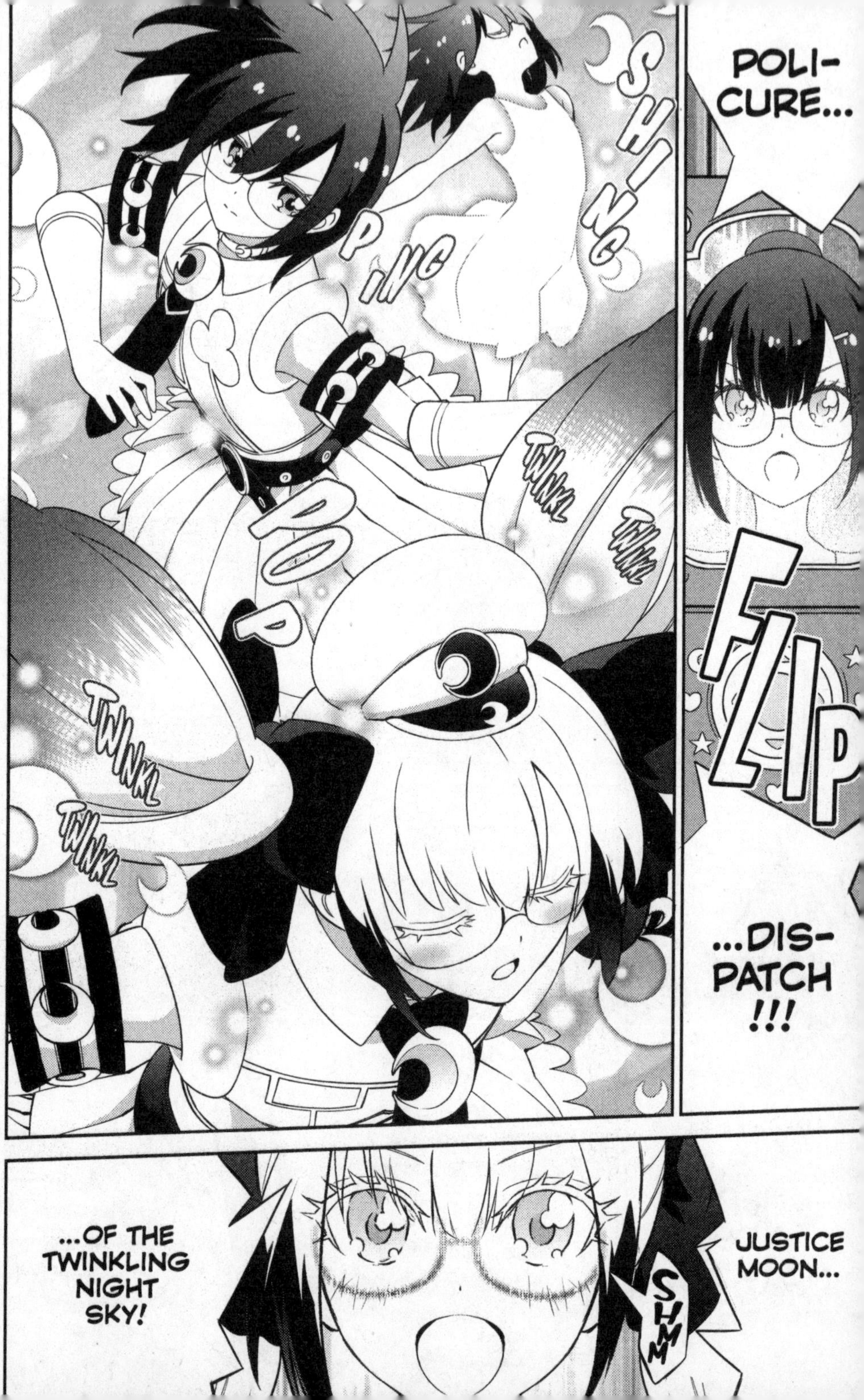
POLI-
CURE...
FLIP
...DIS-
PATCH
!!!
SHING
PING
POP
TWINKL
TWINKL
TWINKL
TWINKL
JUSTICE
MOON...
SHMM
...OF THE
TWINKLING
NIGHT
SKY!

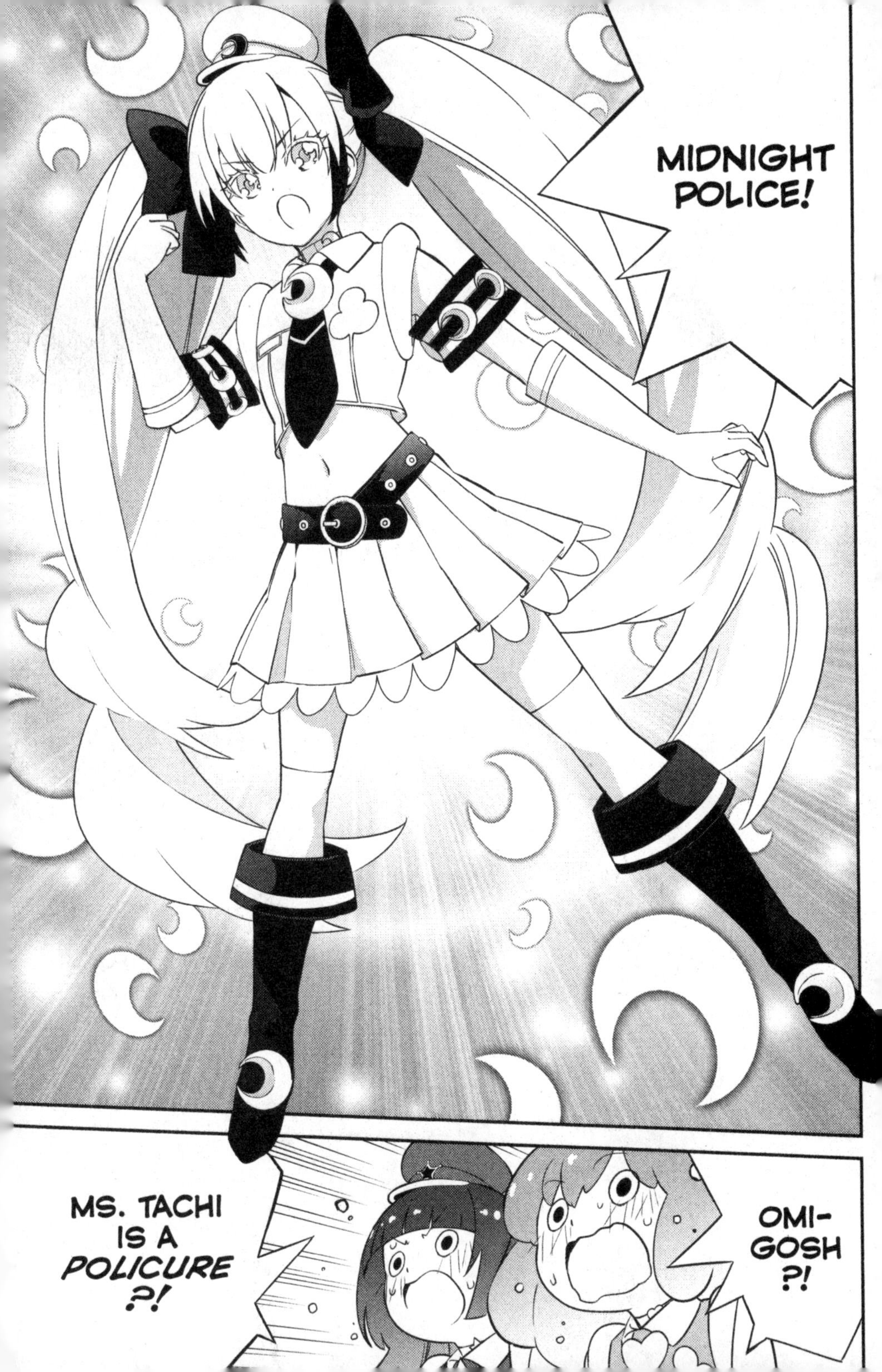
MIDNIGHT POLICE!
OMI-GOSH ?!
MS. TACHI IS A *POLICURE* ?!

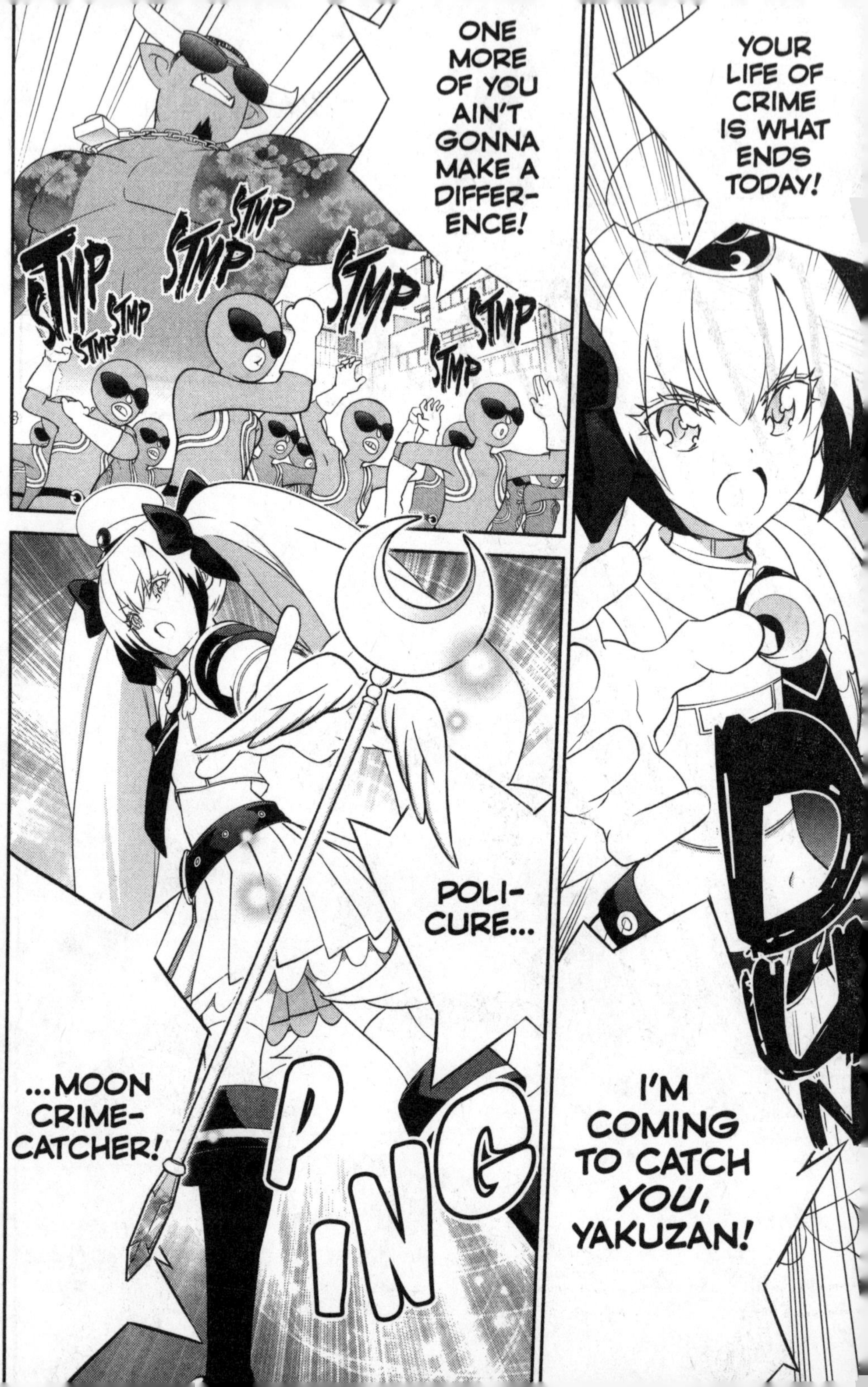
YOUR LIFE OF CRIME IS WHAT ENDS TODAY!
I'M COMING TO CATCH *YOU*, YAKUZAN!
ONE MORE OF YOU AIN'T GONNA MAKE A DIFFER-ENCE!
STMP STMP
STMP STMP STMP
STMP
STMP STMP
POLI-CURE...
...MOON CRIME-CATCHER!
PING

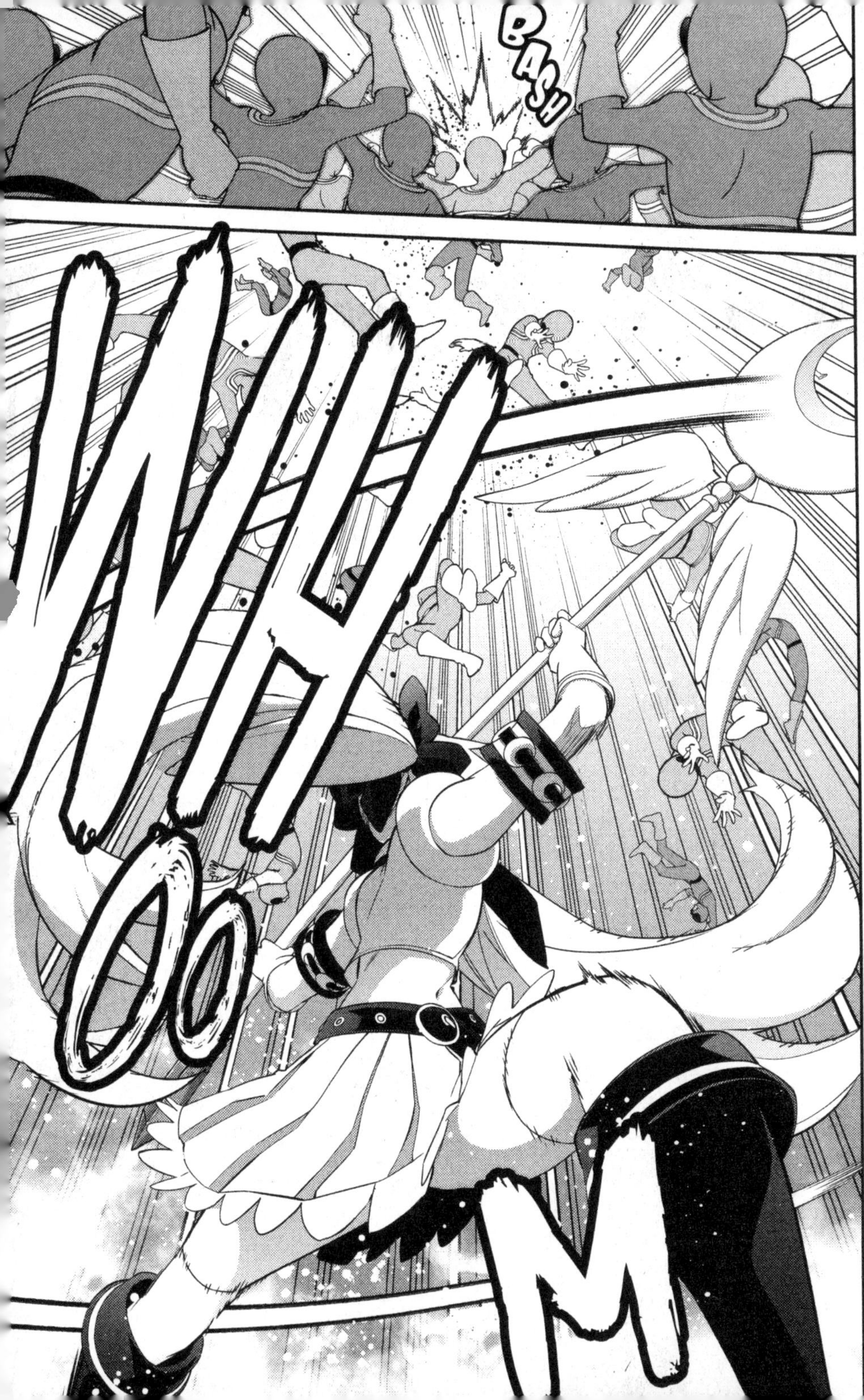
BASH
WHOOM

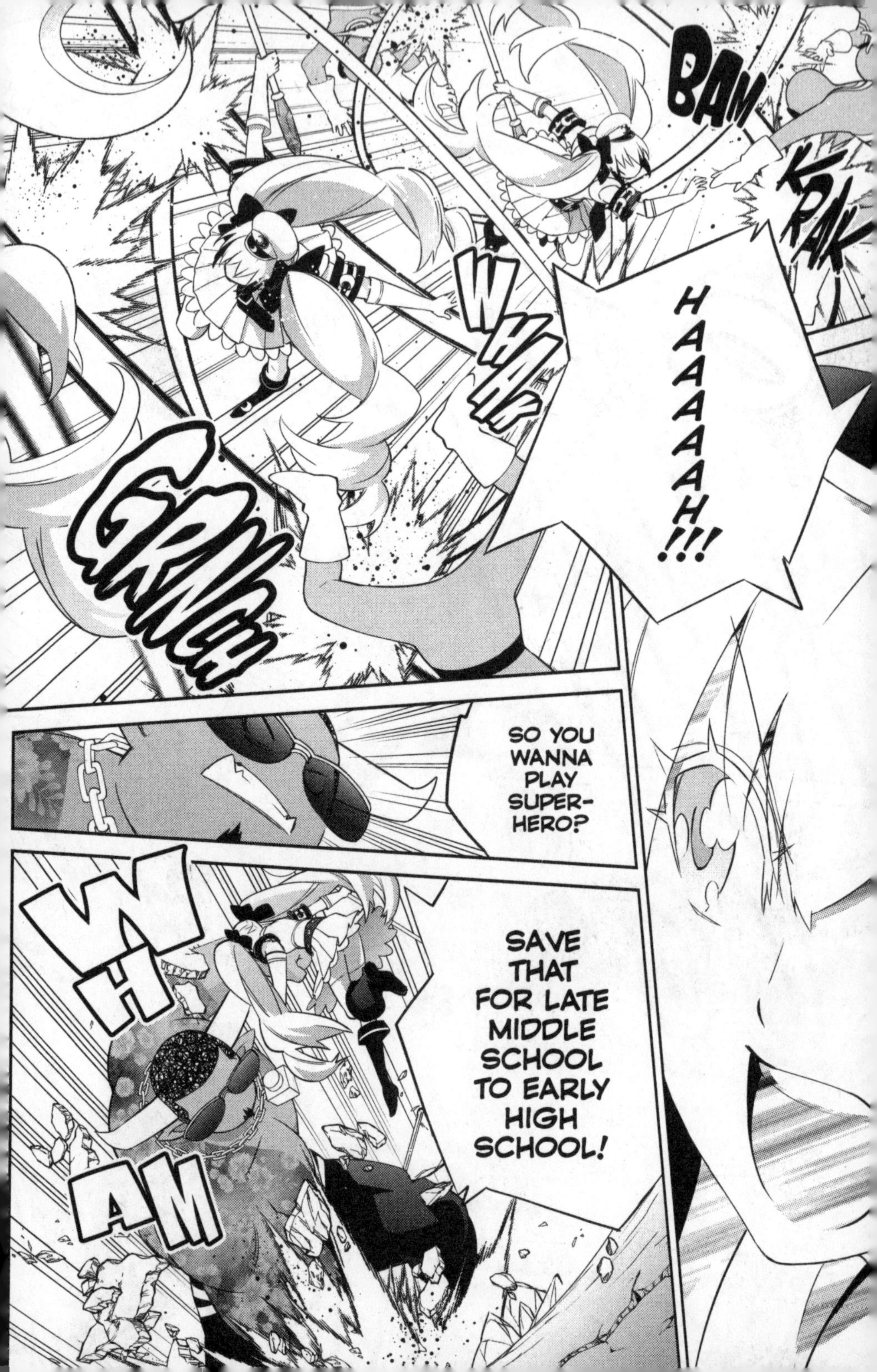
BAM
KRAK
HAAAAAAH!!!
WHAP
GRNCH
SO YOU WANNA PLAY SUPER-HERO?
SAVE THAT FOR LATE MIDDLE SCHOOL TO EARLY HIGH SCHOOL!
WH
AM

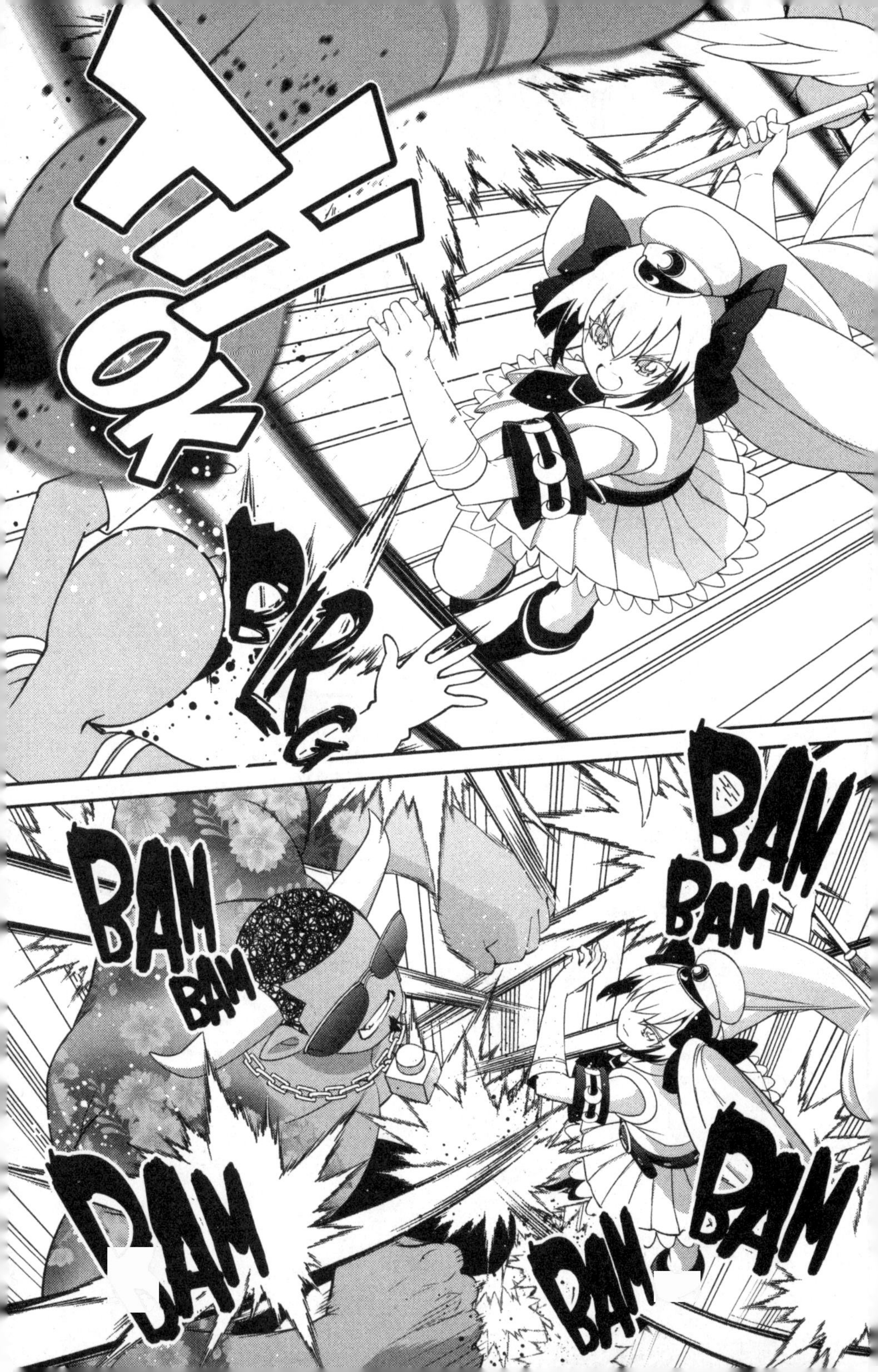
THOK
BAM
BAM
BAM
BAM
BAM
BAM
BAM

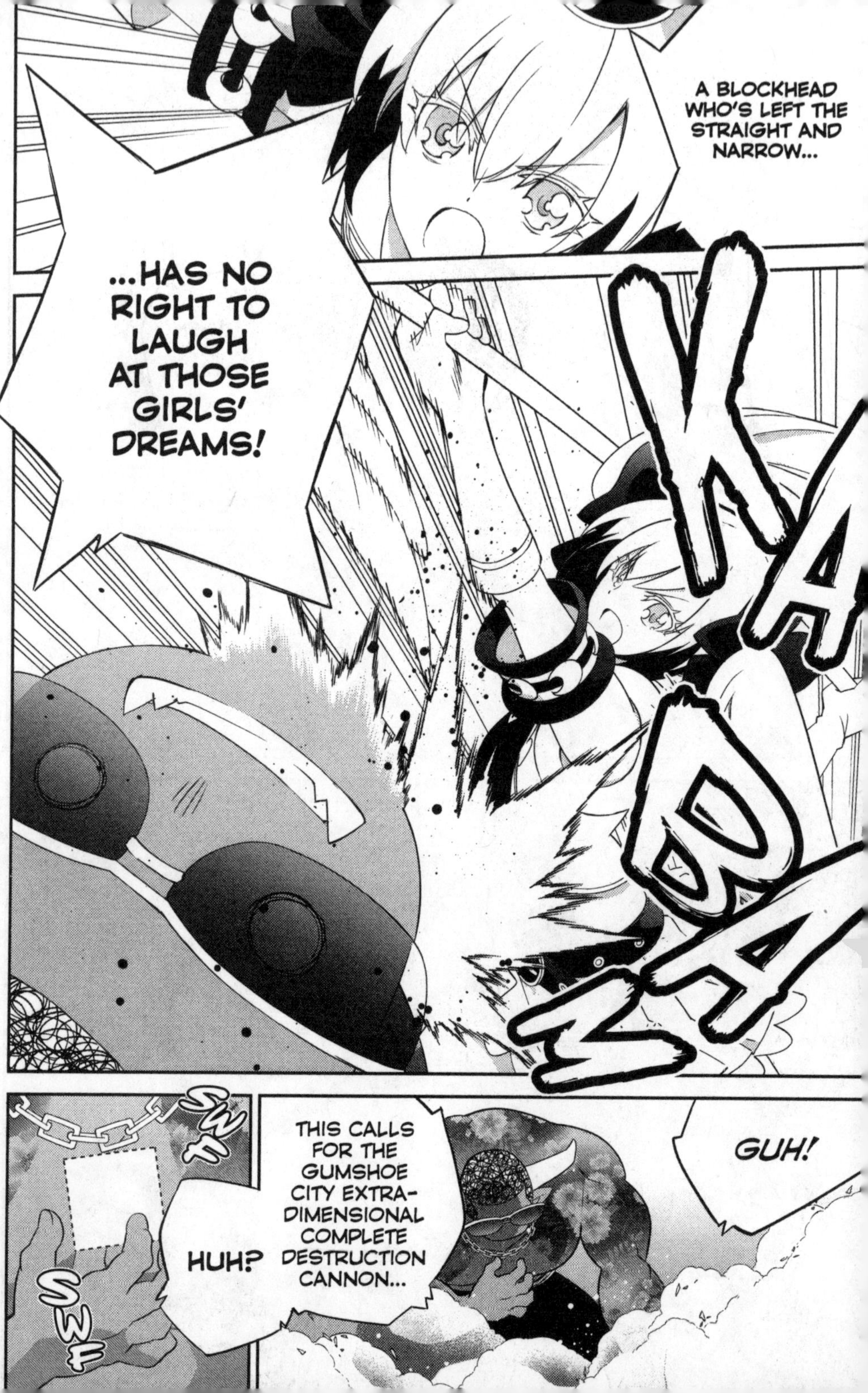
A BLOCKHEAD WHO'S LEFT THE STRAIGHT AND NARROW...
...HAS NO RIGHT TO LAUGH AT THOSE GIRLS' DREAMS!
KABAM
GUH!
THIS CALLS FOR THE GUMSHOE CITY EXTRA-DIMENSIONAL COMPLETE DESTRUCTION CANNON...
SWF
HUH?
SWF

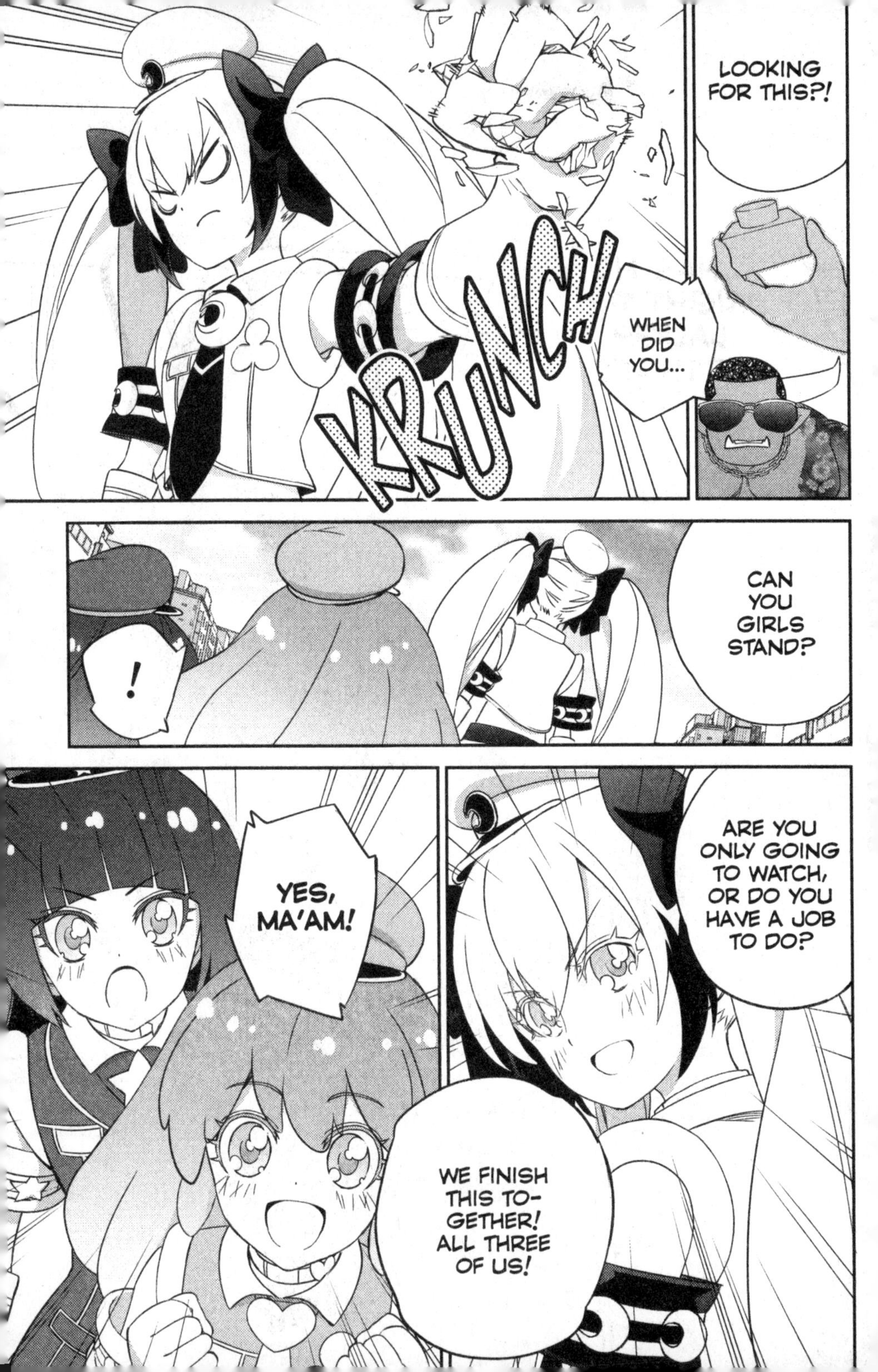
LOOKING FOR THIS?!
WHEN DID YOU...
KRUNCH
CAN YOU GIRLS STAND?
!
ARE YOU ONLY GOING TO WATCH, OR DO YOU HAVE A JOB TO DO?
YES, MA'AM!
WE FINISH THIS TO-GETHER! ALL THREE OF US!

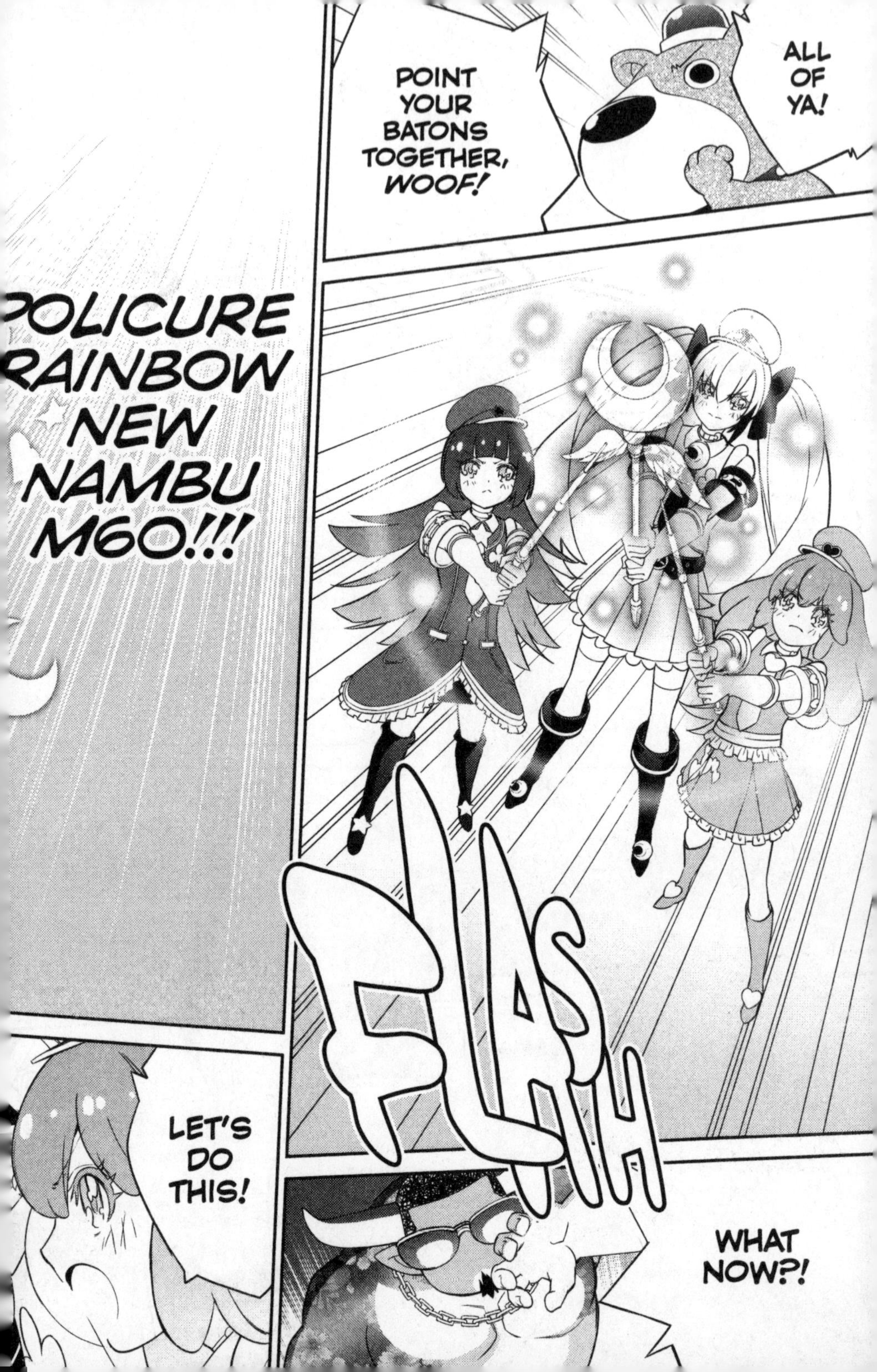
ALL OF YA!
POINT YOUR BATONS TOGETHER, WOOF!
FLASH
POLICURE RAINBOW NEW NAMBU M60!!!
WHAT NOW?!
LET'S DO THIS!

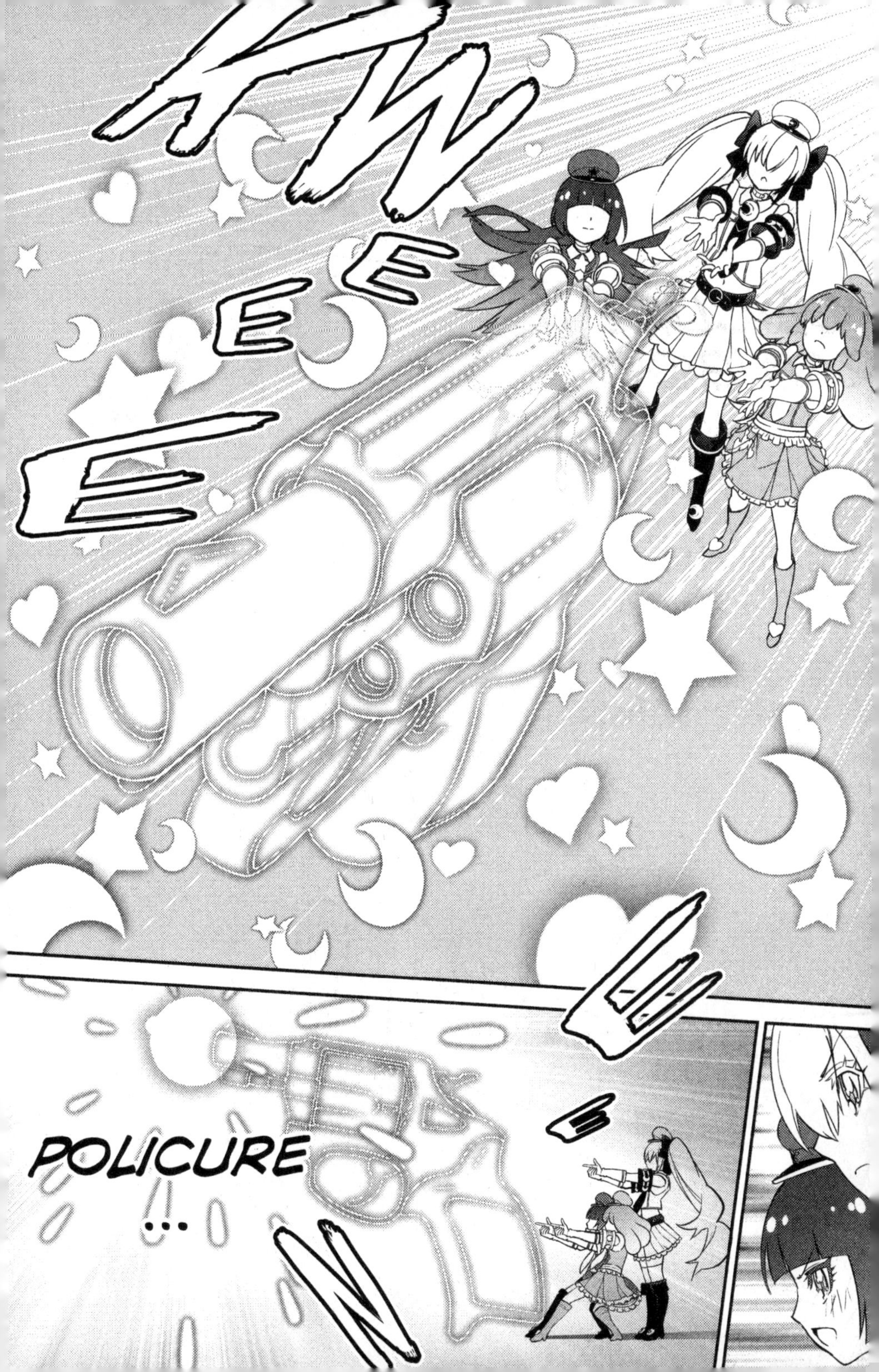
KWEEEE
EEN
POLICURE
...

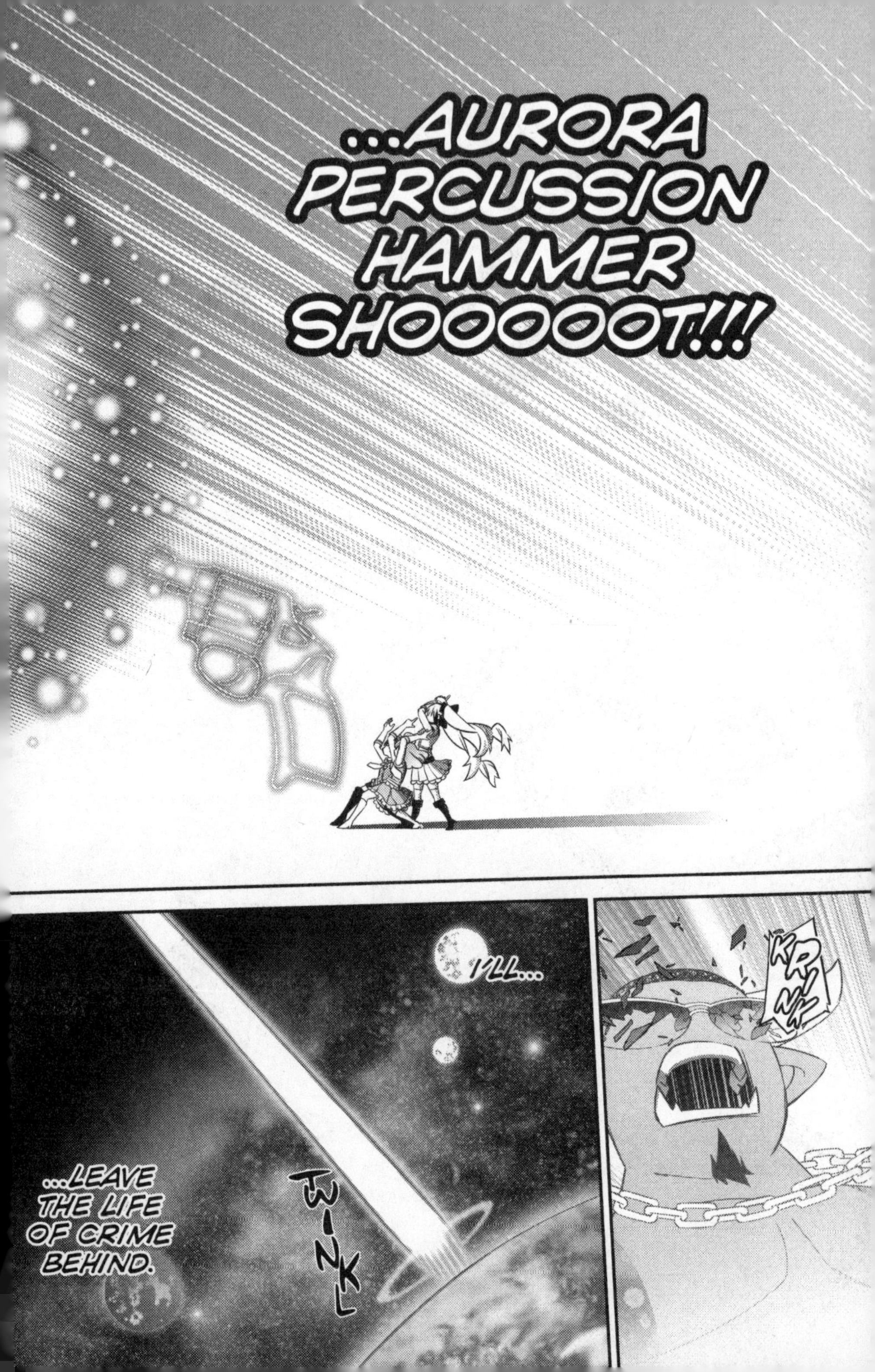
...AURORA PERCUSSION HAMMER SHOOOOOT!!!
KRINK
I'LL...
...LEAVE THE LIFE OF CRIME BEHIND.
TWINKL

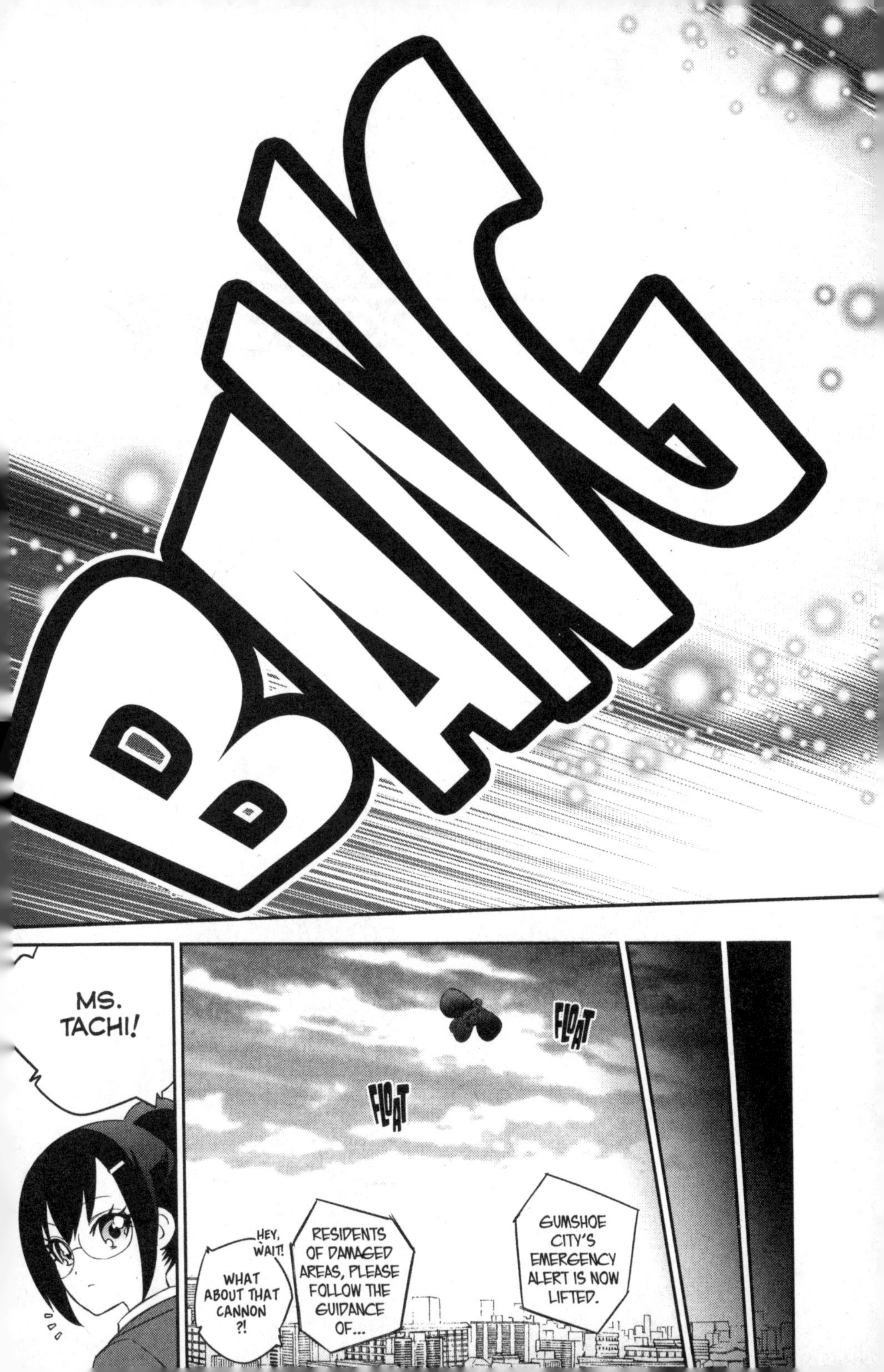
BANG
FLOAT
FLOAT
GUMSHOE CITY'S EMERGENCY ALERT IS NOW LIFTED.
RESIDENTS OF DAMAGED AREAS, PLEASE FOLLOW THE GUIDANCE OF...
HEY, WAIT!
WHAT ABOUT THAT CANNON ?!
MS. TACHI!

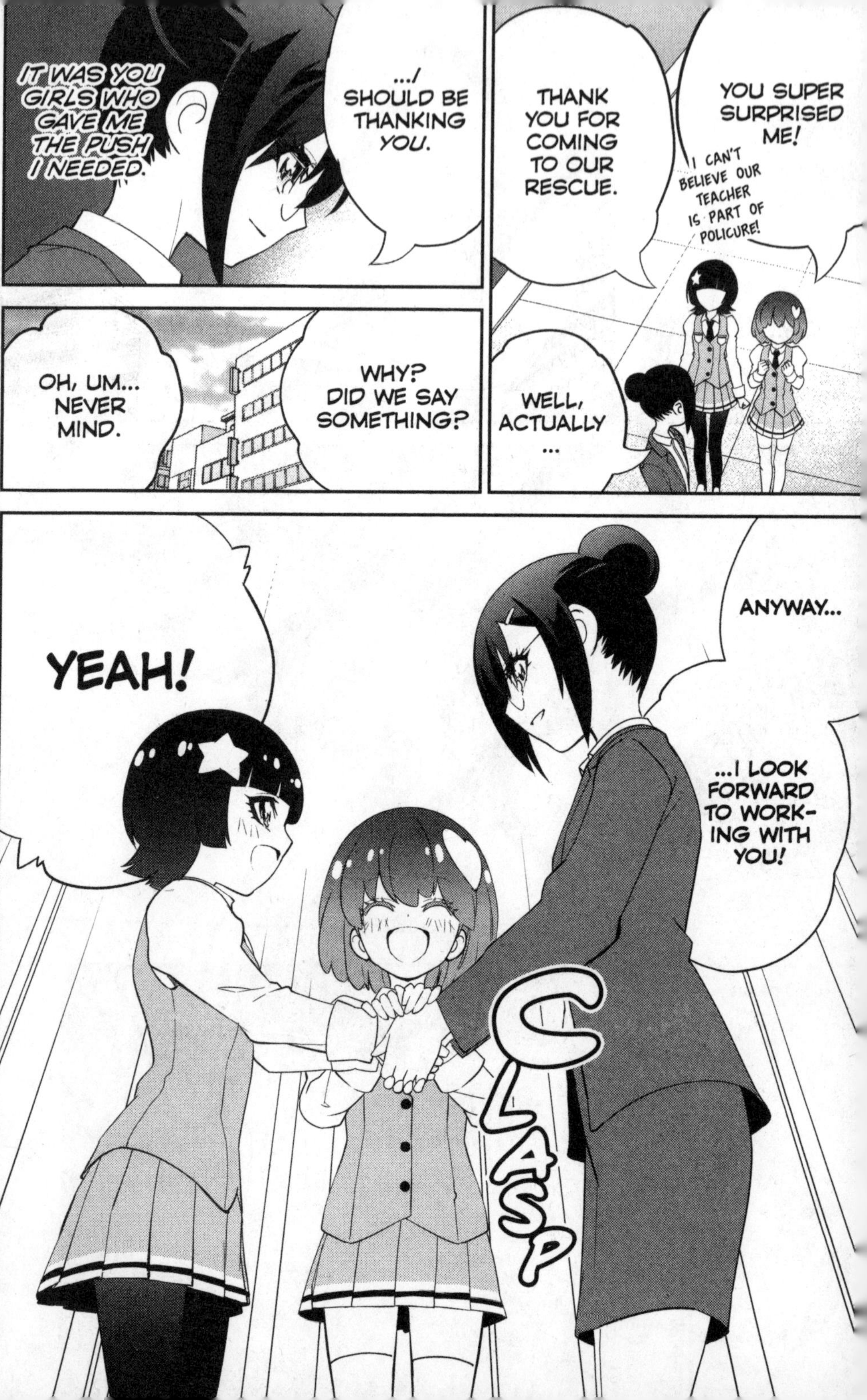
YOU SUPER SURPRISED ME!
I CAN'T BELIEVE OUR TEACHER IS PART OF POLICURE!
THANK YOU FOR COMING TO OUR RESCUE.
WELL, ACTUALLY ...
...I SHOULD BE THANKING YOU.
IT WAS YOU GIRLS WHO GAVE ME THE PUSH I NEEDED.
WHY? DID WE SAY SOMETHING?
OH, UM... NEVER MIND.
ANYWAY...
...I LOOK FORWARD TO WORK-ING WITH YOU!
YEAH!
CLASP

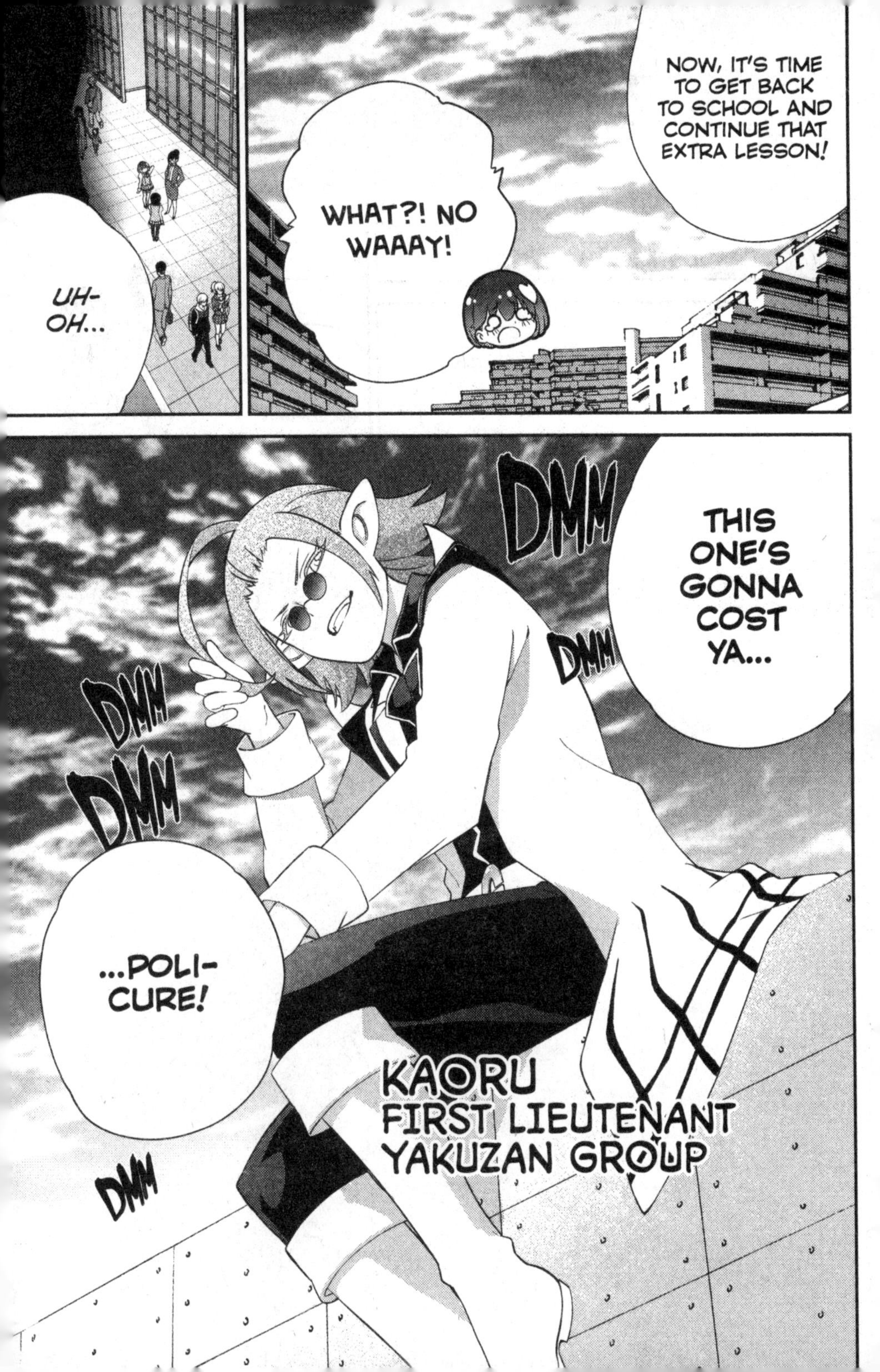
NOW, IT'S TIME TO GET BACK TO SCHOOL AND CONTINUE THAT EXTRA LESSON!
WHAT?! NO WAAAY!
UH-OH...
DMM
THIS ONE'S GONNA COST YA...
DMM
DMM
DMM
...POLI-CURE!
KAORU
FIRST LIEUTENANT
YAKUZAN GROUP
DMM

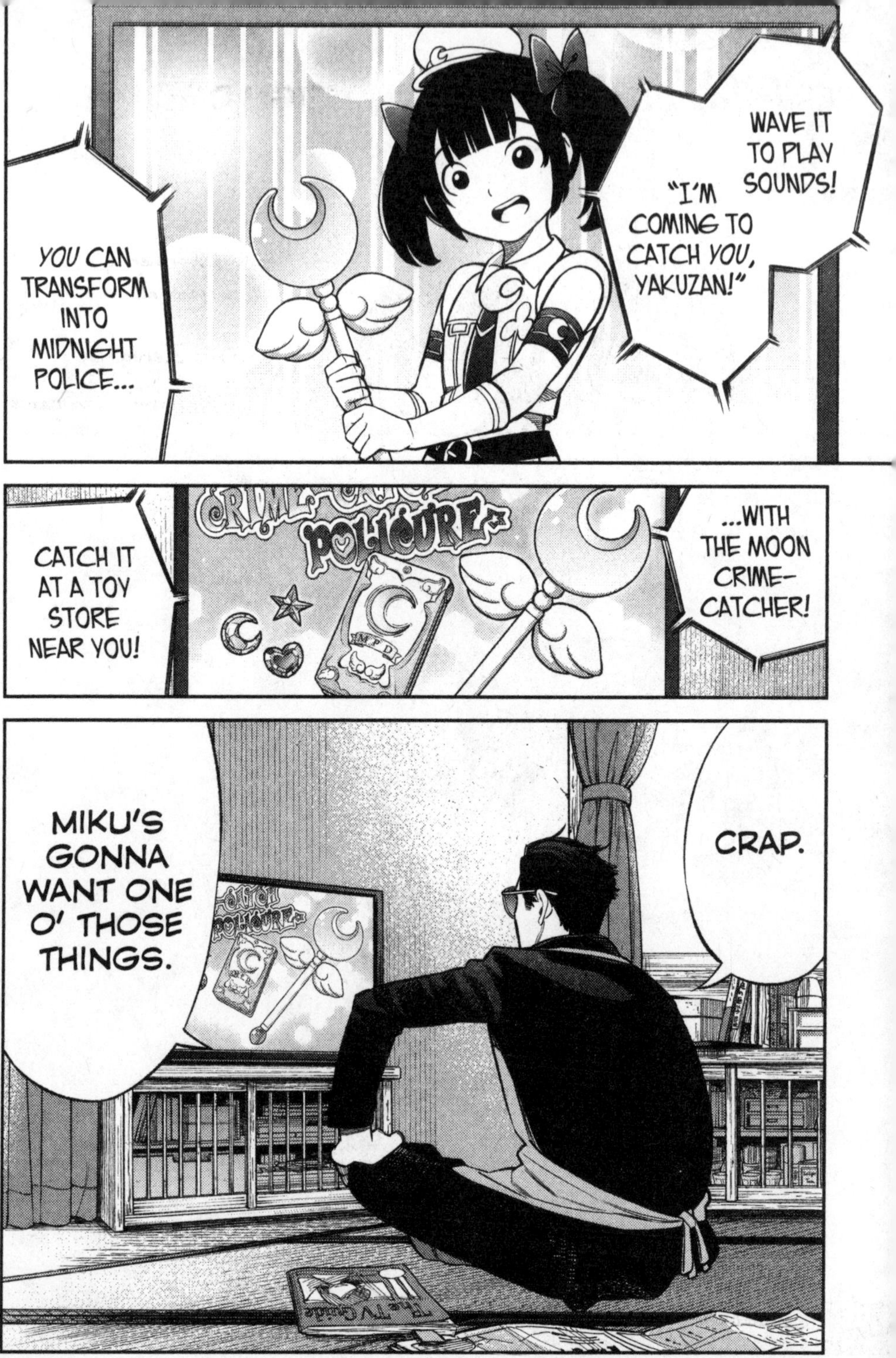
WAVE IT TO PLAY SOUNDS!
"I'M COMING TO CATCH *YOU*, YAKUZAN!"
YOU CAN TRANSFORM INTO MIDNIGHT POLICE...
...WITH THE MOON CRIME-CATCHER!
CATCH IT AT A TOY STORE NEAR YOU!
CRAP.
MIKU'S GONNA WANT ONE O' THOSE THINGS.

THE END

CRIME-CATCH POLICURE ★ / DESIGN DOCUMENTS

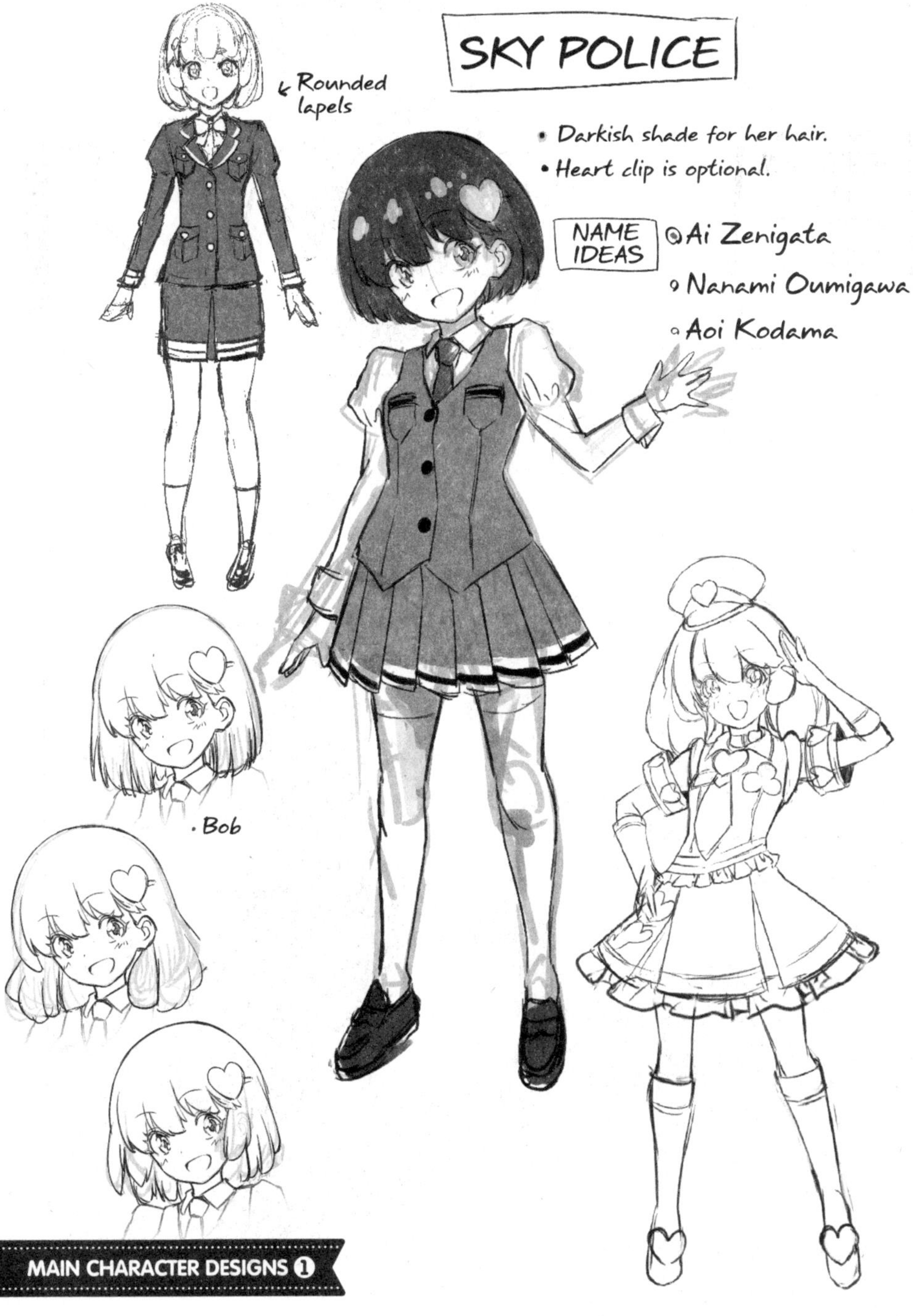

SKY POLICE
Rounded lapels
• Darkish shade for her hair.
• Heart clip is optional.
NAME IDEAS
◎ Ai Zenigata
○ Nanami Oumigawa
○ Aoi Kodama
• Bob

MAIN CHARACTER DESIGNS 1

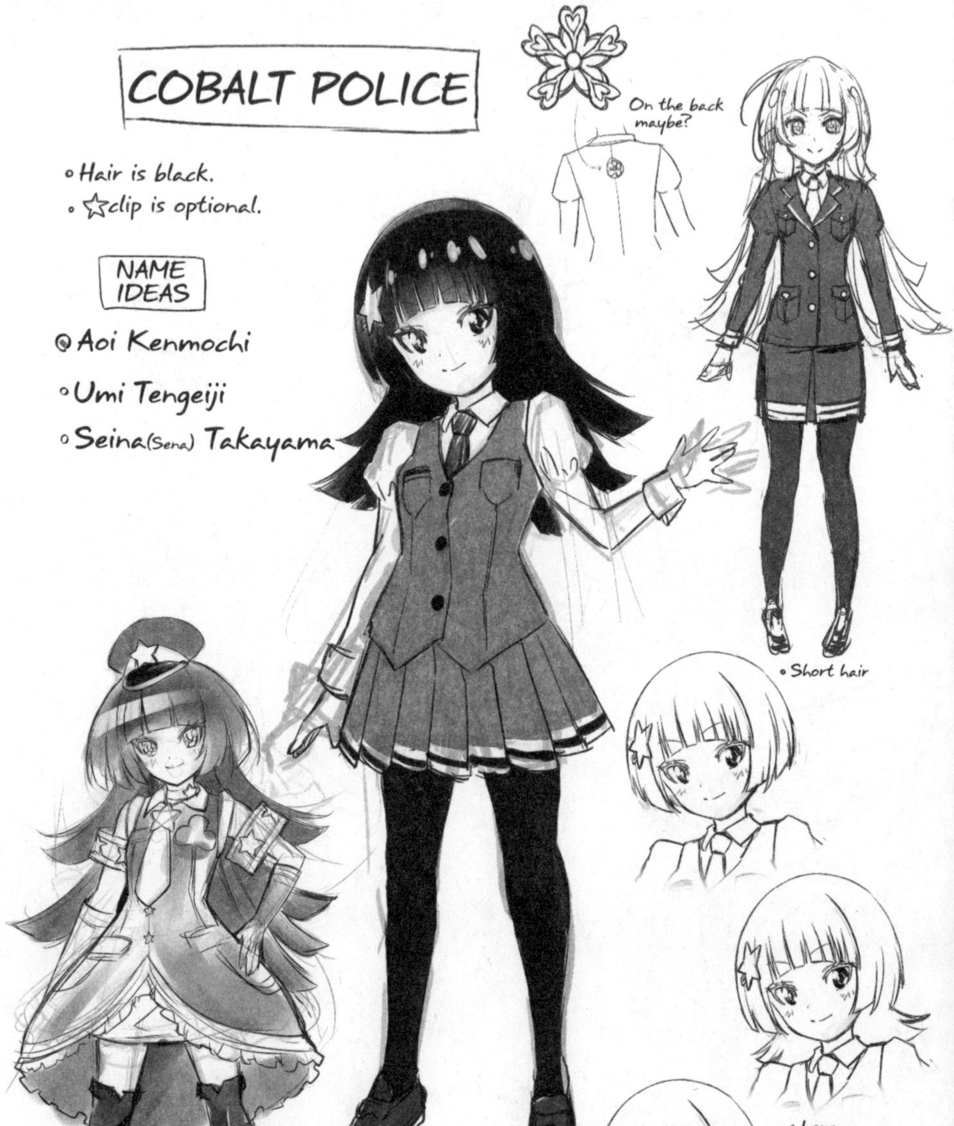
COBALT POLICE
Hair is black.
☆clip is optional.
NAME IDEAS
Aoi Kenmochi
Umi Tengeiji
Seina(Sena) Takayama
On the back maybe?
Short hair
Long (looks a lot like Benio)

MAIN CHARACTER DESIGNS 2

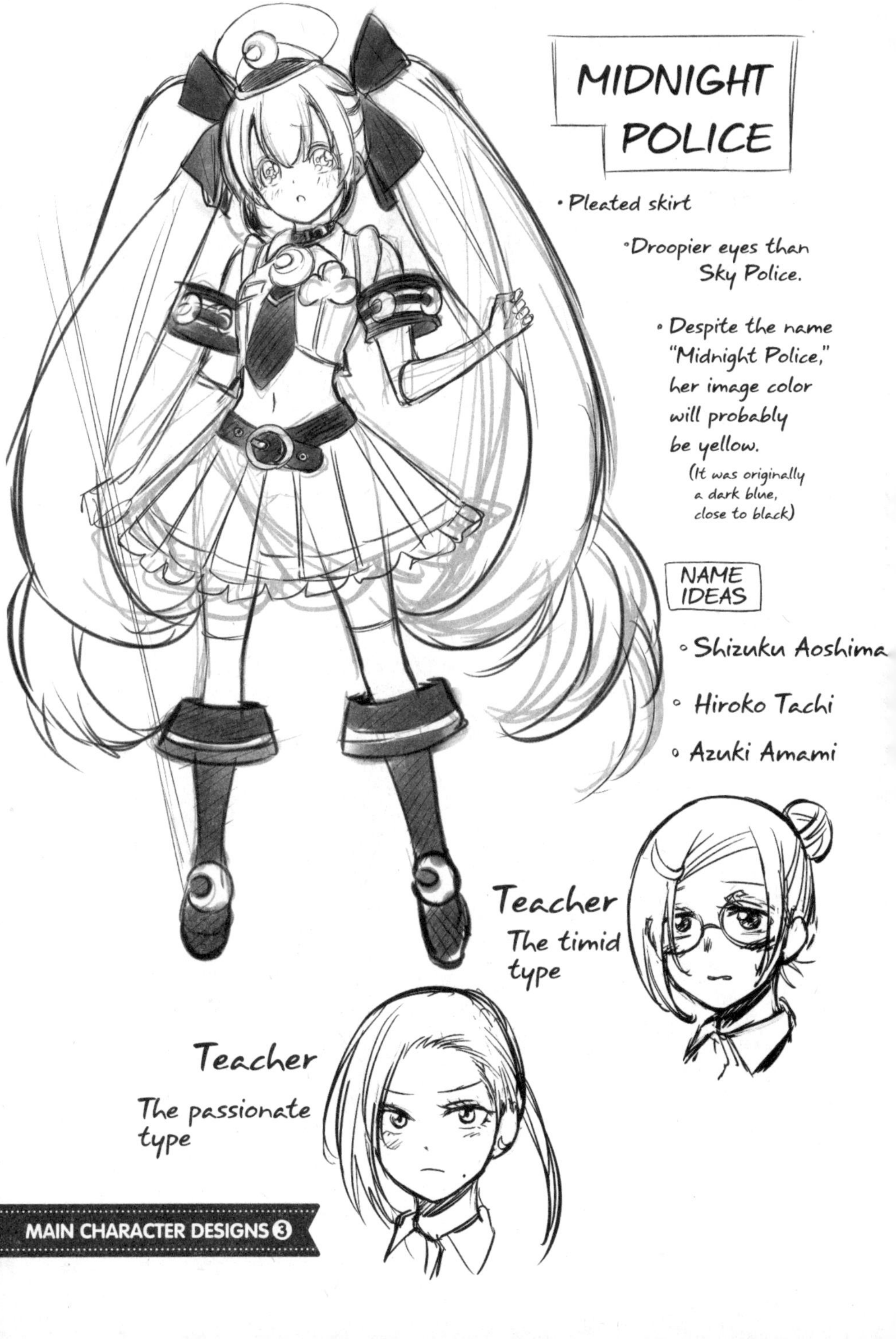
MIDNIGHT POLICE
• Pleated skirt
• Droopier eyes than Sky Police.
• Despite the name "Midnight Police," her image color will probably be yellow.
(It was originally a dark blue, close to black)
NAME IDEAS
◦ Shizuku Aoshima
◦ Hiroko Tachi
◦ Azuki Amami
Teacher
The timid type
Teacher
The passionate type

MAIN CHARACTER DESIGNS 3

OFFICER IMAGERY

- Gigantic upper half.

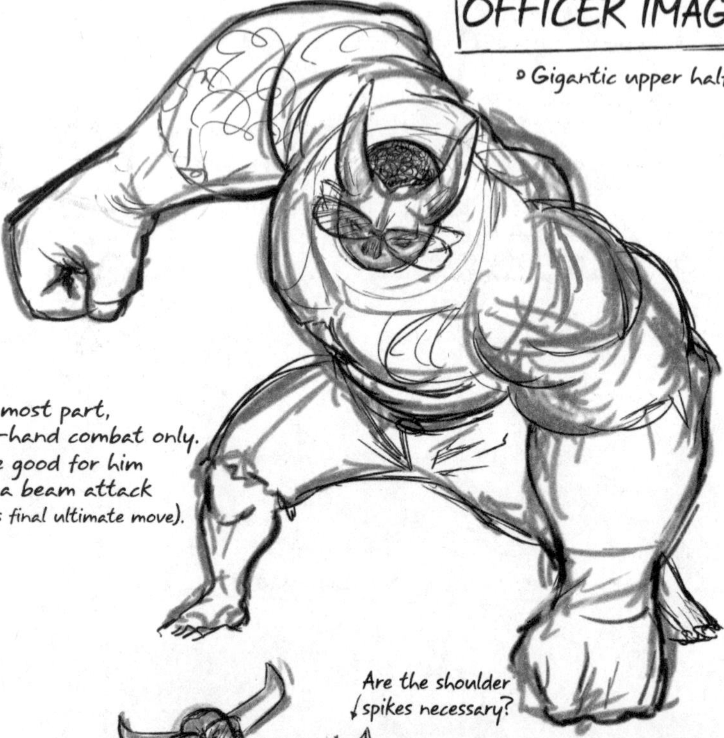

- For the most part, hand-to-hand combat only.
- Might be good for him to have a beam attack (like as his final ultimate move).

Are the shoulder spikes necessary?

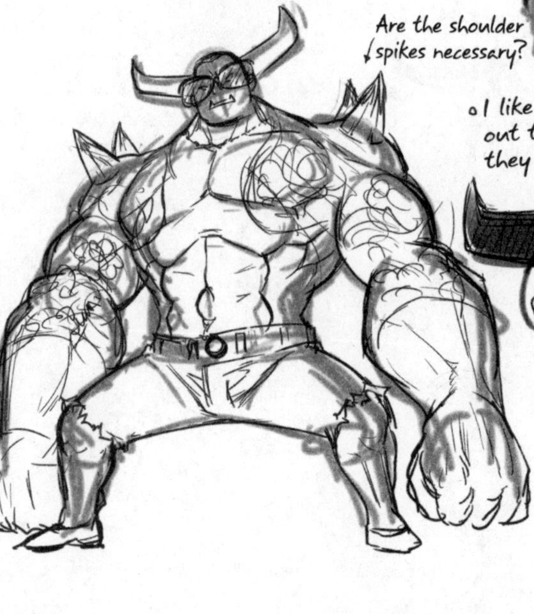

- I like the horns growing out to the sides better—they look dumber.

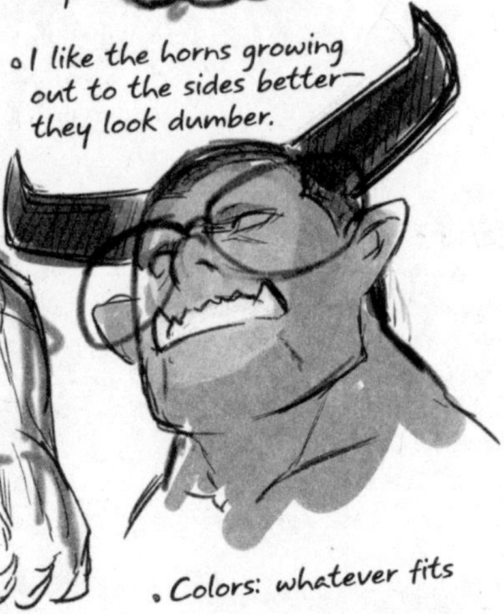

- Colors: whatever fits
- On the manga pages, we'll shade his skin with screentone.

TRANSFORMATION ITEM

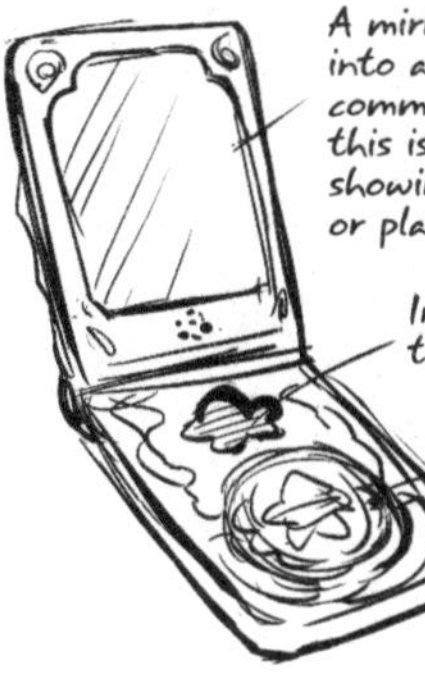

A mirror. Can also turn into a communicator by voice command. On the toy version, this is an LED screen for showing the characters or playing mini games.
Insert Cure Badge here to transform.
The Policure logo. A button you can press. Lights up when transforming.

Policure (Police) Notebook

Star Policure Mirror

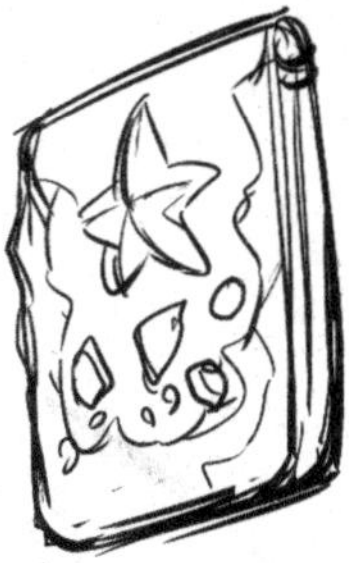

Cure Badges

Shiny, sparkly, gemstone-like collectibles.
Normally worn as accessories.

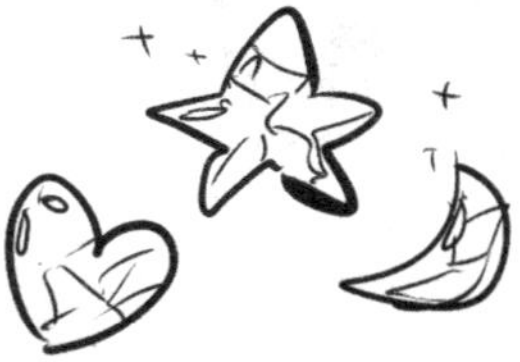

WEAPON

XX City Complete Destruction Cannon

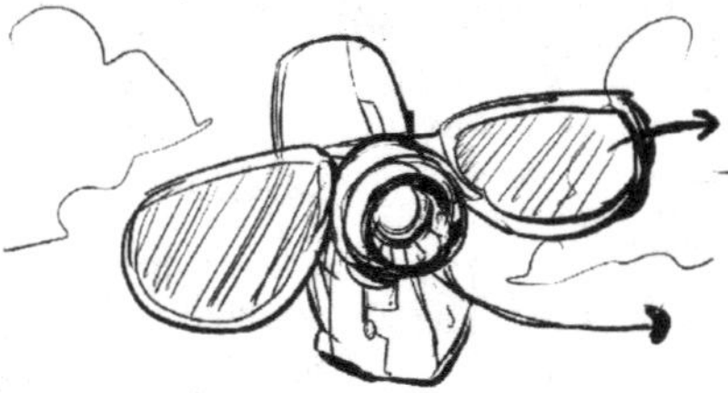

Sunglasses shape
Energy absorption panel

Floats high in the sky. Shoots an ultra-powerful beam that can vaporize a city in an instant.

Sake Cup Energy Supply Antenna

An antenna that fires negative energy. Installed on the peak of the mountain behind the city. Destroy it and the negative energy supply is completely cut off.

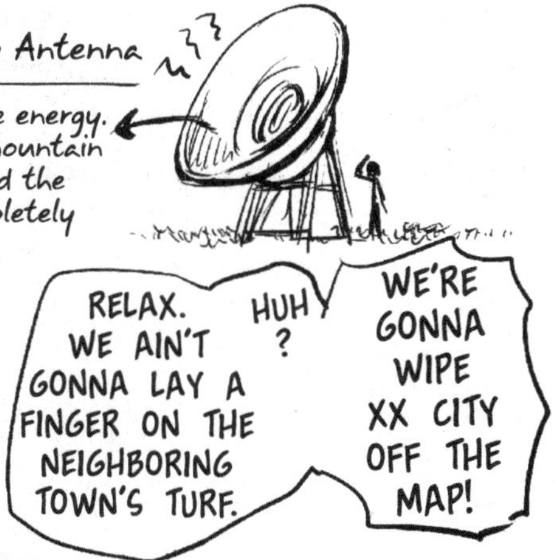

WE'RE GONNA WIPE XX CITY OFF THE MAP!
HUH?
RELAX. WE AIN'T GONNA LAY A FINGER ON THE NEIGHBORING TOWN'S TURF.

STAFF

ART
YOSHIAKI SUKENO / TAKUMI KIKUTA / TAKUMI KABA
KOPPY / YUKIYA YAMAZAKI / NATSUKI ISE

KOUSUKE OONO
MIDORINO / KZK

DESIGN
YUICHI UMEDA + RYOSUKE TAKEUCHI [crazy force]

EDITING
ARIMASA NISHIKAWA

SPECIAL THANKS
TOEI ANIMATION

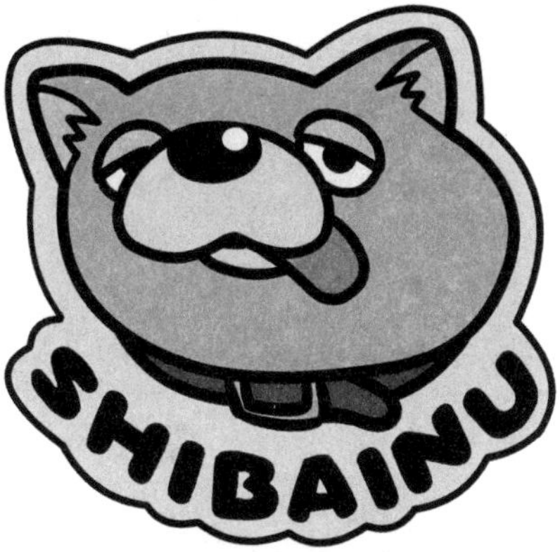
SHIBAINU

My pet Shiba Inu was the model for the Shiba Inu on Tatsu's apron, but the design lost its original form as I refined it. I'm fond of that indescribably derpy face.

KOUSUKE OONO

Kousuke Oono began his professional manga career in 2016 in the manga magazine *Monthly Comics @ Bunch* with the one-shot "Legend of Music." Oono's follow-up series, *The Way of the Househusband*, is the creator's first serialization as well as his first English-language release.

The Way of the House Husband

VOLUME 8

VIZ SIGNATURE EDITION

STORY AND ART BY
KOUSUKE OONO

TRANSLATION: Amanda Haley
ENGLISH ADAPTATION: Jennifer LeBlanc
TOUCH-UP ART & LETTERING: Bianca Pistillo, James Gaubatz
DESIGN: Alice Lewis
EDITOR: Jennifer LeBlanc

GOKUSHUFUDO volume 8
© Kousuke Oono 2018
All Rights Reserved
English translation rights arranged
with SHINCHOSHA PUBLISHING CO.
through Tuttle-Mori Agency, Inc, Tokyo

Printed in Canada

Published by VIZ Media, LLC
P.O. Box 77010
San Francisco, CA 94107

10 9 8 7 6 5 4 3 2 1
First printing, August 2022

VIZ MEDIA   VIZ SIGNATURE
viz.com   vizsignature.com

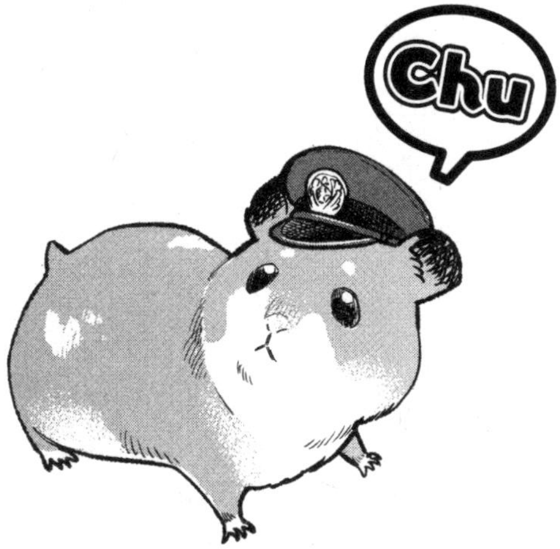
Chu

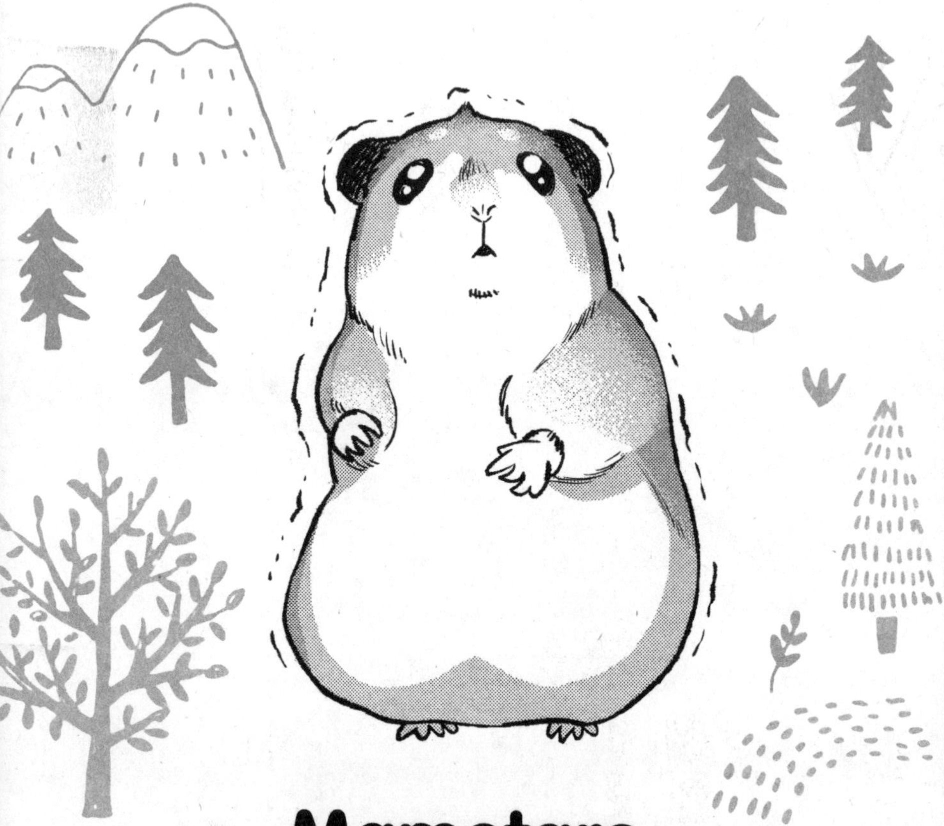

Mametaro

Golden hamster (*Mesocricetus auratus*)

LENGTH: 6 inches LIFE SPAN: 2 to 3 years

Also known as the Syrian hamster, the golden hamster is a relatively large member of the hamster family. Because they are highly territorial, keeping multiple golden hamsters in a small cage can lead to scraps. They are native to arid regions in the Middle East, where they live in burrows dug deep underground.